YOUR COMMODORE 64:™

A Guide to the
Commodore 64™ Computer

YOUR COMMODORE 64:™
A Guide to the
Commodore 64™ Computer

John Heilborn
Ran Talbott

Osborne/McGraw-Hill
Berkeley, California

Disclaimer of Warranties and Limitation of Liabilities

The authors have taken due care in preparing this book and the programs in it, including research, development, and testing to ascertain their effectiveness. The authors and the publisher make no expressed or implied warranty of any kind with regard to these programs or the supplementary documentation in this book. In no event shall the authors or the publisher be liable for incidental or consequential damages in connection with or arising out of the furnishing, performance, or use of any of these programs.

C-64 is a trademark of Commodore Business Machines, Inc. *Your Commodore 64™ User Guide* is not sponsored or approved by or connected with Commodore Business Machines, Inc. Commodore Business Machines, Inc., makes no warranty, expressed or implied, of any kind with regard to the information contained herein, its accuracy, or completeness.

Datassette is a trademark of Commodore Business Machines, Inc.

C= is a registered trademark of Commodore Business Machines, Inc.

Published by
Osborne/McGraw-Hill
2600 Tenth Street
Berkeley, California 94710
U.S.A.

For information on translations and book distributors outside of the U.S.A., please write to Osborne/McGraw-Hill at the above address.

YOUR COMMODORE 64™

1234567890 DODO 89876543

ISBN 0-88134-114-2

Cover illustration by Terry Hoff
Cover design by Yashi Okita
Text design by KLT van Genderen
Unless otherwise mentioned, all photos by Richard Cash

Dedication

The authors would like to dedicate this book to Heinz Max and Ingeborg Heilborn and to Bill and Jo Talbott, without whom we would not have been possible.

ACKNOWLEDGMENTS

No book is ever the work of just the authors and, of course, this book is no exception. We would like to express our thanks to the following people without whose help this work would never have become a reality:

Michael Tomczyk, whose enthusiasm and insight during a brief meeting in Santa Clara got the whole thing started.

Bill Hindorff, whose technical assistance helped clarify many of the lesser known aspects of the C-64.

Larry Ercolino, who provided a first-hand encounter in telecommunications and a seemingly never-ending supply of support and information.

There were many others who also provided help when we needed it the most, and often at times that were quite inconvenient. Some of these are Pat McAllister, Jeff Hand, Andy Finkel, Neil Harris, Steve Murri, Steven Moser, and John Stockman.

Finally, we wish to express our thanks to Denise Penrose whose editorial guidance was invaluable in helping us complete this book.

JH
RT

Contents

Introduction

The Commodore 64 is one of a new breed of computers. Despite its low price and small size, it has more features than larger and more expensive computers did even a few years ago.

If you want to solve math problems, the C-64 can run them for you. If you need to type letters or mailing lists, the C-64 will do the job quickly and easily.

But in addition to these functions, common to most computers, the C-64 offers color text and graphics.

Furthermore, the C-64 can produce tones within a range of nine octaves. These can be combined to imitate anything from the patter of rain to a cannonade.

Chapter 1 explains how to unpack and set up the C-64 and its accessories. It contains a description of all the controls on the C-64, from connectors to keyboard functions.

Chapter 2 guides you through the C-64 screen editor and explains the two operating modes of the C-64: immediate mode and programmed mode. This is followed by an introduction to the Datassette, the 1541 disk drive, and the 1525 printer.

Chapter 3 introduces you to programming. All the BASIC instructions are covered as well as the concepts of loops, branching, Boolean operators, floating point versus integer numbers, and scientific notation. The chapter also describes variable types and the construction of arrays.

Advanced BASIC programming is the subject of Chapter 4. It will teach you practical applications of concepts covered in Chapter 3. You will learn how to write screen display programs, include cursor movement and string variables as commands in your programs, and develop easy-to-use I/O intensive programs requiring considerable data entry. Chapter 4 also discusses the C-64's real time clock and random number generator.

Chapter 5 is a tutorial on game controllers. It will show you how to use the keyboard as a game controller and how to write programs that access a joystick or paddle controller.

Chapter 6 covers graphics. It explains how the video display works, how colors are produced, and how to put characters on the screen. You will learn how to animate pictures and produce high-resolution graphics using BASIC.

Chapter 7 discusses sound generation on the C-64 including the C-64 sound registers, the components of sound, and how to use them. You will learn how to program music into the C-64 and how to save it for playback later on.

Chapter 8 explains the operation of the major C-64 peripherals: the Datassette, 1541 disk drive, and 1525 printer. It contains a complete discussion of data file creation, program storage, and high-level disk operations. It also discusses all the printer commands including double width characters, reverse printing, and high-resolution graphics.

The appendixes contain tables on all the details discussed in the text, from the system architecture and block diagrams to the memory maps. You will also find diagrams showing pinouts for all of the connectors as well as color, screen, and sound value tables.

Introducing the Commodore 64 Computer

When you first unpack the C-64, you will find the equipment shown in Figure 1-1:

- The C-64 computer
- Power supply (large plastic box)
- TV switch box
- Video cable

While your system may include additional components, all systems include this basic equipment. This chapter identifies each component and connector provided by Commodore and introduces the function of each.

Place the C-64 on a flat surface such as a table. Make sure that you have room to put a television near the C-64, ideally directly behind it.

REAR AND SIDE PANEL

All of the switches, connectors, and interfaces are located at the side and back of the C-64 computer. These components are labeled in Figure 1-2. It is important that you learn the function and location of each component as you hook up the computer to avoid damaging it by using connections incorrectly.

1

FIGURE 1-1. Equipment packed with the Commodore 64

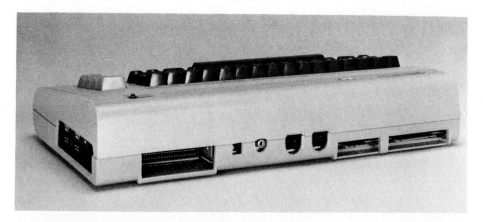

FIGURE 1-2. Rear/side view of the Commodore 64

Power Switch

Make sure the C-64 is OFF at this point. The power switch is located on the right side of the computer. It is a two-position "rocker" switch.

When you turn the power switch ON, the C-64 will display a dark screen for a short time. During this period it is *initializing* itself; that is, it is checking out its internal systems and memory.

When you turn the power OFF, all programs and data in memory that were not stored onto either diskette or tape will be lost.

Power Connector

The power supply has two cables attached to it. One plugs into any standard 110 volt AC outlet. The other plugs directly into the power connector next to the ON/OFF switch on the side of the C-64.

Game Ports

These connectors are used for the various game controllers available for the C-64, as well as for the light pen and some special application devices. ATARI joysticks and paddles will work with this port, as well as those made by Commodore.

Parallel User Port

The parallel user port is a connector that allows you to hook up devices (such as the VIC modem) to the C-64.

More advanced users may use this connector for custom applications as well, since the signals coming from it can be programmed directly by the C-64.

Cassette Interface

The cassette interface is used to connect the Datassette, which is a special digital tape recorder. You can use it to store and reload programs and data into the C-64. The Datassette is described later in this chapter.

Serial Port

The serial port is used to connect the computer to the model 1525 printer, the 1541 disk drive, and other devices using a serial input/output configuration. Instructions for connecting the printer and disk drive to the C-64 are provided later in this chapter.

Video Ports

The C-64 produces the sound and pictures displayed on your television by combining them into a signal called *composite video*. This signal is sent out through the video port.

A video monitor (a television without a tuner) is able to convert the composite video directly into pictures and sound. Connect a monitor to the monitor video port. A television, however, must be tuned to a particular channel. That signal is produced and combined with the composite video by the built-in RF (radio frequency) modulator. Connect your TV to the TV video port.

When you use the C-64 you can select either channel 3 or channel 4 by flipping the channel switch on the back of the computer.

Expansion Interface

The expansion interface gives you access to the computer's memory lines.

Video Display

When you first power up the C-64 it displays 25 rows with 40 characters per row. The computer generates these characters by lighting the appropriate pattern of dots within an 8 × 8 matrix. This is illustrated in Figure 1-3. The C-64's character set is quite extensive, containing 256 letters, numbers, and symbols. It is also possible to program custom characters for special applications. This will be discussed in Chapter 6.

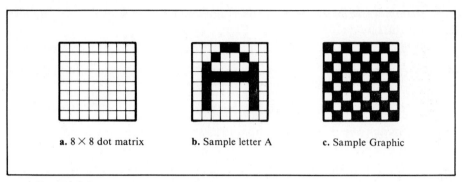

a. 8 × 8 dot matrix   b. Sample letter A   c. Sample Graphic

FIGURE 1-3. The 8 × 8 dot matrix

POWER UP

Connect the TV switch box to the back of the television by attaching one end of the cable with the phono jacks (Figure 1-4) to the switch box.

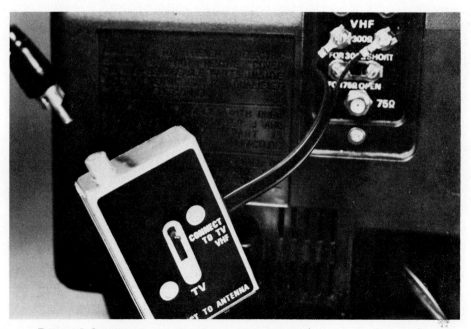

FIGURE 1-4. Television switch box and connections

Connect the larger plug of the video cable to the round five-pin video port on the back of the C-64 (see Figure 1-2).

Finally, plug the power supply cord into the C-64 power connector. *Do not turn on the C-64 yet!*

To start using your C-64, follow these steps:

1. Plug the AC power cord into a wall outlet.

2. Switch the power ON. The power switch is located on the right side near the AC plug.

3. Wait for the READY display. This can take several seconds, during which the C-64 is going through a self-checking and initialization process.

The following display should now appear:

If you not not get this display, turn the power OFF, wait about ten seconds, and turn the power ON again. If you still don't get this display, check the connections. If that does not help, contact your Commodore dealer.

THE KEYBOARD

In almost every application the keyboard is used to communicate with the C-64. The keys are arranged much like those on a standard typewriter. Unlike typewriter keys, however, the C-64's keys can be used to access as many as three or four different symbols, characters, or functions.

The keys on the C-64 may be classified by function as follows:

- Alphabetic keys
- Numeric keys
- Special symbol keys
- Graphic keys
- Function keys
- Cursor control keys

Alphabetic Keys

The alphabetic keys include the 26 letters of the alphabet in both upper and lower case. When the C-64 is powered up, letters are displayed in upper-case. To display lower-case letters, press the COMMODORE and SHIFT keys simultaneously. If you are typing lower-case letters and wish to insert an occasional upper-case letter, use the SHIFT key as you would on a typewriter. Press SHIFT-COMMODORE again to return to upper-case mode.

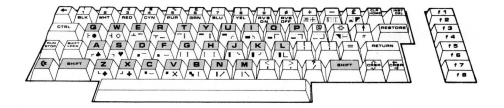

Numeric Keys

The numeric keys are used to enter the digits 0 through 9.

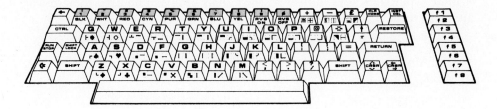

Special Symbol Keys

The special symbol keys include the following standard punctuation marks: ! ' " . , ; : ?. They also include the following mathematical symbols: + = / * ↑ = (note that a slash is used for division, an asterisk for multiplication, and an up arrow for exponentiation). Other special symbols available on the C-64 include # $ & @ % £ π < > [ ] ←.

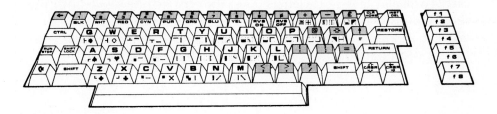

Graphic Keys

The C-64 also has 62 graphic symbols that may be accessed through the SHIFT or COMMODORE function keys. Using these graphic symbols, you can create fairly sophisticated display drawings.

The graphic symbols and their names are listed in Table 1-1. Similar symbols have been grouped to make graphic options immediately obvious. Note that the square enclosing each of the graphic symbols shown in Table 1-1 and Figure 1-3 is not actually part of the symbol, but has been added to show the symbol's location within its 8 × 8 grid.

TABLE 1-1. Graphic Character Keys

Line Horizontal

Key	Description
T	Top
E	3/4 Top
D	2/3 Top
C	Near Middle
.	Middle
F	2/3 Bottom
R	3/4 Bottom
@	Bottom

Line Vertical

Key	Description
G	Left
T	3/4 Left
G	2/3 Left
B	Near Middle
=	Middle
H	2/3 right
Y	3/4 right
M	Right

Thin Bar

Key	Description
Y	Top
P	Bottom
H	Left
N	Right

Thick Bar

Key	Description
U	Top
O	Bottom
J	Left
L	Right

Half Block

Key	Description
K	Left
T	Bottom

Triangle Solid

Key	Description
Z	Top Left
.	Top Right

Quarter Block Solid

Keys	Description
V C	Top Left, Top Right
F D	Bottom Left, Bottom Right
B	Diagonal

Quarter Block Open (Angle)

Keys	Description
X Z	Top Left, Top Right
S A	Bottom Left, Bottom Right

Corner

Keys	Description
O P	Top Left, Top Right
L @	Bottom Left, Bottom Right

Rounded Corner

Keys	Description
U I	Top Left, Top Right
J K	Bottom Left, Bottom Right

Suit

Keys	Description
A S	Spade, Heart
Z X	Diamond, Club

T

Key	Description
E	Top
R	Bottom
W	Left
Q	Right

Symbol

Key	Description
V	X
+	Cross
N	Diagonal Acute
M	Diagonal Grave

Grid

Key	Description
↑	Full
⊒	Half Left
⊏	Half Bottom

Circle

Key	Description
W	Outline
Q	Solid

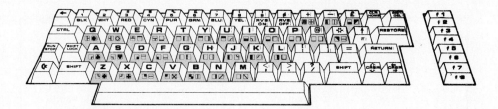

Function Keys

Any key that "does something," rather than "prints something" is a function key. For instance, CTRL-RED (pressing the CTRL and RED keys simultaneously) doesn't print anything, but instead causes all subsequent characters to be displayed in red on the screen.

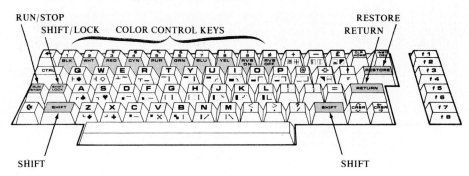

SHIFT

The SHIFT key is used in conjunction with any other key on the keyboard to access that key's "shifted" function or character. Most keys have both a shifted and unshifted character or function. For example, shifted lower-case letters become upper-case letters, and a shifted CRSR UP/DOWN causes the cursor to move up.

There are two identical SHIFT keys on the C-64 keyboard. One is at the lower left corner of the keyboard, while the other is at the lower right.

SHIFT LOCK

You may occasionally need a continuous string of shifted characters. To make this operation easier, the C-64 has a SHIFT LOCK key that is similar to the SHIFT LOCK on a typewriter. Pressing the SHIFT LOCK key until it clicks will lock the keyboard into shifted mode. Pressing it until it clicks again will unlock the shifted mode.

Unless the C-64 is running a program, RUN/STOP does nothing. Pressing SHIFT and RUN/STOP loads and executes a program from the C-64 Datassette.

RETURN

The RETURN key is much like the carriage return key on a typewriter. It causes the cursor (the flashing square that indicates where the next character will appear) to return to the left-hand margin of the next line.

The RETURN key is also used to enter instructions in BASIC. After keying in a line of your program, you press RETURN to enter that line into memory.

A RETURN executed while the cursor is on the bottom line of the screen will cause the entire screen to scroll up, moving the cursor to the beginning of the new blank line generated by the scroll.

```
10 PRINT "NOW IS THE"
20 PRINT "TIME FOR"
30 PRINT "ALL GOOD"
40 PRINT "PEOPLE"
50 READ X
90 A=B+C+D
100 IF A=1 THEN 10
110 IF A=20 THEN 50
120 PRINT "START"
```

```
20 PRINT "TIME FOR"
30 PRINT "ALL GOOD"
40 PRINT "PEOPLE"
50 READ X
90 A=B+C+D
100 IF A=1 THEN 10
110 IF A=20 THEN 50
120 PRINT "START"
```

REVERSE ON/OFF

The RVS ON and RVS OFF keys allow you to exchange the light and dark parts of the characters on the screen. The default mode for this function is RVS OFF. The RVS ON is like the negative of a photograph. To reverse the characters, press CTRL and RVS ON at the same time. All subsequent characters entered will be displayed in reverse. To switch back again, press CTRL and RVS OFF.

NORMAL PRINT

RUN/STOP

In the unshifted mode, the RUN/STOP key will stop any program that is being executed, returning control of the computer to the keyboard. It will also display the number of the program line that was being executed before the stop instruction was received.

To demonstrate this, enter the following short program:

```
10 X = 0
20 PRINT X
30 X = X + 1
40 GOTO 20
99 END
```

Now type **RUN** and press RETURN. You should see a string of numbers scrolling down the left side of your screen. After pressing RUN/STOP your screen should look like the following:

```
0
1
2
3
4
5
6
7
8
9
10
11
12
13
14
15
16
17
18

BREAK IN 20
■
```

Unless the C-64 is running a program, RUN/STOP does nothing. Pressing SHIFT and RUN/STOP loads and executes a program from the C-64 Datassette.

RESTORE

If pressing the RUN/STOP key alone does not stop a program, then press RUN/STOP and RESTORE simultaneously. If this does not work, turn the power off and then on.

COLOR CONTROL KEYS

Along the top of the keyboard, just under the number keys (1-8), are located the eight color control keys: black, white, red, cyan (light blue), purple, green, blue, and yellow. These keys change the color of the characters being typed on the display. To use these keys you must press CTRL and the color you wish to use. For example, when you first power up the C-64, your screen comes up with a cyan border, blue inner field, and light blue letters. By pressing CTRL and PUR together, you will begin typing purple letters. By pressing the COMMODORE key and color keys together you can get eight more colors.

Cursor Control Keys

The remaining keys move the cursor. They are described individually below.

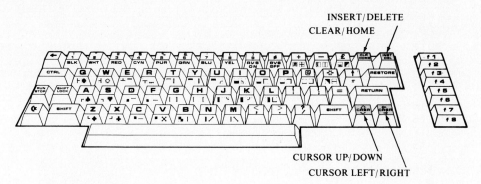

CLEAR/HOME

In the unshifted mode, pressing the CLR/HOME key will make the cursor jump to the top left-hand corner of the screen (the *home* position). To demonstrate this, type **LIST** and press RETURN. You should see a listing of the program you entered in the last section. If you turned the computer off since entering the program, reenter it now. After typing **LIST** you will find the cursor beneath the listing, after the word READY.

```
LIST

10 X = 0
20 PRINT X
30 X = X + 1
40 GOTO 20
99 END
■
```

Press the CLR/HOME key. The cursor should jump to the top left-hand corner of the screen.

```
■IST

10 X = 0
20 PRINT X
30 X = X + 1
40 GOTO 20
99 END
```

In the shifted mode, the CLR/HOME key will not only return the cursor to the home position, but will also erase anything that was on the screen (clear the screen). Type **LIST** again. Now press SHIFT and press CLR/HOME simultaneously.

CURSOR UP/DOWN

Unshifted, the CRSR UP/DOWN key causes the cursor to move down the screen a single line. Holding down the CRSR UP/DOWN key causes the cursor to move down until it reaches the bottom of the screen. If the cursor is on the bottom line of the screen and the unshifted CRSR UP/DOWN is pressed, the entire screen will be scrolled up and the cursor will be positioned at the bottom line.

LIST your program again. Now press the CRSR UP/DOWN key several times, or hold it down. When the cursor reaches the bottom of the screen, all the lines on the screen will move up from one to four lines. This is because the logical length of the lines is 80 characters, but the display is only 22 characters wide. The *logical length* of a line is the number of characters the C-64 can handle internally on each numbered line. Therefore, depending on how much of a line is left when the cursor reaches the bottom of the screen (regardless of what is actually displayed) the screen will scroll up one logical line, producing an effective scroll of one to four partial lines.

```
LIST

10 X = 0
20 PRINT X
30 X = X + 1
40 GOTO 20
99 END
■
```

```
30 X = X + 1
40 GOTO 20
99 END
■
```

In the shifted mode, the CRSR UP/DOWN key moves the cursor up one line at a time. When the cursor reaches the top of the screen, it stays there. The screen will not automatically scroll down (move all the lines down one or more positions).

CURSOR LEFT/RIGHT

In the unshifted mode, the CRSR LEFT/RIGHT key will move the cursor right one character position. Press the CRSR LEFT/RIGHT key and hold it down. Notice what happens when the cursor reaches the end of a line. It jumps to the leftmost position of the next line down.

```
10 PRINT "THE QUICK BROWN FO█
 JUMPED OVER THE DOG"
```

```
10 PRINT "THE QUICK BROWN FOX
█JUMPED OVER THE DOG"
```

Pressing the SHIFT and CRSR keys together will move the cursor left one character position. When the cursor reaches the left-hand border, it jumps to the rightmost column of the next line up. This is called *wraparound*. It allows you to continue entering lines that are more than 22 characters long without your having to press RETURN. This is similar to having an automatic carriage return.

If the cursor is at the right-hand edge of the bottom line and CRSR RIGHT is pressed, the screen will scroll up a line. The wraparound feature advances the cursor to the beginning of the next line, effectively producing a CRSR DOWN.

The CRSR UP/DOWN and CRSR LEFT/RIGHT keys are used to move the cursor over text without changing the text. To alter the text, move the cursor to the character you wish to correct. Typing another character will replace the existing one, allowing you to edit text easily on the screen.

INSERT/DELETE

The INST/DEL key is used to insert or delete characters on the screen. In the unshifted mode, the INST/DEL key deletes the character to the left of the cursor. It also moves the rest of the characters in the line left one space and adjusts any other characters in the 80-column logical line of which it is a part.

```
10 PRINT "BIG BROOM"

10 PRINT "BIG BROM"
```

If you press SHIFT and INST/DEL together, the computer will insert a space on the screen. All characters to the right of the cursor will be moved one position to the right.

```
10 A=B+C+D-(4#/F)

10 A=B+C+D-(4# /F)
```

PROGRAMMABLE FUNCTION KEYS

In addition to the keys we have just covered, the C-64 has four programmable, dual-function keys. They are labeled f1/f2, f3/f4, f5/f6, and f7/f8. The functions of these keys are specified by the user.

Programming the Function Keys

Most of the function keys can be put into PRINT statements in the program mode. For instance, instead of pressing CTRL and RED in the immediate mode to print in red, you could put the control functions in a PRINT statement such as

```
10 PRINT "(CTRL)(CYAN)HAPPY VALENTINES DAY(CTRL)(RED)(HEART)"
```

When you **RUN** this line, it will print the words HAPPY VALENTINE'S DAY in light blue (cyan), followed by a red heart.

With the exception of SHIFT, SHIFT/LOCK, RETURN, RUN/STOP, and RESTORE, any of the function keys can be programmed into PRINT statements.

When the function keys are programmed into PRINT statements they appear on the screen as reverse characters. Table 1-2 shows these symbols.

TABLE 1-2. Special Function Keys

⬚	CLEAR SCREEN	◣	CYAN	▬	f1
⬚	HOME	▓	PURPLE	◤	f2
⬚	CURSOR UP	⬚	GREEN	▬	f3
⬚	CURSOR DOWN	⬅	BLUE	◣	f4
▮▮	CURSOR LEFT	⬚	YELLOW	▮▬	f5
▮⬚	CURSOR RIGHT	⬚	REVERSE ON	◢	f6
▪	BLACK	▬	REVERSE OFF	▮▮	f7
⬚	WHITE	▮▮	DELETE	▬▪	f8
▪▪	RED				

THE COMMODORE DATASSETTE

You will soon find that entering all of your programs by hand is tedious. A data recorder will solve this problem. There are two units that will work with your C-64; both are basically the same. One is the original PET/CBM digital cassette drive, and the other is the VIC Datassette (Figure 1-5). One advantage the Datassette has over the older unit is a tape counter. This makes it easier to locate programs on your tapes. The operation and installation of these two units is the same. To use them, follow these instructions.

Look at the cassette interface on the back of the C-64 (Figure 1-2). The connector has an offset slot between two of the contacts, as shown in Figure 1-6.

The Datassette has a plug with a divider that fits over the connector and

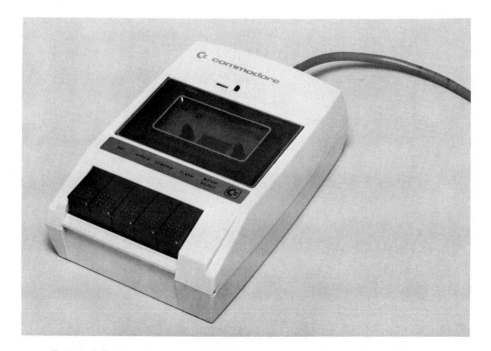

FIGURE 1-5. Commodore Datassette

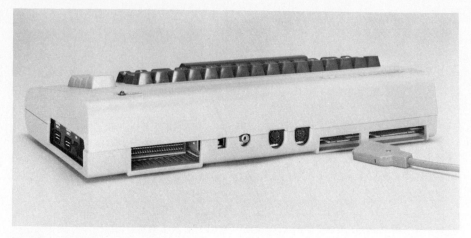

FIGURE 1-6. Datassette connector

into the slot. This makes it difficult to connect it incorrectly, but it *can* be done, so be careful. In general, you may find a connector difficult to remove once it is on, but it is rare to have trouble installing one if it is positioned correctly. If the divider slides over the slot, you can be sure a proper connection has been made.

To connect the Datassette to the C-64, follow these steps:

1. Turn the power OFF.
2. Hold the plug so the divider will mate with the connector slot.
3. Gently push the plug onto the interface. Do not force the connection.
4. Make sure the connection fits securely.
5. Turn power ON.

Testing the Datassette

Before you go any further, you should check the mechanical operation of the Datassette. Here is a simple test you can use to make sure that all of the control functions are operating properly.

1. Turn the C-64 ON. Make sure that none of the cassette keys are depressed and that the cassette drive motor is not running.

2. Open the cassette door on the top of the unit by pressing the STOP/EJECT key on the Datassette. While looking inside the unit, press the PLAY key on the Datassette. You should see the tape heads (Figure 1-7) move out toward the spindles. At the same time, the pinch roller should move out, touch the capstan roller, and begin rotating counterclockwise.

3. Again press the STOP/EJECT key on the Datassette. The tape heads should pop back out of view and the spindles should stop rotating.

4. Press the F.FWD (Fast Forward) key. The tape heads should remain hidden and the take-up spindle (on the right) should begin spinning counterclockwise very fast.

5. Pressing STOP/EJECT once should stop the take-up spindle.

6. Press the REW (Rewind) key. The supply spindle (on the left) should begin spinning clockwise very fast.

7. Press the STOP/EJECT key once. The supply spindle should stop spinning.

8. Very gently press the REC (Record) key. The key should be locked.

9. Get an unused tape. Look at the back of the cassette. It should have two small tabs blocking the write-protect holes (Figure 1-8).

Pressing the PLAY and RECORD keys simultaneously should start the take-up spindle rotating; the head assembly should move out and contact the tape, which should start moving.

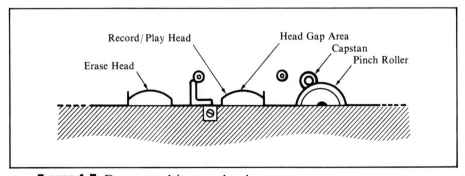

FIGURE 1-7. Datassette drive tape head

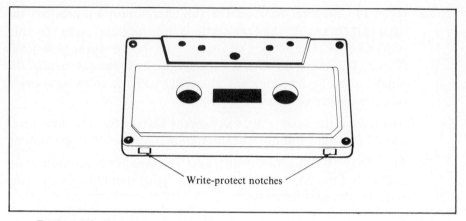

Write-protect notches

FIGURE 1-8. Write-protect notches

If you can perform all these steps, your cassette recorder is ready to begin operation. If some or all of the above tests fail, check the following:

· Make sure the power is ON.
· Press only one key at one time (except when checking the record function).
· Press the keys down until they click into place.

If you are still unsuccessful, contact your Commodore dealer.

Cleaning and Demagnetizing
Tape Heads

The head assembly of the Datassette can be seen by opening the drive door with the power OFF and depressing the PLAY key. Doing this will allow you access to the heads for maintenance. Refer to Figure 1-7 for the locations of the components mentioned in this section.

The tape heads are the devices that make contact with the tape and either read or write data. Since the tape is actually in contact with the heads, some of the oxide coating on the tape will be transferred to the heads during normal operation. To assure proper operation of the Datassette it is necessary to clean this oxide film from the heads periodically using a cotton swab soaked in denatured alcohol. Clean both heads, the capstan, and the pinch roller. Allow the area to dry completely before closing the cover.

The process of reading and writing onto a magnetic surface such as a cassette tape results in the build-up of residual magnetism on the heads of the cassette recorder. Because of this build-up, it is a good idea to demagnetize the heads each time you clean them. Skipping this step in your regular maintenance may eventually result in sufficient loss of fidelity to cause both read and write errors in your programs.

To demagnetize the heads, you will need a tape head demagnetizer such as the one in Figure 1-9. This is an inexpensive unit that can be purchased at most audio equipment stores.

The Datassette should be OFF when you are demagnetizing the tape heads. Open the cassette drive door and press the PLAY key. Make sure the demagnetizer is at least two feet away from the Datassette before plugging it in. Plug in the demagnetizer and *slowly* move it toward the Datassette until it touches one of the heads. Gently move it around on one head surface and then the other. Then touch all the metal surfaces near the heads and *slowly* move back away from the Datassette. When you are at least two feet away, unplug the demagnetizer.

PHOTO BY JOE MAURO

FIGURE 1-9. A typical tape head demagnetizer

Care of Cassette Tapes

When you use a new tape, balance the tension on the tape by fast forwarding it to the end and then rewinding it to the beginning. This will help prevent load errors.

Buy short tapes: 15 to 30 minutes at most. This will not only reduce your search time when running programs from the middle of your tapes, but will ensure that you are using thicker and stronger tapes that are less likely to stretch or break with use. Stay away from bargain brands; they tend to cause load errors more often than high-quality, low-noise tapes.

Store your cassettes in a cool, dry place, away from any magnetism.

NOTE: One of the most hazardous places to store tapes is on or near your television, which produces a magnetic field strong enough to alter the data they contain. Never touch the oxide coating on the tape itself; the surface is easily scratched and can be damaged by the oils on your hands.

Cassette Tape Write-Protect

You can avoid recording (writing) over programs you want to save by *write-protecting* them. Look at Figure 1-8; each cassette tape has two write-protect tabs, one tab for each side of the tape. Breaking out a tab locks out the REC (Record) key on the Datassette. Should you decide, after breaking out a write-protect tab, that you do want to record a program on that side of a tape, simply put a piece of tape over the write-protect opening.

DISK DRIVES

The C-64 can use the model 1541 disk drive (Figure 1-10) which has been designed to interface directly with the C-64 through its serial port. Table 1-3 shows the specifications for the 1541 disk drive.

The 1541 disk drive can store 174,848 bytes of data per diskette. It does this by putting more blocks of data on the outer (longer) tracks of the diskette than do other disk drives.

FIGURE 1-10. 1541 disk drive

Connecting Disk Drives

To connect a disk drive to the C-64 computer, follow these steps:

1. Unplug the computer's power cord from the electrical outlet.
2. Connect the interface cable supplied with the disk drive to the serial port on the back of the C-64.
3. Plug the disk drive's power cord into an AC outlet.
4. Plug the C-64's power cord into an AC outlet.
5. Check all your connections. If they look good, then proceed to the power-on test.

Power-On Test

To perform a power-on test, follow these steps:

1. Turn the C-64's power ON. Wait until it has completed its initialization.
2. Open the disk drive door and make sure the drive is empty.
3. Turn the disk drive's power ON.

TABLE 1-3. 1541 Disk Drive Specifications

Storage	
Total disk capacity	174,848 bytes per diskette
Number of program names	144 per diskette
Sectors per track	17–21
Bytes per sector	256
Number of tracks	35
Number of sectors	683 (664 blocks free)
Disk Memory	
2114 (4)	2K RAM
Mechanical specifications:	
Dimensions	
Height	97 mm
Width	200 mm
Depth	374 mm
Electronic specifications:	
Power requirements	
Voltage	100, 120, 220, or 240 VAC
Frequency	50 or 60 Hz
Power	25 Watts
Media:	
Diskettes	Standard mini 5-1/4", single-sided, single-density

ADAPTED FROM COMMODORE BUSINESS MACHINES

Indicator Lights

The 1541 disk drive has two indicator lights on its front panel. The green one will glow when power is applied to the unit. The red one is the disk activity indicator. It will glow when the drive is running and flash if there is an error condition.

Loading and Unloading Diskettes

Figure 1-11 illustrates the various parts of a floppy diskette. The magnetic surface itself is a disk made of a thin, flexible plastic similar to the material used in cassette tapes. This fragile disk is enclosed in a protective jacket. The jacket is then placed in an envelope that protects the read/write slot.

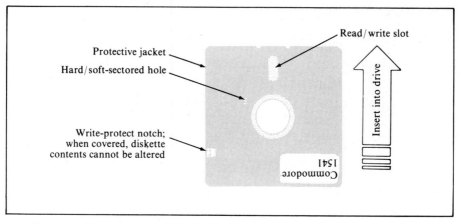

FIGURE 1-11. Floppy diskette

As mentioned earlier, the 1541 disk drive puts more data onto a single diskette than almost any other disk drive. The way it does this is by putting more blocks of data (*sectors*) into the data tracks that are near the outside of the diskette. Some disk drives put the same number of sectors on each track. Of those that do this, there are some that use *hard-sectored* diskettes. These diskettes have a series of evenly spaced holes near their center. The disk drive uses these holes to position the sectors. Since the 1541 does not have regularly spaced sectors, it does not use these holes. The 1541 uses only *soft-sectored* diskettes (those with only one hole in them).

To determine what kind of diskette you have, follow this procedure (see Figure 1-12):

1. Take the diskette out of its envelope (not the jacket), and hold it by its edges.

2. Gently insert two fingers into the center hole.

3. Rotate the diskette with the two fingers in the center hole until a small hole in the diskette aligns with the outer small hole in the jacket.

4. Continue rotating the diskette inside the jacket. If you find only one hole, the diskette is soft-sectored. If you find more than one hole it is hard-sectored and cannot be used with the 1541 disk drive.

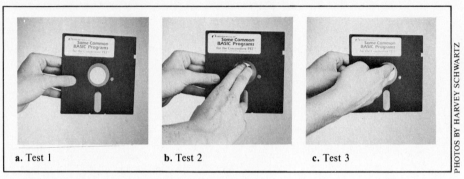

a. Test 1   **b.** Test 2   **c.** Test 3

PHOTOS BY HARVEY SCHWARTZ

FIGURE 1-12. Test for soft-sectored diskette

Loading the Drive

Perform the following steps to load the 1541 disk drive:

1. Make sure the disk drive is OFF (the red activity light is *not* lit).

2. Hold the diskette by its jacket. Do not touch the exposed sections of the diskette! The diskette's label should be facing up, with the write-protect notch (Figure 1-11) on your left.

3. Carefully slide the diskette into the front slot until you hear a click. If it doesn't slide in smoothly, pull it out and try again. Forcing it can damage both the diskette and the drive.

4. With two fingers, firmly press down on the latch until it locks down.

Unloading the Drive

To unload the 1541 disk drive, follow these steps:

1. Make sure the disk drive is OFF (the red activity light is *not* lit).

2. Using two fingers, give the latch a quick press downward and release it. It should pop up, and the diskette should pop slightly forward out of the drive slot.

3. Hold the diskette gently with your thumb and forefinger and withdraw it from the drive. *Do not bend or force the diskette!*

4. Put the diskette back into its envelope.

FLOPPY DISKS

If handled properly, floppy diskettes are a convenient method of storing data. They are, however, quite fragile, and it is just as easy to write over important data as it is to write it in the first place.

Care of Diskettes

Diskettes must be handled with care. All of your information will be stored on them, and once a diskette is damaged, it is virtually impossible to retrieve this information. Here are some hints which will help you protect your diskettes.

1. Whenever the diskette is out of the disk drive, place it in its protective envelope.
2. *Never* remove a diskette from its protective jacket!
3. When you label your diskettes, use only a felt-tip pen. Pencils or ball-point pens may damage the diskette.
4. Do not touch or try to clean the diskette surface. This will damage it.
5. Do not smoke while using diskettes. Tobacco ash or smoke residue will damage the diskette surface.
6. *Keep diskettes away from all magnetic fields!* Even placing them on top of your television set or disk drive can cause some distortion of the data stored on the diskette.
7. Do not expose your diskettes to heat or sunlight.

Diskette Write-Protection

You can prevent the information on your diskettes from being overwritten by write-protecting them. To do this, simply cover the write-protect notch (Figure 1-11) with the adhesive labels that came with your diskettes, or with a piece of opaque tape.

If you remove the write-protect notch cover, you will be able to write to the diskette again.

THE 1525 GRAPHIC PRINTER

While you can use almost any printer with the C-64 through the parallel port or by installing an IEEE 488 interface, the 1525 Graphic Printer operates directly with the C-64 (Figure 1-13). The 1525 can print any standard C-64 character or symbol, both normal and reversed, and it can be programmed to print dot graphics.

The 1525 prints characters using a 7 × 5 dot matrix and a 7 × 6 dot matrix for special symbols. Table 1-4 shows the specifications for the 1525 Graphic Printer.

Connecting the Printer

Follow the steps outlined below to connect the 1525 Graphic Printer to the C-64:

1. Unplug the computer's power cord from the electrical outlet.
2. Look at the back of the C-64. There are two round, similar connectors in the center of the back. The one with five pins is the video

FIGURE 1-13. Model 1525 graphic printer

TABLE 1-4. 1525 Printer Specifications

1. General Specifications

A. Print head . . . . 5×7 dot matrix impact dot matrix print (unihammer method)

B. Character set . . . . Upper and lower case characters, numerals, symbols, and C-64 graphics characters

C. Graphic mode . . . . 7 dots per column

E. Character codes . . . . C-64 8-bit code

G. Print speed . . . . 30 characters per sec

H. Maximum line width . . . . .80 columns

I. Character spacing . . . . 12 characters per inch

J. Linefeed spacing . . . . 6 dots . . . . Character mode

9 dots . . . . Graphic mode

7.5 linefeeds/sec . . . . Graphic mode

M. Paper width . . . . 4.5 to 8.5 inches acceptable

N. Copies . . . . (Maximum) Original plus 2 copies

O. Inked ribbon . . . . Built-in cassette type

P. Physical specifications . . . . 234.D×420 W×136 H

Q. Weight . . . . Approximately 4.5 kg

2. Electrical Specifications

A. Power . . . . .120V AC

15 watts max

port. The other connector has six pins. It is the serial port. Plug the printer cable (Figure 1-14) into the serial port.

3. The other end of the cable plugs into the six-pin plug on the back of the 1525 printer.

4. Turn the C-64 ON and wait for it to initialize (the READY display will appear on the screen).

5. Turn on the 1525 Graphic Printer. The red power light on the top of the printer should glow and the print head should travel to the center of the carriage and return to the left.

6. Move the switch on the back of the printer marked T-5-4 to the "T" position (Figure 1-15). The printer should begin printing the entire C-64 character set.

    The printer should continue printing this until you either turn the power OFF or switch the T-5-4 switch to "4" or "5."

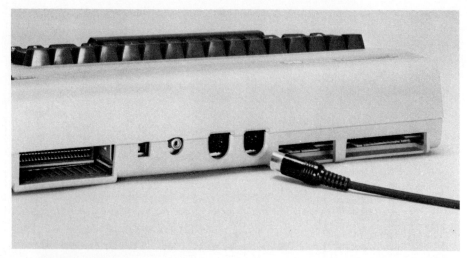

FIGURE 1-14. Printer cable and serial port

FIGURE 1-15. T-5-4 switch

7. Move the T-5-4 switch to the "4" position. The printer should stop printing the test printout.

If the printer does not operate as described above, recheck all your connections and repeat the procedure described above. If you are still unsuccessful, consult your Commodore dealer.

Installing the Ribbon

Perform the following steps to install the printer ribbon:

1. Lift off the clear plastic sound cover (Figure 1-16).
2. The small tab on each ribbon cassette should face forward. Making sure that the ribbon is not twisted (as shown in Figure 1-17), rock each ribbon cassette to the outside of the machine and press it down into position.
3. Rotate the ribbon cam out of the way and feed the ribbon between the cam and its backing plate (Figure 1-18).
4. Replace the front cover and the clear sound cover.

To remove a ribbon, simply reverse the above procedure.

Paper Insertion

The 1525 Graphic Printer uses a continuous form that can be from 4.5 to 8½ inches wide. It is sprocketed on both sides and can have as many as three parts (one original and two copies) as long as the total thickness does not exceed 0.2 mm.

The following steps show how to insert paper into the 1525 Graphic Printer:

1. Turn the printer OFF and unplug its power cord.
2. Lift off the clear plastic sound cover.
3. Open the paper guides (Figure 1-19).
4. Insert the paper from the rear of the printer through the paper chute.
5. Continue feeding the paper in by hand until it emerges at the front of the printer.

FIGURE 1-16. Removing the front cover of the 1525 printer

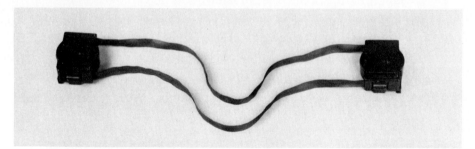

FIGURE 1-17. Ribbon cassettes

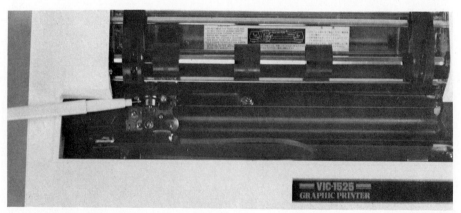

FIGURE 1-18. Ribbon cam assembly

6. Lift the paper-bail and feed the paper underneath it, adjusting the bail glides so they will be evenly spaced across the width of the paper.

7. Pull the paper through from the front and align the paper guides so the sprocket holes on the paper mate with the sprockets on the guides.

   NOTE: The paper should not be too tightly stretched or the sprocket holes may tear; however, if the paper is too loose, it will wrinkle and bind inside the paper feed mechanism.

8. Close the paper guides and replace the clear plastic sound cover.

9. Advance the paper using the thumbwheel, making sure the paper moves smoothly through the feed mechanism.

10. Plug in the printer and turn it ON.

Print Head

You may adjust the force of the print head to compensate for paper thickness and ribbon wear as follows:

1. Turn the printer OFF and unplug its power cord.

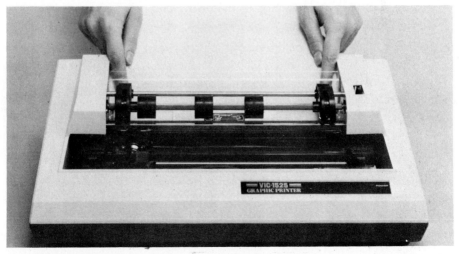

FIGURE 1-19. Loading paper into the 1525 printer

Figure 1-20. Print head pressure adjustment

2. Remove the clear sound cover and the brown front cover from the printer. (To remove the front cover, it will be necessary to press in and up on the two thumb rests molded into the front of the cover.)

3. Looking down at the top of the print head you will see the pressure adjustment lever (Figure 1-20).

4. The lever should be in one of the three position holes. To adjust the force of the print head, lift the adjustment lever and put it into one of the other holes. Do not leave the adjustment lever between any of the holes; it must be resting in one of them to maintain its adjustment.

Operating the C-64 2

This chapter will introduce you to the basic operation of the C-64 and some of its peripheral devices: the Datassette, the 1541 disk drive, and the 1525 printer. It is especially important for you to become comfortable with the C-64's keyboard and display and to become familiar with the computer's two modes of operation: *immediate* and *program* modes.

IMMEDIATE MODE

When you turn on the C-64 it is operating in immediate mode. The flashing cursor signifies that the computer is waiting for instructions and also shows where the next character you type on the keyboard will appear on the screen.

In immediate mode, you can use the C-64 as you would a calculator. You enter *statements*—instructions to display information, perform a calculation, or carry out some other function. When you enter a statement and press the RETURN key, the C-64 processes, or *executes*, the statement. First, though, the C-64 checks your entry for *syntax*—the correct combination of characters in a statement. If the syntax is correct, the statement executes. If it isn't correct, the following message appears:

```
?SYNTAX

ERROR

READY.

■
```

If you get a syntax error message, check your statement for typographical errors.

Immediate mode does what its name implies: any statements you enter will execute immediately after you press RETURN.

The PRINT statement is the most frequently used immediate mode statement. PRINT instructs the C-64 to display whatever follows it. For example, PRINT will display the results of calculations such as

```
PRINT 360+199+1000
```

which, in this case, would be 1559.

PRINT will also display characters or entire strings of characters. A *string* is a sequence of characters that can include letters, numbers, spaces, and symbols. To display a string such as

```
AND MILES TO GO BEFORE I SLEEP
```

on the C-64's screen, you would type the following immediate mode statement and press RETURN:

```
PRINT"AND MILES TO GO BEFORE I SLEEP"
```

The string has quotation marks around it; anything enclosed in quotation marks in a PRINT statement will display literally as a string of characters.

For example, a PRINT statement such as

```
PRINT"360+199+1000"
```

will not calculate anything. The computer will display a string of characters, which in this case is three numbers connected by plus signs. Conversely, the statement

```
PRINT AND MILES TO GO BEFORE I SLEEP
```

will not display anything except a syntax error message. The syntax of a PRINT statement always expects numeric or string information to follow. The word AND does not represent a number and is not in quotes; therefore, the C-64 rejects the statement.

You can abbreviate PRINT by using a question mark. The following statements produce the same result:

```
PRINT"GODFREY CAMBRIDGE"
```

or

```
?"GODFREY CAMBRIDGE"
```

Screen Editing

One of the most powerful features of the C-64 is its screen editor. The key to using the C-64's editing capabilities is the cursor. You can move the cursor in four directions: up, down, left, and right. You can also insert or delete characters anywhere on the screen, or even clear the entire screen using a single keystroke.

EDITING TEXT ON THE CURRENT DISPLAY LINE

Occasionally, you may notice a mistake on a line you are currently entering. You can correct mistakes on a line you are entering by backspacing to the error and correcting it. For example,

```
OUR BUDGEY
```

was intended to display as OUR BUDGET. You can change the Y to a T easily enough. Type in the line above and use the SHIFT and CURSOR LEFT/RIGHT keys to position the cursor over the Y.

```
OUR BUDGE▉
```

```
OUR BUDGET
```

To change the Y to a T, simply type **T**. This replaces the old letter and moves the cursor one position to the right.

BACKSPACING WITH THE DELETE KEY

If you just entered a character that you would like to retype, press the INST/DEL key to remove the incorrect character, and then continue typing.

When you used the CRSR LEFT/RIGHT key, the cursor simply moved over the characters on the screen without changing them. Try the following example using the INST/DEL key:

```
OUR BUDGE█

OUR BUDGET█
```

SHIFTING AND DELETING TEXT WITH THE DELETE KEY

In the following example, the word BUDGET has been entered with two U's. It will be necessary to delete one of the U's and move the text to the left to close up the extra space left by the U.

To do this, use the CRSR LEFT/RIGHT key to position the cursor over the D and press the INST/DEL key once. This key erases the letter to the left of the cursor, deleting the U and shifting the text to fill the space.

```
OUR BU█DGET

OUR B█DGET
```

SHIFTING TEXT TO INSERT CHARACTERS

In the example below, we need to change OUR BUDGET to OUR FAMILY BUDGET. To do this, use the CRSR LEFT/RIGHT key to position the cursor over the space between OUR and BUDGET.

FAMILY has six letters and you will also need a space at the end of the word. Hold down the SHIFT key and press INST/DEL seven times. This will produce seven spaces between the two words. You may now type **FAMILY** between OUR and BUDGET.

Remember, when you are inserting characters, the character directly under the cursor is the one that will be shifted to the right. You must also remember to enter enough spaces for each word you add, plus a space between each word.

```
OUR█BUDGET

OUR█        BUDGET

OUR FAMILY█BUDGET
```

EDITING TEXT BETWEEN QUOTATION MARKS

If you are editing text enclosed in quotation marks you will need to take certain precautions because anything entered within a string will be incorporated into it (with the exception of quotation marks, RETURN, and RUN/STOP). This "quote mode" enables you to enter special characters, but it can be frustrating when you merely want to fix an error in a statement. For example, the following line should say PRINT "HOT DOGS FOR SALE". Enter the line exactly as shown; do not type end quotes or press RETURN. Try to make the necessary change to "HOYT".

```
PRINT "HOYT DOGS FOR SALE
```

When you tried to backspace to correct "HOYT", the computer printed a reverse vertical bar. To backspace when editing text in quotation marks, you will need to exit the quote mode. One way to do this is to type another set of quotes. While you must enter quote mode to enter a string, you must exit quote mode to edit the string.

Another method of escaping from the quote mode is to hold SHIFT down and press RETURN. This will move the cursor down one line, allowing you to move the cursor up and make any changes you like.

While this may seem like an unwelcome "feature," you can write programs using cursor keys. For instance, the immediate mode statement

```
HELLO DOWN THERE
PRINT ".THELLO DOWN THERE"
```

displays the text above the PRINT statement instead of below it, as would normally be the case.

Arithmetic Calculations

The C-64 can perform the four standard mathematical operations: addition, subtraction, multiplication, and division. The symbols for addition and subtraction are the familiar plus sign and minus sign, but an asterisk is used for multiplication and a slash for division. Therefore, to multiply 4 by 4 you would enter

    PRINT 4*4

or

    ?4*4

To divide 8 by 2 you would enter

    PRINT 8/2

or

    ?8/2

PROGRAM MODE

In both immediate mode and program mode, you enter statements and the computer responds to them. However, immediate mode statements are very limited. If you were to press the CLEAR SCREEN key, your statement would be gone.

The immediate mode examples you entered earlier in this chapter were simple, one-line programs, and they do not do much. Once you become familiar with your computer you will want to write longer programs. BASIC programs can be hundreds of statements long; program mode statements should not be as expendable as immediate mode statements. Therefore, the C-64 stores program mode statements in main memory. Program mode statements are more powerful than immediate mode statements because they execute "under their own power." In immediate mode the computer executes one statement and then waits for you to key in another statement. In program mode, statements execute automatically in an order that you specify.

Program Entry

Programs may be entered using the keyboard or loaded into memory through the Datassette or disk drive. Each statement entered through the keyboard has a corresponding line number. When you press RETURN at the end of each statement, that line is stored in the C-64's memory.

You can use any line numbers between 0 and 63999. When you enter lines in your programs, they will execute in the order they are *numbered*, not the order in which they are entered. For instance, if you entered the lines

```
100 PRINT "CRAMDEN!"
90 PRINT "RALPH"
75 PRINT "THE WINNER IS"
```

they would execute in the following order:

```
THE WINNER IS
RALPH
CRAMDEN!
```

It doesn't matter that there are gaps between the numbers used; C-64 BASIC keeps the line numbers in order as you enter them. You should leave some numbers unused between your program lines so you can add statements later. All of this will be covered in greater detail in Chapter 3.

Running a Program

The RUN statement causes the computer to execute any program that is in memory. Enter the following program:

```
10 X=0
20 PRINT X
30 X=X+1
40 GOTO 20
```

The GOTO at line 40 tells the computer to return to line 20 and execute the instruction there.

Typing **RUN** begins execution at the lowest line number in your program.

```
RUN
0
1
2
3
4
5
```

```
6
7
8
9
10
11
12
13
14
15
16
17
18
19
20
21
```

RUN followed by a line number starts execution of your program beginning with the specified line number.

```
RUN 30
22
23
24
25
26
27
28
29
30
31
32
33
34
35
36
37
38
39
40
41
42
43
```

USING THE DATASSETTE

The Datassette saves you the time and tedium of keying in programs over and over again. The Datassette will store BASIC programs and retrieve them when you need them.

The operations the Datassette will perform go well beyond the scope of this chapter. Chapter 8 explores the full potential of the Datassette for storing and retrieving data.

Saving a Program

Make sure the short program you entered in the last section is still in memory by typing **LIST**. If it isn't, reenter it. To save it on a cassette, type

```
SAVE"RALPH"
```

The C-64 will respond with

```
PRESS RECORD & PLAY ON TAPE
```

Press PLAY and RECORD simultaneously. If you press just the PLAY key, the C-64 will send data to the Datassette but nothing will be stored on tape. After you press PLAY and RECORD, the C-64 will respond with

```
OK
SAVING RALPH
```

While the C-64 is saving the program on the Datassette, the cursor disappears. When it is finished, the Datassette will stop, the C-64 will display the READY message, and the flashing cursor will return.

Verification

After you save a program on the Datassette, it is a good idea to verify that it was properly recorded. Occasionally, poor quality tapes or slight mechanical fluctuations may cause a program to be incorrectly recorded. To protect yourself from losing programs, always verify them immediately after you store them.

To verify a program, follow these steps.

1. Rewind the tape and press the STOP/EJECT key.

2. Type **VERIFY**, followed by the program's name, and press RETURN.

A typical verify dialog with the C-64 may look like the following:

```
VERIFY "RALPH"

PRESS PLAY ON TAPE
OK

SEARCHING FOR RALPH
FOUND RALPH


VERIFYING
OK
READY.
```

If the program was not saved properly, you will get an error message. If this happens, you should SAVE it again and reverify it.

Loading a Program

To load a program from the Datassette, simply type **LOAD program name.** The C-64 will respond by displaying

```
PRESS PLAY ON TAPE
```

After you press the PLAY key, the C-64 will display OK and then

```
SEARCHING FOR
```

When you load a program from the Datassette, you do not need to enter a program name. If you simply type **LOAD**, the computer will load the first program it reaches on the tape. Using a program name causes the computer to look for the file named, skipping any others it finds.

After a program is loaded from tape, you can leave the PLAY key depressed if you will be loading more information from the tape at a later time. However, if you do not intend to load another program from tape soon, it is a good idea to press STOP to release the PLAY key so you will not accidently try to SAVE a program while the Datassette is in the play mode. The C-64 can detect when a Datassette key has been pressed, but it cannot distinguish which key was pressed. Therefore, if PLAY and RECORD are pressed (to SAVE a program) and you attempt to LOAD, the Datassette will erase the program instead of reading it.

You may occasionally have trouble loading a program from tape. Instead of displaying

    READY.

the C-64 may display the following message:

    ?LOAD
    ERROR
    READY.
    ■

If this happens, rewind the tape and try loading it again. Try this several times if necessary. If this does not work, there may have been an undetected problem when the program was saved. Always VERIFY programs after you SAVE them, and if they are important or have taken considerable time to enter, make one or more backup copies.

One way to reduce errors during the SAVE procedure is to fast-forward a new tape to the end, and then rewind it to the beginning before storing anything on it. This winding and rewinding process will tend to make the tape move through the tape mechanism more smoothly. This is because when tapes are manufactured they are wound onto their spools at high speed. This process often puts some tension on the tape, and the first time it is unwound it may jump a bit as it moves through the mechanism. It may also pull and stick slightly in the cassette. Although these effects are not usually noticeable in audio applications, they can cause data errors on computer tapes.

Before entering a LOAD instruction, be sure to rewind the tape to a point before your program begins; otherwise the C-64 will never find it. A good practice is to note the number of the tape counter at the beginning of your program and write it down on the tape label beside the name of the program. This will also save time when you LOAD programs, since the computer will not need to go through as much tape before reaching the program you want.

LOAD and RUN

Pressing SHIFT and RUN/STOP together will automatically LOAD and RUN the next program on the Datassette. This works only when the computer is in the immediate mode (not executing an instruction from within a program).

OPERATING THE 1541 DISK DRIVE

If you have been using a cassette drive, you will appreciate how much time can be saved over entering programs by hand each time you wish to run them. The 1541 disk drive can save you even more time because of its much greater flexibility and faster data access time. This section will cover the basic operation of the disk drive, listing the diskette directory, and loading and running programs from a diskette. The disk operations and statements will be covered in detail in Chapter 7.

Loading a Program

To load a program from a diskette in the 1541 disk drive, type **LOAD "file name",8**.

The "8" above is the device number of the disk drive. This device number is set at the factory. The C-64 will display SEARCHING FOR "file name". The disk drive will activate, and the red light on the front of the drive will come on. If the program is on the diskette, the C-64 will also display

```
LOADING
READY.
```

If not, you will see

```
?FILE NOT FOUND
ERROR
READY.
```

If you are not sure of the exact name of a particular file, or don't know what is on your diskette, type

```
LOAD"$",8
```

and the disk directory will be loaded into memory. To display the directory, type

```
LIST
```

and the directory will appear on the screen.

```
0 ▮▮▮▮▮▮▮▮▮▮▮▮▮▮▮▮▮▮▮▮▮▮▮▮
5     "UNIVERSAL WEDGE"   PRG
8     "UNIT TO UNIT"      PRG
3     "CHANGE 1541"       PRG
```

```
11     "COPY 1540-1541"   PRG
27     "PRINTER DEMO"      PRG
12     "SEQUENTIAL"        PRG
11     "PERFORMANCE TEST"  PRG
5      "CHECK DISK"        PRG
17     "LOGIC DIAGNOSTIC"  PRG

■
```

To recall any program from diskette, it is absolutely necessary to enter the file name exactly as it is found on the directory. Therefore, it is generally helpful to list the disk directory before loading any programs.

Look at the directory in the previous display. The top row (in reverse letters) shows the name of the diskette and its ID number. The disk drive always stores this number, and each time a diskette is accessed it compares the ID number with the number it has stored from the last disk operation. If the numbers are the same, the disk drive assumes that the same diskette is being accessed and simply performs its operation (SAVE or LOAD). If the number on the diskette does not match the one in the disk drive's memory, the disk drive will create a map of all the files on the diskette and update its ID memory. This process is called initialization.

As long as no two diskettes have the same ID number, the disk drive will always initialize itself automatically when you change diskettes. If you have two diskettes that have the same ID number, you should manually initialize the disk drive by using the following command:

```
OPEN 1,8,15,"I0"
```

Remember, you need to initialize only when you change diskettes, and then only if the ID and name of the current diskette are the same as that of the new diskette.

Note that once a program has been loaded into memory, whether from tape, from diskette, or by hand, the computer will treat it in the same manner so the procedures for running, listing, and making changes to the program remain the same.

Formatting a Diskette

Before you can record any data on a new diskette, you must first prepare it using a process called formatting. The computer stores and retrieves data from the diskette by accessing special locations, called sectors,

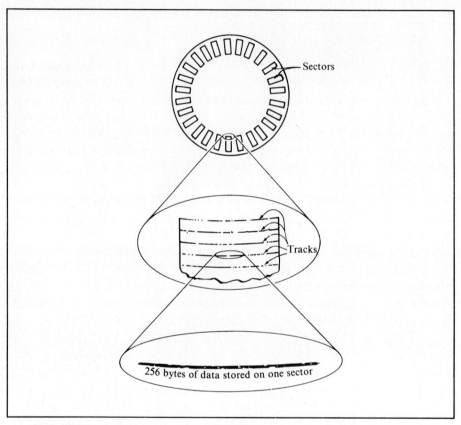

FIGURE 2-1. A diskette's recorded surface

on the diskette. These locations are laid out on the diskette before any data can be stored on it. Each sector is a small part of the tracks on the diskette. Tracks are similar to the grooves in a phonograph record, but are arranged in concentric circles rather than as a spiral. Figure 2-1 shows what the tracks on a diskette might look like if you could see them. Each track is divided into smaller pieces, called sectors, each of which may contain up to 256 bytes of data. When you buy a new diskette, it is not divided into these sectors and will not accept anything you try to record on it. Diskettes are not formatted when you buy them because each disk drive manufacturer uses a slightly different format on its diskettes. The C-64 diskette must be formatted on a C-64 disk drive.

Here are two methods of formatting a diskette.

Method 1:
>   OPEN 1,8,15
>   PRINT#1,"Ndrive no.:disk name,ID no."

Example:

```
OPEN 1,8,15
PRINT#1,"N:NEW DISK,01"
```

The drive number may be omitted when there is only one disk drive connected to the C-64.

Method 2:
>   OPEN 1,8,15,"Ndrive no.:disk name,01"

Example:

```
OPEN 1,8,15,"N:NEW DISK,01"
```

Again, the drive number may be omitted in one-drive systems.

If you have a diskette that has been used before and you wish to completely erase it and then prepare it for use as a new diskette, you may simply type **OPEN1,8,5,"Ndrive no.:disk name"**.

Example:

```
OPEN 1,8,15,"N:NEW DISK"
```

As before, the drive number is not necessary in one-drive systems, and in this case the ID number is intentionally left out. The new disk name is put onto the diskette, and the old ID number is used. All the programs and data stored on the diskette will be erased. Do not confuse this operation with initialization, which sets up the disk and drive for use together. Formatting will erase everything from your diskette.

Saving a Program

Saving a program onto a diskette is nearly the same as saving a program onto tape using the Datassette. The major difference is in the wording (syntax) of the command. To save a program on diskette, type the command **SAVE" <program name >",8**.

If you only have one disk drive you may delete the drive number. For example, to save the "RALPH" program from earlier in this chapter, enter it and type

```
SAVE "RALPH",8
```

The disk drive should activate, the red light on its front should light, the video screen should show

```
SAVING RALPH
```

and the cursor should disappear. When the program has been saved, the screen will show the READY message and the cursor will return.

After you save any program it is a good idea to verify it, as with programs stored on tape. To verify RALPH, which you stored on diskette, type

```
VERIFY"RALPH",8
```

The screen will display

```
SEARCHING FOR RALPH
VERIFYING
OK

READY.
```

if the program was successfully saved. If not, you will get the ?VERIFY error message. If this occurs, try saving and verifying again.

Occasionally, there will be flaws on a diskette's surface. If you try to save a program and cannot get it to save properly, there may be a slight defect in the track and sector being accessed. Try another diskette in this case.

OPERATING THE 1525 GRAPHIC PRINTER

You may use the C-64 graphic printer to print the data from your programs and to list the programs themselves. The printer may be addressed in either immediate or program mode.

The OPEN Statement

Before you can send data to the printer, you must open a channel to it. This is done using the following OPEN statement **OPEN number between 1 and 255,4**.

The first number (between 1 and 255) is the number you will use to address the printer. The second number is the printer's device number. It is always 4.

Here is an example of a printer OPEN statement.

```
OPEN 1,4
```

You would now send all the data to be printed by the printer to channel 1 by typing

```
PRINT#1, "HOW NOW BROWN COW"
```

The printer should print HOW NOW BROWN COW and return, advancing the paper one row.

In a program, you could alternately print to the printer and the video screen by simply typing **PRINT** when you want output to the screen, and **PRINT#1** when you want the output printed on the printer. PRINT always outputs to the primary device (the screen, for example, or another device selected by a CMD instruction). PRINT# outputs to a file specially OPENed to that device number.

The CMD Statement

If you had a program that displayed all its data on the screen and you wanted it to print everything on the printer instead, you could accomplish this by adding two lines to the beginning of the program.

```
OPEN 1,4
CMD 1
```

The OPEN statement opens a channel to the printer, and the CMD statement sends all output to the printer. By doing this, every PRINT statement is automatically sent to the printer.

The CMD statement also allows you to produce a printed listing of a diskette's directory. To do this, type

```
LOAD"$",8
```

This will load the directory into memory. Now type

```
OPEN 1,4
CMD 1
LIST
```

This will generate a complete directory listing on the printer. This will also allow you to produce a printed copy of your disk directory, should you want to put it in the envelope with the diskette.

To exit from the CMD mode, enter **PRINT# device no.**

The CLOSE Statement

After you have finished using the printer, you must close the channel to it. To do this, type **CLOSE channel no.**   If you OPENed channel 1 (as we did above), type

```
CLOSE 1
```

After using a CMD statement, you will need to precede the CLOSE statement with a PRINT# statement.

Here is an example.

```
OPEN 1,4
CMD 1
    .
    .
    .
PRINT#1 : CLOSE 1
```

This will ensure that all files are properly closed. Failing to do this may cause file errors.

Programming the C-64 Computer **3**

This chapter will teach you how to program your C-64 using BASIC, its built-in language. If you are already familiar with BASIC, Appendixes G and H will serve as comprehensive reference to each statement in the language. If you are a beginner, start with this chapter. It will give you the background necessary to continue through the rest of the book.

ELEMENTS OF A PROGRAMMING LANGUAGE

Program statements must be written following a well-defined set of rules. These rules, taken together, are referred to as *syntax*. There are many different sets of rules that define how program statements are written. Each set of rules applies to a different programming language. All of the syntax rules described in this book apply only to C-64 BASIC.

Programming languages are as varied as spoken languages. In addition to BASIC, other common programming languages are Pascal, FORTRAN, COBOL, APL, PL/M, PL-1, and FORTH. Uncommon programming languages number in the hundreds.

Unfortunately, programming languages, like spoken languages, have dialects. A BASIC program written for your C-64 may not run on another computer, even if the other computer is also programmable in BASIC. These variations in the language syntax are due to the computer's limitations or special features. However, having learned how to program your C-64 in BASIC, you will have little trouble learning any other computer's BASIC dialect.

Some programming language syntax rules are obvious. The addition and subtraction examples in Chapter 2 use obvious syntax. You do not have to be a programmer to understand these simple calculation statements. However, most syntax rules seem arbitrary, and sometimes they are. For example, why use "*" to represent multiplication? One would normally use "✕" for multiplication; but the computer would have no way of differentiating between the use of the "✕" sign to represent multiplication or to represent the letter "x." Therefore nearly all computer languages use the asterisk (*) to represent multiplication. Division is universally represented by a slash (/). Since the standard division sign (÷) is not present on computer or typewriter keyboards, some other character had to be selected. The slash was probably chosen because it made the program expression look like a fraction.

BASIC statement syntax deals separately with line numbers, data, and instructions to the computer. We will describe each in turn.

Line Numbers

As we have already stated, in programmed mode every line of a BASIC program must have a unique line number. The first line of the program must have the smallest line number, while the last line must have the largest. In between, line numbers must be in ascending order. The C-64 computer forces this upon you: no matter where you enter a line on the display, the C-64 will move it to its proper sequential position. Consider an existing program with the following line numbers:

```
120
130
140
150
160
170
180
190
```

If you enter a new statement with line number 165, the new statement will initially appear below the existing line 190, but the computer will automatically insert this statement between lines 160 and 170. This may be illustrated as follows:

Line numbers displayed when you entered line 165	Lines stored and redisplayed thus
120	120
130	130
140	140
150	150
160	160
170	165
180	170
190	180
	190
165	

If the line number for a new statement duplicates an existing line number, the old statement will be replaced.

C-64 BASIC allows line numbers to range between 1 and 63999. The C-64 computer interprets digits appearing at the beginning of any line as the line number. If the line number is larger than 63999, a syntax error message appears, since you have violated one of the syntax rules for C-64 BASIC.

All BASIC dialects require line numbers to be assigned in ascending order, as described above. However, the largest line number allowed varies from one dialect of BASIC to the next.

You use line numbers as *addresses,* identifying locations within a program. This is an important concept, since every program will contain the following two types of statements:

1. Statements that create or modify data.
2. Statements that control the sequence in which operations are performed.

The idea that operations specified by a program must be performed in some well-defined sequence is a simple enough concept. Program execution normally begins with the first statement in the program and continues sequentially. This may be illustrated as follows:

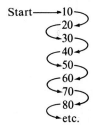

Most programs, however, contain some nonsequential execution sequences. That is when line numbers become important, because they are used to identify a change in execution sequence. This may be illustrated as follows:

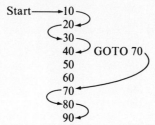

Data

The statement or statements following a line number specify operations the computer is to perform, as well as data that must be used while performing these operations. We will now describe the types of data you may encounter in a C-64 BASIC program.

There are two kinds of numbers that can be stored in C-64 computers: floating point numbers (also called real numbers) and integers.

FLOATING POINT NUMBERS

Floating point is the standard number representation used by C-64 computers. All arithmetic is done using floating point numbers. The name refers to the decimal point's ability to float, allowing fractions with different numbers of digits. A floating point number can be a whole number, or a fractional number preceded by a decimal point. The number can be negative (−) or positive (+). If the number has no sign it is assumed to be positive. Here are some examples of floating point numbers that are equivalent to integers.

```
5
−15
65000
161
0
```

Here are examples of floating point numbers that include a decimal point.

```
0.5
0.0165432
−0.0000009
1.6
24.0055
−64.2
3.1416
```

Note that if you put commas in a number, you will get a syntax error message. For example, use 65000, not 65,000.

ROUNDOFF

Numbers always have at least eight digits of precision; they can have up to nine, depending on the number. C-64 BASIC rounds off additional significant digits. Usually it rounds up when the next digit is more than 5 and rounds down when the next digit is 4 or less, but there are some roundoff quirks.

Here are some examples.

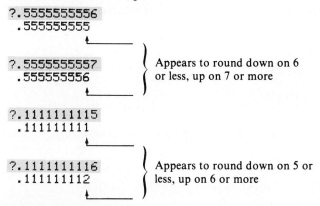

```
?.5555555556
.555555555
```

```
?.5555555557
.555555556
```
Appears to round down on 6 or less, up on 7 or more

```
?.1111111115
.111111111
```

```
?.1111111116
.111111112
```
Appears to round down on 5 or less, up on 6 or more

SCIENTIFIC NOTATION

Large floating point numbers are represented using scientific notation. When numbers with ten or more digits are entered, C-64 BASIC automatically converts these numbers to scientific notation.

```
READY.
?1111111114
 1.11111111E+09

READY.
?1111111115
 1.11111112E+09
```

A number in scientific notation has the following form:

numberE+ee

where

number   is an integer, fraction, or combination, as illustrated above. The "number" portion contains the number's significant digits; it is called the "coefficient." If no decimal point appears, it is assumed to be to the right of the coefficient.

E   is always the letter E. It substitutes for the word "exponent."

+   is an optional plus sign or minus sign.

ee   is a one-digit or two-digit exponent. The exponent specifies the magnitude of the number: the number of places to the right (positive exponent) or to the left (negative exponent) that the decimal point must be moved to give the true decimal point location.

Here are some examples.

Scientific Notation	Standard Notation
2E1	20
10.5E+4	105000
66E+2	6600
66E−2	0.66
−66E−2	−0.66
1E−10	0.0000000001
94E20	9400000000000000000000

Scientific notation is a convenient way of expressing very large or very small numbers. C-64 BASIC prints numbers ranging between 0.01 and 999,999,999 using standard notation, but numbers outside of this range are printed using scientific notation. Here are some examples.

```
?.009
 9E-03

READY.
?.01
 .01

READY.
?999999998.9
 999999999

READY.
?999999999.6
 1E+09
```

Even using scientific notation there is a limit to the size of a number that C-64 BASIC can handle. The limits are

Largest floating point number: +1.70141183E+38
Smallest floating point number: +2.93873588E−39

Any number of a larger magnitude will give an overflow error. The following are examples of overflow errors:

```
?1.70141183E+38
 1.70141183E+38

READY.
?-1.70141183E+38
-1.70141183E+38

READY.
?1.70141184E+38

?OVERFLOW ERROR
READY.
?-1.70141184E+38

?OVERFLOW ERROR
```

No Overflow error

Overflow error

A number that is smaller than the smallest magnitude will yield a zero result. This may be illustrated as follows:

```
?2.93873588E-39
 2.93873588E-39

READY.
?-2.93873588E-39
-2.93873588E-39

READY.
?2.93873587E-39
0

READY.
?-2.93873587E-39
0
```

An integer is a number that has no fraction or decimal point. The number can be negative (−) or positive (+). An unsigned number is assumed to be positive. Because of the way in which they are stored in the computer, integer numbers must have values in the range −32768 to +32767.

```
0
1
44
32699
−15
```

Any integer can also be represented as a floating point number, since integers are a subset of floating point numbers. C-64 BASIC automatically converts integer numbers to floating point before using them in arithmetic.

STRINGS

The word string is used to describe data that consists of characters. This can be anything that is not interpreted as a number.

We have already used strings as messages to be displayed on the C-64's screen. A string consists of one or more characters enclosed in double quotation marks.

```
"HI!"
"SYNERGY"
"12345"
"$10.44 IS THE AMOUNT"
"22 UNION SQUARE, SAN FRANCISCO, CA"
```

Within a string you can include any alphabetic or numeric characters, special symbols or graphic characters, cursor control characters (CLR/ HOME, CRSR UP/DOWN, CRSR LEFT/RIGHT), and the RVS ON/OFF key. The only keys that cannot be used within a string are RUN/STOP, RETURN, and INST/DEL.

All characters within the string are displayed as they appear. The cursor control, color control, and RVS ON/OFF keys, however, normally do not print anything themselves. To show that they are present in a string, certain reverse field symbols are used, as shown in Table 3-1.

Strings are entered as part of a statement. A statement must fit within an 88-character line, so the longest string you can enter at the keyboard will have less than 88 characters, since there must be room for the line number.

Strings of up to 255 characters can be stored in memory. Long strings are generated by concatenation, the joining together of shorter strings. This will be explained later in this chapter.

TABLE 3-1. Special String Symbols

Function		Key	String Symbol
Reverse On	CTRL	RVS ON	▩ (Reverse R)
Reverse Off	CTRL	RVS OFF	■ (Reverse Shifted R)
Home Cursor		CLR HOME	▤ (Reverse S)
Clear Screen	Shifted	CLR HOME	⌙ (Reverse Shifted S)
Cursor Down		↑ CRSR ↓	▨ (Reverse Q)
Cursor Up	Shifted	↑ CRSR ↓	▢ (Reverse Shifted Q)
Cursor Right		⇐ CRSR ⇒	▮ (Reverse])
Cursor Left	Shifted	⇐ CRSR ⇒	▮▮ (Reverse Shifted])

VARIABLES

The concept of a variable is easy to understand. Consider the following statements:

```
100 A=B+C
200 ?A
```

These two statements cause the sum of two numbers to be displayed. The two numbers are whatever B and C represent at the time the statements are executed. In the following example

```
90 B=4.65
95 C=3.72
100 A=B+C
200 ?A
```

B is assigned the value 4.65, while C is assigned the value 3.27. Therefore, A equals 8.37.

VARIABLE NAMES

Variable names can be used to represent string data or numeric data. If you have studied elementary algebra, you will have no trouble understanding the concept of variables and variable names. If you have never studied algebra, then think of a variable name as a name that is assigned to a mailbox. Anything that is placed in the mailbox becomes the value associated with the mailbox name.

A variable name can have one, two, or three characters. The following character options are allowed:

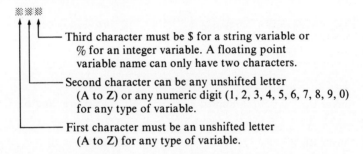

Third character must be $ for a string variable or % for an integer variable. A floating point variable name can only have two characters.

Second character can be any unshifted letter (A to Z) or any numeric digit (1, 2, 3, 4, 5, 6, 7, 8, 9, 0) for any type of variable.

First character must be an unshifted letter (A to Z) for any type of variable.

Thus the last character of the variable name tells C-64 BASIC which type of data the variable represents.

Note that unshifted letters are used for the first and second label characters. Depending on the model of C-64 computer, unshifted letters may be upper-case or lower-case. Either way, they are the letters displayed when the SHIFT key is not being depressed.

Floating point variables are the ones most frequently used in C-64 BASIC. Here are some examples of floating point variable names,

    A
    B
    C
    A1
    AA
    Z5

integer variable names,

    A%
    B%
    C%
    A1%
    MN%
    X4%

and string variable names.

A$
M$
MN$
M1$
ZX$
F6$

Variable names can have more than two alphanumeric characters, but only the first two characters count. Therefore BANANA and BANDAGE are interpreted as the same name, since both begin with BA. C-64 BASIC allows variable names to have up to 86 characters, but such large names are impractical. Four to eight characters is a more realistic limit; long names may actually make it harder to read your program. The names below illustrate the way C-64 BASIC "sees" long variable names.

MAGIC$	*interpreted as*	MA$
N123456789	*interpreted as*	N1
MMM$	*interpreted as*	MM$
ABCDEF%	*interpreted as*	AB%
CALENDAR	*interpreted as*	CA

If you use variable names with more than two characters, keep the following points in mind:

1. Only the first two characters plus the identifier symbol ($ or %) are significant. Do not use extended names like LOOP1 and LOOP2; these are interpreted as the same variable: LO.

2. C-64 BASIC has a number of reserved words which have special meaning within a BASIC statement. Reserved words include BASIC statements, such as PRINT, and others which we will discuss later. No variable name can contain a reserved word embedded anywhere in the name. For example, you cannot use PRINTER as a variable name, because BASIC would see it as "PRINT ER." This problem usually shows up as a syntax error in a line that looks correct. Table 3-4 is a complete list of reserved words.

3. Additional characters use up memory space that you might need in longer programs. On the other hand, longer variable names make programs easier to read. PARTNO, for example, is more meaningful than PA as a variable name describing part numbers in an inventory program.

Operators

The BASIC statement

```
100 ?10.2+4.7
```

tells the C-64 to add 10.2 and 4.7, and then display the sum. The statement

```
250 C=A+B
```

tells the C-64 to add the two floating point numbers represented by the variable names A and B, and to assign the sum to the floating point number represented by the variable name C.

The plus sign specifies addition. The plus sign is referred to as an *operator*. It is an arithmetic operator, since addition is an arithmetic operation. There are two other types of operators: relational operators and Boolean operators. These take a little more explanation, since they reflect conditions and decisions, rather than arithmetic.

Table 3-2 summarizes the BASIC operators. We will examine each group of operators in turn, beginning with arithmetic operators.

TABLE 3-2. Operators

	Precedence	Operator	Meaning
	High 9	( )	Parentheses denote order of evaluation
Arithmetic Operators	8	↑	Exponentiation
	7	—	Unary minus
	6	*	Multiplication
	6	/	Division
	5	+	Addition
	5	—	Subtraction
Relational Operators	4	=	Equal
	4	< >	Not equal
	4	<	Less than
	4	>	Greater than
	4	< = or = <	Less than or equal
	4	> = or = >	Greater than or equal
Boolean Operators	3	NOT	Logical complement
	2	AND	Logical AND
	1 Low	OR	Logical OR

ARITHMETIC OPERATORS

An arithmetic operator specifies addition, subtraction, multiplication, division, or exponentiation. Arithmetic operations are performed using floating point numbers. Integers are automatically converted to floating point numbers before an arithmetic operation is performed, and the result is automatically converted back to an integer if an integer variable represents the result.

The data operated on by any operator is referred to as an operand. Arithmetic operators each require two operands, which may be numbers, numeric variables, or a combination of both.

Addition (+). The plus sign specifies that the data (or operand) on the left of the plus sign is to be added to the data (or operand) on the right. For numeric quantities this is straightforward addition.

The plus sign is also used to "add" strings. In this case, however, the plus sign does not add the values of the strings. Instead, the strings are joined together, or *concatenated,* to form one longer string. The difference between numeric addition and string concatenation can be visualized as follows:

Addition of numbers: num1+num2 = num3
Addition of strings: string1+string2 = string1string2

Using concatenation, strings containing up to 255 characters can be developed.

"FOR"+"WARD"	results in "FORWARD"
"HI"+ " "+"THERE"	results in "HI THERE"
A$+B$	results in concatenation of the two strings represented by string variable labels A$ and B$
"1"+ CH$+E$	results in the character "1," followed by concatenation of the two strings represented by string variable labels CH$ and E$

If A$ is set equal to "FOR" and B$ is set equal to "WARD," then A$+B$ would generate the same results as "FOR"+ "WARD."

Should you try to build a string longer than 255 characters, a STRING TOO LONG error is flagged.

Subtraction (—). The minus sign specifies that the operand on the right of the minus sign is to be subtracted from the operand on the left of the minus sign. For example,

4—1	results in 3
100—64	results in 36
A—B	results in the variable represented by label B being subtracted from the variable represented by label A
55—142	results in —87

The unary minus operator identifies a negative number. For example,

—5	
—9E4	
—B	
4——2	Note that 4 —— 2 is the same as 4+2

Multiplication (*). An asterisk specifies that the operand on the right of the asterisk is to be multiplied by the operand on the left of the asterisk. For example,

100 * 2	results in 200
50 * 0	results in 0
A * X1	results in multiplication of two floating point numbers represented by floating point variables labeled A and X1
R% * 14	results in an integer represented by integer variable label R% being multiplied by 14

In the examples above, if variable A is assigned the value 4.2 and variable X1 is assigned the value 9.63, then the answer would be 40.446. A and X1 could hold integer values 100 and 2 to duplicate the first example; however, the two numbers would be held in the floating point format as 100.0 and 2.0, since A and X1 are floating point variables. In order to multiply 100 by 2, representing these numbers as integers, the example would have to be A% * X1%.

Division (/). The slash specifies that the operand on the left of the slash is to be divided by the data (or operand) on the right of the slash.

10/2	results in 5
6400/4	results in 1600
A/B	results in the floating point number assigned to variable A being divided by the floating point number assigned to variable B
4E2/XR	results in 400 being divided by the floating point number represented by label XR

The third example, A/B, can duplicate the first or second examples, even though A and B represent floating point numbers. The integer numbers would be held in floating point form, however. A%/B% could exactly duplicate either of the first two examples.

Exponentiation (↑). The up arrow specifies that the operand on the left of the arrow is raised to the power specified by the operand on the right of the arrow. If the data (or operand) on the right is 2, the number on the left is squared; if the data (or operand) on the right is 3, the number on the left is cubed; and so on. The exponent can be any number, variable, or expression, as long as the exponentiation yields a number in the allowed floating point range. For example,

2↑2	results in 4
12↑2	results in 144
1↑3	results in 1
A↑5	results in the floating point number assigned to variable A being raised to the 5th power
2↑6.4	results in 84.4485064
NM↑ −10	results in the floating point number assigned to variable NM being raised to the negative 10th power
14↑F	results in 14 being raised to the power specified by floating point variable F

ORDER OF EVALUATION

An expression may have multiple arithmetic operations, as in the following statement.

A+C * 10/2↑2

When this occurs, there is a fixed sequence in which operations are processed. First comes exponentiation (↑), followed by sign evaluation, followed by multiplication and division (* /), then by addition and sub-traction (+ −). Operations of equal precedence are evaluated from left to right. This order of operation can be overridden by the use of parentheses. Any operation within parentheses is performed first. For example,

4+1 * 2	results in 6
(4+1) * 2	results in 10
100 * 4/2−1	results in 199
100 * (4/2−1)	results in 100
100 * (4/(2−1))	results in 400

When parentheses are present, C-64 BASIC evaluates the innermost set first, then the next innermost, and so on. Parentheses can be nested to any level, and may be used freely to clarify the order of operations being performed in an expression.

RELATIONAL OPERATORS

Relational operators represent the following conditions: greater than (>), less than (<), equal (=), not equal (< >), greater than or equal (> =), and less than or equal (< =).

1 = 5−4	results in true (−1)
14 > 66	results in false (0)
15 > = 15	results in true (−1)
A < > B	the result will depend on the values assigned to floating point variables A and B

C-64 BASIC arbitrarily assigns a value of 0 to a "false" condition and a value of −1 to a "true" condition. These 0 and −1 values can be used in equations. For example, in the expression (1 = 1) * 4, the equation (1 = 1) is true. True equates to −1, therefore the expression is the same as (−1) * 4, which results in −4. You can include any relational operators within a C-64 BASIC expression. Here are some more examples.

25+(14 > 66)	is the same as	25+0
(A+(1 = 5−4)) * (15 > = 15)	is the same as	(A−1) * (−1)

Relational operators can be used to compare strings. For comparison purposes, the letters of the alphabet have the order A < B, B < C, C < D, and so on. Strings are compared one character at a time, starting with the leftmost character.

"A" < "B"	results in true (−1)
"X" = "XX"	results in false (0)
C$ = A$+B$	result will depend on the string values assigned to the three string variables C$, B$, and A$

When operating on strings, C-64 BASIC generates a value of −1 for a "true" result, and a value of 0 for a "false" result.

("JONES" >"DOE") +37	is the same as −1+37
("AAA" < "AA") * (Z9−("OTTER" > "AB"))	is the same as 0 * (Z9−(−1))

BOOLEAN OPERATORS

Boolean operators give programs the ability to make logical decisions. There are three Boolean operators in C-64 BASIC: AND, OR, and NOT.

A simple supermarket shopping analogy can serve to illustrate Boolean logic. Suppose you are shopping for breakfast cereals with two children.

The AND Boolean operator says that a cereal is selected only if child A *and* child B select the cereal.

The OR Boolean operator says that a cereal will be selected if *either* child A *or* child B selects the cereal.

The NOT operator generates a logical opposite. If child B insists on disagreeing with child A, then child B's decision is always *not* child A's decision.

Table 3-3 summarizes the way in which Boolean operators handle numbers. This table is referred to as a truth table.

Boolean operators primarily control program logic. Here are some examples.

IF A = 100 AND B =100 GOTO 10
   If both A and B are equal to 100, branch to line 10
IF X< Y AND B> = 44 THEN F = 0
   If X is less than Y and B is greater than or equal to 44,
   then set F equal to 0
IF A = 100 OR B = 100 GOTO 20
   If either A or B has a value of 100, branch to line 20

IF X < Y OR B > = 44 THEN F = 0
   F is set to 0 if X is less than Y or B is greater than 43
IF A = 1 AND B = 2 OR C = 3 GOTO 30
   Take the branch if both A = 1 and B = 2; also take
   the branch if C =3

A single operand can be tested for true or false. An operand appearing alone has an implied "< >0" following it. Any nonzero value is considered true; a zero value is considered false.

IF A THEN B = 2
IF A < > 0 THEN B = 2
   The above two statements are equivalent
IF NOT B GOTO 100
   Branch if B is false, i.e., equal to zero. This is
   probably better written as
IF B = 0 GOTO 100

All Boolean operations use integer operands. If you perform Boolean operations using floating point numbers, the numbers are automatically converted to integers. Therefore, the floating point numbers must fall within the allowed range of integer numbers.

If you are a novice programmer, you are unlikely to use Boolean operators in the manner that we are about to describe. If you do not understand the discussion, skip to the next section.

Table 3-3. Boolean Truth Table

The AND operation results in a 1 only if both numbers are 1
1 AND 1 = 1
0 AND 1 = 0
1 AND 0 = 0
0 AND 0 = 0
The OR operation results in a 1 if either number is 1
1 OR 1 = 1
0 OR 1 = 1
1 OR 0 = 1
0 OR 0 = 0
The NOT operation logically complements each number
NOT 1 = 0
NOT 0 = 1

Boolean operators operate on integer operands one binary digit at a time. C-64 BASIC stores all numbers in binary format, using two's complement notation to represent negative numbers. Therefore we can illustrate an AND operation as follows:

43 AND 137 = 9

$89_{16} \rightarrow 10001001$
$2B_{16} \rightarrow 00101011$
$09_{16} \rightarrow 00001001$

Here is an OR operation.

43 OR 137 = 171

$89_{16} \rightarrow 10001001$
$2B_{16} \rightarrow 00101011$
$AB_{16} \rightarrow 10101011$

Here are two NOT operations.

NOT 43 = 212

$2B_{16} \rightarrow 00101011$
$D4_{16} \rightarrow 11010100$

NOT 137 = 118

$89_{16} \rightarrow 10001001$
$76_{16} \rightarrow 01110110$

If operands are not integers, they are converted to integer form; the Boolean operation is performed, and the result is returned as a 0 or 1.

If a Boolean operator has relational operands, then the relational operand is evaluated to -1 or 0 before the Boolean operation is performed. Thus the operation

A = 1 OR C < 2

is equivalent to

$$\left\{ \begin{matrix} -1 \\ \text{or} \\ 0 \end{matrix} \right\} \text{OR} \left\{ \begin{matrix} -1 \\ \text{or} \\ 0 \end{matrix} \right\}$$

Consider this more complex operation.

IF A = B AND C < D GOTO 40

First the relational expressions are evaluated. Assume that the first expression is true and the second one is false. The statement then becomes

IF −1 AND 0 GOTO 40

Performing the AND yields a 0 result.

IF 0 GOTO 40

Recall that a single term has an implied "< >0" following it. The expression therefore becomes

IF 0 < > 0 GOTO 40

Thus, the branch is not taken.

In contrast, a Boolean operation performed on two variables may yield any integer number.

IF A% AND B% GOTO 40

Assume that A% = 255 and B% = 240. The Boolean operation 255 AND 240 yields 240. The statement, therefore, becomes

IF 240 GOTO 40

or, with the "< >0",

IF 240 < > 0 GOTO 40

Therefore, the branch will be taken.

Now compare the following assignment statements:

A = A AND 10
A = A < 10

In the first example, the current value of A is logically ANDed with 10, and the result becomes the new value of A. A must be in the integer range −32768 to +32767. In the second example, the relational expression A < 10 is evaluated to −1 or 0, so A must end up with a value of −1 or 0.

Arrays

Arrays are used in many types of computer programs. If you are not already familiar with arrays, you will need to learn about them. The information that follows will be very important to your programming efforts.

Conceptually, arrays are very simple. When you have two or more related data items, instead of giving each data item a separate variable name, you give the collection of related data items a single variable name. Then you select individual items using a position number, which in computer jargon is referred to as a subscript, or index.

A grocery list, for example, may have six items from the meat and poultry department, four fruit and vegetable items, and three dairy products. These three groups of items could each be represented by a single variable name as follows:

MP$(0) = "CHOPPED SIRLOIN"	FV$(0) = "ORANGES"
MP$(1) = "CHUCK STEAK"	FV$(1) = "APPLES"
MP$(2) = "NEW YORK STEAK"	FV$(2) = "BEANS"
MP$(3) = "CHICKEN"	FV$(3) = "CARROTS"
MP$(4) = "SALAMI"	
MP$(5) = "SAUSAGES"	DP$(0) = "MILK"
	DP$(1) = "CREAM"
	DP$(2) = "COTTAGE CHEESE"

MP$ is a single variable name that identifies all meat and poultry products.
FV$ identifies fruits and vegetables, while DP$ identifies dairy products.

A subscript follows each variable name. Thus a specific data item is identified by a variable name and an index.

Notice that the first index value in the examples above is 0, not 1. Subscripts in BASIC start from 0 because this simplifies the programming of many scientific and mathematical problems. Many people are uncomfortable with this practice, however. If you don't feel at home with using element 0 of an array, simply ignore it and start with a subscript of 1. You will waste a little memory space, but you are less likely to make programming mistakes if you are not trying to "adapt" yourself to the machine.

We could take the array concept one step further, specifying a single variable name for the entire grocery list, using two indexes. The first index (or subscript) specifies the product type, and the second index specifies the item within the product type. This is one way in which a single grocery list variable array with two subscripts could replace the three arrays with single subscripts illustrated above.

```
GL$(0,0) = MP$(0)   GL$(1,0) = FV$(0)   GL$(2,0) = DP$(0)
GL$(0,1) = MP$(1)   GL$(1,1) = FV$(1)   GL$(2,1) = DP$(1)
GL$(0,2) = MP$(2)   GL$(1,2) = FV$(2)   GL$(2,2) = DP$(2)
GL$(0,3) = MP$(3)   GL$(1,3) = FV$(3)
GL$(0,4) = MP$(4)
GL$(0,5) = MP$(5)
```

Arrays can represent integer variables, floating point variables, or string variables. However, a single array variable can only represent one data type. In other words, a single variable cannot mix integer and floating point numbers. One or the other can be present, but not both.

Arrays are a useful shorthand means of describing a large number of related variables. Consider, for example, a table containing ten rows of numbers, with twenty numbers in each row. There are 200 numbers in the table. How would you like it if you had to assign a unique name to each of the 200 numbers? It would be far simpler to give the entire table one name and identify individual numbers within the table by their table location. That is precisely what an array does.

Arrays can have one or more *dimensions*. An array with a single dimension is equivalent to a table with just one row of numbers. The dimension identifies a number within the single row. An array with two dimensions yields an ordinary table with rows and columns: one dimension identifies the row, the other dimension identifies the column. An array with three dimensions yields a "cube" of numbers, or perhaps a stack of tables. Four or more dimensions yield an array that is hard to visualize, but mathematically no more complex than a smaller-dimensioned array.

Let us examine arrays in detail.

A single-dimension array element has the following form:

name(i)

where

    name is the variable name for the array. Any type
            of variable name may be used
      i is the array index to that element. i must
          start at 0.

A single-dimension array called A, having five elements, can be visualized as follows:

```
A(0) ┌─────────┐
     │         │
A(1) ├─────────┤
     │         │
A(2) ├─────────┤
     │         │
A(3) ├─────────┤
     │         │
A(4) ├─────────┤
     └─────────┘
```

The number of elements in the array is equal to the highest index number plus 1. This takes array element 0 into account.

A two-dimension array element has the following form:

name(i, j)

where

name is the variable name of the array
  ı is the column index
  j is the row index.

A two-dimension string array called A$, having two column elements and three row elements, might be visualized as follows:

```
A$(0,0) ┌────────┬────────┐ A$(0,1)
        │        │        │
A$(1,0) ├────────┼────────┤ A$(1,1)
        │        │        │
A$(2,0) ├────────┼────────┤ A$(2,1)
        └────────┴────────┘
```

The size of the array is the product of the highest row dimension plus 1, multiplied by the highest column dimension plus 1. For the array above, it is $3 \times 2 = 6$ elements.

Additional dimensions can be added to the array.

name (i,j,k,...)

Arrays of as many as 11 elements (index 0 to 10 for a single-dimension array) may be used routinely in C-64 BASIC. Arrays containing more than 11 elements need to be specified in a *dimension statement*. Dimension statements are described later in this chapter. If you do not enter the subscript for an array in your program, it will be treated as a separate variable by C-64 BASIC. This can lead to hard-to-find bugs in your program. You should not exploit this distinction in your programs: other languages and other dialects of BASIC do not work in the same way. This technique could cause confusion for other programmers trying to read your code. Even you might later decide you had mistakenly left out the subscript, and try to fix the "error."

BASIC Commands

In Chapter 2 we described a number of commands that can be entered at the keyboard in order to control C-64 computer operations. RUN is one such command. Commands can all be executed as BASIC statements.

You are unlikely to execute commands out of BASIC statements when you first start writing programs. However, when you start writing very large programs you may run out of memory space. Then you must break a program into a number of smaller modules and execute them one at a time.

Reserved Words

All of the character combinations that define a BASIC statement's operations, and all functions, are called reserved words. Table 3-4 lists the C-64 BASIC reserved words. You will encounter many of these reserved words in this chapter, but others are not described until later chapters.

When executing BASIC programs, the C-64 computer scans every BASIC statement, seeking out any character combinations that make up reserved words. The only exception is text strings enclosed in quotes. This can cause trouble if a reserved word is embedded anywhere within a variable name. The C-64 computer cannot identify a variable name by its location in a BASIC statement. Therefore, you should be very careful to keep reserved words out of your variable names. This is particularly important with the short reserved words that can easily slip into a variable name.

Some reserved words are shown in Table 3-4 with an asterisk. These words are added to BASIC by certain plug-in cartridge programs supplied by Commodore. They can be used in standard C-64 BASIC programs without causing an error. Nevertheless, it is a good idea not to use these reserved words in any C-64 BASIC program. You may at some point want to upgrade your C-64 with a new cartridge or change a program so that it runs on another C-64 using one.

TABLE 3-4. Reserved Words

Word	Standard Character Set	Alternate† Character Set	Word	Standard Character Set	Alternate† Character Set	Word	Standard Character Set	Alternate† Character Set
	Abbreviations			Abbreviations			Abbreviations	
ABS	AI	aB	NEXT	N⁻	nE	TIME$		
AND			NOT			TO	U♥	uS
ASC	A♥	aS	ON			USR	V♠	vA
ATN	AI	aT	OPEN	O⁻	oP	VAL	V⁻	vE
CHR$	C I	cH	OR			VERIFY	W♠	wA
CLOSE	CLΓ	cl0	PEEK	P⁻	pE	WAIT		
CLR	CL	cL	POKE	PΓ	pO			
CMD	C∖	cM	POS					
CONT	CΓ	c0	PRINT	?	?			
COS			PRINT#	P_	pR			
DATA	D♠	dA	READ	R⁻	rE			
DEF	D⁻	dE	REM	RE♥	reS			
DIM	D∖	dI	RESTORE	REI	reT			
END	E∕	eN	RETURN	R∖	rI			
EXP	E♠	eX	RIGHT$	R∕	rN			
FN			RND	R,	rU			
FOR	FΓ	f0	RUN					
FRE	F_	fR	SAVE	S♠	sA			
GET	G⁻	gE	SGN	SI	sG			
GET#			SIN	S∖	sI			
GOSUB	GO♥	goS	SPC	S⁻	sP			
GOTO	GΓ	g0	SQR	S●	sQ			
IF			ST					
INPUT			STATUS	ST⁻	stE			
INPUT#	I∕	iN	STEP	SI	sT			
INT			STOP	ST_	stR			
LEFT$	LE_	leF	STR$	S I	sY			
LEN			SYS	T♠	tA			
LET	L⁻	lE	TAB					
LIST	L∖	lI	TAN	T I	tH			
LOAD	LΓ	l0	THEN					
LOG			TI					
MID$	M∖	mI	TIME					
NEW			TI$					

†The C-64's alternate character set is activated by pressing the SHIFT and COMMODORE keys simultaneously.

BASIC Word Abbreviations

You learned early in this book that the BASIC statement PRINT could always be entered from the keyboard by the abbreviation " ? ". This is expanded by the C-64 BASIC interpreter to the full word PRINT.

Most BASIC commands, statements, and functions can be abbreviated using the first two characters of the keyword, with the second character entered in shifted mode. With the C-64's normal character set (that is, upper-case or graphic characters), the second character appears as a graphic character. For example, the abbreviation for LIST appears as

L◥

1I

C-64 BASIC makes no distinction between the two abbreviations. Either one is expanded to the word LIST.

If a two-letter abbreviation is ambiguous (does ST mean STEP or STOP?), the two-letter abbreviation is assigned to the most frequently used keyword, and the other word (or words) are either not abbreviated or are abbreviated using the first three characters, with the third entered in shifted mode. For STEP and STOP, for example, STOP is abbreviated as

sT

SI

STEP is abbreviated as

stE

ST⁻

To abbreviate STEP, type an unshifted (upper-case) **S**, an unshifted **T**, and a shifted **E**.

The following sample input lines use two- and three-letter abbreviations wherever possible. All abbreviated words are expanded to the full spelling when you list the programs.

```
                           ──────── Press SHIFT ⊑ for lower case.
10 1E a=10
20 b=a aN 14+eX(2)
30 dI c(5)
40 fO i=0 to 5
50 rE c(i)
60 nE
70 dA 1,6,2,4,10,5,16
```

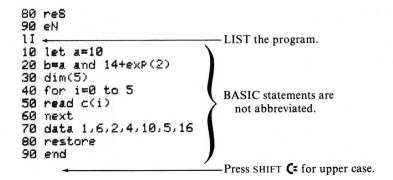

```
80 reS
90 eN
1I ←─────────────────── LIST the program.
10 let a=10
20 b=a and 14+exP(2)
30 dim(5)
40 for i=0 to 5
50 read c(i)              BASIC statements are
60 next                      not abbreviated.
70 data 1,6,2,4,10,5,16
80 restore
90 end
   ←─────────────────── Press SHIFT C⁼ for upper case.
```

After pressing SHIFT and the keys simultaneously, you will see the abbreviations displayed with graphics in the place of the shifted characters. The expanded listing will display upper-case letters.

Refer to Table 3-4. The expansions from abbreviations for the two functions SPC and TAB include the left parenthesis. This means that if you use the abbreviation for either of these, you must not type in the left parenthesis. For example,

```
10 ?sP(5)
```

expands to

```
10 Print sPc((5)
           ‿
```

Syntax error results from two
left parentheses

The correct sequence to key in is

```
10 ?sP5)
```

This parenthesis rule applies only to the SPC and TAB functions and is a format inconsistency you will have to watch for when abbreviating these function names. For all other functions, you key in both parentheses. For example,

```
10 ?rN(1)
```

BASIC Statements

The operation performed by a statement is specified using reserved words (see Table 3-4).

Statements are not described in detail in this chapter. Refer to Appendixes G and H for complete descriptions of all statements recognized by C-64 BASIC. This chapter introduces you to programming concepts, stressing the way statements are used.

Remarks

It is appropriate that any discussion of BASIC statements begin by describing the only BASIC statement which the computer will ignore: the remark. If the first three characters of a BASIC statement are REM, the computer ignores the statement entirely. So why include such a statement? The answer is that remarks make your program easier to read.

If you write a short program with five or ten statements, you will probably have little trouble remembering what the program does—unless you leave it around for six months and then try to use it again. If you write a longer program with 100 or 200 statements, you are quite likely to forget something very important the very next time you use the program. After you have written dozens of programs, you cannot possibly remember each one in detail. The solution to this problem is to document your program by including remarks that describe what the various parts of the program do.

Good programmers use plenty of remarks in all of their programs. In all of this chapter's program examples we will include remarks that describe what is going on, simply to get you into the habit of doing the same thing yourself.

Remark statements have line numbers like any other statement. A remark statement's line number can be used like any other statement's line number.

Assignment Statements

Assignment statements let you assign values to variables. You will encounter assignment statements frequently in every type of BASIC program. Here are some examples of assignment statements.

```
90 REM INITIALIZE VARIABLE X
100 LET X=3.24
```

In statement 100, floating point variable X is
assigned the value 3.24

```
150 X=3.24
```

Equivalent to statement 100 above; the LET is optional
in all assignment statements

```
215 A$="ALSO RAN"
```

The string variable A$ is assigned the two
text words ALSO RAN

Notice that the first assignment statement (line 100) begins with the word "LET", but the other two don't. Originally, all assignment statements had to start with LET. The idea was that the computer could identify the type of statement by looking at the first word. Today, all but a few dialects of BASIC have dropped this requirement. Although LET is not required by C-64 BASIC, it is still a reserved word and cannot appear in a variable name.

Here are three statements that assign values to array variable DP$(I), which we encountered earlier when describing arrays.

```
200 REM DP$(I) IS THE DAIRY PRODUCTS SHOPPING LIST
    VARIABLE
210 DP$(0)="MILK"
220 DP$(1)="CREAM"
230 DP$(2)="COTTAGE CHEESE"
```

Remember, you can put more than one statement on a single line. The three DP$ assignments could be placed on a single line as follows:

```
200 REM DP$(I) IS THE DAIRY PRODUCTS SHOPPING LIST
    VARIABLE
210 DP$(0)="MILK":DP$(1)="CREAM":DP$(2)="COTTAGE CHEESE"
```

A colon must separate adjacent statements appearing on the same line.

Assignment statements can include any of the arithmetic or relational operators described earlier in this chapter.

```
90 REM THIS IS A DUMB WAY TO ASSIGN A VALUE TO V
100 V=3.24+7.96/8.5
```

This statement assigns the value 4.17647059 to floating point variable V. It is equivalent to these three statements

```
90 REM X AND Y NEED TO BE INITIALIZED SEPARATELY FOR
    LATER USE
100 X=7.96
110 Y=8.5
120 V=3.24+X/Y
```

which could be written on one line as follows:

```
100 X=7.96:Y=8.5:V=3.24+X/Y
```

Here are assignment statements that perform the Boolean operations described earlier in this chapter.

```
90 REM THESE EXAMPLES WERE DESCRIBED EARLIER IN
    THE CHAPTER
100 A%=43 AND 137
200 B%=43 OR 137
```

The following example shows how a string variable could have its value assigned using string concatenation:

```
100 V$="COTTAGE"
200 W$="CHEESE"
300 DP$(2)=V$+" "+W$
400 REM DP$(2) IS ASSIGNED THE STRING VALUE
    "COTTAGE CHEESE"
```

DATA AND READ STATEMENTS

When a number of variables need data assignments, the DATA and READ statements should be used rather than the LET statement. Consider the following example:

```
5 REM INITIALIZE ALL PROGRAM VARIABLES
10 DATA 10,20,-4,16E6
20 READ A,B,C,D
```

The statement on line 10 lists four numeric data values. These four values are assigned to four variables on line 20. After the statements on lines 10 and 20 have been executed, A = 10, B = 20, C = 4, and D = 16×10^6.

If you have one or more DATA statements in your program, you can visualize them as building a "column" of numbers. For example, a DATA statement that contains a list of ten numbers would build a ten-entry column. Two DATA statements, each with a list of five data items, would build exactly the same column. This may be illustrated as follows:

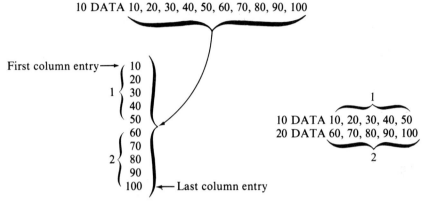

The first READ statement executed in a program starts at the first column entry, assigning each value to corresponding variables named in the READ statement. The second and subsequent READ statements take values from the column, starting at the point where the previous READ statement left off. This may be illustrated as follows:

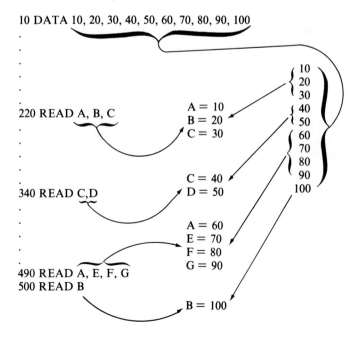

RESTORE STATEMENT

You can at any time send the pointer back to the beginning of the numeric column by executing a RESTORE statement. Here is an example of the use of RESTORE.

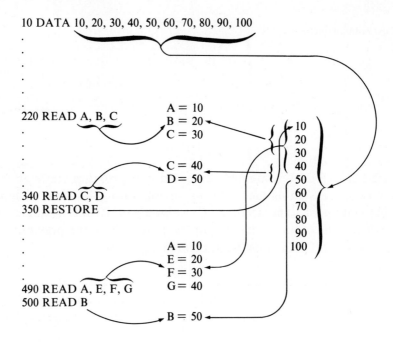

10 DATA 10, 20, 30, 40, 50, 60, 70, 80, 90, 100

220 READ A, B, C

A = 10
B = 20
C = 30

C = 40
D = 50

340 READ C, D
350 RESTORE

A = 10
E = 20
F = 30
G = 40

490 READ A, E, F, G
500 READ B

B = 50

10
20
30
40
50
60
70
80
90
100

Dimension Statement

C-64 BASIC normally assumes that a variable has a single dimension, with index values of 0 through 10. This generates an 11-element array. If you want a single dimension with more or fewer than 11 elements, then you must include the array variable in a dimension (DIM) statement. You also must include the array in a dimension statement if it has two or more dimensions, no matter what number of elements the array has. The following example provides dimensions for one-dimension array variables MP$, FV$, and DP$. We used these variables in our earlier discussion of arrays.

```
DIM MP$(5),FV$(3),DP$(2)
```

The two-dimension grocery list variable, GL$, would be dimensioned as follows:

```
DIM GL$(3,5)
```

A DIM statement can provide dimensions for any number of variables, providing the statement fits within an 80-character line.

The number or numbers following a variable name in a DIM statement is equal to the largest index value that can occur in that particular index position. But remember, indexes begin at 0. Therefore, MP$(5) dimensions the variable MP$ to have six values, not five, since indexes 0, 1, 2, 3, 4, and 5 will be allowed. GL$ (3,5), likewise, specifies a two-dimension variable with 24 entries, since the first dimension can have values 0, 1, 2, and 3, while the second dimension can have values 0 through 5.

Once you have declared an array variable in a DIM statement, you must subsequently reference the variable with the specified number of subscripts; each subscript must have a value between 0 and the number specified in the DIM statement. If any of these syntax rules are broken, you will get a syntax error.

Branch Statements

Statements within a BASIC program normally execute in ascending line number order. This execution sequence was explained earlier in this chapter when we described line numbers. Branch statements change this execution sequence.

GOTO STATEMENT

GOTO is the simplest branch statement. It allows you to specify the statement that will be executed next. Consider the following example:

```
20 A=4.37
30 GOTO 100
40
50
60
70
80
90
100
110
  .
  .
```

The statement on line 20 is an assignment statement; it assigns a value to floating point variable A. The next statement is a GOTO; it specifies that program execution must branch to line 100. Therefore, the instruction execution sequence surrounding this part of the program will be line 20, then line 30, then line 100.

Of course, some other statement should branch back to line 40. Otherwise the statement on line 40 would never be executed by program logic, as illustrated above.

You can branch to any line number, even if the line has nothing but a remark on it. However, the computer ignores the remark, so the effect is the same as branching to the next line. For example, consider the following branch:

```
20 A=4.37
30 GOTO 70
40
50
60
70 REM THERE IS A REMARK, AND
80 NOTHING ELSE ON THIS LINE
90
 .
 .
```

The program branches from line 30 to line 70. There is nothing but a remark on line 70, so the computer moves on to line 80, executing the statement on this line. Even though you can branch to a remark, you might as well branch to the next line. This may be illustrated as follows:

```
20 A=4.37
30 GOTO 80
40
50
60
70 REM THERE IS A REMARK, AND
80 NOTHING ELSE ON THIS LINE
90
 .
 .
```

COMPUTED GOTO STATEMENT

There is also a computed GOTO statement that lets program logic branch to one of two or more different line numbers, depending on the current value of a variable. Consider the following illustration:

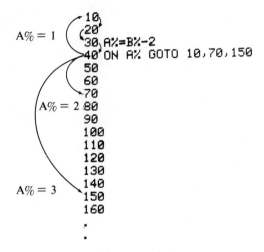

The statement on line 40 is a computed GOTO. When this statement executes, the program will branch to statement 10 if variable A% = 1, to statement 70 if variable A% = 2, or to statement 150 if A% = 3. If A% has any value other than 1, 2, or 3, the program will not branch. Notice that variable A% is assigned a value in statement 30. The value assigned to A% depends on the current value of variable B%. The illustration does not show how variable B% is computed, but as long as B% has a value of 3, 4, or 5, the statement on line 40 will cause a branch.

To test the computed GOTO statement, key in the following program:

```
10 B%=4
20 PRINT B%
30 A%=B%-2
40 ON A%GOTO 10,70,150
70 PRINT B%
80 B%=5
90 GOTO 30
150 PRINT B%
160 B%=3
170 GOTO 20
```

Now execute this program by typing **RUN** on any blank line. Do not type **RUN** on a line that is already displaying something. If you do, you will get a syntax error and the program will not be executed.

Can you account for the sequence in which digits are displayed? Try rewriting the program so that each number is displayed once, in the sequence 345345345...

Control Statements

In every program, the sequence of the statements executed is every bit as important as the statements themselves. C-64 BASIC has several statements that control the way a program executes, hence the name "control statements."

Control statements redirect the execution sequence of a program. Some control statements choose one of many paths program logic can take; others execute several statements a specified number of times.

FOR-NEXT Statement

GOTO and computed GOTO statements let you create any type of statement execution sequence that your program logic requires. But suppose you want to reexecute an instruction (or a group of instructions) many times. For example, suppose array variable A(I) has 100 elements and each element needs to be assigned a value ranging from 0 to 99. Writing a hundred assignment statements would be tedious. It is far simpler to reexecute one statement 100 times. This can be done using the FOR and NEXT statements.

```
10 DIM A(99)
20 FOR I=0 TO 99 STEP 1
30 A(I)=I
40 NEXT I
```

Statements between FOR and NEXT execute repeatedly. In this case a single assignment statement appears between FOR and NEXT, so this single statement is reexecuted repeatedly.

To demonstrate how FOR-NEXT loops work, we will display the A(I) values created within the loop. Key in the following program:

```
10 DIM A(99)
20 FOR I=0 TO 99 STEP 1
30 A(I)=I
35 PRINT A(I)
40 NEXT I
50 REM IF YOU HAVE A GOTO STATEMENT THAT BRANCHES TO
   ITSELF, THE
70 REM COMPUTER EXECUTES AN ENDLESS LOOP; IN EFFECT,
   IT WAITS
90 GOTO 90
```

Now key in **RUN**. One hundred numbers display, starting at 0 and ending at

99. Press the STOP key to terminate program execution.

Statements between FOR and NEXT reexecute the number of times specified by the index value directly after FOR. In the illustration above this index variable is I. I increases in value from 0 to 99 in increments of 1. The first time the assignment statement is executed, I will equal 0 and the assignment statement on line 30 will be executed as follows:

```
30 A(0)=0
```

I increases by the *step*, or increment, size, which is specified on line 20 as 1. I therefore equals 1 the second time the assignment statement on line 30 is executed. The assignment statement has effectively become

```
30 A(1)=1
```

I continues to increment by the specified step value until the maximum value of 99 is reached or exceeded.

The step value does not have to be 1; it can have any value. Change the step value to 5 on line 20 and reexecute the program. Now the assignment statement is executed only 20 times, since incrementing I by 5 nineteen times will take it to 95 (the 20th increment will take it to 100, which is more than the maximum value of 99).

The step size does not have to be positive. But if the step size is negative, the initial value of I must be larger than the final value of I. For example, if the step size is –1 and we want to initialize 100 elements of A(I) with values ranging from 0 to 99, then we would have to rewrite the statement on line 20 as follows:

```
10 DIM A(99)
20 FOR I=0 TO 99 STEP -1
30 A(I)=I
35 PRINT A(I);
40 NEXT I
80 GOTO 80
```

Execute this program to test the negative step.

In this example the initial and final values for I, and the step size, are treated as integers. You must, however, represent these three values using floating point variables or expressions. Expressions will be evaluated to a floating point result. The floating point result will be converted to an integer using the round-off rules described earlier in this chapter.

Because round-off rules can cause problems, you are strongly urged to use beginning values, ending values, and step sizes as integers. Do not use expressions, since this unnecessarily complicates the program. If you must calculate one of these values, it is simpler and faster to do so in a separate statement.

If the step size is 1 (which is frequently the case), you do not have to include a step size definition. In the absence of any definition, C-64 BASIC assumes a step size of 1. Therefore, the statement on line 20 could be rewritten as follows:

```
10 DIM A(99)
15 REM USE A STEP SIZE OF 1
20 FOR I=0 TO 99
30 A(I)=I
35 PRINT A(I);
40 NEXT I
80 GOTO 80
```

Also, you do not need to specify the index variable in the NEXT statement. But if you do, it will make your program easier to read.

NESTED LOOPS

The FOR-NEXT structure is referred to as a *program loop,* since statement execution loops from FOR to NEXT and back to FOR. This loop structure is very common; almost every BASIC program that you write will include one or more such loops. Loops are so common that they are frequently nested. The statement sequence occurring between FOR and NEXT can be of any length; it can run to tens or even hundreds of statements. And within these tens or hundreds of statements, additional loops may occur. The following illustration shows a single level of nesting:

```
10 DIM A(99)
20 FOR I=0 TO 99
30 A(I)=I
40 REM DISPLAY ALL VALUES OF A(I) ASSIGNED THUS FAR
50 FOR J=0 TO I
60 PRINT A(J)
70 NEXT J
80 NEXT I
90 GOTO 90
```

Complex loop structures appear frequently, even in relatively short programs. Here is an example showing the FOR and NEXT statements, but none of the intermediate statements.

```
50 FOR I=1 TO 10
60 FOR X=25 TO 347 STEP 3
.
100 FOR A=9 TO 0 STEP -1
.
140 NEXT A
200 FOR B=25 TO 100 STEP 5
.
280 NEXT B
300 NEXT X
.
500 FOR Y=1 TO 20 STEP 2
.
600 FOR P=10 TO 20
.
650 NEXT P
700 NEXT Y
.
1000 FOR Z=1 TO 10
.
1090 NEXT Z
1200 NEXT I
```

The outermost loop uses index I; it contains three nested loops that use indexes X, Y, and Z. The first loop contains two additional loops which use indexes A and B. The second loop contains one nested loop using index P. The third loop contains no nested loops. Each nested loop must have a different index variable name. Statement execution sequences may be illustrated as follows:

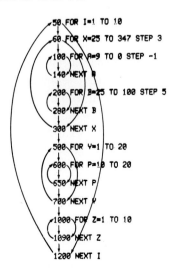

Loop structures are easy to visualize and use. There is only one common error to watch out for: do not terminate an outer loop before you terminate an inner loop. For example, the following loop structure is illegal:

```
 50 FOR I=1 TO 10
 60 FOR X=25 TO 347 STEP 3
100 NEXT I
200 NEXT X
```

If you do not include the index variable in the NEXT statement, program logic will automatically terminate loops correctly, since there is only one possible correct loop termination each time a NEXT statement is encountered.

Every program must have the same number of FOR and NEXT statements, since every loop must begin with a FOR statement and end with a NEXT statement. For example, suppose there are two FOR statements, but only one NEXT statement. The second FOR statement constitutes an inner loop that will execute correctly. But the outer loop has no NEXT statement to terminate it, so the program will execute incorrectly. Too many NEXT statements will also cause a syntax error.

Subroutine Statements

Once you start writing programs that are more than a few statements long, you will quickly find short routines that are used repeatedly. For example, suppose you have an array variable (such as A(I)) that is reinitialized frequently at different points in your program. Would you simply repeat the three instructions that constitute the FOR-NEXT loop described earlier? Since there are only three instructions, you may as well do so.

Suppose you have to initialize the array and then execute ten or eleven instructions that process array data in some fashion. If you had to use this loop many times within one program, rewriting ten to fifteen statements each time you wished to use the loop would take time, but more importantly, it would waste a good deal of computer memory. This may be illustrated as follows:

Start of program ⟶

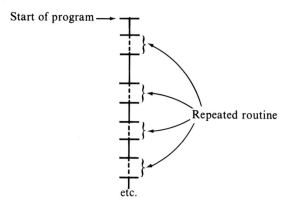

etc.

Repeated routine

To solve this problem, you could separate out the repeated statements and branch to them. This group of statements is referred to as a *subroutine*.

But a problem arises. Branching from your program to the subroutine is simple enough, since the subroutine starts at a given line number. However, where do you branch back to at the end of the subroutine? You could execute a GOTO statement whenever you wish to branch to a subroutine.

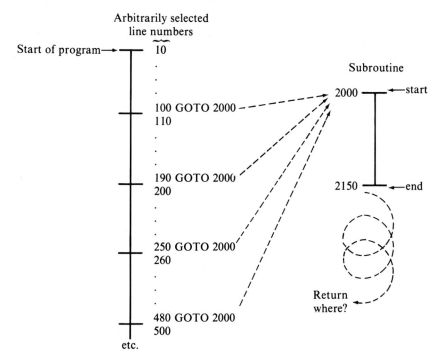

This statement branches in the same way as a GOTO, but GOSUB remembers the line number to which it should return. This is illustrated in the following section.

GOSUB STATEMENT

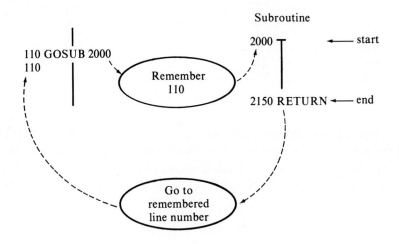

The RETURN statement causes a branch back to the line number that the GOSUB statement remembered. The three-statement loop that initializes array A(I), if converted into a subroutine, would appear as follows:

```
10 REM MAIN PROGRAM
20 REM YOU CAN DIMENSION A SUBROUTINE'S VARIABLE IN
30 REM THE MAIN PROGRAM.  IT IS A GOOD IDEA TO DIMENSION
50 REM ALL VARIABLES AT THE START OF THE MAIN PROGRAM.
60 DIM A(99)
70 GOSUB 2000
80 REM DISPLAY SOMETHING TO PROVE THE RETURN OCCURRED
90 PRINT "RETURNED"
100 GOTO 100
2000 REM SUBROUTINE
2010 FOR I=0 TO 99
2020 A(I)=I
2030 PRINT A(I);
2040 NEXT I
2050 RETURN
```

NESTED SUBROUTINES

Subroutines can be nested. That is to say, a subroutine can itself branch to, or *call*, another subroutine, which in turn can call a third subroutine, and so on. You do not have to do anything special in order to use nested subroutines. Simply branch to the subroutine using a GOSUB statement; each subroutine ends with a RETURN statement. C-64 BASIC will remember the correct line number for each nested return. The following program illustrates nested subroutines:

```
10 REM MAIN PROGRAM
20 REM YOU CAN DIMENSION A SUBROUTINE'S VARIABLE IN
30 REM THE MAIN PROGRAM.  IT IS A GOOD IDEA TO DIMENSION
50 REM ALL VARIABLES AT THE START OF THE MAIN PROGRAM.
60 DIM A(99)
70 GOSUB 2000
80 REM DISPLAY SOMETHING TO PROVE THE RETURN OCCURRED
90 PRINT"RETURNED"
100 GOTO 100
2000 REM FIRST LEVEL SUBROUTINE
2010 FOR I=0 TO 99
2020 A(I)=I
2030 GOSUB 3000
2040 NEXT I
2050 RETURN
3000 REM NESTED SUBROUTINE
3010 PRINT A(I)
3020 RETURN
```

This program moves the ?A(I) statement out of the subroutine and puts it into a nested subroutine. Nothing else changes.

COMPUTED GOSUB STATEMENT

Since GOTO and GOSUB statement logic is very similar, it will not come as any surprise that there is a computed GOSUB statement akin to the computed GOTO statement. The computed GOSUB statement allows you to branch to one of two or more subroutines, depending on the value of an index. Consider the following statement:

```
90
100 ON A GOSUB 1000,500,5000,2300
110
```

When the statement on line 100 is executed, if A = 1 the subroutine beginning at line 1000 is called. If A = 2 the subroutine beginning at line 500 is called. If A = 3 the subroutine beginning at line 5000 is called. If A = 4 the subroutine beginning at line 2300 is called. If A has any value other than 1, 2, 3, or 4, the program will merely continue executing at line 110. The computed GOSUB statement remembers the next line number (in this case, 110). It does not matter which of the subroutines is called; the called subroutine's RETURN statement will branch back to the stored line number (in this case, 110).

You can nest computed GOSUB statements, just as you can nest standard GOSUB statements.

IF-THEN Statement

The arithmetic and relational operators described earlier in this chapter are frequently used in IF-THEN statements. This gives a BASIC program decision-making capabilities. Following IF you enter any expression. If the expression is true, the statement(s) following THEN are executed. However, if the expression is false the statement(s) following THEN are not executed. Here are three simple examples of IF-THEN statements.

```
10 IF A=B+5 THEN PRINT MSG1
40 IF CC$<"M" THEN IN=0
50 IF Q<14 AND M<>M1 GOTO 66
```

The statement on line 10 causes a PRINT statement to be executed if the value of floating point variable A is five more than the value of floating point variable B. The PRINT statement will not be executed otherwise. The statement on line 40 sets floating point variable IN to 0 if string variable CC$ is any letter of the alphabet in the range A though L. The statement on line 50 causes program execution to branch to line 66 if floating point variable Q is less than 14 and floating point variable M is not equal to floating point variable M1. Otherwise, program execution will continue with the statement on the next line (GOTO can substitute for THEN).

If you do not understand the evaluation of expressions following IF, then refer to the discussion of these expressions at the beginning of this chapter.

Input/Output Statements

There are a variety of BASIC statements that control the transfer of data to and from the computer. Collectively, these are referred to as input/output statements. The simplest input/output statements control data input from the keyboard and data output to the display. There are also more complex input/output statements that control data transfer between the computer and peripheral devices such as cassette units, diskette units, and printers. These more complex input/output statements are described in Chapter 8.

Since we have already encountered the PRINT statement, we will discuss this statement first.

PRINT STATEMENT

You can use the word PRINT or a question mark to create a PRINT statement.

Why use PRINT instead of DISPLAY or some abbreviation of the word display? The answer is that in the early sixties, when the BASIC programming language was being created, displays were very expensive and generally unavailable on medium- or low-cost computers. The standard computer terminal had a keyboard and a printer. Information was printed where today it is displayed; hence the use of the word "print" to describe a statement that causes a display.

The PRINT statement will display any data. Text must be enclosed in quotes. For example, the following statement will display the single word "TEXT":

```
10 PRINT "TEXT"
```
or
```
10 ?"TEXT"
```

To display a number, you place the number, or a variable name, after PRINT. This may be illustrated as follows:

```
10 A%=10
20 ?5,A%
```

The statement at line 20 displays the number 5 and then the number 10 on the same line.

You can display a mixture of text and numbers by listing the information to be displayed after PRINT. Use commas to separate individual items. The following PRINT statement displays the words "ONE", "TWO", "THREE", "FOUR", and "FIVE", followed by the numeral for each number:

```
10 ?"ONE",1,"TWO",2,"THREE",3,"FOUR",4,"FIVE",5
```

If you separate variables with commas, as above, then the C-64 computer automatically assigns 11 character spaces for each variable displayed. In other words, it splits each line into two halves. Try executing the statement illustrated above in immediate mode to prove this to yourself. If you want the display to remove the empty spaces, separate the variables with semicolons, as follows:

```
10 PRINT "ONE";1;"TWO";2;"THREE";3;"FOUR";4;"FIVE";5
```

Enter this statement in immediate mode and display it to see how the semicolon works.

A PRINT statement automatically advances to the next line of the display unless you suppress it. You can suppress this feature by putting a comma or a semicolon after the last variable. A comma after the last variable will continue the display at the next 11-character space boundary. To illustrate this, enter and run the following program:

```
10 PRINT "ONE";1;"TWO";2
20 PRINT "THREE";3
```

Now add a semicolon to the end of the statement on line 10 and again execute the program by typing **RUN**. The two lines of display will now occur on a single line.

We have been illustrating the numerals by inserting them directly into the PRINT statement. You can, if you wish, display the contents of variables instead. Try entering and running the following program, which uses variable A%(I) to create digits:

```
10 FOR I=1 TO 5
20 A%(I)=I
30 NEXT
40 PRINT "ONE";A%(1);"TWO";A%(2);"THREE";A%(3);
   "FOUR";A%(4)
50 GOTO 50
```

You can put the displayed words into a string array and move the PRINT statement into the FOR-NEXT loop by changing the program as follows:

```
10 DATA "ONE","TWO","THREE","FOUR","FIVE"
20 FOR I=1 TO 5
30 A%(I)=I
40 READ N$(I)
50 PRINT N$(I);A%(I);
60 NEXT
70 GOTO 70
```

The program shown above is not well written. A%(I) can be eliminated, and N$ need not be an array variable. Can you rewrite the program using N$ and removing A%(I) entirely?

QUOTES IN STRINGS

Although most BASIC programs will not need to print quotation marks, there are some that do, such as "electronic typewriters" or other programs that deal with words rather than numbers.

Since quotation marks indicate the beginning and end of strings, you cannot put them in the middle of a string. You can, however, put a quotation mark into a string or a PRINT statement using the BASIC function CHR$. CHR$ acts like an array of all the possible characters. You supply a subscript, and CHR$ returns the character corresponding to that number. The values of the subscripts and the characters they produce are listed in Appendix E. The value for a quotation mark is 34. Using CHR$, you can print a quotation mark with a statement such as

```
100 PRINTCHR$(34);"THIS IS DISPLAYED IN QUOTES";CHR$(34)
```

If you PRINT a string containing control characters, such as CRSR UP or HOME, you must take an additional step. In Chapter 2 we described the quote mode. In quote mode, cursor movement keys are translated into special characters so they can be stored in strings. This allows your program to perform these functions while it is running.

"Quote mode" also applies to output. To allow you to LIST programs containing these control characters, the portion of BASIC that puts information on the display "watches" for quotes. When it finds a quotation mark, it goes into quote mode and displays control characters in the reversed form you see when typing them into a program. This can do unpleasant things to a carefully planned display.

You can escape from quote mode while printing just as you do when typing in a program: with a second quotation mark or a RETURN. Since programs that print quotation marks usually print them in pairs, you will seldom see a problem. If your program must print only one, you can use CHR$ to delete the first one, and then print another to leave quote mode.

```
100 PRINTCHR$(34);CHR$(20);CHR$(34);"▓RVS QUOTED STRING▉";
    CHR$(34)
```

CHR$(20) deletes the first quotation mark. Only the second one will appear on the screen.

PRINT FORMATTING FUNCTIONS

We use the word *formatting* to describe the process of arranging information on a display (or a printout) to make it easier to understand or more pleasing to the eye. Given the PRINT statement and nothing else, formatting could become a complex and painful chore. For example, suppose you want to display a heading in the middle of the top line of the display. Does that mean displaying space codes until you reach the first heading character position? Not only would that be time-consuming and likely to cause errors, but it would also waste a lot of memory, since each space code must be converted into a computer instruction. Fortunately, C-64 BASIC provides three PRINT formatting aids: the SPC, TAB, and POS functions.

SPC FUNCTION

SPC is a space-over function. You include SPC as one of the terms in a PRINT statement. After the letters SPC you include, in parentheses, the number of character positions that you wish to space over. For example, you could display a heading beginning at the leftmost character position of the display as follows:

```
10 PRINT"HEADING"
```

To center the heading on the screen you would first space over eight character positions, as follows:

```
10 PRINT SPC(8);"HEADING"
```

Notice the semicolon after the SPC function. A comma after SPC will start displaying text at the next 11-character boundary following the number of spaces specified by SPC.

When you include the SPC function in a PRINT statement you simply cause the next printed or displayed character to be moved over by the number of positions specified after SPC; no other PRINT statement syntax is changed.

TAB FUNCTION

TAB is a tabbing function similar to typewriter tabbing.

Suppose you want to print or display information in columns. You must first calculate the character position of the line where each column is to begin. This may be illustrated as follows:

Column Number
↓
```
0                 13
JONES, P. J.      431-25-6277
BURKE, P. L.      447-71-7614
ROBINSON, L.W.    231-80-8421
etc.              etc.
```

In the illustration above, columns begin at character positions 0 and 13. Now, instead of computing space codes as you go from line to line, following each column entry you simply insert a TAB function in the PRINT statement.

Consider one line of the display illustrated above. Counting character positions, you could display the line without tab stops, as follows:

```
10 PRINT "JONES,P.J.    431-25-6277"
```

Instead of inserting space codes, you could use the space function and shorten the statement, as follows:

```
10 PRINT "JONES,P.J.";SPC(3);"431-25-6277"
```

But tabbing is easier because you tab to a known column number instead of counting spaces.

Note that the entries in the third and fourth columns are numbers that were entered as text. Try rewriting the PRINT statement to display these as numbers. The numbers no longer align as they did when they were displayed as characters (in Chapter 5 we discuss the quirks associated with display formatting). In this case, numbers leave a space for a negative sign, and they do not display zeros occurring after the decimal point. That is why there are differences.

POS FUNCTION

POS returns the current cursor position. The position is returned as a number, equal to the column number where the cursor is blinking. Write the POS function as **POS(0)**.

The following statement demonstrates the capability of POS:

```
10 PRINT"CURSOR POSITION IS";POS(0)
```

Execute this statement in immediate mode. The display will appear as follows:

```
?"CURSOR POSITION IS";POS(0)
CURSOR POSITION IS 18
```

The cursor was at character position 18 after displaying CURSOR POSITION IS. If you add some spaces after IS and before the closing quotes, you will change the number 18 to a larger number.

INPUT STATEMENT

When an INPUT statement is executed, the computer waits for input from the keyboard; until the computer receives this input, nothing else will happen.

An INPUT statement begins with the word INPUT, which is followed by a list of variable names. Entered data is assigned to the named variables. The variable name type determines the form in which data must be entered. A string variable name (ending with a $) can be satisfied only by text input; any number of text characters can be entered for a string variable. To demonstrate string input, key in the following short program and run it:

```
10 INPUT A$
20 PRINT A$
30 GOTO 10
```

Upon executing an INPUT statement, the computer displays a question mark, then waits for your entry. The program illustrated above displays any text which you enter as you enter it. The text is also displayed a second time because of the PRINT statement on the next line. The first display occurs when the INPUT statement on line 10 is executed. The second display is in response to the PRINT statement on line 20.

You input integer or floating point numeric data by listing the appropriate variable names following INPUT. Separate individual entries with commas. The comma is not used for punctuation in an INPUT statement. The following example inputs a text word, an integer number, and a floating point number, then displays these three entries. Enter and run the program.

```
10 INPUT A$,A,A%
20 PRINT A$,A,A%
30 GOTO 10
```

You must enter some text followed by a comma, then an integer number followed by a comma, then a floating point number followed by RETURN. Any departure from this input sequence will cause an error; following an error the computer displays two question marks. You will have to reenter the data in the correct format. If the computer then displays a question mark with the message REDO FROM START, enter the data again.

Now rewrite the PRINT statement so that A$, A, and A% are in an order that differs from the INPUT statement. Rerun the program.

As we discussed earlier, any integer can be represented using a floating point number. Therefore, you can input an integer value for a floating point variable. You cannot input a floating point value for an integer variable, however. You cannot enter text for an integer or a floating point number, but you can enter a number for a text variable; the number will be interpreted as characters rather than a numeric value. Try these variations to satisfy yourself that you understand the data entry options.

The INPUT statement is very fussy; its syntax is too demanding for any normal human operator. Imagine the office worker who knows nothing about programming. On encountering the types of error messages that can occur if one comma is out of place, one may well give up in despair. You are therefore likely to spend a lot of time writing "idiot-proof" data entry programs; these are programs that are designed to watch out for every conceivable type of mistake an operator can make when entering data. An idiot-proof program will cope with errors in a way that the operator can understand. Chapter 4 describes data entry programming in detail.

One simple trick worth noting is the INPUT statement's ability to display data. You can precede each item of data entry with a short message telling the operator what to do. The message appears in the INPUT statement as text between quotes. A semicolon must occur after the text to be displayed and before the first input variable name. Here is an example.

```
10 INPUT "ENTER THE NUMBER 1";N
20 IF N<>1 THEN GOTO 50
30 PRINT "OK"
40 GOTO 40
50 PRINT "NO, DUMMY,"
60 GOTO 10
```

This program prints a message, then waits for a single data entry.

The *prompting* feature of INPUT does have a pitfall, however: if the prompt string is too long, BASIC tries to read the prompt along with the input typed at the keyboard. This will happen only if the prompt extends beyond the end of a row on the screen. To avoid this problem, always make sure your prompts are less than 22 characters long. The problem can also arise if the INPUT statement follows a PRINT statement that ends with a semicolon. Since the prompt starts in the middle of the line, it must be short enough to ensure that it does not "overflow" to the next row of the display.

If you inadvertently make a prompt too long, you may find yourself trapped. BASIC will keep telling you to "REDO" your response, then display the prompt again. To escape from this trap, use the DEL key to delete the prompt, then type your response. The only other way is to press the RUN/STOP and RESTORE keys simultaneously. This aborts the program.

"PRESETTING" THE RESPONSE TO INPUT

After printing your prompt, INPUT prints a question mark and a space. Anything to the right of that space on the screen is treated as if it were typed from the keyboard. By adding backspaces to your prompt, you can "preset" the response so that the user need only press RETURN. To use this feature, add two spaces to your prompt string, followed by the response. Then use CRSR LEFT to move the cursor back to the first of the added spaces. When INPUT prints its question mark and space, they will replace your two spaces, positioning the cursor on the response. If the user simply presses RETURN, INPUT will read the response you have set up on the screen.

You can also preset responses by assigning a value in advance to the variable you will INPUT. If the user responds with just a RETURN, the value already in the variable is not changed. Note, however, that if you INPUT multiple variables, this is an all-or-nothing proposition: if the value for the first variable is typed in, values for all variables must be given.

GET STATEMENT

The GET statement inputs a single character. No carriage return is needed. The single character input can be any character the C-64 recognizes, or it can be a numeric value between 0 and 9. The entry will be interpreted as a character if a string variable name follows GET. Type in the following program and run it:

```
10 GET A$
20 PRINT A$
30 GOTO 10
```

When you run this program, everything will race off the top of the display. Each time you press a key, the character typed will also race off the top of the screen. This is because GET does not wait for a character entry, but assumes the entry is there. You can make GET wait for a specific character by testing for the character as follows:

```
10 GET A$
20 IF A$<>"X" THEN GOTO 10
30 PRINT A$
40 GOTO 10
```

This program waits for the letter X to be entered. Nothing else will do.

GET can also be programmed to wait for any keyboard entry. This program logic makes use of the fact that the GET statement string variable is assigned a null character code until a character is input at the keyboard. The null code, 00, cannot be entered from the keyboard, but can be specified within a program using two adjacent quotation marks (" "). Here is the necessary program logic.

```
10 GET A$
20 IF A$="" THEN GOTO 10
30 PRINT A$
40 GOTO 10
```

If the GET statement specifies an integer or floating point variable, the input is interpreted as a numeric digit. The integer or floating point variable appearing in a GET statement is assigned a value of 0 until data input is received. But since you can enter 0 at the keyboard, program logic has no way of knowing whether the 0 represents a valid entry or the absence of any entry. This can present problems to programming logic that checks for an entry, as shown above. GET statements therefore usually receive string characters.

Programs use the GET statement most frequently when generating dialog with an operator. For example, a program may wait for an operator to indicate that he or she is there by entering a specific character (for example, "Y" for "yes"). Here is the appropriate program logic.

```
10 PRINT "OPERATOR! ARE YOU THERE? TYPE Y FOR "YES"
20 GET A$
30 IF A$<>"Y" THEN GOTO 20
40 PRINT "OK, LET'S GET ON WITH IT"
```

Notice that this sequence never displays the character entered at the keyboard. Try rewriting the program so that any character entered in the GET statement is displayed.

PEEK and POKE Statements

PEEK and POKE are two C-64 BASIC statements that you will encounter in later chapters. The C-64 computer has 65,536 individual memory locations, each of which can store a number ranging between 0 and 255. (This strange upper bound is in fact 2^8-1.) All programs and data are converted into sequences of numbers which are stored in this fashion.

The PEEK statement lets you read the number stored in any C-64 computer memory location. Consider the following PEEK statement:

```
10 A%=PEEK(200)
```

This statement assigns the contents of memory location 200 to variable A%. The PEEK argument may be a number, as shown, an integer variable name, or an integer expression, but it must evaluate to the address of a memory location.

The POKE statement writes data into a memory location. For example, the statement

```
20 POKE 8000,A%
```

stores the contents of variable A% in memory location 8000. Each POKE argument may be a number, a variable, or an expression with a value between 0 and 255. A floating point value is automatically converted to an integer.

You can PEEK into read/write memory or read-only memory, but you can POKE only into read/write memory. Read-only memory, as its name implies, can have its contents read, but cannot be written into.

END and STOP Statements

The END and STOP statements halt program execution. You can continue execution by typing **CONT**. You do not have to include END or STOP statements in your program, but these statements do make programs easier to use.

In many of the programming examples given in this chapter we have used a GOTO statement that branches to itself in order to stop program execution. For example, the statement

```
50 GOTO 50
```

will execute endlessly since the GOTO statement selects itself for the execution. We could replace this statement with a STOP statement. When a STOP statement is executed, the following message will appear:

```
BREAK IN XXXX
```

Then execution stops. XXXX is the line number of the STOP statement. If you have more than one STOP statement in your program, use the line number to identify which one was executed.

FUNCTIONS

Another element of C-64 BASIC is the *function*, which in some ways looks like a variable, but in other ways acts more like a BASIC statement.

Perhaps the simplest way of illustrating a function is to look at an example in an assignment statement.

```
10 A=SQR(B)
```

The variable A has been set equal to the square root of the variable B. SQR specifies the square root function. Here is a string function.

```
20 C$=LEFT$(D$,2)
```

In this example the string variable C$ is set equal to the first two characters of string variable D$.

Functions can substitute for variables or constants anywhere in a BASIC statement, except to the left of an equal sign. In other words, you can say that A = SQR(B), but you cannot say that SQR(A) = B.

We have already used four functions. SPC, TAB, and POS are system functions used with the PRINT statement to format displays. PEEK is also a function.

The discussion that follows shows you how to use functions. A brief incomplete summary of the C-64 BASIC functions is presented here, but complete descriptions of all functions are given in Appendixes G and H.

You specify a function using an abbreviation (such as SQR for square root), followed by *arguments* enclosed in parentheses. In the case of A = SQR(B), SQR requires a single argument, which in this case is the variable B. For C$ = LEFT$(D$,2), LEFT$ specifies the function; the two arguments D$ and 2 are enclosed in parentheses. Generally stated, any function will have one of the following two formats:

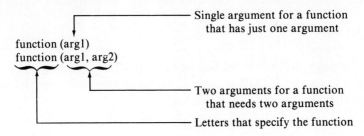

A few functions need three arguments. Each function argument can be a constant, a variable, or an expression.

A function appearing in a BASIC statement is evaluated before any operators. Every function in a BASIC statement is reduced to a single numeric or string value before any other part of the BASIC statement is evaluated. For example, in the following statement the SQR and SIN functions are evaluated first:

```
10 B=24.7*(SQR(C)+5)-SIN(0.2+D)
```

Suppose SQR(C) = 6.72 and SIN(0.2 + D) = 0.625. The statement on line 10 will first be reduced to

```
10 B=24.7*(6.72+5)-0.625
```

This simpler statement is then evaluated.

Arithmetic Functions

Here is a list of the arithmetic functions that can be used with C-64 BASIC.

INT	Converts a floating point argument to its integer equivalent by truncation.
SGN	Returns the sign of an argument: +1 for a positive argument, −1 for a negative argument, 0 for 0 argument.
ABS	Returns the absolute value of an argument. A positive argument does not change; a negative argument is converted to its positive equivalent.
SQR	Computes the square root of the argument.

EXP	Raises the natural logarithm base e to the power of the argument (e^{arg}).
LOG	Returns the natural logarithm of the argument.
RND	Generates a random number. There are some rules regarding use of RND; they are described in Chapter 5.
SIN	Returns the trigonometric sine of the argument, which is treated as a radian quantity.
COS	Returns the trigonometric cosine of the argument, which is treated as a radian quantity.
TAN	Returns the trigonometric tangent of the argument, which is treated as a radian quantity.
ATN	Returns the trigonometric arctangent of the argument, which is treated as a radian quantity.

The following example uses an arithmetic function:

```
10 A=2.743
20 B=INT(A)+7
30 PRINT B
40 STOP
```

When you execute this program, the result displayed is 9, since the integer value of A is 2. As an exercise, change the statement on line 10 to an INPUT statement. Change line 40 to GOTO 10. Now you can enter a variety of values for A and watch the integer function at work. Use this program to experiment with various functions.

Here is a more complex example using arithmetic functions.

```
10 INPUT A,B
20 IF LOG(A)<0 THEN A=1/A
30 PRINT SQR(A)*EXP(B)
40 GOTO 10
```

If you understand logarithms, then as an exercise change the statement on line 20, replacing the LOG function with arithmetic functions that perform the same operation.

The argument of a function can be an expression; the expression itself may contain functions. For example, change line 30 to the following statement and rerun the program:

```
30 PRINT SQR(A*EXP(B)+3)
```

Now experiment with arithmetic functions by creating PRINT statements that make complex use of arithmetic functions.

String Functions

String functions allow you to manipulate string data in a variety of ways. You may never need to use some of the arithmetic functions, but you must make the effort to learn every string function.

Here is a list of the string functions that can be used with C-64 BASIC.

STR$ Converts a number to its equivalent string of text characters.

VAL   Converts a string of text characters to their equivalent number (if such a conversion is possible).

CHR$ Converts an 8-bit binary code to its equivalent ASCII character.

ASC   Converts an ASCII character to its 8-bit binary equivalent.

LEN   Returns the number of characters contained in a text string.

LEFT$ Extracts the left part of a text string. Function arguments identify the string and its left part.

RIGHT$ Extracts the right part of a text string. Function arguments identify the string and its right part.

MID$ Extracts the middle section of a text string. Function arguments identify the string and the required mid part.

String functions let you determine the length of a string, extract portions of a string, and convert between numeric, ASCII, and string characters. These functions take one, two, or three arguments. Here are some examples.

```
STR$(14)

LEN("ABC")

LEN(A$+B$)

LEFT$(ST$,1)
```

System Functions

In the interest of completeness, C-64 BASIC system functions are listed below. They perform operations that you are unlikely to need until you are an experienced programmer. The only system function you are likely to use fairly soon is the time-of-day function. If you print many variations of a report (or any other material) in a single day, you may wish to print the time of day at the top of the report. That way you can tell the sequence in which these reports were generated.

PEEK Fetches the contents of a memory byte.

TI\$,TI Fetches system time, as maintained by a program clock.

FRE Returns available free space—the number of unused read/write memory bytes.

SYS Transfers to subsystem.

USR Transfers to user assembly language program.

User-Defined Functions

In addition to the many functions that are a standard part of C-64 BASIC, you can define your own arithmetic functions, providing they are not very complicated. User-defined string functions are not allowed. Here is an example of a short program that uses a DEF FN (define function) statement.

```
10 DEFFNP(X)=100*X
20 INPUT A
30 PRINT A,FNP(A)
40 GOTO 20
```

Following the DEF FN entry you can have any valid floating point variable name. In this case P was entered, therefore the function name becomes FNP. If the variable name were AB, the function name would be FNAB.

In the DEF FN statement, a single variable, enclosed in brackets, must follow FN. This is the only variable name that can appear to the right of the equal sign. This variable name is used within the DEF FN statement only; you can use it in the body of the program without affecting the function.

Advanced BASIC Programming **4**

Although the previous chapter covered most of the inner workings of C-64 BASIC, you will find that there is much more to be learned about programming. Whereas Chapter 3 covered the language itself, this chapter and those that follow will provide programming techniques and hints that will help you get the most out of your C-64.

Because this chapter concerns itself with more advanced programming, program examples and explanations will be longer. You will probably want to enter and run each example in order to better understand the concepts being discussed.

Many of the program examples covered in this chapter are designed for use in programs you write yourself. Some are written as subroutines, and others can be turned into subroutines with minor changes.

PROGRAMMING WITH STRINGS

A string can do much more than simply contain data that cannot be expressed in numeric form. String operations and functions give you the ability to change and manipulate data.

Concatenating Strings

Strings can contain alphabetic or numeric characters or combinations of these. When handling strings, it may be useful to link shorter strings end-to-end in a chain-like fashion to create one large string. This linking process, as you may recall, is called concatenation.

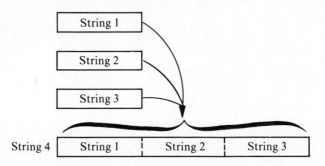

Suppose, for example, you want to create one large string, Z$, containing the alphabet A through Z. To do this, you can link the last character of A$, shown below, to the first character of J$, and the last character of J$ to the first character of S$.

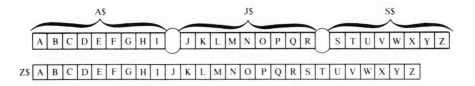

When a plus sign appears between two numeric expressions, it adds the values of the expressions. However, the plus sign will concatenate strings when string variables appear on either side of it.

The same is not true of the minus sign. Strings cannot be separated or "de-concatenated" in the same way they are concatenated; they cannot be "subtracted" the way they are "added."

For instance, to create string X$, containing the contents of J$ and S$ from our original strings A$, J$, S$, and Z$, it would be incorrect to type

```
X$=Z$-A$ ←——————— Incorrect
```

Try it yourself. Enter the values of **A\$, J\$, S\$**, and **X\$ = Z\$—A\$** into the C-64 as shown. The computer will respond with the message ?TYPE MIS-MATCH ERROR IN LINE 50.

```
10 A$="ABCDEFGHI"
20 J$="JKLMNOPQR"
30 S$="STUVWXYZ"
40 Z$=A$+J$+S$
50 X$=Z$-A$  ←——————— Incorrect attempt to get J through Z string
60 PRINT A$

RUN

?TYPE MISMATCH
 ERROR IN 50
```

The correct way to extract part of a larger string is to use string functions. With the LEFT\$, MID\$, and RIGHT\$ functions, it is possible to extract any portion of a string. In our example, the letters J through Z can be extracted as follows:

```
50 X$=RIGHT$(Z$,17)
```

XS=
RIGHT$(| A | B | C | D | E | F | G | H | I | J | K | L | M | N | O | P | Q | R | S | T | U | V | W | X | Y | Z | 17)

XS = | J | K | L | M | N | O | P | Q | R | S | T | U | V | W | X | Y | Z |

The 17 points to the 17th character from the right (RIGHT\$) as the first character of the string and includes the rest of the characters to its right. The string may also be built by concatenating J\$ and S\$.

```
50 X$=J$+S$
```

XS = | J | K | L | M | N | O | P | Q | R | + | S | T | U | V | W | X | Y | Z |

XS = | J | K | L | M | N | O | P | Q | R | S | T | U | V | W | X | Y | Z |

Numeric Strings

A numeric string is a string whose contents can be evaluated as a number. Numeric strings can be created in two different ways, each yielding slightly different results.

When numeric variables are assigned to numeric strings using the STR$ function, the sign value preceding the number (blank if positive, − if negative) is transferred along with the number. This is shown in the following short program:

```
10 AB=12345
20 PI= -1*3.14159265
30 T$=STR$(AB)
40 N$=STR$(PI)
50 PRINT "AB=";AB
60 PRINT "T$=";T$
70 PRINT "N$=";N$
```

```
RUN                          Space left for sign value
AB= 12345
T$= 12345
N$=-3.14159265
```

However, if a number is entered enclosed in quotation marks, or if the number is entered as a string with an INPUT or READ statement, then the numeric string is treated like any other alphabetic or graphic string. No blank for a positive sign value is inserted before the number. This is demonstrated in the following program:

```
10 AB=12345
20 T$="12345"
30 READ R$
40 DATA 12345
50 PRINT "AB=";AB
60 PRINT "T$=";T$
70 PRINT "R$=";R$
```

```
RUN
AB= 12345        ←————— Space inserted
T$=12345         ←————— No space inserted
R$=12345         ←————— No space inserted
```

Concatenate the two numeric strings **T$** and **Q$** to make a new numeric string W$ so that the string W$ contains the ten digits 1,2,3,4,5,6,7,8,9,0. Here is one possibility:

```
10 T=12345
20 Q=67890
30 T$=STR$(T)
```

```
40 Q$=STR$(Q)
50 W$=T$+Q$          ──────────── Create new string W$
60 PRINT "W$=
```

```
RUN
W$= 12345 67890
```

Why are there blanks before the 1 and 6? The T$ and Q$ string were originally positive numeric variables T and Q. When T and Q were converted from numbers into strings, the blank sign positions were transferred along with the numbers.

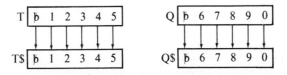

Therefore, when T$ and Q$ are concatenated, the new string W$ contains a first-digit blank, and an embedded blank before the first digit of Q$.

To get rid of the blanks, go back to the separate strings T$ and Q$. Look again at the contents of T$ and Q$ above. The only values we want in W$ are the numbers to the right of the sign value in both T$ and Q$. With the LEFT$, MID$, and RIGHT$ commands, you can select any character or group of characters from within a given string. We want all the characters to the right of the first character, which is the sign value (either blank or −). T$ = MID$(T$,2) does the trick.

Since the first digit needed is in the second position of the string, the C-64 is instructed to use only the values starting in the second position. We can concatenate T$ and Q$ and drop the leading blanks all in one statement.

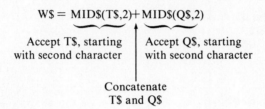

$$W\$ = MID\$(T\$,2) + MID\$(Q\$,2)$$

| Accept T\$, starting with second character | Accept Q\$, starting with second character |

Concatenate
T\$ and Q\$

Our example program, amended to eliminate the sign digits, appears as follows:

```
10 T=12345
```

T   =   ⌷12345

```
20 Q=67890
```

Q   =   ⌷67890

```
30 T$=STR$(T)
```

T\$ = | ⌷ | 1 | 2 | 3 | 4 | 5 |

```
40 Q$=STR$(Q)
```

Q\$ = | ⌷ | 6 | 7 | 8 | 9 | 0 |

```
50 W$=M$(T$,2)+MID$(Q$,2)
```

W\$ = T\$ | 1 | 2 | 3 | 4 | 5 | + Q\$ | 6 | 7 | 8 | 9 | 0 |

W\$ = | 1 | 2 | 3 | 4 | 5 | 6 | 7 | 8 | 9 | 0 |

```
60 PRINT "W=";W$
```

```
RUN
W$=1234567890
```

INPUT AND OUTPUT PROGRAMMING

It is usually easy for beginning programmers to become acquainted with how BASIC calculates numbers. When writing programs that receive input from the keyboard and display data on the screen, however, the programming becomes trickier.

Nearly every program requires some kind of input from the keyboard. If you are the person operating the computer, you can probably put together some INPUT statements that get the required data and process it in your program. But if someone else is operating the computer, sooner or later the wrong key will be pressed or an incorrect entry will be made. Every computer operator will make mistakes at some time. You should write programs that allow for conceivable human errors.

The same is true for output programming. If you display the results of a program with a set of PRINT statements, those results have to be readable to the person looking at the display. This does not happen by hacking away at program statements until the output looks a little better; you must give it some thought while you are writing the program.

Assume that you want to write a program that inputs names and addresses. You could write a program to do this quickly and easily enough.

```
10 REM NAME/ADDRESS PROGRAM
20 DIM NM$(20),AD$(20),CS$,(20),ZC$(20)
21 REM ARRAYS ARE:
22 REM NM$() FOR NAME
23 REM AD$() FOR ADDRESS
24 REM CS$() FOR CITY AND STATE
26 REM ZC$() FOR ZIP/POSTAL CODE
30 FOR I=1 TO 20
40 INPUT "NAME:";NM$(I)
50 INPUT "ADDRESS:";AD$(I)
60 INPUT "CITY, STATE:";CS$(I)
70 INPUT "ZIP/POSTAL CODE:";ZC$(I)
80 NEXT I
90 END
```

Here is an example of how the program would appear on the display.

```
RUN
NAME:? NAM THANG
ADDRESS:? 2000 CONSTITUTION DR.
CITY, STATE:? CASTRO VALLEY, CA.
?EXTRA IGNORED
ZIP/POSTAL CODE:? 91912
NAME:? PETER BILT
ADDRESS:? 200 KNOW PL.
CITY, STATE:? AMARILLO, TEXAS
?EXTRA IGNORED
ZIP/POSTAL CODE:? 65432
```

In this program, the C-64's screen is unformatted. The screen width is 40 characters; most names and addresses entered would wrap around to the line below the original entry because the entry message, or *prompt*, takes up several spaces on the input line.

While running this program, the person entering names and addresses might discover a mistake in a name after pressing RETURN. But the operator can't go back to fix the name when the program is asking for address input.

Other problems with this program are obvious if you enter and run it. The display is not very easy to read. One entry for a name and address follows another, all the way down the screen. This kind of clutter will increase the possibility of incorrect entries.

The INPUT statement on line 60 will cause the program to fail if the operator puts a comma between the city and state when entering them. The city and state have to be entered without a comma between them. Try entering a city and state separated by a comma (for example, **OAKLAND, CALIFORNIA**). This is what you get.

```
ADDRESS:? OAKLAND, CALIFORNIA
?EXTRA IGNORED
```

Recall from Chapter 3 that the INPUT statement allows you to enter more than one item of data on a single line, as long as each one is separated by a comma. Therefore, when **OAKLAND, CALIFORNIA** was entered, C-64 BASIC interpreted it as two separate strings when only one string was expected—hence the ?EXTRA IGNORED message. In addition to the error message, the program stored only OAKLAND and discarded CALIFORNIA, which was considered "extra" input.

Screen Layout

Starting the display at row 0, column 0 (the upper left corner), the rightmost column is 39, and the lowest row is 24. The screen layout in this grid form is a set of *coordinates*. A coordinate is the point at which a particular column and row intersect on the display.

Column

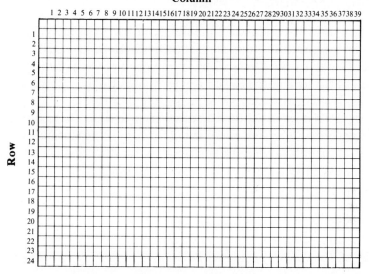

A coordinate on the C-64 screen is expressed as (*row,column*). That is, the coordinate of the 12th row and 20th column will be expressed as (11,19). The first column of the fourth row is (3,0), and so on. (Remember that the row and column numbers start at 0, not 1.)

The coordinates (11,19) would appear at this point on the screen.

Column

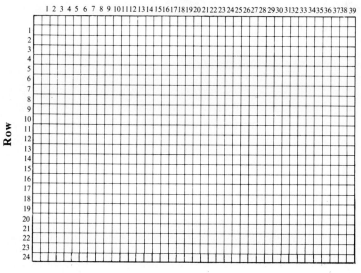

Creating a Formatted Display

Keep in mind the maximum possible length of each entry. For instance, a name with a job title, such as "MAJOR SEIDELL—DIRECTOR OF STRATEGIC OPERATIONS", will wrap around to the next display line. Allow space for such entries when you format a display. Centering prompts on the display will also make it appear more orderly.

Formatted displays should be used in programs that require a good deal of data entry. Three distinguishing features of proper data entry techniques are a readable, uncluttered display, clear directions to the operator, and the ability of the operator to correct mistakes.

Programming Cursor Movement

If you encountered the C-64's quote mode while entering program statements, you will already know how to program cursor movement.

If you edit a program statement containing a string constant, C-64 BASIC will interpret a control key as an actual character within the string you are trying to edit. For example, when you press the CRSR UP/DOWN key between the quotes in a string, it will appear as an inverse-video Q on the screen. Instead of moving the cursor up or down one line as you intended, C-64 BASIC inserted the CRSR UP/DOWN key into the string. If you print the string containing the cursor control character, the cursor will move down.

The statement

```
1010 R$="◖◖◖◖◖◖◖◖◖◖◖◖◖◖◖◖◖◖◖◖◖◖"
```

sets up a string of 22 CRSR DOWN characters which, when printed by a PRINT statement, will move the cursor down 22 rows. Likewise, a string containing 21 CRSR/RIGHT characters will move the cursor to the right 21 spaces.

```
1020 C$="▮▮▮▮▮▮▮▮▮▮▮▮▮▮▮▮▮▮▮▮▮"
```

These strings containing the cursor control characters will allow you to display a character anywhere on the display screen.

A CURSOR MOVEMENT SUBROUTINE

With three strings containing the cursor control characters to move to the home position, down, and to the right, it is possible to move to any coordinate position on the C-64 display. How?

The coordinates of the upper left corner of the screen are (0,0). You can move the cursor anywhere by printing a string containing the CLR/HOME control key, followed by strings that move the cursor down and to the right. Here is an example.

```
10 REM PROGRAMMED CURSOR MOVEMENT
20 PRINT "⌑":REM CLEAR THE SCREEN
30 R%=20:C%=4:GOSUB 1000
40 PRINT "IGNORANCE IS BLISS"
50 GOTO 50
1000 REM CURSOR POSITIONING SUBROUTINE
1010 R$="▮▮▮▮▮▮▮▮▮▮▮▮▮▮▮▮▮▮▮▮▮▮"
1020 C$="▮▮▮▮▮▮▮▮▮▮▮▮▮▮▮▮▮▮▮▮▮"
1030 PRINT "⌑"; :REM MOVE CURSOR TO (0,0)
1040 PRINT LEFT$(R$,R%);LEFT$(C$,C%);
1050 RETURN
```

Line 20 clears the screen, removing any old text from the display. (This has nothing to do with cursor positioning; it is just "housekeeping" to make a cleaner display.) The integer variables R% and C% on line 30 stand for "row" and "column." The three statements combined on line 30 set the row (20) and the column (4), followed by a GOSUB that moves the cursor to the coordinates (20,4).

You may not understand why the cursor must go to (0,0) first. In order for the program to move the cursor to the correct coordinates, it has to know how many rows and columns the cursor is from the coordinates you selected. The easiest and most efficient way to do this is to move to (0,0) first, because the program will always know exactly how many times the cursor must move in order to reach the coordinates (in this case, 20 rows down and 4 columns right).

Let's take the cursor movement subroutine apart line by line, starting with lines 1010 and 1020. These two lines are assignment statements that set up (initialize) the cursor movement strings. R$ contains 22 CRSR DOWN control characters; C$ contains 21 CRSR RIGHT characters.

Line 1030 prints the CLR/HOME character, thus positioning the cursor at (0,0). Line 1040 does the real work: it uses the LEFT$ string function to print the first 20 characters in R$, then the first 10 characters in C$.

This cursor movement subroutine will be an integral part of creating and using formatted displays.

The CHR$ Function: Programming Characters in ASCII

If you cannot press a key to include a character within a text string, you can still select the character by using its ASCII value.

The CHR$ function translates an ASCII code number into its character equivalent. This is the format of the CHR$ function.

```
PRINT CHR$(xxx)
```
ASCII number from 0 to 255 of desired character or control

To obtain the ASCII code for a character, refer to Appendix B. Scan the columns until you find the desired character or cursor control, then note the corresponding ASCII code number. Insert this number between the two parentheses of the CHR$ function. For example, to create the symbol $ from its ASCII code, look up ASCII code for $ in Appendix B. You will notice that $ has two ASCII values: 36 and 100. Which value should you use? Either number works. But for good programming technique, once you select one number over the other, use that number consistently throughout the program. Insert 36 into the CHR$ function as follows:

```
PRINT CHR$(36)
```

Try displaying this character ($) in immediate mode:

```
PRINT CHR$(36)
$
```

Now try displaying ASCII code 100.

```
PRINT CHR$(100)
$
```

The result is the same. Experiment in immediate mode using any ASCII code from 0 to 255.

You can use the CHR$ function in a PRINT statement as follows:

```
10 PRINT CHR$(36);CHR$(42);CHR$(166)

RUN
$*▦
```

The CHR$ function lets you include otherwise unavailable characters such as RETURN, INST/DEL, and the quote character (") in a PRINT statement's parameters.

You can also use the CHR$ function to check for special characters such as RETURN and INST/DEL. Suppose a program must check character input at the keyboard, looking for a RETURN key. You could check for a RETURN (which has an ASCII code of 13) as follows:

```
10 GET X$:IF X$<>CHR$(13) THEN 10
```

This test would be impossible if you tried to put RETURN between quotation marks.

```
20 IF X$<>"[ RETURN ]" THEN 10
```

Impossible

This does not work, because pressing the RETURN key following the first set of quotation marks automatically moves the cursor to the next line.

```
20 IF X$<>"        Press RETURN key
```

If you attempt to program the INST/DEL or the RETURN key, you will encounter some surprising results.

The INSERT key is programmable. Inside the quotation marks of a PRINT statement, it displays as ▮.

If you try to program the DELETE key in a PRINT statement you will merely erase the previous character, unless the DELETE key occurs within a sequence of inserted characters.

The DELETE key may be entered following an INSERT, but doing so is not very useful. The only common use of this feature is in concealing program lines during a listing (hiding answers for a test, for instance). Hidden data can be easily rediscovered in several ways, however, so using DELETE characters within program lines is not advisable.

The RETURN character in a PRINT statement will immediately move the cursor out of the statement and to the next line.

Data Entry (Input)

Data entry should be programmed in functional units. A mailing list program, for example, requires names and addresses to be entered as data. You should treat each entire name and address as a single functional unit rather than separate data items. In other words, your program should ask for the name and address, allowing the operator to enter all of this information and then change any part of it. When the operator is satisfied that the name and address are correct, the program should process the entire name and address. The program should then ask for the next name and address.

It is bad programming practice to break data input into its smallest parts. In a mailing list program, for example, it would be bad programming practice to ask for just the name, process this data as soon as it is entered, and then ask for each line of the address, treating each piece of the name and address as a separate functional unit. This approach makes programs difficult to change and also renders them less readable.

The goal of any data entry program should be to make it easy for an operator to spot errors and to give the operator as many chances as possible to fix them.

PROMPTING MESSAGES

Any program that requires data entry should prompt the operator by asking questions. Questions are usually displayed on a single line and require a simple response such as "yes" or "no." For example, a prompt message such as ANY CHANGES (Y OR N)? would clearly indicate the question and the available choices.

An operator responds to this message by pressing the Y or N key. Good programming practice dictates that entries other than Y or N not be accepted. If the operator replies **Y** to the ANY CHANGES prompt, another prompt will display, such as WHAT ENTRY LINE TO CHANGE (1-6)?. In this case, one of six entry lines could be changed; all the operator needs to do is enter the number corresponding to the line that was entered in error. Of course, with this approach each entry line on the display should have an identifying number.

This type of data entry should be written in subroutines, so the main program is not clogged up with prompting messages. Also, because a limited number of choices is allowed, a subroutine could contain the logic necessary to check the entry against permitted responses.

This has two implications.

1. The subroutine must receive parameters from the calling program. For example, if a message asks the operator to enter a number, the calling program should pass the minimum and maximum allowed numbers to the subroutine as parameters.
2. The subroutine must return the operator's response to the calling program. This variable may be a character (for example, Y or N), a word (such as yes or no), or a number.

A subroutine that prompts for a reply of **Y** for "yes" or **N** for "no" uses a PRINT statement to ask the question, followed by a GET to receive a one-character response. Since you may have many questions in a program which require a response of "yes" or "no," the subroutine should also allow for a prompt to be passed to the subroutine from the main program in a string variable. Here are the necessary statements.

```
3000 REM ASK A QUESTION AND RETURN A RESPONSE OF Y OR
     N IN YN$
3010 PRINT ""
3020 PRINT "DO YOU WANT TO MAKE ANY CHANGES? ";
3030 GET YN$: IF YN$<>"N" AND YN$<>"Y" THEN 3030
3040 PRINT YN$
3050 RETURN
```

The string variable QU$ must be set in the program that calls the subroutine. The subroutine is generalized; that is, it displays any prompt sent to it by the main program. The response is returned to the main program in the string variable YN$.

Now consider dialog that allows an operator to enter a number. Assume that the main program passes to the subroutine the lowest allowable numeric entry in LO% and the highest in HI%. Once the operator enters a number within range, the subroutine will return the entered number in NM%. Here is the subroutine that gets the keyboard entry, checks it against LO% and HI% values, and then passes it back to the main program in NM%.

```
3500 REM ASK FOR A NUMERIC SELECTION
3510 REM RETURN THE NUMBER IN NM%
3520 REM NM% MUST BE <= HI% AND >= LO%
3530 PRINT QU$;
```

```
3540 GET C$:IF C$=" " THEN 3540
3550 NM%=VAL(C$)
3560 IF NM%<LO% OR NM%>HI% THEN 3540
3570 PRINT C$;
3580 RETURN
```

Write a short program that sets values for HI% and LO%, and then goes to subroutine 3500. Add the previous subroutine and run it.

Can you change the subroutine so that it accepts two-digit input? Try to write this modified program for yourself. If you cannot do it, wait until the next section, where you will find the necessary subroutine in the program that controls the input of a date.

ENTERING A VALID DATE

Most programs at some point need relatively simple data input—more than a simple yes or no, but less than a full screen display. Consider a date.

You must be careful with such apparently simple data entry. In all likelihood, the date will be just one item in a data entry sequence. By carefully designing data entry for each small item, you can avoid having to restart a long data entry sequence whenever the operator messes up a single entry.

The date is to be entered as follows:

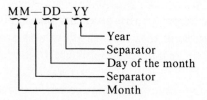

The dashes separating the month, day, and year could be slashes or any other appropriate character. In Europe, the day of the month precedes the month.

You should program data entry so that it is pleasing to the operator's eye. The operator should be able to see immediately where data is to be entered, what type of data is required, and how far the data entry process has proceeded. A good way of showing where data is to be entered is to display the entry line in inverse video. For example, the program that asks for a date might create the following display:

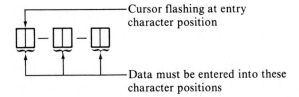

You can create such a display with the following statement:

10 PRINT"<CLR><CRSR↓ ><CRSR↓ >";TAB(20);"<RVS ON>bb
    <RVS OFF> — <RVS ON> bb <RVS OFF> — <RVS ON>
    bb <RVS OFF>";CHR$(13);"<CRSR↑ >";TAB(20);

b represents a space code

The PRINT statement above includes cursor controls that position the date entry to begin at column 6 in row 3. The PRINT statement also clears the screen so that no residual display surrounds the request for a date. After displaying the data entry line, the PRINT statement moves the cursor back to the first position of the entry line by using the RETURN and CRSR UP characters, followed by a TAB to position 6 on the current display line.

Try using an INPUT statement to receive entry of the month. This can be done as follows:

```
20 INPUT M$;
```

Enter statements in lines 10 and 20, as illustrated above, and execute them. The INPUT statement will not work. Aside from the fact that a question mark displaces the first entry line character, the INPUT statement picks up the rest of the line following the question mark. Unless you overwrite the entire date entry display—which requires entering a very large number—you will get an error message each time you press the RETURN key, because C-64 BASIC is accepting everything on the line as if it were a keyboard entry.

This is an occasion to use the GET statement.

```
10 PRINT "▩▩▩▩ ▦—▦ ▦—▦ ▦";CHR$(13);"]";
20 GET C$:IF C$=" "THEN 20
30 PRINT C$;:MM$=C$
40 GET C$:IF C$=" "THEN 40
50 PRINT C$;:MM$=MM$+C$
60 STOP
```

These statements accept two-digit input. The input displays in the first part of the date. The two-digit input needs no RETURN or other terminating character. The program automatically terminates the data entry after two characters are entered.

Two-digit entries are needed for the month, the day, and the year. Rather than repeating statements in lines 20 through 50, you could put these statements into a subroutine and branch to it three times, as follows:

```
10 PRINT "[CLR][DOWN][DOWN][DOWN] ■-■ ■-■ ■";CHR$(13);"[UP]";
20 GOSUB 1000:MM$=TC$:PRINTTAB(3)
30 GOSUB 1000:DD$=TC$:PRINTTAB(6)
40 GOSUB 1000:YY$=TC$
50 STOP
1000 REM TWO CHARACTER INPUT SUBROUTINE
1010 GET C$:IF C$=""  THEN 1010
1020 PRINT C$;
1030 GET CC$:IF CC$="" THEN 1030
1040 PRINT CC$
1050 TC$=C$+CC$
1060 RETURN
```

The variables MM$, DD$, and YY$ hold the month, day, and year entries, respectively. Each entry is held as a two-character string. You should empty the input buffer before accepting the first input; otherwise, any prior characters in the input buffer will be read by the first GET statement in the two-character input subroutine. You need to empty the buffer only once before the first GET statement.

There are two ways to help the operator recover from errors while entering a date.

- The program can automatically test for valid month, day, and year entries.
- The operator can restart the data entry by pressing a specific key.

The program can check that the month lies between 01 and 12. The program will not bother with leap years, but will check for the maximum number of days in the specified month. Any year from 00 through 99 is allowed. Any invalid entry restarts the entire date entry sequence. Also, if the operator presses the RETURN key, the entire date entry sequence restarts.

The final date entry program now appears in Figure 4-1.

Notice that the date is built up in the 8-character string DT$ as month, day, and year are entered.

```
5 REM ROUTINE TO ACCEPT AND VERIFY A DATE
10 PRINT "■■■■ ■-■ ■-■ ■";CHR$(13);"■";
50 GOSUB 1000:REM GET MONTH
60 IF C$=CHR$(13) OR CC$=CHR$(13) THEN 10
70 DT$=TC$:PRINT TAB(3)
80 REM CHECK FOR VALID MONTH
90 M%=VAL(TC$)
95 IF M%<1 OR M%>12 THEN 10
100 IF M%<1 OR M%>12 THEN 10
110 REM GET NUMBER OF DAYS IN MONTH
120 D%=31
130 IF M%=2 THEN D%=28
140 IF M%=4 OR M%=6 OR M%=9 OR M%=11 THEN D%=30
150 GOSUB 1000: REM GET DAY
160 IF C$=CHR$(13) OR CC$=CHR$(13) THEN 10
170 DT$=DT$+"-"+TC$:PRINT TAB(6)
190 REM CHECK FOR VALID DAY
200 IF VAL(TC$)<1 OR VAL(TC$)>D% THEN 10
210 GOSUB 1000: REM GET YEAR
220 DT$=DT$+"-"+TC$
230 IF C$=CHR$(13) OR CC$=CHR$(13) THEN 10
240 REM CHECK FOR VALID YEAR
270 STOP
1000 REM TWO CHARACTER INPUT SUBROUTINE
1010 GET C$: IF C$="" THEN 1010
1011 IF VAL(B$)>100 THEN PRINT"T"
1015 IF C$=CHR$(13) THEN 1050
1016 IF C$<"0" OR C$>"9" THEN 1010
1020 PRINT C$;
1030 GET CC$:IF CC$="" THEN 1030
1035 IF CC$=CHR$(13) THEN 1050
1036 IF CC$<"0" OR CC$>"9" THEN 1030
1040 PRINT CC$;
1050 TC$=C$+CC$
1060 RETURN
```

FIGURE 4-1. Simple program to enter and verify a date

Three questions are asked of data as it is entered.

· Is the character a RETURN?
· If the character is not a RETURN, is it a valid digit?
· Is the two-character combination a valid month for the first entry, a valid day for the second entry, or a valid year for the third entry?

The RETURN has been selected as an abort (restart) character. By replacing CHR$(13) in lines 60, 160, 230, and 1035, you can select any other abort character. When the operator presses the selected abort key, the entire date entry sequence restarts. You must check for the abort character in the two-character input subroutine (at line 1035), since you want to abort after the first or second digit has been entered.

The main program also checks for an abort character in order to branch back to the statement in line 10 and restart the entire date entry sequence. You could branch out of the two-character input subroutine and to the statement in line 10 in the calling program, thereby eliminating the abort character test in the calling program, but this is a bad practice. Every subroutine should be treated as a module, with specified entry point(s) and standard subroutine return points.

Using GOTO to branch between the subroutine and the calling program is likely to be a source of programming errors. If you branch out of the subroutine and back to the calling program without going through the RETURN, you are making yourself vulnerable to all kinds of subtle errors that you will not understand until you are an experienced programmer.

Program logic that tests for nondigit characters can reside entirely in the two-character input subroutine. This program ignores nondigit characters. Statements in lines 1016 and 1036 test for nondigit characters by comparing the ASCII value of the input character and the ASCII values for the allowed numeric digits.

Logic to check for valid month, day, and year must exist within the calling program since each of these 2-character values has different allowed limits.

The statement in line 100 tests for a valid month. Statements in lines 120, 130, and 140 compute the maximum allowed day for the month entered. The statement in line 200 checks for a valid day. The check for a valid year in line 260 is very simple.

A numeric equivalent of the month is generated in line 90, but not for the day or the year. This is because the day and year are not used very often, but the month is used in lines 90 through 140. You will save both memory and execution time by using a numeric representation of the month.

It does take more time to write a good data entry program that checks for valid data input, allowing the operator to restart at any time. Is the extra time worthwhile? By all means, yes. You will write a program once, while an operator may have to run the program hundreds or thousands of times. Thus, by spending extra programming time once, you may save operators hundreds or thousands of delays.

Formatted Data Input

The best way of handling multi-item data entry is to display a form and then fill it in as data is entered. Consider the formatted name-and-address display earlier in this chapter.

```
ENTER NAME AND ADDRESS
❚❚  NAME: ▇▇▇▇▇▇▇▇▇▇▇
❚  STREET:
❚  CITY:
❚❚  STATE:
❚  ZIP:
❚  PHONE:
```

Each entry line has a corresponding number. The form displays the number in inverse video. The operator enters data starting with item 1 and ending with item 6. The operator can then change any specific data entry line.

The following statements clear the screen and display the initial form:

```
10 REM NAME AND ADDRESS DATA ENTRY
20 REM DISPLAY THE DATA ENTRY
30 PRINT "❚ENTER NAME AND ADDRESS"
40 PRINT "❚1❚   NAME:"
50 PRINT "❚2❚ STREET:"
60 PRINT "❚3❚   CITY:"
70 PRINT "❚4❚  STATE:"
80 PRINT "❚5❚    ZIP:"
90 PRINT "❚6❚  PHONE:"
```

The program listed in Figure 4-2 is a more complete version of the name-and-address program. It uses the display format shown above. Key in the program if you wish. It will help you gain a better understanding of the program's structure and how it works as it is explained line by line.

In order to format the display itself, lines 10 through 90 print each entry

```
10 REM NAME AND ADDRESS DATA ENTRY
20 REM DISPLAY THE DATA ENTRY
30 PRINT " ENTER NAME AND ADDRESS"
40 PRINT " 1   NAME "
50 PRINT " 2   STREET "
60 PRINT " 3   CITY "
70 PRINT " 4   STATE "
80 PRINT " 5    ZIP "
90 PRINT " 6   PHONE "
100 EDITING%=0
200 REM GET 12 CHARACTER NAME
210 R%=3:C%=9:LN%=12:GOSUB 8000
220 NA$=CC$
230 IF EDITING% THEN 500
250 REM GET STREET
260 R%=4:C%=9:LN%=12:GOSUB 8000
270 SR$=CC$
280 IF EDITING% THEN 500
300 REM GET 12 CHARACTER CITY
310 R%=5:C%=9:LN%=12:GOSUB 8000
320 CI$=CC$
330 IF EDITING% THEN 500
350 REM GET 12 CHARACTER STATE
360 R%=6:C%=9:LN%=5:GOSUB 8000
370 IF EDITING% THEN 500
400 REM GET 5 CHARACTER ZIP CODE
410 R%=7:C%=9:LN%=5:GOSUB 8000
420 ZI$=CC$
430 IF EDITING% THEN 500
450 REM GET PHONE NUMBER
460 R%=8:C%=9:LN%=12:GOSUB 8000
470 PH$=CC$
500 REM ASK IF ANY CHANGES ARE TO BE MADE
510 EDITING%=-1
520 R%=10:C%=0:GOSUB 9000
530 QU$="ANY CHANGES?   ▮"
540 GOSUB 3000:REM GET "Y" OR "N"
550 IF C$="N" THEN PRINT "◻";:END
560 REM ASK WHICH LINES NEED CHANGING
570 QU$="WHICH LINE (1-6)?:   ▮"
580 R%12:LO%=1:HI%=6
590 GOSUB 3500
600 ON NM% GOTO 200,250,300,350,400,450
610 GOTO 520
3000 REM ASK A QUESTION AND RETURN A RESPONSE OF Y OR
     N IN C$
3020 PRINT QU$;
3030 GOSUB 5000:REM GET A CHARACTER
```

FIGURE 4-2. Name and address entry program

```
3040 IF C$<>"Y" AND C$<>"N" THEN 3030
3050 PRINT C$;
3060 RETURN
3500 REM ASK FOR A NUMERIC SELECTION
3510 REM RETURN SELECTION IN NM%
3520 REM NM% MUST BE LESS THAN HI% AND MORE THAN LO%
3530 REM CALLING PROGRAM MUST SET HI%,LO% AND QU$,
     THE QUESTION ASK'ED
3540 GOSUB 9000:REM POSITION THE CURSOR
3550 PRINT QU$;
3560 GOSUB 5000: REM GET A CHARACTER
3570 NM%=VAL(C$)
3580 IF NM%<LO% OR NM%>HI% THEN 3560
3590 PRINT C$;
3600 RETURN
5000 REM DISPLAY FLASHING CURSOR AND GET CHARACTER
5010 FOR I=0 TO 60
5020 IF I=0 THEN PRINT "█ █";
5030 IF I=30 THEN PRINT " █";
5040 GET C$: IF C$<>"" THEN I=60
5050 NEXT I
5060 IF C$="" THEN 5000
5070 RETURN
8000 REM INPUT SUBROUTINE
8020 SP$="
8040 GOSUB 9000
8060 PRINT "█";LEFT$(SP$,LN%);"█";
8070 GOSUB 9000: REM POSITION THE CURSOR
8100 CC$=""
8110 GET C$:I C$="" THEN 8110
8120 IF C$=CHR$(13) THEN 8200
8130 IF C$=CHR$(20) THEN 8160
8140 IF LEN(CC$)<LN% THEN CC$=CC$+C$:PRINT C$;
8150 GOTO 8110
8160 IF CC$="" THEN 8110
8170 PRINT"██ █";
8175 REM DELETE CHARACTER FROM STRING CC$
8180 CC$=LEFT$(CC$,LEN(CC$)-1)
8190 GOTO 8110
8200 IF LN%>LEN(CC$) THEN PRINT LEFT$(SP$,LN%-LEN(CC$));
8210 RETURN
9000 REM CURSOR POSITIONING SUBROUTINE
9010 R$="█████████████████████████"
9020 C$="█████████████████████████"
9030 PRINT "█";:REM MOVE CURSOR TO (0,0)
9040 PRINT LEFT$(R$,R%);LEFT$(C$,C%);
9050 RETURN
9500 GOSUB 5000:PRINT C$;:GOTO 9500
```

FIGURE 4-2. Name and address entry program (continued)

line. The RVS ON control character precedes each PRINT statement line number, and the RVS OFF character follows it. These characters do not display anything by themselves, and they do not take up space on the display. They do change the display mode; thus, any characters following the RVS ON will display in inverse video. Likewise, any characters following the RVS OFF will display in normal video.

THE DATA ENTRY SEQUENCE

Once the entry lines are displayed, the entries start at the NAME line. The program displays a black bar, showing where the entry should start, as well as how long the entry will be.

The operator can back up on the entry line by pressing the INST/DEL key to correct any typing errors. When the entry is complete, the operator presses RETURN and the program goes to the next entry line.

This data entry sequence translates into the following BASIC statements:

```
200 REM GET 12 CHARACTER NAME
210 R%=3:CX=9:LN%=12:GOSUB 8000
220 NA$=CC$
230 IF EDITING% THEN 500
250 REM GET STREET
260 R%=4:CX=9:LN%=12:GOSUB 8000
270 SR$=CC$
280 IF EDITING% THEN 500
300 REM GET 12 CHARACTER CITY
310 R%=5:CX=9:LN%=12:GOSUB 8000
320 CI$=CC$
330 IF EDITING% THEN 500
350 REM GET 12 CHARACTER STATE
360 R%=6:CX=9:LN%=5:GOSUB 8000
370 IF EDITING% THEN 500
400 REM GET 5 CHARACTER ZIP CODE
410 R%=7:CX=9:LN%=5:GOSUB 8000
420 ZI$=CC$
430 IF EDITING% THEN 500
450 REM GET PHONE NUMBER
460 R%=8:CX=9:LN%=12:GOSUB 8000
470 PH$=CC$
```

There is some uniformity to these statements, which are in six separate groups. The groups start at lines 200, 250, 300, 350, 400, and 450, each corresponding to an entry the operator is to make. Each group begins with a REM statement.

Lines 200 through 230 have the same structure as any of the other five statement groups.

```
200 REM GET 12 CHARACTER NAME
210 R%=3:C%=9:LN%=12:GOSUB 8000
220 NA$=CC$
230 IF EDITING% THEN 500
```

Line 210 assigns values to variables and performs a GOSUB to line 8000. Line 8000 is a data entry subroutine; it uses variables R% and C% to specify where on the screen the data entry will occur. LN% contains the maximum length of the entry. Line 220 assigns the entered data to NA$, the string variable to hold the name.

Line 230 is a logical test which you can ignore for now; it will be explained shortly.

Now check the group starting at line 250. Although the values assigned to R%, C%, and LN% may differ and line 270 is not exactly the same, the structure of lines 250-280 is identical to that of lines 200-270. This is the case for all of the other statement groups.

EDITING DATA ENTRY LINES

Once all six lines are entered, the program displays ANY CHANGES? and waits for a response of Y or N. If the response is **N**, the program will clear the screen and end. If the response is **Y**, the program will ask which entry line needs to be changed. At this point, the operator can change any entry lines at random until all lines are correct.

The following lines of the data entry program in Figure 4-2 perform these steps:

```
500 REM ASK IF ANY CHANGES ARE TO BE MADE
510 EDITING%=-1
520 R%=10:C%=0:GOSUB 9000
530 QU$="ANY CHANGES?    ■"
540 GOSUB 3000:REM GET "Y" OR "N"
550 IF C$="N" THEN PRINT "◻";:END
560 REM ASK WHICH LINES NEED CHANGING
570 QU$="WHICH LINE (1-6)?:   ■"
580 R%12:LO%=1:HI%=6
590 GOSUB 3500
600 ON NM% GOTO 200,250,300,350,400,450
610 GOTO 520
```

Line 510 is of special interest because it "switches on" the editing line 590 calls it. The subroutine returns the number of the entry line to change (1, 2, 3, 4, 5, or 6) in the integer variable NM%, and program logic proceeds to line 600.

The ON-GOTO statement on line 600 uses the number entered in NM% to change one of the six name-and-address lines by branching back to any of the six statement groups. EDITING% plays a critical part here, because the logical test at the end of each statement group will now cause a branch directly to line 500, which is the start of the ANY CHANGES? routine. If EDITING% was zero, this would not happen. Program logic would plod along to the next entry line unconditionally. Try changing line 510 to **EDITING% = 0**, and note the difference in operation.

DATA ENTRY SUBROUTINES

There are six subroutines in this program. Each subroutine has a specific function. One of the subroutines is not used by the main program, but is called by the other subroutines.

First look at the subroutine starting at line 3000 and ending at line 3060. This asks a question that requires a Y or N response. The subroutine displays the question which was passed to it in string variable QU$. It calls the subroutine at line 5000, which in turn gets a character from the keyboard. If the character is Y or N, the subroutine ends and returns the response in C$.

```
3000 REM ASK A QUESTION AND RETURN A RESPONSE OF Y OR
     N IN C$
3020 PRINT QU$;
3030 GOSUB 5000:REM GET A CHARACTER
3040 IF C$<>"Y" AND C$<>"N" THEN 3030
3050 PRINT C$;
3060 RETURN
```

But why use a subroutine to get a character when a GET statement would suffice?

A GET statement checks the keyboard for a keypress, but it gives no clear sign to the operator that a character should be entered. The subroutine at line 5000 flashes the cursor while waiting for a keypress, thus making it more obvious that the C-64 is waiting for some kind of entry. Besides, the get character subroutine is used by another subroutine in this program. It makes sense to relegate this low-level function to another subroutine.

The subroutine starting at line 3500 and ending at line 3600 asks for a single-digit numeric entry. In the name-and-address program, the only numeric entry is the number of the line to change, which ranges from 1 to 6.

```
3500 REM ASK FOR A NUMERIC SELECTION
3510 REM RETURN SELECTION IN NM%
3520 REM NM% MUST BE LESS THAN HI% AND MORE THAN LO%
3530 REM CALLING PROGRAM MUST SET HI%,LO% AND QU$,
     THE QUESTION ASKED
3540 GOSUB 9000:REM POSITION THE CURSOR
3550 PRINT QU$;
3560 GOSUB 5000: REM GET A CHARACTER
3570 NM%=VAL(C$)
3580 IF NM%<LO% OR NM%>HI% THEN 3560
3590 PRINT C$;
3600 RETURN
```

This subroutine must have several variables set by the main program before it is called. First, the maximum and minimum allowable values of the entry should be in integer variables HI% and LO%. Second, the subroutine displays a question to the operator contained in QU$, which also has to be set before calling the subroutine.

This subroutine positions the cursor to a given screen position, and the coordinates of that position need to be passed to the subroutine in the variables R% and C%. Line 3540 calls the subroutine at line 9000, which positions the cursor. Line 3550 displays the prompt, and line 3560 calls the "get keyboard entry" subroutine.

The subroutine at line 5000 needs no parameters. It simulates a flashing cursor while waiting for a keyboard entry. A FOR-NEXT statement on line 5010 starts a timing loop that displays an inverse-video space for the first 30 times through the loop. Once the index variable I reaches 30, the statement on line 5030 erases the cursor. During this time, the subroutine is constantly checking the keyboard for an entry. If a key is pressed, the statement on line the subroutine the loop by setting I to 60, and the subroutine ends, passing back the entered character in C$

```
8000 REM DISPLAY FLASHING CURSOR AND GET CHARACTER
8010 FOR I=0 TO 60
8020 IF I=0 THEN PRINT " ";
8030 IF I=30 THEN PRINT " ";
8040 GET C$: IF C$<>"" THEN I=60
8050 NEXT I
8060 IF C$="" THEN 8000
8070 RETURN
```

The subroutine starting at line 8000 and ending at line 8210 is designed to position the cursor and accept a string entry of a specified length. This subroutine therefore needs to know the screen coordinates (row and column) of the entry and the length of the entry before it can begin.

$LN\%$ contains the length of the entry in characters. $R\%$ and $C\%$ contain the row and column of the entry. A variable SP$ is assigned 22 spaces and is used at two points in the subroutine.

Next the cursor-positioning subroutine is called by the GOSUB statement on line 8040. Line 8060 prints the RVS ON character, followed by a block of inverse-video spaces that show the length of the entry to the operator, and then the RVS OFF character.

```
8000 REM INPUT SUBROUTINE
8020 SP$="                      ":REM 22 SPACES
8040 GOSUB 9000
8060 PRINT " ";LEFT$(SP$,LN%);" ";
8070 GOSUB 9000: REM POSITION THE CURSOR
8100 CC$=""
8110 GET C$:IF C$="" THEN 8110
8120 IF C$=CHR$(13) THEN 8200
8130 IF C$=CHR$(20) THEN 8160
8140 IF LEN(CC$)<LN% THEN CC$=CC$+C$:PRINT C$;
8150 GOTO 8110
8160 IF CC$="" THEN 8110
8170 PRINT"   ";
8175 REM DELETE CHARACTER FROM STRING CC$
8180 CC$=LEFT$(CC$,LEN(CC$)-1)
8190 GOTO 8110
8200 IF LN%>LEN(CC$) THEN PRINT LEFT$(SP$,LN%-LEN(CC$))
8210 RETURN
```

Statements on lines 8100 through 8150 accept a character from the keyboard. If the character entered is RETURN—that is, equal to CHR$(13)—the entry is complete. A branch to line 8200 occurs. Any part of the black bar on the entry line disappears, and the subroutine returns with the full entry contained in CC$. The subroutine also checks for the INST/DEL key; if this key was pressed, the subroutine branches to line 8170.

If the character entered is neither RETURN nor INST/DEL, then the character entered in C$ is concatenated to CC$, which contains all of the characters entered so far. Notice the logical test on this line.

```
8110 IF LEN(CC$)<LN% THEN CC$=CC$+C$:PRINT C$;
```

If the length of CC$ is not yet equal to the maximum number of characters allowed for the entry (in LN%), then C$ is tacked onto the end of CC$, the character entered is displayed on the screen, and a branch back to the GET statement occurs. If the maximum entry length was reached, the character in C$ is simply ignored.

What do the statements on lines 8160 through 8190 do? A branch to these statements occurs if the operator presses the INST/DEL key.

If the operator presses INST/DEL but the entry string CC$ is empty, then no characters need to be deleted. The IF-THEN statement on line 8160 checks for this condition and branches back to line 8110 if no characters need to be deleted. Otherwise, program logic continues with line 8170.

Line 8170 prints the CRSR LEFT and RVS ON characters to position the cursor on the last character entered, a space (in inverse video) that wipes out that character, then a RVS OFF and a CRSR LEFT. What all this does is move left, delete the last character entered, and move left once again to the space.

Line 8180 deletes the last character of CC$ by measuring the length of CC$ using the LEN function, subtracting 1, and reassigning CC$ all of its original characters except the last.

Once the character is deleted from the screen and from CC$, the subroutine branches back to the GET statement on line 8110.

You should study the name-and-address program carefully and understand the data entry aids that have been included. They are as follows:

· Reversing the field on the current entry line clearly indicates what data is expected and how many characters are available.
· An operator does not have to fill in all the characters on an entry line. When the operator presses the RETURN key, the balance of the entry is filled out with blanks.
· At any time the operator can backspace and correct errors on an entry line by pressing the INST/DEL key.

Here are some data entry precautions that could be added:

· Check the ZIP code for any nondigit entry. However, postal codes outside the U.S.A. (Canada, for example) do allow alphanumeric entries.
· Many cautious programmers will ask the question: ARE YOU SURE? when an operator responds with "no" to the question ANY CHANGES?. This gives the operator who accidentally touched the wrong key a second chance.
· You might add a key that aborts the current data entry and restores the prior value. For example, if the operator presses the wrong number to select a field that must be changed, the example program forces the operator to reenter the line.

Try modifying the name-and-address entry program to include the additional safety features described above.

THE REAL-TIME CLOCK

Another C-64 computer feature is the real-time clock. This clock keeps real time in a 24-hour cycle by hours, minutes, and seconds. The reserved string variable TIME$, or TI$, keeps track of the time.

Setting the Clock

To set the clock, use the following format:

TIME$ = "hhmmss"

where:

hh is the hour between 0 and 23
mm is the minutes between 0 and 59
ss is the seconds between 0 and 59

For hh, enter the hour of the day from 00 (12 A.M.) to 23 (11 P.M.). The C-64 computer is on a 24-hour cycle so that you can distinguish between A.M. and P.M. The hours from 00 to 11 designate A.M., and the hours from 12 to 23 designate P.M., returning to 00 at midnight. At midnight, when one 24-hour cycle ends and another begins, hh, mm, and ss are all set to zero.

When initializing TIME$ to the actual time, type in a time a few seconds in the future. When that actual time is reached, press the RETURN key to set the clock.

```
TIME$="120150"
```

Accessing the Clock

To retrieve the time, type the following in immediate mode:

```
?TIME$
```

The computer will display the time in hhmmss format.

```
?TIME$
120200
```

The C-64 computer clock keeps time until it is turned off. The clock must be reset when the computer is turned on again.

Real-Time Clock Operation

The C-64 computer actually keeps track of time in *jiffies*. A jiffy is 1/60 of a second. TIME, or TI, is a reserved numeric variable that automatically increments every 1/60 of a second. TIME is set to zero on start-up and is set back to zero after 51,839,999 jiffies. TIME$ is a string variable that is generated from TIME. When TIME$ is called, the computer displays time in hours, minutes, and seconds (hhmmss); that is, it converts jiffy time to real time.

Notice that TIME$ and TI$ are not the string representations of TIME and TI, they are numbers representing real time, calculated from jiffy time (TIME, TI). The conversion is done as follows: each second is divided into 60 jiffies. One minute is composed of 60 seconds. One hour is made up of 60 minutes. Thus, one second is 60 jiffies, one minute is 3600 jiffies, and one hour is 216,000 jiffies, as illustrated.

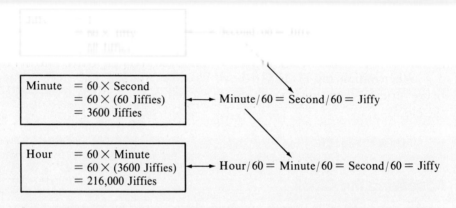

$$\text{Minute} = 60 \times \text{Second} = 60 \times (60 \text{ Jiffies}) = 3600 \text{ Jiffies} \quad\longleftarrow\quad \text{Minute}/60 = \text{Second}/60 = \text{Jiffy}$$

$$\text{Hour} = 60 \times \text{Minute} = 60 \times (3600 \text{ Jiffies}) = 216,000 \text{ Jiffies} \quad\longleftarrow\quad \text{Hour}/60 = \text{Minute}/60 = \text{Second}/60 = \text{Jiffy}$$

The following program converts jiffy time (J) into real time, shown as hours (H), minutes (M), and seconds (S). A complete program follows the statement descriptions.

```
10 J=TI
20 H=INT(J/216000)
```
Calculate hours. Integer function takes only whole number.

```
30 IF H<>0 THEN J=J-H*216000
```
If any hours, subtract number of jiffies in one hour by H to leave remaining jiffies.

```
40 M=INT(J/3600)
```
Calculate minutes. Integer function takes only whole number.

```
50 IF M<>0 THEN J=J-M*3600
```
If any minutes, subtract number of jiffies in minutes by 7 to leave remaining jiffies.

```
60 S=INT(J/60)
```
Calculate seconds. Integer function takes only whole number.

```
5 PRINT":REAL TIME":PRINT:PRINT
10 J=TI
15 T$=TIME$
20 H=INT(J/26000)
00 IF H<>0 THEN J=J-H*216000
40 M=INT(J/3600)
50 IF M<>0 THEN J=J-M-3600
60 S=INT(J/60)
70 H$=RIGHT$(STR$(H),0)
80 M$=RIGHT$(STR$(M),2)
90 S$=RIGHT$(STR$(S),1)
100 PRINT"H:M:S: ";H$;":";M$;":";":";S$
105 PRINT"TIME$: ";T$
110 PRINT "▧▨▨▨";:GOTO 10
```

In this program, statements 70 through 90 convert the numeric answers into proper form for tidy printing. Statement 100 prints both the real time calculated from the program, and TIME$, the real time calculated automatically by the computer. Notice that the result is the same in both cases.

To get an idea of jiffy speed and the conversion from the jiffy clock to the standard clock, type in the following program, which displays the running time of both TIME$ and TIME (TI).

```
5 REM **RUNNING CLOCKS**
10 PRINT":REAL TIME: ":PRINT:PRINT"JIFFY TIME:"
20 FOR I=1 TO 235959
30 :PRINT"▨";TAB(13);TIME$
40 :FOR J=1 TO 60 STEP 2
50 :PRINT"▧▨▨";TAB(12);TI
60 :NEXT
70 NEXT
```

The FOR-NEXT loop for TIME in line 40 increments by STEP 2 (every two jiffies) for the following reasons:

- Displaying 60 jiffies a second is too fast to read, and
- Displaying a jiffy takes longer than incrementing the jiffy. This delays the loop, so the TIME$ display is slower than it should be. By incrementing and printing every other jiffy, you can minimize this delay problem. Run this program and you will see that jiffies increment to 60 within each second. Run this program without STEP 2 in line 40 and see the time delay when printing TIME$.

    Real time: 006604
    Jiffy time: 25500

Keeping time in jiffies is useful for timing program speed. This lets you test the efficiency of a program. Consider the following short program:

```
10 PRINT"***KEYBOARD TEST**":PRINT
20 FOR I=32 TO 127
30 PRINT CHR$(I);
40 NEXT I
50 FOR J=161 TO 255
60 PRINT CHR$(J);
70 NEXT J
80 PRINT:PRINT:PRINT"**END TEST**"
```

You can compute execution time for this program as follows:

1. TI (or TIME) is assigned to a variable at the start of the time test.
2. TI (or TIME) is checked at the end of the time test. Subtract the first value of TI from the new TI value. This will give you the amount of jiffy time it took to process the program in question.

The following listing adds these steps:

```
10 PRINT"]**KEYBOARD TEST**":PRINT
15 A=TI
20 FOR I=32 TO 127
30 PRINT CHR$(I);
40 NEXT
50 FOR J=161 TO 255
60 PRINT CHR$(J);
70 NEXT
80 PRINT:PRINT:PRINT"**END TEST**"
100 PRINT:PRINT"TI = ";TI-A
```

As the program continues, TI increments 60 times every second. Line 100 subtracts the first value of TI (A) from TI's latest value. It took 41 jiffies to display the keyboard characters. Divide jiffy time (41 jiffies) by 60 (the number of jiffies in a second).

$41/60 = 0.6833$

Thus, it took 0.6833 seconds to run the program.

RANDOM NUMBERS

Random numbers may be used in games you program on your C-64; they have more practical uses in statistics and other areas as well. The C-64 will generate random numbers with the RND function.

RND provides a real number between 0 and 1. This number is actually *pseudo*-random; that is, it is not truly random. However, that is a point raised by statisticians. The number is a close approximation of randomness.

To determine the degree of randomness the RND function will have, you provide a starting number, or *seed*. If you use zero as the seed, that is, RND(0), the values it generates are based on three separate internal clocks. The odds against all three clocks having the same values twice in a row are very high; therefore, any number generated can be considered random.

The sequence of most random numbers generated will always be the same. The only exceptions are RND(0) and RND(TI). Numbers that are very nearly random may be obtained using a random seed of 0. A predictable pattern of numbers may be obtained by using a negative number as a seed.

It may not seem very useful to have a random number with such a small range of values. To obtain larger numbers, multiply the random number by the maximum value you want. For instance, to get a random number between 0 and 100, multiply the random number by 100. Type in the following program:

```
1 REM RANDOM
5 X=100:REM MULTIPLIER TO SET MAXIMUM RANGE
10 R1=RND(0):REM GET RANDOM NUMBER
20 R2=X*R1:REM MULTIPLY TO DESIRED RANGE OF NUMBERS
50 PRINT" RAW    #";R1
55 PRINT"RANGED #";R2
```

Type **RUN** and press the RETURN key. The computer will choose a "raw" or random number, multiply it by 100, and display it.

```
RAW    # .672457317
RANGED # 67.2457317
```

Set X to a positive number less than 100, then type **RUN** to see a different ranged number. Try setting X to any negative real number and running the program again. This gives you a negative random number with zero as the greatest possible value.

If you need the result to be rounded to the nearest whole or decimal number, add the following lines to the program you just entered:

2 Y=3 REM DECIMAL DIGITS WANTED IN NUMBER
40 R4=INT(X*R1*10↑Y.5)/10↑Y:REM ROUND TO Y DECIMAL
   PLACES
50 PRINT" RAW #";R1
60 PRINT"RANGED #";R4
70 PRINT"ROUNDED ";R3
65 PRINT"ROUNDED DECIMAL";R4

The variable Y controls the number of decimal digits of precision in the
rounded decimal number. Your results will be similar to the following.

RAW # .473473311

```
RANGED # 67.2457317
ROUNDED  67
ROUNDED DECIMAL 67.246
```

Generating Random Dice Throws

Random numbers are generated in the range 0 through not quite 1 (the
limit of 1, in calculus terms). You will have to convert the random number to
whatever range you require. Suppose numbers must range from 1 to 6 (as in
one die number of a dice game). You will need to multiply the random
number by 6.

6 * RND(1)

This returns a real number in a range just greater than 0 but less than 6. Add
1 to get a number between 1 and 6.

6 * RND(1) + 1

Then convert the number to an integer. This discards any fractional part of a
number, returning the number in the range 1 to 6 but in integer form.

INT(6 * RND(0) + 1)
or:
A% = 6 * RND(0) + 1

The general cases for converting the RND fraction to whole number
ranges are shown below.

INT (RND(0) * N)   Range 0 to N
INT (RND(0) * N + 1)   Range 1 to N
INT (RND (0) * N + M)   Range M to N

Now experiment with a variety of different random number ranges by
modifying the statements illustrated above.

The program below shows −TI being used to generate a random seed. This program calculates numbers in the range M to N. In this program, the values of M and N are set in line 10 for a given program run. Note that these values can be negative. In the following example, the display is an unending sequence of random numbers between −50 and +50. (Press the STOP key to end the program.) A different sequence of numbers will be printed each time the program runs, since −TI provides a random seed. Note that the X value returned from RND(−TI) is displayed instead of the TI value.

```
10 M=50:N=50
20 X=RND(-TI):PRINT X
30 FOR I=1 TO 8
40  :C%=(N-M+1)*RND(1)+M
50  :PRINT C%
60 GOTO 30:REM PRINTS NEW RANDOM NUMBERS

RUN
 8.27633085E-06
-14
 29
 7
 35
-32
-12
 48
-18
```

To illustrate different number ranges, change the values of M and N in line 10 of the above program. For example, make M = 1 and N = 6; this will generate an unending sequence of random numbers between 1 and 6.

Random Selection of Playing Cards

A quick scan of the display above shows that numbers repeat within the first 100 generated. That is, 101 numbers will not include every number in the range −50 to +50 with no duplications. This is fine in, say, a dice game, but for other applications you may need to produce random numbers in a certain range where every number occurs and there are no duplications. Dealing from a deck of cards is one such application. Once a card has been selected, it cannot be selected again during the same deal.

The program below shows one way to program shuffling a deck of

cards on the C-64. This program fills a 52-element table D% with the numbers 1 through 52 in random sequence. (Element D%(0) is not used.) The
cards can be pegged to the random numbers in any way, such as

A = 1 2 = 2 ... Q = 12 K = 13

Spades = 0, Hearts = 13, Diamonds = 26, Clubs = 42

With this scheme, the Ace of Spades = 1 + 0 = 1, the Queen of
Spades = 12 + 0 = 12, the three of Hearts = 3 + 13 = 16, and so on.

In the shuffle program, a 52-element flag table FL keeps track of
whether a card has been chosen. PRINT statements are inserted to display
the seed value, followed by the numbers, in a continuous-line format. Note
that exactly 52 numbers are displayed and that no number is repeated. Each
program run will produce a new random sequence.

```
10 DIM A(53)
20 E=52
30 FOR R=0 TO 51
40 A(R)=R
50 NEXT R
60 B=INT(RND(0)*E)
70 PRINT A(B),
80 FOR R=B TO E
90 A(R)=A(R+1)
100 NEXT R
110 E=E-1
120 IF E>0 THEN 60

RUN
 43          25          39          10          4          18
   13           3     37         15         35         45
     5       38       27         0       33       34        40
       1     46       27       22       48       26       23        16
   8       21     7       47     32     9     2     30
     36     6     51     29     44     28     19
       11       17       24       12       50       20
```

You will find several uses for random numbers in the programs you
write, especially if you write game programs. In the next two chapters you
will see how to fully utilize your C-64's capabilities as a game machine.

CHAPTER 5

Game Controllers

The programs we have described so far have communicated with you in a "stop and go" fashion; that is, they stopped and waited for you to type something at the keyboard, then acted on it. This is fine for balancing a checkbook or typing letters, but many C-64 applications require a different style of communication. A program that simulated airplane flying wouldn't be realistic if the plane stopped in midair while the "pilot" typed instructions. To make this type of program more realistic (and less tedious to use), the C-64 takes its directions from a different source. Instead of receiving instructions through the keyboard, the C-64 can use *game controllers,* the joystick and paddle controllers similar to those used in arcade games.

In this chapter we'll show you how to write programs that use these game controllers. We'll also describe how to use the keyboard "on the run," eliminating the stop and wait steps. If you don't have a joystick, our keyboard example illustrates how to simulate one.

155

THE JOYSTICK CONTROLLER

    The joystick, like old-fashioned airplane control sticks, controls both up-and-down and side-to-side motion. It does so with four switches: Up, Down, Left, and Right. Inside the joystick are "fingers" that push these switches as the stick is moved.

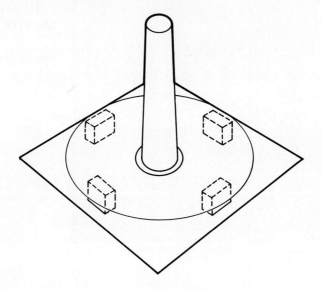

If the stick is moved up, down, or to one side, only one switch is closed.

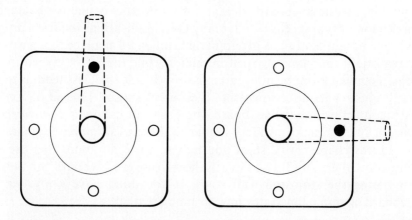

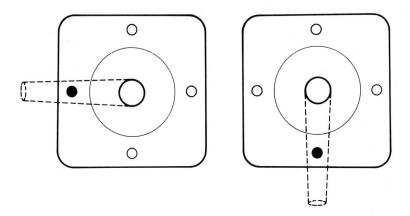

If the stick is moved diagonally, two of the switches are closed.

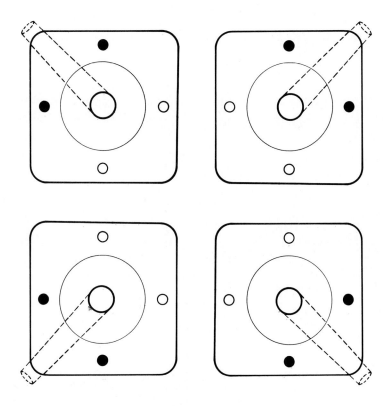

There is also a Fire button, which has its own switch. Using the method described in the following sections, your program can tell whether these switches are open or closed and thus determine which way the joystick is pointing. By moving the joystick, you can direct elements on the screen.

The CIA Chips

The joystick is connected to the C-64 through integrated circuits called Complex Interface Adapters (CIAs). Certain pins of the CIA chips connect to the "outside world." These pins receive a signal sent to them (input) or send a signal out to another device (output). Circuitry in the CIA chip enables the C-64 to set or examine the signals on these pins using memory locations. The signals can be read and controlled through PEEKs and POKEs in BASIC.

Testing the Joystick Switches

The CIA's input/output pins are divided into two groups of eight. Each group can be set or examined through a single memory location, with one bit in that location representing each pin. The switches for control port 1 are connected to one group of pins, and the switches for control port 2 are in another group.

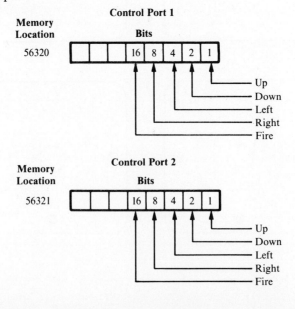

Since the four directory switches and the Fire button are in the same memory location, the numbers in the boxes are used with the AND operator to isolate the bit for a particular switch from the others PEEKed from the same memory location. This use of AND was discussed in the "Boolean Operators" section of Chapter 3. In the result of the AND operation, all bits except the one we want to look at will be forced to a 0 value. (This is called *masking*. Just as you use masking tape to cover up woodwork while painting the walls, computer programs use bit masks to cover up the bits they don't want to test.) For example, the following statement determines if the Fire button of control port 1 is being pushed:

```
10 FB = (PEEK(56320) AND 16) = 0
```

"AND 16" eliminates the other switch values by "covering up" all bits except 16. The program then compares the result to 0. The joystick switches supply a 0 signal to their VIA pins when the switch is closed and a 1 when open. When the switch is closed, the button is being pushed.

Let's look at the AND operation in binary.

```
PEEK location 56320        00000110
AND bit number 16          00001000
                           _____
                           00000000
```

The result of the AND is 0, since 1 AND 0 is always 0. The switch is closed, the signal is 0, and the button is pushed.

Try entering and running the following program to see how moving the joystick affects location 56320:

```
10 PRINT PEEK(56320)
20 FOR I=1 TO 250 : NEXT I : REM WAIT ABOUT HALF A
   SECOND
30 GOTO 10
```

The program checks and displays the value in memory location 56320 every half second. As you move the joystick, notice the changes in the values displayed on the screen. When a switch in the joystick is closed, its mask value (16, 8, 4, 2, or 1) is subtracted from the displayed number. To look at the other joystick, replace 56320 in line 10 with 56321.

A Complete Joystick Scanner

We will now look at the programming necessary to convert the joystick's bit locations to physical movement. If you write one program that uses a joystick, you will probably write others, so we'll provide a standard subroutine that can be typed into any program. This subroutine sets three variables for the main program.

XI   The X Increment. Controls movement to the right or left.

YI   The Y Increment. Controls movement up or down.

FB   Tells whether the Fire Button was pressed.

XI is set to −1 for left, +1 for right, and 0 for neither. YI is set to −1 for down, +1 for up, and 0 for neither. If the Fire button is pressed, FB will be a 1; otherwise, it will be a 0.

```
63000 XT% = PEEK(56320) AND 31
63020 XI = SGN(XT% AND 4) - SGN(XT% AND 8)
63030 YI = SGN(XT% AND 2) - SGN(XT% AND 1)
63040 FB = 1 - SGN(XT% AND 16)
```

This program uses some tricks to make it run faster. Let's examine its operation line by line.

63000   Reads the joystick in control port 1 and uses the technique described above to preserve the keyboard scanner.

63020   These two lines derive the X and Y increments from
63030   the switch values. To reduce the amount of time needed to calculate them, the SGN function is used. This returns a 1 if the switch is off and a 0 if it is on. This is faster than comparing the result of the AND to zero.

63040   Gets the value of the Fire button.

63050   Returns to the main program.

USING THE JOYSTICK SCANNER

The following simple program illustrates the capabilities of the joystick scanner. It moves an object around on the screen in response to the movement of the stick.

TABLE 5-1. Paddle Controller Memory Locations

Location	Contents
54297	Left Paddle Position
54298	Right Paddle Position
56320	Paddles A&B Fire Buttons
56321	Paddles C&D Fire Buttons

```
100 PRINT "⬛";
200 GOSUB 63000
300 IF XI=0 AND YI=0 THEN 200
400 PRINT CHR$(20); : REM DELETE CHAR ON SCREEN
500 IF XI=-1 THEN PRINT "⬛";
600 IF XI= 1 THEN PRINT "⬛";
700 IF YI=-1 THEN PRINT "⬛";
800 IF YI= 1 THEN PRINT "⬛";
900 GOTO 200
```

THE PADDLE CONTROLLERS

The paddle controllers derive their name from their use in the early ping-pong style video games. Each controller consists of a variable resistor called a *potentiometer* or *pot*. The potentiometer is controlled by a knob and by a switch similar to the Fire button on the joystick. Like the joystick, the paddle interface is compatible with controllers like those made by Atari.

The value of the "pot" is read by the SID chip in the C-64 and converted to a number between 0 and 255. The switches, on the other hand, are read by the CIAs, using two of the joystick pins. (Table 5-1 lists the location and contents of paddle control memory.)

Before you can read the values of the four pots, you will need to disable the keyboard scanner. This can be done by using a simple two-byte machine language routine. Then, when you need to read the paddles, just SYS to your routine and read the paddles. NOTE: You must perform the SYS and read the paddles in the same BASIC line or else the keyboard scanner will be re-enabled.

The following routine will read the four paddle values and assign them to variables A, B, C & D:

```
10 PRINT "<CLEAR/HOME>"
20 POKE 8000, 120 : POKE 8001, 96
30 SYS 8000 : POKE 56320, 64 : A=PEEK(54297) : B=PEEK(54298)
40 SYS 8000 : POKE 56320, 128 : C=PEEK(54297) : D=PEEK(54298)
```

The Fire buttons on the paddle controllers can be read from locations 56320 and 56321. By adding to the following routine, the variables FA, FB, FC, and FD will indicate whether the Fire buttons are being pressed. A zero indicates that the button is being pressed.

```
70 FA = SGN(PEEK(56320) AND 4)
80 FB = SGN(PEEK(56320) AND 8)
90 FC = SGN(PEEK(56321) AND 4)
100 FD = SGN(PEEK(56321) AND 8)
```

KEYBOARD COMMUNICATION USING
THE GET STATEMENT

In Chapter 3 we introduced the GET and INPUT statements. Many of the examples so far have used the INPUT statement. Those programs are the "stop and go" kind; if they need information from the keyboard, they have to wait for it. If you want to write an "action" program that receives instructions from the keyboard, you can use the GET statement.

Like INPUT, the GET statement reads information from the keyboard. But that's where the similarity ends. The main differences are as follows:

1. INPUT reads one or more complete numbers or strings. GET reads only a single keystroke.
2. Using INPUT, the program waits for you to press RETURN. If nothing is typed, your program will wait indefinitely. GET, on the other hand, never waits; if no key was pressed the program tells you so, but keeps on running.
3. When you are typing in response to an INPUT statement, the "?" prompts you for input, and the characters you type appear on the screen. GET has no prompt and doesn't echo what you type.

In other words, with a GET statement a program can determine whether a key has been pressed, but won't wait if no key is pressed. If the person using the program types nothing, the program can determine this and make decisions based on it.

GET Statement Syntax

The syntax of GET, shown in the following line, is quite simple:

GET *variable name*

No options are available. You must have exactly one variaable in the "list." Unlike INPUT, no prompt string is allowed. You can, however, easily display a prompt string: use a PRINT statement terminated with a semicolon to stop the C-64 from printing a RETURN.

```
10 PRINT "THIS IS A PROMPT:";
20 GET A$
```

The variable used with GET can be any type (integer, floating point, or string), but a string variable works best. There are two reasons for this.

1. If a numeric variable is used, BASIC attempts to interpret any key pressed as a number. If you type something other than a number, a syntax error occurs and the program stops.

2. If no key has been pressed, the numeric variable is assigned a value of 0. The program has no way of determining whether no key was pressed or a "0" was typed.

With a string variable, you can GET almost any key, including the cursor control keys and RETURN. (The STOP and RESTORE keys can't be read, and the various shifts and the CTRL key operate as usual.) If no key is pressed, GET assigns an empty string to the variable and your program detects this. If you want to wait until something is typed in, use a line like the following:

```
10 GET A$ : IF A$ = "" THEN 10
```

Notice that there is no space between the quotes, resulting in an empty string. If the variable you GET is equal to this empty string, then no key was pressed.

Echoing Keystrokes

As mentioned earlier, characters entered with GET do not appear on the screen. Sometimes, however, you need to see what you type. This can be accomplished by adding a PRINT statement to the program.

```
10 GET A$ : IF A$ = "" THEN 10
20 PRINT A$;
30 GOTO 10
```

The simple program above will echo to the screen exactly what is typed at the keyboard. Pressing the STOP key will stop the program.

The Keyboard as Joystick

This section is presented in a "case study" form. Rather than start with the program listing, we will first show you some of the steps taken in designing it. Following these steps will help you to understand both the program listings and the programming process itself.

Our make-believe joystick will act just like the ones made by Commodore. You can make it point in various directions (left, right, up, down, and diagonally) by pressing different keys. It will also have a Fire button, although it can't be pushed while a direction key is being held down.

CHOOSING THE KEYS

We will first select the keys that will make up the joystick. Nine keys are needed: eight for the various pointing directions and one for the Fire button. The keys should be arranged so that they are easy to use. The arrangement below uses the keys that are naturally under the right hand when touch-typing. Their circular pattern is easy to learn and remember.

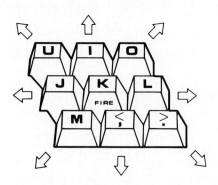

DESIGNING THE INTERFACE
TO THE MAIN PROGRAM

Now let's take a look at the programming necessary to interpret the keys and simulate the joystick. The subroutine should be compatible with the one described for the actual joystick so that you can write programs that work with either. This subroutine will set the same three variables for the main program.

XI   The X Increment. Controls movement to the right or left.

YI   The Y Increment. Controls movement up or down.

FB   Tells whether the Fire Button was pressed.

XI is set to −1 for left, +1 for right, and 0 for neither. YI is set to −1 for down, +1 for up, and 0 for neither. If the K key is pressed, FB will be a 1; otherwise, it will be a 0.

LOADING THE TABLES

The program will interpret the keys by looking them up in a table. It uses other tables for the XI and YI values. These tables will be stored as arrays in the program. The first array (KT$) contains the values of the keys that make up our joystick. The other two arrays contain the values of XI and YI that correspond to those keys. For example, KT$(5) contains the letter "U", which means "up and left," so XT(5) contains −1, and YT(5) contains 1. To save time when scanning the keyboard, we'll build these tables in a separate subroutine that is executed only once at the beginning of the program.

```
62000 REM KEY TABLE VALUES
62100 DATA I,O,L,".",",",M,J,U
62200 REM X INCREMENT VALUES
62300 DATA 0,1,1,1,0,-1,-1,-1
62400 REM Y INCREMENT VALUES
62500 DATA 1,1,0,-1,-1,-1,0,1
62600 FOR I=0 TO 7: READ KT$(I): NEXT
62700 FOR I=0 TO 7: READ XT(I): NEXT
62800 FOR I=0 TO 7: READ YT(I): NEXT
62850 REM MAKE ALL KEYS REPEAT
62900 POKE 650, 128
```

Your program must call this subroutine before attempting to use the "joystick" in order to translate the keys correctly.

When using this routine, be careful where you place the DATA statements. Remember that the READ statement starts with the first DATA statement in the program. If you put additional DATA statements in this program, you may find it helpful to separate the ones above from the subroutine and group them with your own to keep them in the right order.

THE KEYBOARD INTERPRETER SUBROUTINE

The subroutine to read the keyboard and translate the key has high statement numbers to force it to the end of the program.

```
63000 XI=0: YI=0: FB=0: LI=0
63010 GET KE$
63020 IF KE$ = "" THEN RETURN
63030 IF KE$ = KT$(LI) THEN YI = YT(LI): XI = XT(LI):
      RETURN
63040 LI = LI+1: IF LI < 8 THEN 63030
63050 IF KE$ = "K" THEN FB = 1
63060 RETURN
```

This subroutine has a few tricky parts, so we will go over it line by line.

63000   XI, YI, and FB are set to zero first. Since there are three places where we RETURN, the old values must be erased before we start.

63010   Checks to see if any key is pressed.

63020   If not, RETURNs, leaving all variables set to zero.

63030   These lines form a loop to scan the key table for
63040   the key that was pressed. A FOR-NEXT loop is not used, since we want to RETURN immediately if the key is found. (Remember that you must always terminate a FOR loop with a NEXT, and we want to stop this loop as soon as possible.)

63050   Checks for the Fire button.

63060   RETURNs to main program.

USING THE KEYBOARD JOYSTICK

Your program should be entered ahead of statement 62000. You can SAVE a copy of these routines by themselves to use as a base on which to build programs.

To see what can be done with the "keyboard joystick" routines, try using them with the demonstration program below.

```
10 GOSUB 62000
20 A$(0)=" LEFT": A$(1)="        ": A$(2)="RIGHT"
30 B$(0)="DOWN ": B$(1)="        ": B$(2)="UP   "
40 C$(0)="FIRE": C$(1)="▒FIRE▇"
50 POKE 650, 128
100 PRINT "▯"
110 PRINT "▓";A$(XI+1);"/";B$(YI+1);SPC(5);C$(FB)
120 GOSUB 63000
130 GOTO 110
62000 REM KEY TABLE VALUES
62100 DATA I,O,L,".",",",",M,J,U
62200 REM X INCREMENT VALUES
62300 DATA 0,1,1,0,-1,-1,-1
62400 REM Y INCREMENT VALUES
62500 DATA 1,1,0,-1,-1,-1,0,1
62600 FOR I=0 TO 7: READ KT$(I): NEXT
62700 FOR I=0 TO 7: READ XT(I): NEXT
62800 FOR I=0 TO 7: READ YT(I): NEXT
63000 XI=0: YI=0: FB=0: LI=0
63010 GET KE$
63020 IF KE$ = "" THEN RETURN
63030 IF KE$ = KT$(LI) THEN YI = YT(LI): XI = XT(LI):
       RETURN
63040 LI = LI+1: IF LI < 8 THEN 63030
63050 IF KE$ = "K" THEN FB = 1
63060 RETURN
```

Graphics **6**

In this book, "graphics" means the display of pictures, rather than text, data, or programs, on the screen. The "picture" could be a face, an architectural drawing, a geometric shape, or simply an arrangement of text characters.

The C-64 has extensive graphics capabilities. Some of these, such as the built-in graphics characters and the C-64's ability to display text and pictures in color, have been mentioned in the preceding chapters. In this chapter we will cover these features in more detail and describe the C-64's other graphics features, including its ability to use characters you design. As these features are introduced, we will show you programming techniques for using them to produce colorful and animated displays.

The Video Interface Chip

The 6566 Video Interface Chip (VIC-II chip) is a complex integrated circuit that generates the picture and sound that the C-64 produces on your television. (It's called the "VIC-II" because it's an improved version of the original VIC chip that was used in Commodore's VIC 20.)

The VIC-II chip acts as a video interface: it translates computer signals into television signals that produce a picture on the screen.

Your program communicates with the VIC-II chip using PEEK and POKE. Much of the art of C-64 graphics involves knowing what to POKE and where to PEEK. That is the focus of this chapter.

The C-64 Screen

Let's look again at the screen, our canvas for graphics artistry. Figure 6-1 presents a blank screen. Notice that it is divided into two areas, the border and the background. The border frames the background; since television screens do not have straight edges, the border fills the gap between the display and the edge of the television screen. The background is the working area of the screen. Both the text and graphics created by your programs are displayed here. The background consists of 25 rows of 40 characters each, as shown in Figure 6-2. Notice that the rows are numbered from 0 to 24, and the columns from 0 to 39. The formulas for manipulating screen data that we will present

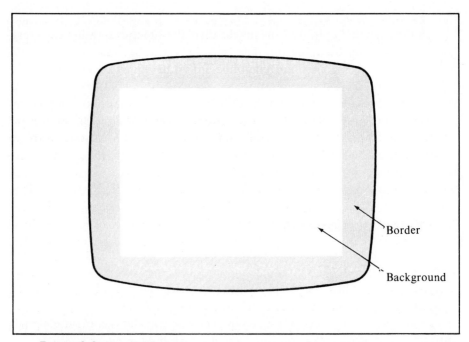

FIGURE 6-1. The C-64 screen

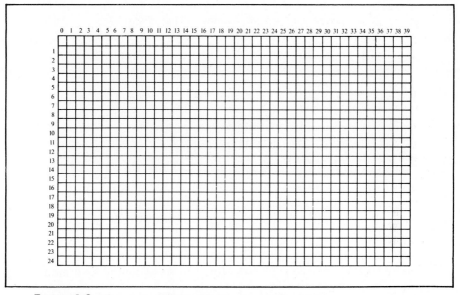

FIGURE 6-2. The screen divided into rows and columns

throughout this chapter are much simpler if you think of the screen as starting at row 0, column 0, rather than row 1, column 1. All the discussions and examples in this chapter will use this numbering convention.

Border, Background, and Character Colors

The colors of the border, background, and the individual characters can be set independently. When the C-64 is powered on (or reset with the RUN/STOP and RESTORE keys), the background is dark blue and the characters and border light blue. You can change these colors at any time.

The background and border colors are stored in the VIC-II chip. They can be changed simply by POKEing a number into a memory location. The border color is controlled by location 53280, while the background color is kept in location 53281. A table of the POKE values for all their possible values is provided in Appendix E.

The color of each character on the screen can be set individually. Each character has its own location in an area called *color memory*. Later in this chapter we will explain how to access this color memory directly, but you can make the C-64 take care of it for you. On the front of the numeric keys 1 through 8 are printed abbreviations for eight of the character colors.

Key	Abbreviation	Color
1	BLK	Black
2	WHT	White
3	RED	Red
4	CYN	Cyan
5	PUR	Purple
6	GRN	Green
7	BLU	Blue
8	YEL	Yellow

To change the color of the characters, press and hold the CTRL key, then press the key for the color you desire. All characters generated at the keyboard or by a program will appear in the color selected. Only characters displayed after you set the new color will be affected; those already on the screen will not be changed.

There are eight other colors that you can choose from, but they are not marked on the keys for you. These colors are set using the Commodore key with the number keys.

Key	Color
1	Orange
2	Brown
3	Light Red
4	Dark Gray
5	Medium Gray
6	Light Green
7	Light Blue
8	Light Gray

To change to one of these colors, press and hold the Commodore key, then press the key for the color you desire. Just as with the "CTRL" colors, only new characters will appear in the new color.

Players and Playfields

Many graphics programs, especially games and simulations, move one or more objects against a fixed background. To avoid confusion with other terms, we will refer to the objects as *players*, and the background as the *playfield*. The C-64 offers a variety of ways to build both players and playfields.

Not all players will move, and the playfield may change. In fact, in some applications the players will stay in one place and the background will move, just as in the old movies where the stagecoach sat still while the painted scenery rolled by behind it.

GRAPHICS WITH THE EXTENDED CHARACTER SET

Simple players can be made using the C-64's built-in graphics characters. These are the shapes and symbols printed on the front of the keys. For example, the following short program will display a drawing of a car on the screen:

```
100 PRINT "□"
200 PRINT " /‾‾\____   "
300 PRINT "/        \  "
400 PRINT "L________J  "
500 PRINT " O      O   "
```

One of the advantages of creating displays with PRINT statements is that you can doodle on the screen in immediate mode until you're satisfied with your player, then build the PRINT statements around it. This is how we built the car in the program above. Let's look at the process step by step, using a simpler example:

Step 1: Clear the screen. Use the SHIFT and CLR/HOME keys (Figure 6-3*a*).

Step 2: Draw the top half of the diamond. Type SHIFT-N, then SHIFT-M (Figure 6-3*b*). Don't press RETURN; if you do, the C-64 will try to execute what you just typed and print a READY message on your picture. (If you type any nongraphics characters, you may also get a ?SYNTAX ERROR message.) To avoid this, type SHIFT-RETURN. The cursor will still move down to the beginning of the next line, but the C-64 will not try to execute your picture.

Step 3: Draw the bottom half of the diamond. Use SHIFT-RETURN to get to the next line. Type SHIFT-M and SHIFT-N to complete the diamond (Figure 6-3*c*).

Step 4: Home the cursor. Press the CLR/HOME key without pressing the SHIFT key (Figure 6-3*d*).

FIGURE 6-3. Drawing a diamond

Step 5: Insert four spaces with the INST/DEL key. This leaves room for a line number, a "?" for PRINT, and a double quote to start a string (Figure 6-3e).

Step 6: Type in the PRINT statement. Enter the line number (10), a question mark, and the double quote (Figure 6-3f).

Step 7: Press RETURN. Don't use SHIFT this time. BASIC stores the first line of the diamond as a program line. Repeat steps 5 through 7 for the second line of the drawing, using a line number of 20 this time.

You now have a program that can be RUN to display the diamond drawing. This method can be used to reproduce almost anything you can sketch on the screen, from a simple square to a complex picture. The only restriction is that you can't completely fill the screen, since you will need room to insert the PRINT statements.

Now experiment a bit with some of your own designs. For the moment, stay away from reversed characters. They require some special handling that we'll cover in the next section.

Using Reversed Characters

You may have already noticed that reversed characters have a special use in PRINT statements: they represent keys that do not generate "normal" characters, such as HOME, the cursor controls, and the color keys. If you enter a reversed character directly into a PRINT statement, one of the following will happen:

· The character will be interpreted as a "special key" to move the cursor, change the color, and so on.

· The character will not match any of the special keys; it will be stored as a nonreversed character when you press RETURN. This will happen even if the character appears between quotes in the program.

To PRINT a single reversed character within a string, enter a RVS ON (CTRL-9) before the reversed character. The character itself must appear in the PRINT statement as a "normal" (nonreversed) character. If you are building PRINT statements from a screen sketch, you can insert the RVS ON using the INST key. Remember that pressing the INST key puts you in quote mode for one character, so the RVS ON will be stored as part of the PRINT statement instead of being executed.

The "reverse on" is reset automatically at the end of the PRINT line. (Remember that a PRINT line can span more than one line on the screen. A RETURN indicates the end of a PRINT line. If a PRINT statement ends with a semicolon, BASIC does not add a carriage return, and characters will still be displayed in reverse.) If normal characters follow the reversed ones on the PRINT line, insert a RVS OFF (CTRL-0) before the first nonreversed character.

To illustrate the problem and solution, we will modify the Diamond program to produce a solid block instead of an outline. Follow the steps displayed in Figure 6-3, but use different characters to make up the player.

· In step 2, after clearing the screen, type RVS ON (CTRL-9), SHIFT-£, and C=-*.

· In step 3, type C=-* and SHIFT-£.

When you list the program, you will notice that the first SHIFT-£ has changed to normal, but the C=-* has not.

```
10 PRINT "◥◣"
20 PRINT "▼"
```

Now run the program, and observe the effect of the reversed C=-*. The second line has turned cyan.

To change the program so it displays what we originally wanted, follow these steps: List the program to display it on the screen. Position the cursor over the SHIFT-£ in line 10 and press SHIFT-INST. This inserts a space, and temporarily puts the C-64 in quote mode. Type CTRL-9 (RVS ON). Since it is in quote mode, the C-64 will insert the RVS ON in the PRINT statement (displayed as a reversed "R"), instead of switching to reversed characters. When the PRINT statement is executed, the reversed R will be recognized and the C-64 will start displaying reversed characters. Change the reversed C=-* to a normal one, so it won't turn the screen cyan again. Move the cursor over and type a C=-* over the old one.

The program should now look like this:

```
10 PRINT "◤◥◣"
20 PRINT "▼"
```

Run the program again, and you will see that the diamond is now correctly displayed.

Adding Color to Your Display

Like reversed characters, color displays require special care. The problem here is somewhat different: the C-64 simply forgets the color of a character once it's off the screen. This happens because the color is not actually part of the character. As mentioned earlier, there is an area in memory set aside to hold the colors of the characters on the screen. When you list your program, the C-64 sets the color for each character to the active character color. When first powered on, it uses blue for the character color. In Chapter 2, you learned how to change the color from the keyboard, using the CTRL key. As we are about to see, your program can also change it. Once a character is gone from the screen, the color memory is reused to show the color of the character that takes its place. Only the character itself is stored as part of the program.

As with reversed characters, this problem is solved by inserting control characters into the program to set the color. For example, to make the diamond red instead of blue, insert a CTRL-3 into line 10 following the "reverse on" (reversed R) so that the line looks like the following:

```
10 PRINT "◆◥◤◣"
20 PRINT "▼"
```

Now run the program. Notice that the entire diamond is red, not just the first line. Color controls, unlike the reverse on control, are not reset when you start a new line. They remain in effect until a new color is set, or until you reset the C-64 with the RUN/STOP and RESTORE keys.

CREATING DISPLAYS WITH POKE

Sometimes it is not practical to use PRINT to build a graphics display. For example, if several players are moving about on the screen, you may need to detect when they collide with each other or with an object on the playfield. Or you might want to have a cursor on the screen when reading characters with GET. For applications like these, you will want to access the display directly. The C-64 allows you to do this using PEEK and POKE.

Screen Memory

The characters displayed on the screen are stored in the C-64's memory. The VIC-II chip reads the image of a character from memory as it is being displayed on the screen. The characters are stored in an area called *screen memory*, and the colors of the characters are stored in *color memory*. Because these areas are part of the C-64's memory, you can use PEEK and POKE to examine and change the contents of the display.

FINDING SCREEN MEMORY

In most computers, the location of screen memory is part of the hardware design and cannot be changed. In the C-64, although the number of rows and columns in screen memory is fixed, its starting point is not. The VIC-II chip uses one of its internal registers to keep track of the start of screen memory and this *pointer* can be changed. Some of the programs we will show you later in this chapter will make use of this capacity. Programs that PEEK and POKE directly into screen memory must be aware of where the screen is. This is easily done. There is a different memory location used by BASIC that tells the C-64 where the screen begins. If you PEEK this memory (location 648), and multiply it by 256, you will get the starting address of screen memory.

```
10 SB=256*PEEK(648)
```

Our sample programs will keep location 648 up-to-date when they move screen memory. If you follow this convention in your programs, you can write programs that work no matter where screen memory is located.

SCREEN MEMORY LAYOUT

The characters you see on the screen are stored in memory as an *array* of 25 *rows* and 40 *columns*. This array is not a BASIC variable. It is simply a 1000-byte area in the C-64's memory that you can access with PEEK and POKE, but you will find it helpful to visualize this area as an array. Each element of this array holds one character from the screen. Element (0,0) contains the character in the upper left corner of the display, and element (24,39) holds the character in the lower right corner.

Once you have found where screen memory starts, using the formula from the preceding section, you can readily calculate where to POKE for a particular character. The formula is

POKE location = start of screen + column + 40 * row

In order to use this formula, you must number screen columns from 0 to 39, and rows from 0 to 24. As an example of this formula, type in the following program:

```
100 SB=256*PEEK(648)
110 REM FILL SCREEN MEMORY WITH "@"
120 FOR I=0 TO 999
130 POKE SB+I,0
140 NEXT I
150 REM WAIT FOR A KEY TO BE PRESSED
160 GET X$
170 IF X$="" THEN 160
180 REM CHANGE BACKGROUND TO BLACK
190 POKE 53281,0
```

Before running the program, clear the screen and list the program, leaving the listing on the screen. Now run the program and observe the results; all the characters on the screen, except spaces, were changed to @'s. In fact, the program changed every character to an @, but those that appear on the screen as spaces are invisible. When BASIC clears the screen, it changes the character color of all characters on the screen to match the background. Then, as each character is printed, the C-64 sets its location in color memory. Since some of the @'s are displayed as blue characters on a blue background, they will be impossible to see. To make them visible, press the space bar. The program will change the background color to black, and the blue @'s will appear. (This program does not work exactly the same way on all C-64's; Commodore made a change to the screen-clearing portion of BASIC after some computers had already been shipped. On your computer, the "invisible" @-signs may appear in white.)

You must be aware of this problem of disappearing characters when using POKE in a display. Your program must ensure that the color of the location you are POKEing is correctly set. The next section describes how to do this.

Color Memory

Earlier in this chapter we mentioned that the colors of the characters on the screen are kept in a special area called color memory. As our most recent example shows, an understanding of how to use color memory is essential when using POKE in displays. So, before proceeding further with POKEing screen memory, let's take a look at color memory.

FINDING COLOR MEMORY

Unlike screen memory, color memory never moves; it is always in locations 55296 through 56295. As with screen memory, there is one location in color memory for each character on the screen. The order of character colors is the same as that of the characters themselves, so the formula used to find a character's location in color memory is like the one used to locate the character in screen memory.

Color memory location = 55296 + column + 40 * row

CONTENTS OF COLOR MEMORY

The color of each character is stored in color memory as a number from 0 to 15. The colors produced by these numbers are as follows:

0	Black	8	Orange
1	White	9	Brown
2	Red	10	Light Red
3	Cyan	11	Dark Gray
4	Purple	12	Medium Gray
5	Green	13	Light Green
6	Blue	14	Light Blue
7	Yellow	15	Light Gray

Unlike other areas of C-64 memory, color memory uses only four bits per location. Only four bits are needed to hold the color number (0 to 15). Since the upper four bits are not used, Commodore did not include a memory chip to hold them. If you POKE a number larger than 15 into a color memory location, the part of it held in those "missing" bits will be lost.

10101010	A binary value of 204, when the upper 4 bits are dropped
1010	is stored as a 12.
11111111	255
1111	becomes a 15.
00000111	A value of 7, however,
0111	is not changed.

Since there is no memory chip to supply the upper four bits when reading color memory locations, they will take on unpredictable values. Remember that a bit must be either a 1 or a 0; even if there is no signal present on a chip's input pin, the chip must assign it some value. With no signal coming into the pins for the upper four bits, the chip arbitrarily gives them either a 1 or a 0 value. When PEEKing color memory, always discard the nonexistent bits. This can be done by using AND to mask them, as described in Chapter 5.

```
10 BY=PEEK(55400) AND 15
```

Screen Display Codes

Once you understand where to POKE to change the display, you will need to know what value to put there. Commodore computers, including the C-64, do not use the same character code in screen memory that they use in programs. Most computers store characters in a standard code called ASCII (American Standard Code for Information Interchange). Commodore computers use an "extended" ASCII for all purposes other than representing characters in screen memory. The "extensions" are graphics characters and certain control codes not used by other manufacturers. Many of the control codes do not have a displayable character associated with them. In order to make as many graphic codes as possible available on the screen, Commodore devised a different code for screen memory. This code eliminates some ASCII characters, and changes the values of others.

Appendix E contains a table showing the screen display codes. If your program is POKEing characters that are set at the time you write it, you can simply look them up in the table. If you do not know in advance what characters you will be POKEing, your program must convert them from ASCII to screen display code. This might be necessary if, for example, your program uses GET to read instructions from the keyboard, and you want to echo the characters in a particular place on the display.

The conversion to screen code can be done with little effort, because the ASCII codes that were changed were moved in blocks of 32 characters. The changes are shown in Table 6-1.

Here is a simple subroutine that takes a key value, KV$, and converts it to a screen code, SC. If the key cannot be translated (a cursor control key, for example), it returns a value of −1. The main program can thus tell the difference between a displayable and a nondisplayable keystroke.

TABLE 6-1. ASCII to Screen Code Conversion

ASCII Code	Screen Code
0-31	None
32-63	Same
64-95	0-31
96-127	64-95
128-159	None
160-191	96-127
192-254	64-126
255	94

```
60000 SC=ASC(KV$)
60010 IF SC<32 THEN SC=-1 :RETURN
60020 IF SC<64 THEN RETURN
60030 IF SC<96 THEN SC=SC-64:RETURN
60040 IF SC<128 THEN SC=SC-32:RETURN
60050 IF SC<160 THEN SC=128:RETURN
60060 IF SC<192 THEN SC=SC-64:RETURN
60070 IF SC<255 THEN SC=SC-128:RETURN
60080 SC=126:RETURN
```

The Moving Dot Revisited

In Chapter 5 we presented a program that moved a dot around the screen as an example of using the joystick. Here, for comparison, is how that program could be written using POKE instead of PRINT. As before, this program is not complete; you must add the appropriate subroutine to use either the keyboard or the joystick for control.

```
100 REM CLEAR SCREEN
110 PRINT"::"
120 REM SET COLOR MEMORY
130 FOR I=55296 TO 56295
140 POKE I,14
150 NEXT I
160 XP=0:YP=0
170 SB=PEEK(648)*256
180 REM MAIN LOOP
190 GOSUB 63000
200 IF (XI=0)AND(YI=0)AND(FB=0)THEN 190
```

```
210 REM ERASE OLD DOT
220 POKE SB+XP+40*YP,32
230 REM CALCULATE NEW X POSTION
240 XP=XP+XI
250 IF XP>39 THEN XP=0
260 IF XP<0 THEN XP=39
270 REM CALCULATE NEW Y POSTION
280 YP=YP+YI
290 IF YP>24 THEN YP=0
300 IF YP<0 THEN YP=24
310 REM POKE NEW DOT
320 POKE SB+XP+40*YP,81
330 GOTO 190
```

ANIMATING YOUR PLAYERS

There are two facets to player animation. The first we have already discussed: moving a player around on the screen. The second involves changing the player itself, so that it appears to be doing something. To animate a player, one or more of the characters that make it up are changed, giving the illusion that it is moving. For example, this program produces a windshield, with wipers that sweep back and forth.

```
10 DLY=150
20 REM BUILD WINDSHIELD
30 PRINT"☐ ╭────╮ "
40 PRINT"│        │"
50 PRINT" ╰────╯ "
60 REM SWEEP WIPERS TO RIGHT
70 FOR I=1 TO 4
80 ON I GOSUB 180,240,300,360
90 FOR J=1 TO DLY : NEXT
100 NEXT
110 REM SWEEP WIPERS TO LEFT
120 FOR I=3 TO 2 STEP -1
130 ON I GOSUB 180,240,300,360
140 FOR J=1 TO DLY : NEXT
150 NEXT
160 GOTO 70
170 REM SHOW WIPERS AT 10 O'CLOCK
180 POKE 1065,77
190 POKE 1066,32
200 POKE 1067,77
210 POKE 1068,32
220 RETURN
230 REM SHOW WIPERS AT 12 O'CLOCK
```

```
240 POKE 1065,32
250 POKE 1066,101
260 POKE 1067,32
270 POKE 1068,101
280 RETURN
290 REM SHOW WIPERS AT 2 O'CLOCK
300 POKE 1065,32
310 POKE 1066,78
320 POKE 1067,32
330 POKE 1068,78
340 RETURN
350 REM SHOW WIPERS AT 3 O'CLOCK
360 POKE 1066,100
370 POKE 1068,100
380 RETURN
```

The program has several major parts. We will look at each in detail. Lines 30 through 50 clear the screen and display the windshield using PRINT statements.

Lines 70 through 100 sweep the wipers from left to right. They are then swept back to the left by lines 120-150. These loops change the display by calling, in turn, subroutines that put the wipers in particular positions by POKEing characters to the screen. Each subroutine erases the wipers from the screen and puts them in a new position.

Two of the most important lines in the program are lines 90 and 140. These FOR-NEXT loops slow down the program. Without such *delay loops,* the display would change too quickly, reducing the movement to a blur. Choosing the lengths of the delay loops is crucial to animation. This is especially true of programs that produce complex movements. When developing such programs, you can expect to spend much of your time fine-tuning the delays to create a display that moves smoothly at the speed you want. Try experimenting with our example program: the length of the delay loops is controlled by the variable DLY and the value of this variable is set in line 10. A lower value shortens the delay loops, making the display change more quickly. Increasing the value lengthens the delay loops, slowing the movement of the wipers.

It is difficult to do complex animation with the built-in character set unless you are working with a very large player. In most cases you must move part of your player an entire character space to move it at all. This makes the motion somewhat jerky unless the player takes up a large portion of the screen. To produce more subtle movements with small players, you must design your own characters. Techniques for making and using your own characters will be discussed later in this chapter.

Combining PRINTed and POKEd Graphics

As we have seen, both the PRINT and the POKE methods have strengths and weaknesses in building graphic displays. For those programs that have players moving against a fixed background, a combination of PRINT and POKE often works best. Using PRINT statements to display graphics on the screen in combination with POKEs that jump to any location on the screen can make the development of a program much easier.

Racetrack Game

Figure 6-4 is a listing of a simple game called Racetrack, an adaptation of a common pencil-and-paper game. This program demonstrates some of the techniques we have discussed so far in this chapter.

```
100 GOSUB 40000
200 CR=15
300 CC=2
356 POKE 53275,254
400 POKE SB+CC+CR*40,0
1000 IF XS<>0 AND TI>XT THEN CC=CC+SGN(XS):XT=TI+60/ABS(XS)
1100 IF YS<>0 AND TI>YT THEN CR=CR+SGN(YS):YT=TI+60/ABS(YS)
1200 IF CC<0 OR CC>39 THEN 4000
1300 IF CR<0 OR CR>24 THEN 4000
1400 POKE BA,32
1500 BA=SB+CC+CR*40
1600 TG=PEEK(BA)
1700 IF TG<>0 AND TG<>32 THEN 5500
1800 POKE BA,0
1900 IF TT>TI THEN 1000
2000 TT=TI+30
2100 POKE V2,129
2200 GOSUB 63000
2300 POKE V2,0
2400 XS=XS+XI : YS=YS+YI
2500 GOTO 1000
4000 IF CC<0 THEN CC=0
```

FIGURE 6-4. Racetrack program

```
4100 IF CC>39 THEN CC=39
4200 IF CR<0 THEN CR=0
4300 IF CR>24 THEN CR=24
4400 BA=SB+CC+CR*40
5000 POKE BA,0
5100 FOR I=1 TO 350 : NEXT I
5200 POKE BA,32
5300 FOR I=1 TO 350 : NEXT I
5400 GET A$: IF A$<>"" THEN 100
5500 GOTO 5000
40000 PRINT"";
40100 SB=256*PEEK(648)
40200 FOR I=55296 TO 56295:POKE I,14:NEXT
40300 XS=0 : YS=0 : XT=0 : YT=0
40400 REM JOYSTICK VARIABLES
40500 JS=56321
40600 UM%=1 : DM%=2 : LM%=4 : RM%=8
40700 REM SET UP SOUND
40800 V2=54283
40900 POKE V2+1,80
41000 POKE 54295,0
41100 POKE 54296,15
41200 PRINT"                                    ";
41300 PRINT"                                    ";
41400 PRINT"                                    ";
41500 PRINT"                                    ";
41600 PRINT"                                    ";
41700 PRINT"                                    ";
41800 PRINT"                                    ";
41900 PRINT"                                    ";
42000 PRINT"                                    ";
42100 PRINT"                                    ";
42200 PRINT"                                    ";
42300 PRINT"                                    ";
42400 PRINT"                                    ";
42500 PRINT"                                    ";
42600 PRINT"                                    ";
42700 PRINT"                                    ";
42800 PRINT"                                    ";
42900 PRINT"                                    ";
43000 PRINT"                                    ";
43100 PRINT"                                    ";
43200 RETURN
63000 SS%=PEEK(JS)
63010 XI=SGN(SS% AND LM%)-SGN(SS% AND RM%)
63020 YI=SGN(SS% AND UM%)-SGN(SS% AND DM%)
63030 RETURN
```

FIGURE 6-4. Racetrack program (continued)

The pencil-and-paper version of Racetrack is played on a sheet of graph paper with the course drawn on it. Here is a typical course:

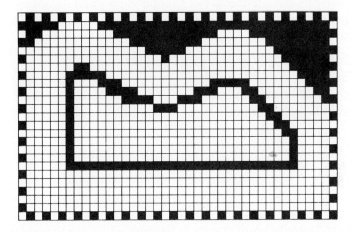

The C-64 version of the game uses one character location on the screen for each square on the graph paper.

The rules of the game are quite simple.

1. The car moves in both the horizontal and vertical dimensions at a speed of a certain number of squares per second. It can move in both dimensions at once. For example, to travel diagonally it can move at a rate of one square up and one square right per second.

2. On each turn (about twice a second), the player can speed up or slow down by a rate of one square per second in each dimension. For example, if a player is moving at a rate of 3 squares up and 1 right, he can change his speed to 4 up, 1 right; 2 up, 1 right; 2 up, 2 right; 2 up, 0 right, and so on.

3. If the car goes off the track, it crashes and the game is over.

The Racetrack program listed in Figure 6-4 is a somewhat crude version of the game, but it does provide some practical examples of techniques you can use in writing graphics and animation programs. It uses PRINT to display a playfield that was originally developed as a screen sketch. It also contains some examples of using POKE to move the player and PEEK to detect collisions. We'll start our examination of the program by introducing the main variables.

Variable Name	Description
CC	*Car Column* — the column number on the screen where the car is to be displayed.
CR	*Car Row* — the screen row where the car is located.
TT	*Test Time* — the value that TI will have when it is time to test the joystick for the next turn.
XS	*X Speed* — the car's speed in the X dimension: negative is toward the left, positive toward the right.
XT	*X Time* — the value of TI when it is time to move in the X dimension.
YS	*Y Speed* — the car's speed in the Y dimension: negative is up, positive is down.
YT	*Y Time* — the value of TI when it is time to move in the Y dimension.

Lines 1000 through 2500 make up the main processing loop of the program. The program runs continuously through the code, looking for something to do. On each pass it checks the current time to see if it should move the car (lines 1000 and 1100) or look at the joystick (line 1600). If any of these things needs to be done, the timer value for the next occasion is also set.

In lines 1200 and 1300 the program checks to ensure that the car has not gone off the screen. Lines 1500 and 1600 make sure that the car is not about to collide with a wall. If either of these is true, the program goes to the "crash" routine at line 4000.

Lines 2100 and 2300 sound a "tock" each time the program tests the joystick. (The C-64's sound capabilities are discussed in Chapter 7.)

The "crash" routine (lines 4000 through 5500) brings the car back onto the screen if it has gone off (lines 4000-4400) and makes it flash at a rate of about once per second (lines 5000-5300). As soon as the user presses any key, line 5400 starts the game over.

Racetrack is both an example of graphics techniques and a basis for your own experiments. You might want to try putting a readout of the number of turns or seconds used in the infield, modifying the course, or making sure that the car has really gone all the way around the course, instead of doubling back to the finish line.

MEMORY "SEGMENTS"

The graphics features we have examined so far have used the screen memory area in locations 1024-2023. However, the more advanced features that we will be discussing access other memory locations as well.

One of the characteristics of the VIC-II chip is that it can only access 16K (16,384) bytes of memory. Since the C-64 has 64K of memory, it would seem that most of it can't be used by the VIC-II.

To circumvent this problem, the engineers at Commodore divided the C-64's 64K of memory into four "segments," each 16K bytes long. They also designed the C-64 so that your program can select which of these four segments the VIC-II will use.

Because most of the first segment (the one selected by the C-64 when it is powered on) is used by BASIC, our program examples will be switching the VIC-II to other segments. The methods for choosing the right segment and switching to it are a bit complex, so we have reserved the explanation of them for the section on "Advanced VIC-II Chip Topics" at the end of this chapter.

However, there are two important points about memory segments you need to understand before continuing with the rest of this chapter. The first is that all the memory areas used by the VIC-II (screen memory and the new ones we'll be telling you about) must be in the same 16K segment.

The second item to remember is that pressing RUN/STOP-RESTORE does not completely reset memory. Location 648, as we mentioned earlier, controls the screen location and RUN/STOP-RESTORE does not restore it to its "power on" value. If something goes wrong while you are running one of our sample programs that moves screen memory (hitting the STOP key, typing error entering the program), it is possible for BASIC to get confused about where screen memory is. If this happens, the screen editor won't work, and the computer won't be properly reset by pressing RUN/STOP-RESTORE.

This sort of confusion will *almost* never happen, but any program that does a lot of POKEing into memory can cause it by changing the wrong location in memory. Before RUNning any of our sample programs, or any program that does many POKEs, be sure you SAVE a copy of it: the typing fingers you save may be your own!

CUSTOM CHARACTER SETS

The C-64 can easily change the shapes of the characters that appear on the screen. Most personal computers require hardware changes to use a different set of characters, but the C-64 allows you to create your own characters, then switch over to your character set with a simple POKE. In this section we will show how the character set is defined, and how to design your own characters and make them appear on the screen.

How Characters are Displayed

First, let's take a brief look at how television works. If you look closely at your television screen, you'll notice that the picture is made up of individual dots arranged in rows. There are about 500 dots on each row and about 500 rows on the screen. Inside the picture tube, a beam of electrons sweeps back and forth, one row at a time, lighting up each dot as it passes. The incoming TV signal determines the brightness and color of each dot. Although the process of generating and receiving a TV signal involves much more, all you need to know is that the television picture is made up of rows of dots. The VIC-II chip generates the TV signals.

Character Memory

This leads us to the question of how the VIC-II chip knows which dots to turn on. You will recall that the characters displayed on the screen are stored in the screen memory area. As it "paints" the screen, the VIC-II chip steps through screen memory, picking up the characters one at a time. To determine which dots to turn on for a particular character, it looks at a table in memory that contains the character shapes. This table was worked out by Commodore and stored in a special memory chip in the C-64. This chip, called a ROM (Read-Only Memory), retains the information that was stored in it at the factory, even when power is turned off. The area occupied by this table is called character memory. With a POKE, your program can tell the VIC-II chip to use a different area for character memory — one that you can fill with your own table. Finally, the VIC-II chip must know what color to make the character. This information comes from color memory. We've already examined the screen and color memory areas, so we'll look at character memory, then discuss how to use these areas to create displays.

FORMAT OF CHARACTER MEMORY

Each character on the screen is made up of a matrix that is eight dots wide and eight high. A magnified view of the letter A, for example, would look like this

The 8×8 format was chosen because each row of the character conveniently fits into one byte of memory, and the eight rows make a nice round number in the computer's binary number system. This format also greatly simplifies custom character design. You can lay out your character on an

ordinary sheet of graph paper, and convert each row to its value and location in character memory.

The eight bytes that make up the rows of a character are stored next to each other in character memory, with the top row first. Each dot on a row corresponds to one bit, with the bit for the leftmost dot having the highest binary value, 128. A bit value of 1 means the dot is "on" (displayed in the character color). A value of 0 means the dot is "off" (displayed in the screen color). This is what the letter A looks like in character memory

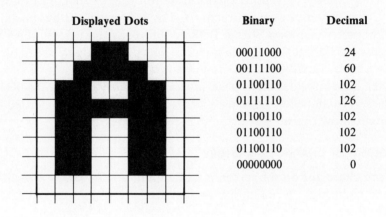

Displayed Dots	Binary	Decimal
	00011000	24
	00111100	60
	01100110	102
	01111110	126
	01100110	102
	01100110	102
	01100110	102
	00000000	0

Here, for comparison, is the checkerboard character:

Displayed Dots	Binary	Decimal
	11001100	204
	00110011	51
	11001100	204
	00110011	51
	11001100	204
	00110011	51
	11001100	204
	00110011	51

Notice that the checkerboard character's dots extend to the edge of the matrix, while the A has space at the sides and bottom. This built-in space is the only space between adjacent characters on the screen. The 8×8 matrices of characters displayed on the screen actually touch those of adjoining characters, making the screen a continuous field of dots. Here is a magnified view of a small section of the screen.

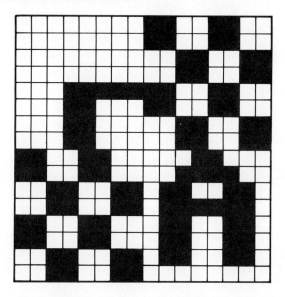

This contact between characters is what enabled us to build players made up of multiple characters. This also means that you must include spaces in some of your character definitions. If, for example, you wanted to display the Greek "lambda" character in a scientific formula, you might define it like this:

Displayed Dots	Binary	Decimal
	00000000	0
	01100000	96
	01100000	96
	00110000	48
	00011000	24
	01101100	108
	11000110	198
	00000000	0

Like Commodore, we left white space at the right and the bottom of the lambda. This makes it line up with the other characters when displayed.

THE MISSING DOTS

Some quick arithmetic will tell you that if there are eight dots in each row of a character, and 40 characters on each line of the screen, this accounts for only 320 dots. We stated earlier that there are about 500 dots on each row of the TV screen. What happened to the others? Some of them are lost because the electron beam in the picture tube actually sweeps a little beyond the edges of the screen. Some of them are taken up by the border of the display. So even though there are over 500 dots on each line of the TV screen, only 320 are available to you.

FINDING A CHARACTER'S DEFINITION IN CHARACTER MEMORY

Character definition shapes are stored in character memory by screen code. The screen code is, in effect, a subscript for the character memory array. Like screen and color memory, the character memory "array" is not a BASIC variable, but simply a way to visualize the character memory area.

As mentioned earlier, the eight bytes that define a character are stored in adjacent locations in color memory, with the top row first and the bottom row last. Here is how the first few bytes of Commodore's built-in character memory, which starts at location 53248, are used.

Location	Contents
53248	Top row of "@"
53249	Second row of "@"
53250	Third row of "@"
53251	Fourth row of "@"
53252	Fifth row of "@"
53253	Sixth row of "@"
53254	Seventh row of "@"
53255	Bottom row of "@"
53256	Top row of A
53257	Second row of A
.	
.	
53263	Bottom row of A

53264   Top row of B
53265   Second row of B

.

.

.

This layout of character memory uses the following formula to find the definition of a particular row for a given character:

Location = start of character memory + row + 8 ∗ screen code

EXPLORING CHARACTER MEMORY

Examining the contents of character memory requires a bit of "trickery." Having the character ROM memory available all the time would take up valuable memory space. Since most programs don't look at it anyway, Commodore designed the C-64 so that character memory is usually hidden. This leaves an extra 4096 bytes available for programs and data, but it also means that a little extra programming is necessary for those programs that do need to see the character definitions.

The following program lets you choose a character and magnify it on the screen. The program also displays other information — such as where the character resides in character memory, and the decimal values of the rows — that will help you become more familiar with how characters are designed.

```
100 POKE 52,128 : POKE 56,128 : CLR
110 REM COPY CHARACTER MEMORY ROM TO RAM
120 POKE 56334,PEEK(56334) AND 254
130 POKE 1,PEEK(1) AND 251
140 FOR I=0 TO 2047:POKE 32768+I,PEEK(53248+I) : NEXT
150 POKE 1,PEEK(1) OR 4
160 POKE 56334,PEEK(56334) OR 1
170 PIX$(0)=" ":PIX$(1)="▨ ■"
180 PRINT"▢CHARACTER MAGNIFIER"
190 REM GET A CHARACTER
200 PRINT "SELECT A CHARACTER";
210 GET KV$:IF KV$="" THEN 210
220 GOSUB 490
230 REM IGNORE UNPRINTABLE CHARACTERS
240 IF SC=128 THEN 210
250 REM FIND CHARACTER'S DEFINITION IN CHARACTER MEMORY
260 CB=32768+8*SC
270 PRINT "▢CHARACTER: ";KV$
280 PRINT "ASCII VALUE: ";ASC(KV$)
290 PRINT "SCREEN VALUE: ";SC
```

```
300 PRINT "CHARACTER STARTS AT: ";CB
310 PRINT
320 REM PRINT MAGNIFIED VIEW
330 PRINT "▓▓             "
340 FOR I=CB TO CB+7
350 ROW=PEEK(I)
360 FR$=RIGHT$(("        "+STR$(ROW)),6)
370 OS$="▓▓ ▓▓"
380 REM TRANSLATE A ROW OF BITS TO A STRING
390 FOR J=7 TO 0 STEP -1
400 BIT=SGN(ROW AND 2↑J)
410 OS$=OS$+PIX$(BIT)
420 NEXT J
430 OS$=OS$+"▓▓ ▓▓"
440 PRINT OS$+FR$
450 NEXT I
460 PRINT "▓▓             ▓"
470 PRINT:PRINT:PRINT:GOTO 200
480 REM TRANSLATE KEYSTROKE TO SCREEN CODE
490 SC=ASC(KV$)
500 IF SC < 32 THEN SC=128: RETURN
510 IF SC < 64 THEN RETURN
520 IF SC < 96 THEN SC=SC-64: RETURN
530 IF SC < 128 THEN SC=SC-32 : RETURN
540 IF SC < 160 THEN SC=128: RETURN
550 IF SC < 192 THEN SC=SC-64 : RETURN
560 IF SC < 255 THEN SC=SC-128: RETURN
570 SC=94: RETURN
```

The tricky part is in lines 120-160 of the program. They make the contents of the character ROM chip visible and copy them into locations 20480 through 24575. The way that this part of the program works is discussed in the section on "Advanced VIC-II Chip Topics" later in this chapter. For now, you should simply enter and use them as they are.

This program will also be helpful in providing practical examples for the next section, so you should save a copy of it.

Designing Characters

A good way to start designing characters is with a sheet of graph paper (4 or 5 lines per inch works best). Draw a square enclosing an area with eight boxes on each side, to match the C-64's 8 × 8 character matrix. Then number the columns, so that it looks like this:

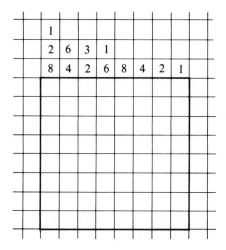

You now have an area that corresponds to one character on the screen, with each box representing one dot.

Now fill in the boxes for the dots that should be "on" (set to the character color). Here is an example of a simple character.

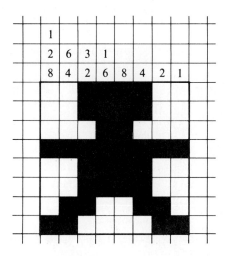

When you are satisfied with the dot pattern, calculate the values of the rows in screen memory. For each row, add the numbers at the top of those columns whose dots are "on." Here are the values for our stick man:

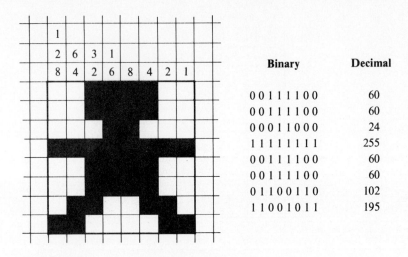

Binary	Decimal
0 0 1 1 1 1 0 0	60
0 0 1 1 1 1 0 0	60
0 0 0 1 1 0 0 0	24
1 1 1 1 1 1 1 1	255
0 0 1 1 1 1 0 0	60
0 0 1 1 1 1 0 0	60
0 1 1 0 0 1 1 0	102
1 1 0 0 1 0 1 1	195

Your new character is now ready for a screen test.

USING YOUR CHARACTERS ON THE C-64

To use your custom characters on the C-64, there are three steps you must take:

1. Your program must set aside an area in memory to hold your character memory.

2. Your character patterns must be loaded into character memory.

3. Your program must tell the VIC-II chip to start using your character memory instead of Commodore's.

In order to simplify your initial experiments, you can start by making a copy of Commodore's characters, replacing them one by one with your own. To get started, enter and run the following program:

```
100 REM RESERVE MEMORY
110 POKE 52,128 : POKE 56,128 : CLR
120 REM POINT VIC-II AT NEW SCREEN
```

```
130 POKE 56576,(PEEK(56576) AND 252) OR 1
140 POKE 53272,32
150 REM POINT BASIC AT NEW SCREEN
160 POKE 648,136
170 PRINT "◤█◣ABCDEFGHIJKLMNOPQRSTUVWXYZ[£]↑←!";
180 PRINT CHR$(34);CHR$(34);CHR$(20);
190 PRINT "#$%&'()*+,-.";
200 PRINT "/0123456789:;<=>?"
210 REM COPY CHARACTER MEMORY ROM TO RAM
220 POKE 56334,PEEK(56334) AND 254
230 POKE 1,PEEK(1) AND 251
240 FOR I=0 TO 2047:POKE 32768+I,PEEK(53248+I) : NEXT
250 POKE 1,PEEK(1) OR 4
260 POKE 56334,PEEK(56334) OR 1
```

We will now examine this program line by line. Line 110 changes two of BASIC's internal pointers to make it appear that less program memory is available. (The method for choosing this POKE value will be explained later.) It also includes a CLR statement, which forces BASIC to erase any variables that have been defined and to adjust its other internal pointers to the reduced memory size. The POKEs and CLR must be done before any variables are defined in the program, or the values assigned to those variables will be lost. It is best to make this statement the first one in any program that defines its own characters.

Lines 130 and 140 tell the VIC-II chip that screen memory starts at location 34816, and character memory at location 32768 (the section "Advanced VIC-II Chip Topics" at the end of this chapter describes how these values are calculated). When these statements are executed, the characters on the screen will change to gibberish because we have not yet filled in our character definitions. Line 160 updates location 648, so BASIC can find our new screen memory.

Lines 170 through 200 set up an area in screen memory where we can see the results of changing character memory by PRINTing the characters that will use our custom character set.

Lines 220 through 260 load our new character memory with the upper-case and graphics characters from the Commodore set. This will take several seconds. When the program starts copying the reversed characters, you can see the characters in the top lines change as their definitions are filled in.

We chose to copy both the nonreversed and reversed characters because the C-64 generates its cursor by turning bit 7 (the "reverse" bit) in the character off and on. If we had copied just the nonreversed characters, the character under the cursor would be changing from the normal nonreversed character to gibberish, because the reversed portion of character memory would not be filled in.

In the examples that follow, we will be making our changes in the reversed characters, leaving the normal characters intact. This will make program listings and immediate mode statements readable on the screen.

As our first experiment, we'll replace the @ sign with our stick man character. To change the character memory for @, enter the following POKE statements. You should type the POKE statement once and keep reusing it with screen editing to avoid rolling the sample characters off the top of the screen.

```
POKE 33792, 60
POKE 33793, 60
POKE 33794, 24
POKE 33795,255
POKE 33796, 60
POKE 33797, 60
POKE 33798,102
POKE 33799,195
```

As each POKE is entered, one row of the @ character is changed, until the @ sign is replaced with our stick man. Now, type CTRL-RVS ON, then @; the C-64 will display a stick man. Press the CRSR LEFT key until the cursor is over the stick man. Instead of changing back and forth between reversed and nonreversed @ signs, the character changes from @ to our stick man and back.

Now you're ready to experiment with characters of your own design. Simply follow the steps we outlined above: POKE the values you calculated on the worksheet into character memory, and use CTRL-RVS ON to make the C-64 display your character from the reversed portion of character memory. We recommend that you experiment with several characters before putting them to work in programs.

Design Aids for Custom Characters

If you expect to make extensive use of custom characters, you will find it helpful to have a character editor utility to help you. Such a program should display the character in both normal and magnified views, allow you to change individual dots, and calculate the POKE values and locations for you.

You can write your own utility or you can purchase one.

If you wish to write your own utility, several parts of the program can be taken from the examples in Chapters 5 and 6 of this book. The Character Magnifier program in this chapter can be used to display the character, and the Moving Dot program can be used as a base for the subroutine to change the dots. (Hint: use a delay loop to flash the magnified dot off and on, and use the Fire button on the joystick to change the dots.)

If you plan to use custom characters only occasionally, using the worksheet to lay out your characters and calculating the POKE values by hand should be sufficient.

Writing Programs that Make Use of Custom Characters

Once you have your characters defined, you will want to put them to work for you in programs. Programs that use custom characters are not much different from those that use the standard character set. You still have the option of using either PRINT or POKE (or both) to build your displays. There are two differences, however: the reduced memory available, and the absence of the standard character set.

HOW TO HANDLE MEMORY LOSS

Custom characters use up memory in two ways. Some memory must be set aside as character memory. In our examples we use an area of 8192 bytes for the sake of simplicity, but you can reduce that considerably. The section "Changing the Location of Screen and Character Memory," near the end of this chapter, explains how to do this. This memory reduction will not be a problem for most programs.

Memory is also needed to hold the program and DATA statements to load your custom characters. This loss will not be large if you use only a few characters, but can be significant if you are defining many. A DATA statement to hold a custom character definition will use from 25 to 40 bytes, depending on the number of digits in its values. Remember that spaces in a DATA statement are stored with the program, so you can reduce the amount of memory used by eliminating them. While we generally recommend that you use spaces in your programs to improve readability, the commas that separate the values in DATA statements can do that job adequately.

You can make more memory available to your main program by splitting it into two programs: one to build the characters and one to do the main work. If you run the character builder first, the program can be replaced by the main program when it is finished. You can even do this automatically, by placing a LOAD statement in the character builder. If you are loading the program from tape, save the character builder first, then the main program (the order does not matter on a disk drive). Make the last two statements of the character builder a CLR and a LOAD.

```
100 REM LOAD CUSTOM CHARACTERS
110 DATA 5,12,17,32
      .
      .
      .
340 REM PROTECT MEMORY
350 POKE 52,128 : POKE 56,128
360 REM FORGET VARIABLES
370 CLR
380 REM GET TO WORK
390 LOAD "MAIN"
```

The C-64 will load and run the program called MAIN. The CLR is needed to erase any variables defined in the character builder. BASIC stores variables in memory immediately after the program text. Because your main program will probably be larger than the character builder, part of it will be stored in the area occupied by the character builder's variables. If the CLR were not there, and you had a variable in the main program with the same name as one in the character builder, BASIC might store values assigned to that variable in the program's area. The result of damaging a program this way is unpredictable, but you can avoid it easily: always include the CLR statement before the LOAD, telling BASIC to "forget" the old variables.

ACCESSING THE BUILT-IN CHARACTER SET

Your program may also need to work around the loss of the standard character set. If your program displays messages, you have two choices: if you are not redefining all 256 characters, simply leave the alphabetic characters intact. If you do need 256 characters, you can switch back and forth between your custom characters and the built-in character set. The section on "Advanced VIC-II Chip Topics," later in this chapter, explains the techniques for switching.

Messages from BASIC itself may still be a problem. If you redefine the alphabetic characters to build players, a simple READY message may look like Egyptian hieroglyphics. This should not cause any serious difficulty except when you are debugging your program. If you interrupt it with the STOP key, or if BASIC finds an error, the messages produced may be somewhat difficult to read. You can return to the normal character set by entering the statements later in this chapter to switch back and forth between character sets from the keyboard. You should also note that RUN/STOP-RESTORE will bring back the normal character set, but leave your custom character memory intact and still protected from BASIC. Unfortunately, it will also clear the screen and erase the error message, so it's not very useful while debugging programs.

Animating Players

A player built from custom characters can be made to move by modifying its patterns in character memory, but this technique will usually be too slow if done in BASIC. (Machine language programs can run fast enough to handle it.) A simpler and faster approach is to define more than one version of the player in character memory. Your program can then make it move by changing the version displayed with a POKE to screen memory.

As an example of this method of animation, we have taken our stick man and put a little meat on his bones by building him with nine characters instead of one.

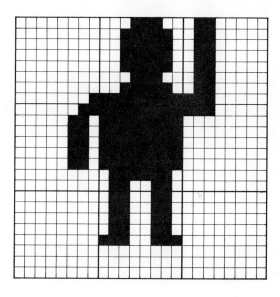

To liven him up a bit, we'll make him wave one arm by defining two more versions of the character that contains it.

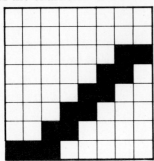 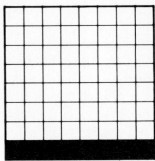

To observe him in action, enter the following program:

```
100 REM RESERVE MEMORY
110 POKE 52,128 : POKE 56,128 : CLR
120 REM POINT VIC-II AT NEW SCREEN AND CHARACTER MEMORY
130 POKE 56576,(PEEK(56576) AND 252) OR 1
140 POKE 53272,32
150 REM POINT BASIC AT NEW SCREEN
160 POKE 648,136
170 REM COPY CHARACTER MEMORY ROM TO RAM
180 POKE 56334,PEEK(56334) AND 254
190 POKE 1,PEEK(1) AND 251
200 FOR I=0 TO 2047:POKE 32768+I,PEEK(53248+I) : NEXT
210 POKE 1,PEEK(1) OR 4
220 POKE 56334,PEEK(56334) OR 1
230 REM CLEAR SCREEN AND SET UP DISPLAY AREA
240 DLY=250 : SB=34816
250 PRINT "◼◼◼AB"
260 PRINT "◼CDE"
265 PRINT "◼FGH"
270 REM LOAD BASIC PLAYER
280 FOR I=33792 TO 33863 : READ X : POKE I,X : NEXT I
290 DATA 0,0,0,0,0,0,0,0
300 DATA 28,62,62,62,62,28,62,255
310 DATA 96,96,96,96,96,96,96,96
320 DATA 3,6,6,6,6,6,0,0
330 DATA 255,255,255,255,255,255,126,102
340 DATA 192,0,0,0,0,0,0,0
350 DATA 0,0,0,0,0,0,0,0
360 DATA 102,102,102,102,231,0,0,0
370 DATA 0,0,0,0,0,0,0,0
380 REM LOAD 'EXTRA ARMS'
390 FOR I=33864 TO 33879 : READ X : POKEI,X : NEXT I
400 DATA 0,0,3,6,12,24,48,224
410 DATA 0,0,0,0,0,0,255,255
```

```
420 POKE SB+2,130
430 FOR I=1 TO DLY : NEXT I
440 POKE SB+2,137
450 FOR I=1 TO DLY : NEXT I
460 POKE SB+2,138
470 FOR I=1 TO DLY : NEXT I
480 POKE SB+2,137
490 FOR I=1 TO DLY : NEXT I
500 GOTO 420
```

When you run this program, the new stick man will be placed in the upper left corner of the screen, and his arm will begin to wave.

Note: There is a long delay preceding the action in this program.

MORE COMPLEX ANIMATION

While the C-64 is capable of much more complex animation than our stick man example shows, the techniques are the same. Your program can, for example, have several players in motion at once, or have one player making different motions simultaneously. Either of these can be done by predefining the movements with several custom characters.

Let's look at an example of two players in motion at once. We'll create another stick man who will wave to the first one. Change the stick man program so that it looks like this:

```
10 REM RESERVE MEMORY
100 CLR:POKE52,128:POKE56,128:CLR
110 GOSUB 10020
120 REM LEFT MAN WAVES
130 FOR J=1 TO 2 : GOSUB 220 : NEXT J
140 REM BOTH MEN WAVE
150 FOR J=1 TO 5 : GOSUB 320 : NEXT J
160 REM RIGHT MAN WAVES
170 FOR J=1 TO 2 : GOSUB 500 : NEXT J
180 REM BOTH MEN REST
190 FOR J=1 TO 1000 : NEXT J
200 GOTO 130
210 REM WAVE LEFT MAN'S ARM ONLY
220 POKE SB+2,130
230 FOR I=1 TO DLY : NEXT I
240 POKE SB+2,137
250 FOR I=1 TO DLY : NEXT I
260 POKE SB+2,138
270 FOR I=1 TO DLY : NEXT I
280 POKE SB+2,137
290 FOR I=1 TO DLY : NEXT I
300 RETURN
```

```
310 REM WAVE BOTH MEN'S ARMS
320 POKE SB+2,130
330 FOR I=1 TO DLY/2 : NEXT I
340 POKE SB+8,137
350 FOR I=1 TO DLY/2 : NEXT I
360 POKE SB+2,137
370 FOR I=1 TO DLY/2 : NEXT I
380 POKE SB+8,138
390 FOR I=1 TO DLY/2 : NEXT I
400 POKE SB+2,138
410 FOR I=1 TO DLY/2 : NEXT I
420 POKE SB+8,137
430 FOR I=1 TO DLY/2 : NEXT I
440 POKE SB+2,137
450 FOR I=1 TO DLY/2 : NEXT I
460 POKE SB+8,130
470 FOR I=1 TO DLY/2 : NEXT I
480 RETURN
490 REM WAVE RIGHT MAN'S ARM ONLY
500 POKE SB+8,137
510 FOR I=1 TO DLY : NEXT I
520 POKE SB+8,138
530 FOR I=1 TO DLY : NEXT I
540 POKE SB+8,137
550 FOR I=1 TO DLY : NEXT I
560 POKE SB+8,130
570 FOR I=1 TO DLY : NEXT I
580 RETURN
590 REM INITIALIZATION
600 REM SET DELAY LOOP LENGTH
610 DLY=100
10020 REM POINT VIC-II AT NEW SCREEN AND CHARACTER MEMORY
10030 POKE 56576,(PEEK(56576) AND 252) OR 1
10040 POKE 53272,32
10050 REM POINT BASIC AT NEW SCREEN
10060 POKE 648,136
10070 REM COPY CHARACTER MEMORY ROM TO RAM
10080 POKE 56334,PEEK(56334) AND 254
10090 POKE 1,PEEK(1) AND 251
10100 FOR I=0 TO 2047:POKE 32768+I,PEEK(53248+I) : NEXT
10110 POKE 1,PEEK(1) OR 4
10120 POKE 56334,PEEK(56334) OR 1
10130 REM CLEAR SCREEN AND SET UP DISPLAY AREA
10140 DLY=250 : SB=34816
10150 PRINT "▨▧▨AB▮   ▨▨AJ"
10160 PRINT "▨CDE▮   ▨CDE"
10170 PRINT "▨FGH▮   ▨FGH"
10180 REM LOAD BASIC PLAYER
10190 FOR I=33792 TO 33863 : READ X : POKE I,X : NEXT I
10191 REM
```

```
10200 DATA 0,0,0,0,0,0,0,1
10210 DATA 28,62,62,62,62,28,62,255
10220 DATA 96,96,96,96,96,96,96,224
10230 DATA 3,6,6,6,6,6,0,0
10240 DATA 255,255,255,255,255,255,126,102
10250 DATA 192,0,0,0,0,0,0,0
10260 DATA 0,0,0,0,0,0,0,0
10270 DATA 102,102,102,102,231,0,0,0
10280 DATA 0,0,0,0,0,0,0,0
10290 REM LOAD 'EXTRA ARMS'
10300 FOR I=33864 TO 33879 : READ X : POKE I,X : NEXT I
10310 DATA 0,0,3,6,12,24,48,224
10320 DATA 0,0,0,0,0,0,0,255
10330 RETURN
```

When you run the program, the stick man on the left side of the screen starts waving. After a moment, the one at the right starts to wave back. Then the man on the left stops waving, followed by the one on the right, and the cycle repeats.

The three subroutines that make the men wave (lines 210, 310, and 490) are the key to the motion. The first one, starting at line 210, makes only the figure on the left wave.

The second subroutine, which begins with line 310, causes both of the men to wave. Notice that the man on the left moves, then the program pauses for about half the time it did when moving just one arm before moving the man on the right. After the right-hand man's arm moves, the program again delays only half as long as before. This keeps the men moving at about the same speed, even though both are waving together. The man on the right also waves in the opposite direction from the man on the left, so they don't appear to be moving in "lock-step" with each other. These small differences make the display more interesting.

The last subroutine, starting at line 490, moves only the right-hand stick man, so the one on the left stops waving.

BIT-MAPPED GRAPHICS

With *bit-mapped* graphics, your program manipulates individual dots on the screen instead of whole characters. Bit-mapping gets its name from the fact that there is an area in memory set aside to represent the contents of the screen on a dot-by-dot basis. Just as cities, parks, and airports are represented by symbols on a geographic map, dots on the screen are represented by bits in memory. Bit-mapping can be used to draw finer lines on the screen or to smooth the motion of a player, since it can move in increments of one dot instead of a whole character space.

Using bit-mapped graphics on the C-64 is much like using custom characters. The VIC-II chip handles them in almost exactly the same way: in each case, it looks up the contents of an 8×8 dot "cell" in a table, and displays the dots one row at a time. The difference lies in how the VIC-II decides where to look in the table; in a character display, it uses the value in screen memory (the "screen code" for the character) to find the entry in character memory. When displaying a bit-mapped screen, the VIC-II steps through the table sequentially. It's as though you had a table of 1000 custom characters, and the screen contained screen codes numbered 0 through 999.

You can still use many of the concepts and tools that you used for custom character displays. The main difference is one of programming technique. Using custom characters, you set up the character memory and change the display by altering screen memory. In bit-mapped displays, "screen memory" stays constant, but "character memory" changes.

To understand bit-mapped graphics, let's review our discussion of character memory, but with a different perspective. From the point of view of text display, we think of screen memory as containing characters to be displayed, with character memory holding the dot patterns that represent the characters. In bit-mapped (*high-resolution*) terms, character memory becomes a dot-by-dot representation of the display, and screen memory is replaced by a counter to remind the VIC-II chip of where it is on the screen. In both cases, the VIC-II chip is doing exactly the same thing: looking up dot patterns in character memory and displaying them on the screen. Only the method for finding the dot pattern in the table process is different. Recall how we built one player from several custom characters in the last section. You can think of bit-mapped graphics as using the entire screen as a single "super player."

High-resolution graphics have two drawbacks. First, they use a large amount of memory: to completely map the screen in high-resolution mode takes 8000 bytes of character memory. Second, bit-mapping is an all or nothing proposition: you can't have bit-mapped graphics and a character display on the screen at the same time. It is possible, however, to experiment with high resolution without losing the character display. Since the bit-mapped display is so similar to a custom character display, we can create a mini-bit-mapped display using only a small portion of the screen. The techniques we used for defining a custom character set can also be used to set up a 64×64 dot area for bit-mapping experimentation.

The steps in preparing this bit-mapped work area are similar to those for establishing a custom character set. The Setup program listed below may seem familiar, because it was written by making some editing changes to the program we used to set up our custom character work area.

```
100 REM HIGH RESOLUTION "SETUP" PROGRAM
110 REM PROTECT CHARACTER MEMORY
120 POKE 52,128 : POKE 56,128 : CLR
130 REM POINT VIC-II AT NEW SCREEN AND CHARACTER MEMORY
140 POKE 56576,(PEEK(56576) AND 252) OR 1
150 POKE 53272,32
160 REM POINT TO NEW SCREEN
170 POKE 648,136 : SB=34816
180 REM COPY CHARACTER MEMORY ROM TO RAM
190 POKE 56334,PEEK(56334) AND 254
200 POKE 1,PEEK(1) AND 251
210 FOR I=0 TO 1023:POKE 32768+I,PEEK(53248+I) : NEXT
220 POKE 1,PEEK(1) OR 4
230 POKE 56334,PEEK(56334) OR 1
240 REM CLEAR "BIT-MAP" AREA IN CHARACTER MEMORY
250 FOR I=33792 TO 34303 : POKE I,0 : NEXT I
260 REM CLEAR SCREEN AND SET UP WORK AREA
270 PRINT "⌂◖HPX (08"
280 PRINT "◖RIQY!)19"
290 PRINT "◖BJRZ";CHR$(34);CHR$(34);CHR$(20);"*2:"
300 PRINT "◖CKS[#+3;"
310 PRINT "◖DLT£$,4<"
320 PRINT "◖EMU]%-5="
330 PRINT "◖FNV↑&.6>"
340 PRINT "◖GOW←/7?"
```

Now the upper left corner of the screen has become a bit-mapped work area in which you can experiment.

Changing the Dots in the Bit-Mapped Work Area

After running the Setup program, the portion of character memory that defines the work area looks like this:

Row	Memory Location	Column 0 1 2 3 4 5 6 7		Memory Location	Column 8 9 10 11 12 13 14 15 · · · ·		Memory Location	Column 56 57 58 59 60 61 62 63
0	34816			34880			35264	
1	34817			34881			35265	
2	34818			34882		· · · ·	35266	
3	34819			34883			35267	
4	34820			34884			35268	
·	·	·	·	·	·		·	·
·	·	·	·	·	·		·	·
·	·			·			·	
60	34876			35240			35324	
61	34877			35241			35225	
62	34878			35242		· · · ·	35226	
63	34879			35243			35227	

To change a dot on the screen, your program must find the right location to POKE, and the value to put there. The 64 bits of the X dimension are broken up into eight bytes of eight bits each. To find the correct column of bytes, use the following formula:

```
450 COL=INT(X/8)
```

Since each column of bytes in our pseudo-display is 64 rows high, the column number must be multiplied by 64. The calculation to find the right location to POKE is

```
460 PL=33792+Y+64*COL
```

The bit within that byte is the remainder of the division by 8 we did to find the column. To calculate the right bit, use

```
460 PL=33792+Y+64*COL
470 BIT=7-(X-COL*8)
```

We subtracted the remainder from 7 because our bit-mapped columns are numbered from left to right, but the bits in a byte are numbered from right to left.

Just knowing the number of the bit is not enough. Because it will be using POKE to change the display, your program must calculate the number that corresponds to that bit. Remember that each bit in the byte represents a power of 2.

Bit Number	7	6	5	4	3	2	1	0
Value for POKE	128	64	32	16	8	4	2	1

Since this is the case, you can easily convert from the bit number to the POKE value using the exponentiation operator.

```
480 PV=2↑BIT
```

Your program cannot simply POKE blindly into the byte it has found because there are seven other bits there that you don't want to disturb. To change just one bit, you must PEEK the byte to be changed, modify only the correct bit, and then POKE it back. To change only a single bit, you can use the AND and OR operators. For example, to set a bit to 0 (making its dot the background color), you can use a variation of the masking technique that was used to isolate the bits for joystick switches.

```
500 POKE PL,PEEK(PL) AND NOT PV
```

Notice the use of the NOT operator. When we were isolating the joystick switches, we used the value of the bit directly. That produced a mask in which the bit we wanted was a 1, and all the others were 0s. This time we are using a mask in which the bit we are interested in is a 0 and all the others are 1s. The AND will force that bit to 0 and leave the others undisturbed. Suppose we want to turn off bit 3 in location 34882, which currently contains a value of 43. We could use a BASIC statement like this:

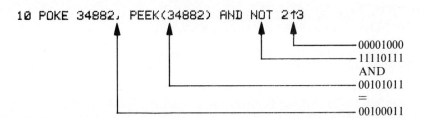

```
10 POKE 34882, PEEK(34882) AND NOT 2↑3
```

```
00001000
11110111
AND
00101011
=
00100011
```

When we POKE the result back into location 34882, only bit 3 has changed. The other bits kept their old values.

To change the dot back to the background color, use the OR operator.

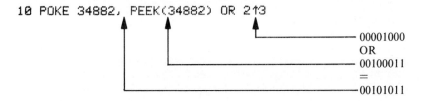

```
10 POKE 34882, PEEK(34882) OR 2↑3
```

```
00001000
OR
00100011
=
00101011
```

As before, only the value of bit 3 is changed.

This is a lot of work just to change one bit. However, since there are only eight bits in a byte, there are only eight possible values for the AND mask and eight for the OR mask. Since there are only eight of each type of mask, it is practical (and much faster) to calculate them in advance and store them in tables. The program fragment that follows can be used as a subroutine in programs that produce bit-mapped displays. It creates two arrays of masks, called M1% (Make 1) and M0% (Make 0).

```
100 FOR I=0 TO 7
110 M1%(I)=2↑I
120 M0%(I)=NOT M1%(I)
130 NEXT I
```

Notice that our array indexes, like our bit numbers, start with 0 because we calculate the bit number using the remainder of a division, which can be 0. The arrays are specified as integer variables because BASIC does Boolean operations with integers.

Using these precalculated masks not only makes programs faster, but also makes them easier to read. Compare our earlier examples for setting and resetting bits with statements that perform the same operations using the table.

```
10 POKE 34882,PEEK(34882) AND M0%(3)
20 POKE 34882,PEEK(34882) OR M1%(3)
```

Even with techniques like precalculating masks, BASIC is usually too slow for animation of bit-mapped displays; there are just too many bits to change in order to move a player around the screen. This kind of high-speed "bit-juggling" is best done in machine language. BASIC is, however, quite useful for displays that don't move, such as drawings and graphs. For example, the following program below will draw a triangle on the screen:

```
100 REM HIGH RESOLUTION "SETUP" PROGRAM
110 REM PROTECT CHARACTER MEMORY
120 POKE 52,128 : POKE 56,128 : CLR
130 REM POINT VIC-II AT NEW SCREEN AND CHARACTER MEMORY
140 POKE 56576,(PEEK(56576) AND 252) OR 1
150 POKE 53272,32
160 REM POINT TO NEW SCREEN
170 POKE 648,136 : SB=34816
180 REM COPY CHARACTER MEMORY ROM TO RAM
190 POKE 56334,PEEK(56334) AND 254
200 POKE 1,PEEK(1) AND 251
```

```
210 FOR I=0 TO 1023:POKE 32768+I,PEEK(53248+I) : NEXT
220 POKE 1,PEEK(1) OR 4
230 POKE 56334,PEEK(56334) OR 1
240 REM CLEAR "BIT-MAP" AREA IN CHARACTER MEMORY
250 FOR I=33792 TO 34303 : POKE I,0 : NEXT I
260 REM CLEAR SCREEN AND SET UP WORK AREA
270 PRINT "⬛⬛HPX (08"
280 PRINT "⬛AIQY!>19"
290 PRINT "⬛BJRZ";CHR$(34);CHR$(34);CHR$(20);"*2:"
300 PRINT "⬛CKS[#+3;"
310 PRINT "⬛DLT£$,4<"
320 PRINT "⬛EMUJ%-5="
330 PRINT "⬛FNV↑&.6>"
340 PRINT "⬛GOW←/7?"
350 REM BUILD MASK ARRAY
360 FOR I=0 TO 7:M1%(I)=2↑I : NEXT I
370 REM DRAW BOTTOM OF TRIANGLE
380 Y=63
390 FOR X=0 TO 63
400 GOSUB 540
410 NEXT
420 REM DRAW LEFT SIDE OF TRIANGLE
430 FOR X=0 TO 30
440 Y = 63-X*2
450 GOSUB 540
460 NEXT
470 REM DRAW RIGHT SIDE OF TRIANGLE
480 FOR X=31 TO 62
490 Y = 63-(62-X)*2
500 GOSUB 540
510 NEXT
520 END
530 REM BIT SETTING SUBROUTINE
540 COL=INT(X/8)
550 PL=33792+Y+64*COL
560 BIT=7-(X-COL*8)
570 POKE PL,PEEK(PL) OR M1%(BIT)
580 RETURN
```

When you run the program you will see that the triangle is drawn much too slowly to be useful in a fast-action game. It would be practical, however, for use in an educational program that displayed geometric shapes.

Using the Entire Screen

The techniques we discussed in the last section work just as well for a full bit-mapped screen. However, we need to change the formulas for finding the right byte to POKE. A subroutine to do the calculation might look like this:

```
100 PL = BM+(40*INT(Y/8))+(Y AND 7)+INT(X/8)
```

We also need to tell the VIC-II to switch to bit-mapped mode. This is controlled by bit 5 in location 53265. When this bit is set to "1," the VIC-II changes to a bit-mapped display. The other bits in this location should be preserved, so use the same masking technique we used for the character memory bytes:

```
100 POKE 53265,PEEK(53265) OR 32
```

There is one more thing you need to know to use bit-mapped graphics: the colors of the dots are specified differently from character displays. You may have wondered what happened to screen memory in bit-mapped mode. Remember that the location in "character memory" doesn't come from screen memory for bit-mapped displays. This leaves screen memory available for other purposes, and it is used to store the color codes. Just as for character displays, a "0" dot in a high-resolution display appears on the screen in the "background" color, and a "1" dot is the "character" color. But screen memory is 8 bits wide, not 4, so there is room for 2 color codes. In bit-mapped mode, each 8×8 dot "cell" has its own "background" and "character" colors. The "background" color is stored in bits 0-3, and the "character" color is in bits 4-7.

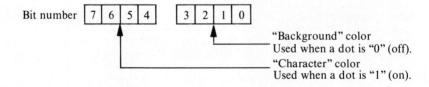

This gives you more freedom in mixing colors on the screen. To calculate the value to POKE for a given location on the screen, use the formula:

```
100 POKE 36867,(PEEK(36867) AND 127) OR ((SB/8) AND 128)
```

Now let's examine how these techniques work in a real program. We've modified our triangle-drawing program to use a bit-mapped screen. If you compare it to the version that used custom characters, you'll see that it hasn't changed much.

```
100 REM BIT MAPPED DISPLAY DEMONSTRATION PROGRAM
110 REM PROTECT BIT MAP MEMORY
120 POKE 52,64 : POKE 56,64 : CLR
130 REM POINT VIC-II AT NEW SCREEN AND BIT MAP MEMORY
140 POKE 56576,(PEEK(56576) AND 252) OR 2
150 POKE 53272,8
160 REM SET VIC-II TO BIT-MAPPED MODE
170 POKE 53265,PEEK(53265) OR 32
180 REM SET POINTER TO BIT MAP AREA
190 BM=24576 : SB=16384
200 REM CLEAR "BIT-MAP" AREA
210 FOR I=BM TO BM+7999 : POKE I,0 : NEXT I
220 REM FILL "SCREEN" MEMORY WITH COLOR CODES
230 FOR I=SB TO SB+999 : POKE I,230 : NEXT I
240 REM BUILD MASK ARRAY
250 FORI=0TO7:M1%(I)=2↑(7-I) : NEXT I
260 REM DRAW BOTTOM OF TRIANGLE
270 Y=63
280 FOR X=0 TO 63
290 GOSUB 530
300 NEXT
310 REM DRAW LEFT SIDE OF TRIANGLE
320 FOR X=0 TO 30
330 Y = 63-X*2
340 GOSUB 530
350 NEXT
360 REM DRAW RIGHT SIDE OF TRIANGLE
370 FOR X=31 TO 62
380 Y = 63-(62-X)*2
390 GOSUB 530
400 NEXT
410 REM WAIT FOR A KEY TO BE PRESSED
420 GET A$ : IF A$="" THEN 420
430 REM ALL DONE. RESTORE SYSTEM TO NORMAL
440 REM GIVE BIT MAP MEMORY BACK TO BASIC
450 POKE 52,128 : POKE 56,128 : CLR
460 REM POINT VIC-II AT ORIGINAL SCREEN AND
    CHARACTER MEMORY
470 POKE 56576,(PEEK(56576) AND 252) OR 3
480 REM RETURN TO CHARACTER MODE
490 POKE 53265,PEEK(53265) AND 223
500 POKE 53272,21
510 END
520 REM BIT SETTING SUBROUTINE
530 PL = BM+(40*(Y AND 248))+(Y AND 7)+(X AND 504)
540 POKE PL,PEEK(PL) OR M1%(X AND 7)
550 RETURN
```

One important difference is that the program goes into a loop when it's finished. When you press any key, it will return to the "normal" VIC-II segment. When using bit-mapped graphics, you must do this in your program: you can't type in the POKEs to do it from the keyboard, because the keyboard and display only work in character display mode.

This program is also too slow for lively animation. However, in the next section we will look at a technique for smooth player movement that can be used in BASIC.

SPRITE GRAPHICS

Using custom characters to animate displays has a drawback in some cases: while the parts of a player can be moved as little as a single dot, the player as a whole can only move a full character space at a time. You could get around this by defining different versions of the player at different offsets in the X and Y directions, but this would use up your 256 possible custom characters very quickly. There is, however, an easier way to get fine-tuned player movement, by using "sprites."

A "sprite" is a special form of player, very similar to the ones we built using custom characters. But it differs in one very important way: sprites are completely independent of the rest of the screen display. Sprites can overlap any character display already on the screen and move about without affecting it.

To understand how sprites work, start by imagining a background displayed on a transparent sheet of glass:

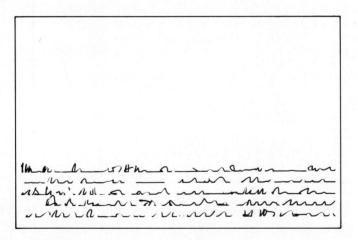

Although we could also put players made up of built-in or custom characters on this display, we'll keep things simple for now by assuming that it's all background. Now, on a second sheet of glass, we'll draw our sprite, an automobile:

Because the glass is transparent, we can put the car in front of the background:

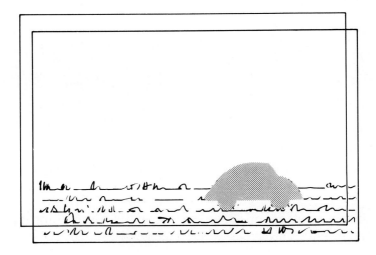

or behind it:

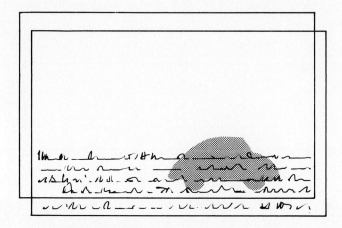

We can also move the glass with the sprite on it, while leaving the background fixed:

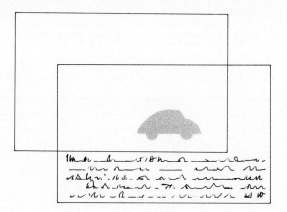

One important difference between sprites and the other types of players we have used so far is that your program does not have to move the sprite around in memory to make it move on the screen. It simply tells the VIC-II where the sprite belongs on the screen by POKEing its position into certain memory locations. This makes sprites much easier to move.

To make the display a bit livelier, we can add more sheets of glass, each with its own sprite. For example, we could add some trees to the scene:

We can arrange these sheets so that the car passes in front of one tree, but behind the other:

Through all this action, the background display remains unchanged, requiring no special action by the programmer to keep track of what should be displayed at a particular location on the screen. The VIC-II chip takes care of that for you.

As many as eight sprites can appear on the screen at any given moment, although you can have many more defined in memory and "waiting in the wings." You may find it helpful to think of the screen as a "frame" that can hold up to eight sheets of "sprite glass" at once, with other sheets nearby, ready to be switched with the ones already in place.

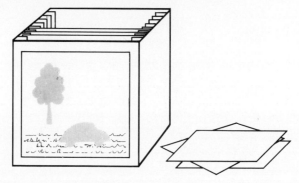

Now let's take a closer look at how sprites work, and how you can paint your own sprite glass, and get it into the "frame."

HOW SPRITES ARE DISPLAYED

Sprites are displayed on the screen in a fashion very similar to ordinary characters. As we discussed earlier, each character is defined by a table in memory, with the bits in each memory location telling the VIC-II chip which dots to turn on and which to turn off. Here, once again, is the table that defines the letter "A".

Displayed Dots	Binary	Decimal
	00011000	24
	00111100	60
	01100110	102
	01111110	126
	01100110	102
	01100110	102
	01100110	102
	00000000	0

The table for a sprite is very similar. The big difference is that a sprite is bigger: sprites are 24 dots wide, and 21 dots high. This requires a bigger table: a sprite table is 3 bytes wide and 21 bytes tall. Let's take the stick man we designed earlier in this chapter, and turn him into a sprite.

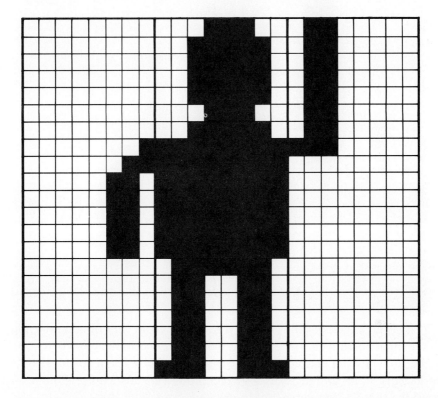

Notice the empty bytes surrounding the stick man. These must be there. The size of a sprite is fixed, just like a character, and the empty space is filled with zeros. This makes a sprite player similar to a player made up of several custom characters. You may find it helpful to think of a sprite as an oversized character.

Sprite Memory

Sprite definitions are stored in memory just like character definitions: the top row first (in the lowest memory locations), followed by the second row, and so on to the 21st row. The three bytes that hold the 24 dots of each row are next to each other in memory. If the definition for our stick man sprite were stored starting at location 32768, it would look like this:

32768	0	⎫
32769	28	⎬ top row
32770	96	⎭
32771	0	⎫
32772	62	⎬ second row
32773	96	⎭
32774	0	⎫
32775	62	⎬ third row
32776	96	⎭
	.	
	.	
	.	
32825	0	⎫
32826	102	⎬ 20th row
32827	96	⎭
32828	0	⎫
32829	102	⎬ 21st row
32830	96	⎭

This arrangement in memory does differ from that of a similar player made up of custom characters. However, the values in the table bytes are the same, so a custom character player can be converted to a sprite with just a little work. The design tools and techniques are also quite similar. We'll examine those a little later in this chapter.

One big difference between sprite memory and the other areas we've looked at is that there is no specific block of memory reserved for sprites. The characters displayed on the screen and the character definition tables are grouped together in their own areas of computer memory. While you can change the starting location of the screen or character memory areas, they can't be split up. You can't, for example, put the definitions of the first 128 characters in locations 32768-33791, and the second 128 in locations 34816-35839.

This sort of restriction does not apply to sprites. The VIC-II chip has a separate pointer for each sprite to the memory locations that contain its definition. So, while all the bytes for each sprite's definition have to be together, the various sprites can be scattered all over the VIC-II's 16K segment of memory.

The ability to store sprite definitions throughout the segment is the secret to keeping sprites available. These sprites can be used not only to expand your "cast of characters," but to animate them, too. We'll examine the techniques for using them a little later.

DESIGNING SPRITES

Since a sprite is so much like a custom character player, you might expect the design processes to be very similar, and indeed they are. Let's begin with a design form, just as we did for custom characters. Start with the long edge of your graph paper running horizontally, and draw a box 24 squares wide and 21 tall, so that it looks like this:

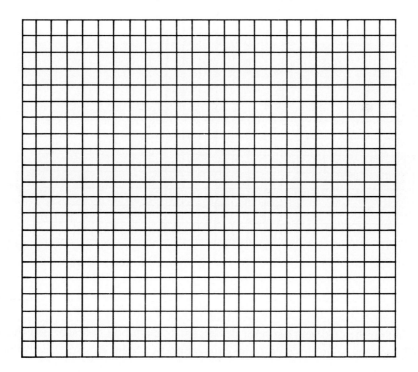

Notice that the box is toward the left edge of the paper, leaving room for calculations on the right. Now divide the box into three columns of 8 squares, and number them like this:

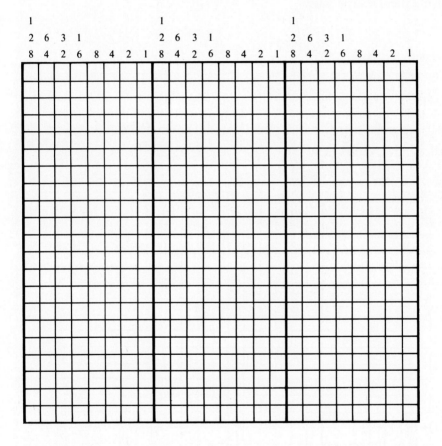

As in the custom character design form, each box corresponds to a dot on the screen. The three columns correspond to bytes in sprite memory.

In practice, the sprite design form works just like the custom character form. Here is our stick man again, designed as a sprite:

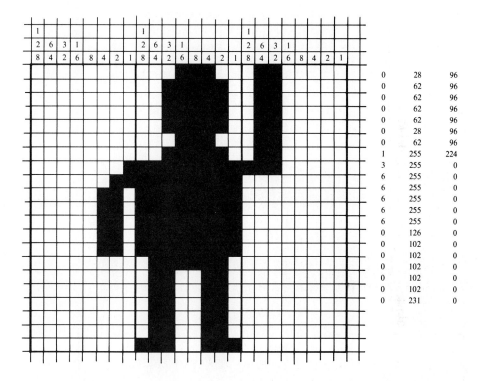

We left the binary values out in this example. As you get more practice in converting the dots to numbers, you will probably want to do the same. We also put in all the zeros for the "empty" bytes. This is a good habit to develop, since it is easy to forget them otherwise.

If you have written or purchased programs to help design players made of custom characters, they can also be used for sprites. Just remember that the bytes are stored in a different order in sprite memory.

Now let's take a look at the programming techniques for using sprites.

PUTTING YOUR SPRITE TO WORK

Once you have designed a sprite, there are several programming steps neccessary to make it work:

1. Reserve memory for your sprite definition.
2. Load the sprite defintion into memory.
3. Tell the VIC-II where the sprite definition is.
4. Tell the VIC-II to start displaying your sprite.
5. Move the sprite onto the screen.

This may sound like a lot of work, but each of these steps is actually quite simple. In the sections that follow, we'll examine each one in turn.

Loading Your Sprite Definition Into Memory

Just as with custom characters, the first steps in a program using sprites are to reserve the memory needed for the definitions, then load them into that memory. This program loads our "stick man" sprite into memory.

```
100 REM RESERVE MEMORY
110 CLR:POKE 52,128:POKE 56,128:CLR
120 REM MOVE SCREEN TO HIGH MEMORY
130 POKE 648,132
140 POKE 56576,(PEEK(56576)AND 252) OR 1
150 PRINT ""
160 REM LOAD SPRITE
170 FOR I=32832 TO 32894 : READ X : POKE I,X : NEXT
180 REM SPRITE DATA, 2 ROWS PER STATEMENT
190 DATA 0,28,96,    0,62,96
200 DATA 0,62,96,    0,62,96
210 DATA 0,62,96,    0,28,96
220 DATA 0,62,96,    0,255,96
230 DATA 3,255,192,  6,255,0
240 DATA 6,255,0,    6,255,0
250 DATA 6,255,0,    6,255,0
260 DATA 0,126,0,    0,102,0
270 DATA 0,102,0,    0,102,0
280 DATA 0,102,0,    0,102,0
290 DATA 0,231,0
```

This program is very similar to the one we used to set up the custom character player. As before, the very first line of the program resets the limits of memory, and does a "CLR" to reset BASIC's internal memory pointers.

The program then POKEs the locations in the CIA (complex interface adapter) chip that control the VIC-II's "segment" of memory, and BASIC's pointer to screen memory. Finally, the program uses a READ loop to load the sprite definition into memory.

Telling the VIC-II Chip Where to Find Your Sprite

Now that the sprite definition is in memory, the VIC-II chip must be told where to find it. As with screen and character memory, there are "pointers" to tell the VIC-II where in its 16K segment the sprite definitions reside. Sprite memory pointers are also incomplete: some of the bits come from memory, and some are calculated by the VIC-II chip. Instead of supplying only three or four bits of the location, sprite definition pointers supply eight of them:

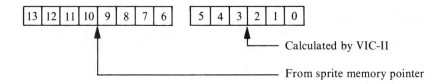

The formula for calculating the POKE value has to change, too. The following BASIC statement will do this:

```
100 PV=SDA/64 AND 255
```

The result of the calculation, "PV", will be assigned the numeric value of the 8 bits to be supplied to the VIC-II. We divide "SDA" (the Sprite Definition Address) by 64 because 6 bits of the location number are calculated by the VIC-II, and 64 is 2 to the 6th power. The division eliminates those calculated bits. The AND operation is used to eliminate bits from the left. Remember that there are 16 bits in the number that identifies a memory location (0-65535), but only 14 bits in a number that identifies a location in the VIC-II's 16K segment. Since a byte can only hold 8 bits, we have to get rid of the others. The AND makes sure that only values 0 through 255 will be POKEd. The two bits that select the right 16K segment are the ones we POKEd into the CIA chip, so we don't have to worry about them being lost.

Let's take a look at this formula in action. We started the definition for our stick man sprite at location 32832. Watch what happens to the bits as the calculation progresses.

1000000001000000	32832
	/64
	=
0000001000000001	513
	AND
0000000011111111	255
	=
0000000000000001	1

The correct value to POKE is 1. What would have happened if we had decided to start our sprite definition at location 32833? The binary value of 32833 is 1000000001000001. The last bit would be lost in our calculation, so the VIC-II would think that the definition started at location 32832. This would give us a strange-looking player, because the last eight dots on each row would be shifted onto the next row. The fact that the VIC-II calculates the last 6 bits of the address limits the locations where a sprite definition can begin in memory.

0
64
128
192
256
320
.
.
.
16192
16256
16320

Now that we know what value to POKE, we need to know where it goes. As we've mentioned before, computers are binary creatures, like numbers that are powers of 2. So even though there are only 1000 visible locations in screen memory, the VIC-II perceives screen memory as being an area of 1024 bytes. The sprite definition pointers are stored in some of the wasted 24 bytes, so the map of screen memory really looks like this:

Offset	Contents
0	Row 0, column 0
1	Row 0, column 1
2	Row 0, column 2
3	Row 0, column 3
.	
.	
.	
997	Row 24, column 37
998	Row 24, column 38
999	Row 24, column 39
1000	Not used
1001	Not used
.	
.	
.	
1014	Not used
1015	Not used
1016	Sprite pointer 0
1017	Sprite pointer 1
1018	Sprite pointer 2
1019	Sprite pointer 3
1020	Sprite pointer 4
1021	Sprite pointer 5
1022	Sprite pointer 6
1023	Sprite pointer 7

In our examples, we are using the segment that starts at location 32768, with screen memory starting at location 33792, so the sprite pointers start at location 34808. To make our stick man sprite 0, the correct POKE location is 34808. The statement to tell the VIC-II chip about our sprite definition is

```
100 POKE 34808,1
```

Type in and execute this statement now. Nothing will change on the screen yet, because we still have a few more steps to go before our sprite can make its entrance.

Enabling and Disabling Sprites

Every location on the character display must contain something. Even if you want nothing to appear, you must display a blank. This is not the case with sprites. They must be enabled (turned on) and disabled (turned off) by your program. Although this requires an extra program step, it does have some advantages. For example, it means you don't have to define a blank sprite if you don't plan to use all eight at the same time. More important, though, is that you can build up your sprite without having it appear on the screen before it's finished.

Sprites are enabled and disabled by bits in location 53269, which is part of the VIC-II chip:

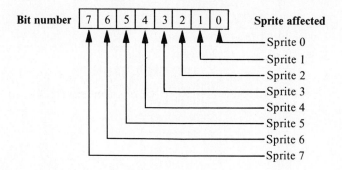

If the bit that controls a sprite is "on" (has a value of 1), the sprite is enabled, and appears on the screen. If the bit is off, the sprite is disabled. To turn the bit for a particular sprite off or on without disturbing the others, use AND and OR for bit-masking, as described earlier. For example, to enable sprite 1, you could use the statement:

```
100 POKE 53269,PEEK(53269) OR 2
```

Remember that you must PEEK the value that is already in the byte, so you will have the values of the other bits to POKE back into it. To disable a sprite, use AND to turn its bit off. The statement

```
100 POKE 53269,PEEK(53269) AND 254
```

will disable sprite 0, making it disappear from the screen. The statement above also PEEKs first to preserve the values of the other bits. Here are the masks to use for enabling and disabling sprites:

Sprite Number	To enable, OR with	To disable, AND with
0	1	254
1	2	253
2	4	251
3	8	247
4	16	239
5	32	223
6	64	191
7	128	127

Now enable our example sprite by entering the statement

```
POKE 53269,PEEK(53269) OR 1
```

Once again, nothing happens to the screen. Our sprite is actually being displayed, but it is behind the border, and now we have to tell the VIC-II to move it onto the screen.

Moving Your Sprite

From our discussions so far, you've probably guessed that sprite positions are expressed in dots, and that dots, like character rows and columns, are numbered from the upper left to the lower right corner. But there is one thing about sprite positioning that may surprise you: the numbering does not start in the visible area of the screen. The lowest numbered dot is actually in the border area!

While this may seem strange at first, there is a very good reason for it. Most of the time, you will not want your sprite to suddenly appear on the screen. Like an actor in a play, your sprite will usually make an entrance, moving onto the screen from behind the border. You can't do this unless you have some way to position the sprite in the border area, so the numbering of the dots actually starts off screen. The numbering looks like this:

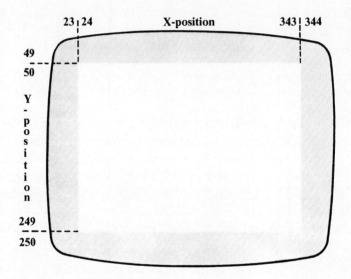

To avoid confusion with screen character positions, we will refer to the dot counts as the "X-position" for left-to-right and "Y-position" for top-to-bottom, rather than as "row" and "column."

Your program controls the X- and Y-positions of sprites by POKEing locations in the VIC-II chip. Each sprite has its own pair of locations.

Sprite Number	X-position location	Y-position location
0	53248	53249
1	53250	53251
2	53252	53253
3	53254	53255
4	53256	53257
5	53258	53259
6	53260	53261
7	53262	53263

To get the sample sprite (sprite 0) onto the screen, enter these statements:

```
POKE 53248,100
POKE 53249,100
```

Try a few more POKEs into these locations, and watch what happens to the position of the sprite. In particular, try POKEing a value of 255 into location 53248, the sprite's X-position.

As you experimented with moving the sprite, you may have noticed that you couldn't get it near the right-hand edge of the screen. Look back at the drawing showing the X- and Y-positioning values, and you'll see why. An X-position value of 255 (the largest number you can POKE into a byte) will only move a sprite about three-fourths of the way across the screen. To move the rest of the way, we need a 9-bit number, which can contain values from 0 through 511.

Since a byte can only hold eight bits, the VIC-II must get the ninth bit from some other location. Eight extra bits are needed (1 for each sprite), so Commodore grouped them together in one location in the VIC-II. These bits are in the same order as the enable bits, allowing us to use the same bit masks used to enable or disable the sprite. To see how this is done, let's look at a complete subroutine that will position a sprite on the screen. This subroutine is given three variables.

SN   The "Sprite Number" (0 through 7)
XP   The X-position of the sprite
YP   The Y-position of the sprite

Such a subroutine might look like this:

```
10000 XL = 53248 + 2 * SN
10010 YL = XL + 1
10020 IF XP > 255 THEN 10050
10030 B9 = PEEK(53264) AND NOT (2↑SN)
10040 GOTO 10060
10050 B9 = PEEK(53264) OR (2↑SN)
10060 XV = XP AND 255
10070 POKE XL,XV : POKE YL,YP : POKE 53264,B9
```

This subroutine probably seems a bit obscure. Let's go over it line by line:

10000   Calculates the memory location to POKE for the X-position.

10010   Calculates the memory location to POKE for the Y-position.

10020   Different masking operations must be done, depending on the value of the 9th bit in the X-position. If XP is less than 256, the 9th bit is a "0."

10030   "B9" is set to the new value for the "bit 9" location in the VIC-II. The exponentiation gives us a mask in which only the bit for the chosen sprite is a 1. The PEEK gets the current value, and the OR turns on the bit.

10040   The GOTO skips over the processing for an X-position that is less than 256.

10050   If the ninth bit is a "0," we must force off the sprite's bit in the "bit 9" location. By using a NOT, we generate a mask in which the sprite's bit is a 0, and all others are 1's. The AND forces the bit off.

10060   The AND with 255 makes sure that we don't try to POKE too big a number into the X-position location.

10070   This line POKEs the position information into the VIC-II chip's locations.

This last line of this subroutine is very important. It is usually not a good programming practice to combine statements on one line, because it makes programs harder to read. One exception we have already mentioned is a short FOR-NEXT loop, such as the delay loops used for animation, where putting everything on one line makes the program easier to follow. In the subroutine above, we combined the POKEs into one line for a different reason: it takes time to do the calculations for the POKE values. If we calculated and POKEd each value separately, it could make the motion of the sprite a little choppy. This is especially true when the X-position goes from 255 to 256. If we POKEd the X-position location, then calculated the bit 9 location value, the sprite would jump off the screen while we were doing the calculation, then jump back on when we POKEd the bit 9 value. Depending on the order in which the calculations and POKEs are done, this might cause a noticeable flicker. While you don't have to follow the order of calculations we used, you will find that you get the most pleasing results by doing the calculations first, then the POKEs.

Animating Sprites

Like custom character players, sprites can be animated by defining different versions and changing the version displayed "on the fly." There is one difference, though; while you can redefine part of a custom character player, you must define a completely new sprite for each position in the animation sequence. In the section on custom character players, we animated our stick man by making him wave. Here's a program that does the same thing with our sprite stick man.

```
900 REM RESERVE MEMORY
1000 CLR:POKE 52,128:POKE 56,128:CLR
1010 REM MOVE SCREEN TO HIGH MEMORY
1020 POKE 648,132
1030 POKE 56576,(PEEK(56576)AND 252) OR 1
1040 PRINT""
1100 REM LOAD SPRITE 1
1200 FOR I=32832 TO 32894 : READ X : POKE I,X : NEXT
1300 REM SPRITE DATA, 2 ROWS PER STATEMENT
1400 DATA 0,28,96,    0,62,96
1401 DATA 0,62,96,    0,62,96
1402 DATA 0,62,96,    0,28,96
1403 DATA 0,62,96,    0,255,96
1404 DATA 3,255,192,  6,255,0
1405 DATA 6,255,0,    6,255,0
1406 DATA 6,255,0,    6,255,0
1407 DATA 0,126,0,    0,102,0
1408 DATA 0,102,0,    0,102,0
1409 DATA 0,102,0,    0,102,0
1410 DATA 0,231,0
2100 REM LOAD SPRITE 2
2200 FOR I=32896 TO 32958 : READ X : POKE I,X : NEXT
2300 REM SPRITE DATA, 2 ROWS PER STATEMENT
2400 DATA 0,28,0,     0,62,0
2401 DATA 0,62,3,     0,62,6
2402 DATA 0,62,12,    0,28,24
2403 DATA 0,62,48,    0,255,224
2404 DATA 3,255,192,  6,255,0
2405 DATA 6,255,0,    6,255,0
2406 DATA 6,255,0,    6,255,0
2407 DATA 0,126,0,    0,102,0
2408 DATA 0,102,0,    0,102,0
2409 DATA 0,102,0,    0,102,0
2410 DATA 0,231,0
3100 REM LOAD SPRITE 3
3200 FOR I=32960 TO 33022 : READ X : POKE I,X : NEXT
3300 REM SPRITE DATA, 2 ROWS PER STATEMENT
3400 DATA 0,28,0,     0,62,0
```

```
3401 DATA 0,62,0,    0,62,0
3402 DATA 0,62,0,    0,28,0
3403 DATA 0,62,255,  0,255,255
3404 DATA 3,255,192, 6,255,0
3405 DATA 6,255,0,   6,255,0
3406 DATA 6,255,0,   6,255,0
3407 DATA 0,126,0,   0,102,0
3408 DATA 0,102,0,   0,102,0
3409 DATA 0,102,0,   0,102,0
3410 DATA 0,231,0
4100 REM ENABLE THE SPRITE
4110 POKE 34808,1
4120 POKE 53269,PEEK(53269) OR 1
4200 REM PUT IT ON THE SCREEN
4210 POKE 53248,100
4220 POKE 53249,100
4300 REM START MAKING IT MOVE
4310 POKE 34808,2
4320 FOR I = 1 TO 250 : NEXT
4330 POKE 34808,3
4340 FOR I = 1 TO 250 : NEXT
4350 POKE 34808,2
4360 FOR I = 1 TO 250 : NEXT
4370 POKE 34808,1
4380 FOR I = 1 TO 250 : NEXT
4390 GOTO 4300
```

Lines 4300 through 4380 are the key to the animation: we POKE
location 34808, which is the sprite definition pointer for sprite 0. No matter
how much of the sprite changes, only one POKE is necessary. If the player's
movements must be complex, as with a figure that walks and waves at the
same time, it is much easier to animate a sprite than a custom character
player. There is a price for this, though; the sprite method will usually require
more memory. In most cases, this will not be a problem, but it is something
you must keep in mind when designing programs.

Now let's liven up the display a bit more. Add these lines to the program:

```
4222 XP=100:YP=100:SN=100
4224 XI=3:YI=3
4300 REM START MAKING IT MOVE
4310 POKE 34808,2
4320 GOSUB 4400
4330 POKE 34808,3
4340 GOSUB 4400
4350 POKE 34808,2
4360 GOSUB 4400
4370 POKE 34808,1
4380 GOSUB 4400
```

```
4390 GOTO 4300
4400 FOR I=1 TO 5
4410 XP=XP+XI
4420 YP=YP+YI
4430 GOSUB 10000
4440 IF XP<21 OR XP>320 THEN XI=-XI
4450 IF YP<51 OR YP >228 THEN YI=-YI
4460 FOR J=1 TO 25:NEXT
4470 NEXT I
4480 RETURN
10000 XL = 53248 + 2 * SN
10010 YL = XL + 1
10020 IF XP > 255 THEN 10050
10030 B9 = PEEK(53264) AND NOT (2↑SN)
10040 GOTO 10060
10050 B9 = PEEK(53264) OR (2↑SN)
10060 XV = XP AND 255
10070 POKE XL,XV : POKE YL,YP : POKE 53264,B9
```

When you RUN the program, the stick man will start to wave again, but this time he drifts around the screen at the same time. When he hits the border, he bounces off it, and heads off in a different direction.

We'll be using modified versions of this program to illustrate other sprite concepts. SAVE a copy of it to reduce wear and tear on your typing fingers.

Coloring Sprites

Just as each location in screen memory has a corresponding location in color memory, each sprite has a location that contains its color. Sprite colors are stored in the VIC-II chip, not in memory. The memory locations that control sprite colors are

Location	Sprite number
53287	0
53288	1
53289	2
53290	3
53291	4
53292	5
53293	6
53294	7

These locations take the same POKE values that color memory locations do.

To see sprite colors in action, change the sprite demonstration program so it looks like this:

```
100 REM RESERVE MEMORY
110 CLR:POKE 52,128:POKE 56,128:CLR
120 REM MOVE SCREEN TO HIGH MEMORY
130 POKE 648,132
140 POKE 56576,(PEEK(56576)AND 252) OR 1
150 PRINT"⌧"
160 REM LOAD SPRITE 1
170 FOR I=32832 TO 32894 : READ X : POKE I,X : NEXT
180 REM SPRITE DATA, 2 ROWS PER STATEMENT
190 DATA 0,28,96,    0,62,96
200 DATA 0,62,96,    0,62,96
210 DATA 0,62,96,    0,28,96
220 DATA 0,62,96,    0,255,96
230 DATA 3,255,192,  6,255,0
240 DATA 6,255,0,    6,255,0
250 DATA 6,255,0,    6,255,0
260 DATA 0,126,0,    0,102,0
270 DATA 0,102,0,    0,102,0
280 DATA 0,102,0,    0,102,0
290 DATA 0,231,0
300 REM LOAD SPRITE 2
310 FOR I=32896 TO 32958 : READ X : POKE I,X : NEXT
320 REM SPRITE DATA, 2 ROWS PER STATEMENT
330 DATA 0,28,0,     0,62,0
340 DATA 0,62,3,     0,62,6
350 DATA 0,62,12,    0,28,24
360 DATA 0,62,48,    0,255,224
370 DATA 3,255,192,  6,255,0
380 DATA 6,255,0,    6,255,0
390 DATA 6,255,0,    6,255,0
400 DATA 0,126,0,    0,102,0
410 DATA 0,102,0,    0,102,0
420 DATA 0,102,0,    0,102,0
430 DATA 0,231,0
440 REM LOAD SPRITE 3
450 FOR I=32960 TO 33022 : READ X : POKE I,X : NEXT
460 REM SPRITE DATA, 2 ROWS PER STATEMENT
470 DATA 0,28,0,     0,62,0
480 DATA 0,62,0,     0,62,0
490 DATA 0,62,0,     0,28,0
500 DATA 0,62,255,   0,255,255
510 DATA 3,255,192,  6,255,0
520 DATA 6,255,0,    6,255,0
530 DATA 6,255,0,    6,255,0
540 DATA 0,126,0,    0,102,0
550 DATA 0,102,0,    0,102,0
560 DATA 0,102,0,    0,102,0
```

```
570 DATA 0,231,0
580 REM ENABLE THE SPRITE
590 POKE 34808,1
600 POKE 53269,PEEK(53269) OR 1
610 REM PUT IT ON THE SCREEN
620 SN=0
630 XP=100 : XI=1
640 YP=100 : YI=1
650 GOSUB 10000
660 REM START MAKING IT MOVE
670 POKE 34808,2
680 GOSUB  760
690 POKE 34808,3
700 GOSUB  760
710 POKE 34808,2
720 GOSUB  760
730 POKE 34808,1
740 GOSUB  760
750 GOTO 660
760 FOR I = 1 TO 5
770 XP = XP+XI
780 YP = YP+YI
790 GOSUB 10000
800 IF XP<21 OR XP > 320 THEN XI = -XI : GOSUB 860
810 IF YP<51 OR YP > 228 THEN YI = -YI : GOSUB 860
820 REM FOR J = 1 TO 25 : NEXT
830 NEXT I
840 RETURN
850 REM MAKE HIM "BLUSH"
860 POKE 53287,10
870 FOR J = 1 TO 250 : NEXT
880 POKE 53287,1
890 RETURN
10000 XL = 53248 + 2 * SN
10010 YL = XL + 1
10020 IF XP > 255 THEN 10050
10030 B9 = PEEK(53264) AND NOT (2↑SN)
10040 GOTO 10060
10050 B9 = PEEK(53264) OR (2↑SN)
10060 XV = XP AND 255
10070 POKE XL,XV : POKE YL,YP : POKE 53264,B9
10080 RETURN
```

Now RUN the program, and watch the results. Each time the man bumps into the wall, he turns red for a moment before continuing.

Sprite Interaction

When sprites move around on the screen, they sometimes overlap each other or objects in the background display. The sprite world is like the real world in that two objects can't occupy the same space at the same time. Only one object can be displayed in a particular dot position at any one moment. The VIC-II has a set of rules to determine which object gets priority when two or more compete for a particular dot. It also has a way to tell your program when two objects collide. In this section, we'll look at those rules and how you can use them in your programs.

Display Priorities

In the introduction to sprites, we described them as figures on sheets of glass. Each sheet can hold only one sprite, so when two sprites try to occupy the same position, one must pass "behind" the other. The rule for determining which one gets priority (passes "in front") is very simple: sprite 0 is always in front of sprite 1, which is in front of sprite 2, and so on. Sprite 7, of course, will pass behind any other sprite. To see this in action, type in and RUN the following program:

```
100 REM RESERVE MEMORY
110 CLR:POKE 52,128:POKE 56,128:CLR
120 REM MOVE SCREEN TO HIGH MEMORY
130 POKE 648,132
140 POKE 56576,(PEEK(56576)AND 252) OR 1
150 PRINT"⊐"
160 REM LOAD SPRITE 0 (DIAMOND)
170 FOR I=32832 TO 32894 : READ X : POKE I,X : NEXT
180 REM SPRITE DATA, 2 ROWS PER STATEMENT
190 DATA 0,0,0,      0,0,0
200 DATA 0,0,0,      0,0,0
210 DATA 0,24,0,     0,60,0
220 DATA 0,126,0,    0,255,0
230 DATA 1,255,128,  3,255,192
240 DATA 7,255,224,  7,255,224
250 DATA 3,255,192,  1,255,128
260 DATA 0,255,0,    0,126,0
270 DATA 0,60,0,     0,24,0
280 DATA 0,0,0,      0,0,0
290 DATA 0,0,0
300 REM LOAD SPRITE 1 (SQUARE)
310 FOR I=32896 TO 32958 : POKE I,255 : NEXT
320 REM ENABLE THE SPRITES
330 POKE 34808,1
340 POKE 34809,2
350 POKE 53269,PEEK(53269) OR 3
360 REM PUT THEM ON THE SCREEN
370 X(0)=50 : XI(0)=3
```

```
380 X(1)=50 : XI(1)=-3
390 YP=150
400 FOR SN=0 TO 1 : XP=X(SN) : GOSUB 10000 : NEXT
410 REM START MAKING THEM MOVE
420 FOR SN = 0 TO 1
430 X(SN) = X(SN)+XI(SN)
440 XP=X(SN)
450 IF X(SN)<21 OR X(SN)> 75  THEN XI(SN) = -XI(SN)
460 GOSUB 10000
470 REM FOR J = 1 TO 25 : NEXT
480 NEXT
490 GOTO 410
10000 XL = 53248 + 2 * SN
10010 YL = XL + 1
10020 IF XP > 255 THEN 10050
10030 B9 = PEEK(53264) AND NOT (2↑SN)
10040 GOTO 10060
10050 B9 = PEEK(53264) OR (2↑SN)
10060 XV = XP AND 255
10070 POKE XL,XV : POKE YL,YP : POKE 53264,B9
10080 RETURN
```

When the program is executed, it creates two simple sprites and moves them back and forth across the screen. The diamond shape is sprite 0 and always passes in front of the square. Notice that the "transparent" part of the diamond doesn't blot out the square; only the "visible" part covers up any of the dots that make up the square. Now interrupt the program and enter these lines:

```
330 POKE 34808,2
340 POKE 34809,1
```

The POKEs switched the sprites, so that the square became sprite 0 and the diamond sprite 1. Now the diamond passes behind the square. Notice that it makes no difference where the sprite is in memory; the only thing that counts is which sprite definition pointer points to it.

The relationships between sprites are only half the story, though. Sprites can also pass in front of, or behind, the background display. To illustrate this, add the following lines to the program:

```
355 REM PUT SQUARE BEHIND BACKGROUND
356 POKE 53275,PEEK(53275) OR 2
```

When you RUN the program, you'll see that the square (sprite 1) passes behind the background, but the diamond (sprite 0) passes in front of both the square and the background display. The secret to this is the POKE in line 356, which clears a bit that tells the VIC-II that sprite 1 has a higher priority than the background. Like many of the other bits that control sprites, there are eight of them, one per sprite, grouped together in one location, number 53275. The least significant bit controls sprite 0, and the most significant bit controls sprite 7:

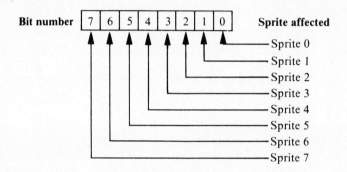

If a sprite's bit in this location is a 0, it takes priority over the background, and passes in front of it. If the bit is a 1, the sprite passes behind the background. The bits are, of course, controlled with bit-masking operations. As always, you must PEEK location 53275 first, to save the values of the other bits. To put sprite 3 behind the background, you would use a statement like

```
100 POKE 53275,PEEK(53275) OR 8
```

To put sprite 7 in front of the background, use

```
100 POKE 53275,PEEK(53275) AND 127
```

Splitting the sprite-to-sprite priorities from the sprite-to-background priorities has a very interesting side effect. Change line 356 of the program to

```
356 POKE 53275,1
```

Now RUN the program, and watch what happens. The square (sprite 1) is in front of the background, and the diamond (sprite 0) is behind it. But the diamond passes in front of the square, because sprite 0 always has priority over sprite 1. So, when the diamond and the square overlap, the background is in front of the part of the square that is covered by the diamond! This makes perfect sense as far as the VIC-II's priority rules are concerned, but don't spend too much time trying to imagine how this works with our "sheets of glass."

Collisions

In the real world, when two cars collide, the results are noisy and messy. Fortunately, things are not that bad in the sprite world. Instead, the VIC-II simply sets some flags to let you know who hit whom.

Being able to detect collisions is very handy for game software. The process of finding overlaps by calculation uses up a lot of computer time, and would slow down the action. However, collision detection is also useful for almost any program that uses sprites to simulate moving objects.

There are two different types of "collisions": one occurs when two sprites overlap, and the other is a result of a sprite passing in front of or behind an object in the background display. Each type of collision is recorded in its own location: location 53279 marks collisons between sprites and the background, and location 53278 contains bits to identify sprites that collide with each other. Like many of the other locations in the VIC-II, each location contains one bit for each sprite, with the least significant bit corresponding to sprite 0, and the most significant being used for sprite 7. This allows you to use the same bit masks for examining these locations that are used to set bits in the "controlling" locations.

Now let's see how collision detection works in a program. The example below uses the diamond and square sprites from our earlier example, but this time they don't pass each other: when they touch, they bounce, and reverse direction. We've also added "walls" in the background that the sprites bounce off when they touch.

```
100 REM RESERVE MEMORY
110 CLR:POKE 52,128:POKE 56,128:CLR
120 REM MOVE SCREEN TO HIGH MEMORY
130 POKE 648,132
140 POKE 56576,(PEEK(56576)AND 252) OR 1
150 PRINT""
160 REM LOAD SPRITE 0 (DIAMOND)
170 FOR I=32832 TO 32894 : READ X : POKE I,X : NEXT
180 REM SPRITE DATA, 2 ROWS PER STATEMENT
190 DATA 0,0,0,     0,0,0
200 DATA 0,0,0,     0,0,0
210 DATA 0,24,0,    0,60,0
220 DATA 0,126,0,   0,255,0
230 DATA 1,255,128, 3,255,192
```

```
240 DATA 7,255,224,  7,255,224
250 DATA 3,255,192,  1,255,128
260 DATA 0,255,0,    0,126,0
270 DATA 0,60,0,     0,24,0
280 DATA 0,0,0,      0,0,0
290 DATA 0,0,0
300 REM LOAD SPRITE 1 (SQUARE)
310 FOR I=32896 TO 32958 : POKE I,255 : NEXT
320 REM BUILD THE WALLS
330 FOR I = 1 TO 8 : PRINT : NEXT
340 FOR I = 1 TO 10 : PRINT"▧            ▧" : NEXT
350 REM ENABLE THE SPRITES
360 POKE 34808,1
370 POKE 34809,2
380 POKE 53269,PEEK(53269) OR 3
390 REM PUT THEM ON THE SCREEN
400 X(0)=60 : XI(0)=2
410 X(1)=35 : XI(1)=-1
420 YP=150
430 FOR SN=0 TO 1 : XP=X(SN) : GOSUB 10000 : NEXT
440 REM START MAKING THEM MOVE
450 FOR SN = 0 TO 1
460 X(SN) = X(SN)+XI(SN)
470 XP=X(SN)
480 GOSUB 10000
490 REM CHECK FOR COLLISION WITH OTHER SPRITE
500 IF PEEK(53278) = 0 THEN GOTO 600
510 REM IMPACT! REVERSE COURSE
520 XI(0) = -XI(0) : XI(1) = -XI(1)
530 REM BACK UP THE SPRITE WE JUST MOVED
540 X(SN) = X(SN) + XI(SN) * 2
550 XP=X(SN)
560 GOSUB 10000
570 REM CLEAR THE SPRITE COLLISION FLAGS
580 DD = PEEK(53278)
590 REM CHECK FOR COLLISION WITH BACKGROUND
600 IF (PEEK(53279) AND 2↑SN) = 0 THEN GOTO 690
610 REM HIT THE WALL! REVERSE COURSE
620 XI(SN) = -XI(SN)
630 REM BACK UP THE SPRITE WE JUST MOVED
640 X(SN) = X(SN) + XI(SN)
650 XP=X(SN)
660 GOSUB 10000
670 REM CLEAR THE BACKGROUND COLLISION FLAG
680 DD = PEEK(53279)
690 NEXT
700 GOTO 440
10000 XL = 53248 + 2 * SN
10010 YL = XL + 1
10020 IF XP > 255 THEN 10050
```

```
10030 B9 = PEEK(53264) AND NOT (2↑SN)
10040 GOTO 10060
10050 B9 = PEEK(53264) OR (2↑SN)
10060 XV = XP AND 255
10070 POKE XL,XV : POKE YL,YP : POKE 53264,B9
10080 RETURN
```

Most of this program should be familiar by now, so we'll concentrate on the parts that use collision detection.

Line 500 PEEKs location 53278, which contains the flags for sprite-to-sprite collisions. In our example, we are using only two sprites, so any nonzero value means that the two have collided. A more complex program, involving many sprites, would use bit-masking to determine which two sprites had collided. To detect a collision between sprites 3 and 5, you can use this statement:

```
100 IF PEEK(53278) AND 40 = 40 THEN GOTO 200
```

Where did the 40 come from? The mask value for sprite 3 is 8, and sprite 5's is 32. By adding 8 and 32, we get a mask that will force off all bits except those for sprites 3 and 5. The comparison to 40 is important, too; it makes sure that both bits are on. If sprite 3 had collided with sprite 2, the PEEK value would be 12 (8 plus 4). If 12 and 40 are ANDed together, the result is 8. This value is not zero, so a simple IF would see a true result. By comparing the result of the AND to 40, we know whether both sprites, or just one of them, were involved in the collision.

Your program should check the collision flags after every sprite move. If it doesn't, it may be difficult to determine exactly who hit whom. For example, if sprites 2 and 3 are colliding in the upper-left corner of the screen, and sprites 0 and 4 are colliding at the same time in the lower-right, a PEEK into location 53278 will return a value of 15, because all four are involved in collisions. In order to figure out which sprites are touching which, your program must resort to the calculations that the collision detection mechanism is designed to eliminate. Checking after each move avoids this extra work.

Line 580 demonstrates another important characteristic of the collision flags. The REM statement in line 570 says that we are clearing the flags, but you would expect that to be done with a POKE, not a PEEK. The reason lies in the electronic design of the VIC-II chip. Whenever a sprite is involved in a collision, its collision flag bit is set. The bit stays set until the collision flag location is examined with a PEEK (there are certain advantages to designing chips this way, and the practice is quite common). If the flag is cleared by PEEKing, why do we have to PEEK again to clear it? As soon as we cleared the flags with the first PEEK, the VIC-II discovered that the sprites were still colliding, so it set them again (it checks every time it scans the display). To clear the flags, we had to move the sprite, then PEEK again. If the flags weren't cleared, we would get a false indication. Even though the two sprites were no longer touching, the VIC-II hadn't communicated to the program, and would remember the collision until it had. Try deleting line 580 from the program, and watch what happens. The program thinks that the two sprites are colliding all the time, so once they touch, they sit there and vibrate, reversing every move.

Although we haven't mentioned the sprite-to-background collision flags, their electronic design is the same as the sprite-to-sprite flags. You'll need to use the same methods to clear them and to avoid false collisions.

FANCY COLORS

While the combination of standard graphics and custom characters will meet the needs of most applications, there are some things that cannot be easily displayed in blue and white (or green and white, or red and green). If you need fine shading in a display, or want to make it more eye-catching, just turning a dot on the screen on or off isn't enough.

The C-64 offers two techniques for making your display more colorful. The first, called "Extended Color Mode," allows you to control the background color for each character on the screen. The second, "Multicolor Mode," gives you the ability to use more than two colors in a given character. Multicolor mode can even be used for high-resolution displays and sprites. In the sections that follow, we'll show you how these techniques work, and how to put them to use in your programs.

Extended Color Mode

On a normal character display, there are two ways to draw attention to a message: you can display it in a different color, or print it in reversed characters. These are effective if the person using the computer is actively involved in reading the display, but there are circumstances where you need a real eyecatcher. One such case might be using the C-64 to control a lab

experiment. It might be necessary for the experimenter to adjust some
equipment across the lab from the computer, or the experiment might run for
a while, leaving time to wash out the test tubes.

If you were already using reversed characters for some other purpose,
such as to highlight instructions for the experiment, you wouldn't want to use
them for an alarm message. You'd want something that really stood out, and
extended color mode does that nicely.

In extended color mode, both the background and character colors are
set for each individual character. The character color is kept in color memory,
just as in a normal display. To set the background color, the VIC-II takes two
bits from screen memory:

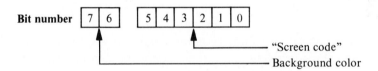

The two bits that control the background color are used to select one of
four locations in the VIC-II chip.

Bit Pair	Location Selected
00	53281 (Background color 0)
01	53282 (Background color 1)
10	53283 (Background color 2)
11	53284 (Background color 3)

"Background color 0" is the color of the background for a normal text
display. These four locations, like color memory, hold a color code from 0
through 15. Bits 4 through 7 are ignored when you POKE them, and you must
AND the value with 15 when you PEEK.

There is a price to be paid for the flexibility of choosing background
colors. With bits 6 and 7 used for the background color, the remaining six bits
only allow 64 different characters. If you want to use reversed characters you
must "trick" the computer into displaying them. Finally, using the extra
colors requires a bit of extra programming. However, the result can be a
program that is much easier to use.

TURNING ON EXTENDED COLOR MODE

It will come as no surprise that extended color mode, like so many of the graphics features we've discussed, is controlled by a bit in a location in the VIC-II chip. When bit 6 of location 53265 is turned on, the display is changed to extended color mode. Try executing this statement:

```
POKE 53265,PEEK(53265) OR 64
```

The first thing you'll see is that the cursor, instead of changing from dark blue to light blue (normal space to reversed space), changes from dark blue to red. Remember that the C-64 turns bit 7 off and on to flash the cursor. On a standard display, this changes the character from normal to reversed. On an extended color display, changing bit 7 changes the location from which the color is taken. When the C-64 is reset, the four background color locations are initialized to dark blue, white, red, and cyan. A "reversed" space (screen code 160) becomes a red space in extended color mode, because bits 7 and 6 contain the values 1 and 0 respectively, taking the background color from location 53283.

For a clear picture of the effects of extended color mode, type in and RUN this program:

```
100 REM TEST EXTD COLOR MODE CONVERTER
110 PRINT"⌂"
120 REM FILL SCREEN
130 SB=256*PEEK(648)
140 FOR I=0 TO 255 : POKE SB+I,I : NEXT
150 REM FILL COLOR MEMORY
160 FOR I=0 TO 255 : POKE 55296+I,1 : NEXT
170 REM SET UP COLORS
180 POKE 53282,4
190 POKE 53283,5
200 POKE 53284,9
210 REM SWITCH EXTENDED COLOR ON AND OFF
220 POKE 53265,PEEK(53265) OR 64
230 FOR I=1 TO 800 : NEXT
240 POKE 53265,PEEK(53265) AND 191
250 FOR I=1 TO 800 : NEXT
260 GOTO 220
```

The program fills the first 256 bytes of screen memory with all 255 possible screen codes, then turns extended color mode on and off. With extended color mode off, the screen contains all 128 uppercase and graphics characters, followed by their reversed counterparts. When extended color mode is turned on, the screen becomes 4 groups of 64 characters each, with each group having a different background color.

The 64 characters appearing on the screen are those with screen codes 0 through 63: the letters, numbers, and punctuation. These are the only characters you can use in messages that are displayed in extended color mode (Appendix E contains a chart of the screen codes for all characters). The six lower bits of a byte can only hold numbers in the range of 0 through 63. If you POKE a larger number into screen memory, it will spill over into bits 6 and 7, and change the background color.

CREATING EXTENDED COLOR DISPLAYS WITH POKE

Screen POKEing in extended color mode works just as it does with the built-in or custom character set. The only difference is that you must add the appropriate color value in bits 6 and 7. Earlier in this chapter, we showed you a sample subroutine to convert CHR$ codes to screen codes. Here is a modified version of that subroutine that does the conversion, then adds the appropriate color code bits. Like the earlier routine, it takes a character in variable KV$, and returns the screen code in SC. For this subroutine, a new variable is needed. This variable, BC, contains the background color (0 through 3) for the character.

```
12000 REM TRANSLATE CHARACTER FOR EXTENDED COLORS
12010 SC=ASC(KV$)
12020 REM BLANK OUT ILLEGAL CHARACTERS
12030 IF (SC<32) OR (SC>95) THEN SC=32+64*BC : RETURN
12040 IF SC>63 THEN SC=SC-64+64*BC : RETURN
12050 SC=SC+64*BC : RETURN
```

This subroutine is much shorter, because only two groups of 32 characters need to be translated. The others are all changed to blanks.

USING PRINT WITH EXTENDED COLORS

At first glance, it might appear that you can't easily PRINT characters with different background colors. Since there are no BASIC commands to handle extended color mode directly, adding the color control bits to characters could quickly turn simple messages into long unreadable strings of CHR$ calls. However, with a bit of the trickery mentioned earlier, you can use PRINT to display extended color messages, and still be able to read your program.

The key to controlling the background color is to control the values of bits 6 and 7 in screen memory. Controlling bit 7 is easy: PRINTing the reverse on and reverse off control characters will force bit 7 to a one or a zero for the following characters. The hard part is bit 6; if we directly PRINTed the 64 characters we can use in extended color mode, bit 6 would always be a 0. This would only give us the use of the usual background color, plus background color 2 (for reversed characters). This may be enough for some programs. If it is, you won't need the trick we are about to describe. But if you want more flexibility, read on.

The trick to using background colors 1 and 3 is somehow to force bit 6 to a value of 1 for the characters to be displayed in those colors. To do this, we'll use a "translation" technique similar to the one we described for converting characters to screen codes. This translation will be necessary in many different parts of the program (wherever we want to PRINT a message), so we've written it as a subroutine:

```
12000 REM TRANSLATE STRING FOR EXTENDED COLORS
12010 REM SET REVERSE IF BC = 2 OR 3
12020 PS$="■" : IF BC >= 2 THEN PS$="▨"
12030 FOR CP=1 TO LEN(MS$)
12040 PC=ASC(MID$(MS$,CP,1))
12050 REM CONVERTS 1 CHARACTER
12060 REM CHECK FOR CONTROL CHARACTERS
12070 IF (PC AND 127) < 32 THEN PS$=PS$+CHR$(PC) : RETURN
12080 REM BLANK OUT ILLEGAL CHARACTERS
12090 IF PC > 95 THEN PC = 32
12100 IF BC=0 OR BC=2 THEN 12150 : REM NO MORE WORK NEEDED
12110 REM FORCE BIT 6 ON FOR BC=1 OR 3
12120 IF PC>63 THEN PC=PC+32
12130 IF PC<64 THEN PC=PC+128
12140 REM ALL DONE. ADD BYTE TO OUTPUT STRING
12150 PS$=PS$+CHR$(PC)
12160 NEXT
12170 RETURN
```

The subroutine takes a *message string,* MS$, and the background color, BC, and uses them to build a *print string*, PS$. The message string is the text of the message you want to print, in simple readable characters. The print string is a string of characters that have been translated, so that the statement

```
400 PRINT PS$
```

will print your message on the right background color. As mentioned earlier, this is somewhat tricky code, so let's go over it in detail.

Bit 7 in screen memory is controlled by reverse on and reverse off characters. Line 12020 starts the print string with a reverse off if the background color is 0 or 1 (bit 7 off), or a reverse on for background colors 2 and 3 (bit 7 on).

Lines 12030 and 12160 form a FOR-NEXT loop that steps the index variable CP through the message string, one character at a time. The lines between them convert one character from the message string, and add it to the print string.

Because BASIC's Boolean and arithmetic operators only work on numbers, line 12040 converts the character being translated to a number with the ASC function.

Line 12070 checks the character to see if it is one of the "control characters" (RETURN, color controls, etc.). Control characters all have values in the ranges of 0 through 31, and 128 through 159. By ANDing the value of the character with 127, we need only do one comparison to find all the control characters. If we do find a control character, we bypass the rest of the translation, and pass it through unchanged.

The characters we can display have ASCII values in the range of 32 through 95. We have screened out those less than 32 with the check for control characters, so line 12090 changes all the ones above that range to spaces.

If the background color is 0 or 2, we're ready: bit 7 will be taken care of by the reverse code we set in line 12020, and bit 6 has been forced to zero. Therefore, line 12100 skips over the rest of the translation for these colors.

Now comes the difficult part. For background colors 1 and 3, we need to make sure that bit 6 is on in screen memory. To do that, we have to change the ASCII code for the character to one that will give us the right value for bit 6. To figure out how to do the translation, we consulted the ASCII and screen code tables in Appendix E and came up with this table:

MS$ code	Screen code needed	PS$ code	Operation
32-63	96-127	160-191	+ 128
64-95	64-95	96-127	+ 32

The first column is the ASCII value of the character in the message string. The second column is the screen code that we need to display that character with bit 6 on. By comparing the screen and character code tables, we found the ASCII values we needed to get those screen codes and the BASIC operation that would translate them. From that information we wrote lines 12120 and 12130.

Now we're almost done. We have in the variable PC the ASCII value that will give us the screen code value we need. Line 12150 finishes the loop by converting PC back to a string value, and concatenating it to the print string. When that's done, we repeat the loop until MS$ is completely translated, then RETURN.

To see the subroutine in action, type in this program, along with the subroutine, and RUN it.

```
100 REM TEST EXTD COLOR MODE CONVERTER
110 POKE 53265,PEEK(53265) OR 64
120 POKE 53281,14
130 POKE 53282,1
140 POKE 53283,5
150 POKE 53284,7
160 PRINT"♥■"
170 MS$="BLUE TEST MESSAGE"
180 BC=0
190 GOSUB 340
200 PRINT PS$
210 MS$="WHITE TEST MESSAGE"
220 BC=1
230 GOSUB 340
240 PRINT PS$
250 MS$="GREEN TEST MESSAGE"
260 BC=2
270 GOSUB 340
280 PRINT PS$
290 MS$="YELLOW TEST MESSAGE"
300 BC=3
310 GOSUB 340
320 PRINT PS$
330 END
340 REM TRANSLATE STRING FOR EXTENDED COLORS
350 REM SET REVERSE IF BC = 2 OR 3
360 PS$="■" : IF BC >= 2 THEN PS$="▩"
370 FOR CP=1 TO LEN(MS$)
380 PC=ASC(MID$(MS$,CP,1))
390 REM CONVERTS 1 CHARACTER
400 REM CHECK FOR CONTROL CHARACTERS
410 IF (PC AND 127) < 32 THEN PS$=PS$+CHR$(PC) : RETURN
420 REM BLANK OUT ILLEGAL CHARACTERS
430 IF PC > 95 THEN PC = 32
440 IF BC=0 OR BC=2 THEN 490 : REM NO MORE WORK NEEDED
450 REM FORCE BIT 6 ON FOR BC=1 OR 3
```

```
460 IF PC>63 THEN PC=PC+32
470 IF PC<64 THEN PC=PC+128
480 REM ALL DONE. ADD BYTE TO OUTPUT STRING
490 PS$=PS$+CHR$(PC)
500 NEXT
510 RETURN
```

The program sets the background colors in lines 120-150, and displays a message in each color. For each color, the process is the same: assign the message to MS$, set the background color in BC, call the subroutine, and PRINT PS$. We could have put the PRINT statement in the subroutine, but we left it out for extra flexibility. Since the main program does the PRINT, it can use features such as tabbing, or ending the PRINT statement with a semicolon to continue PRINTing on the same line. You can even mix background colors on the same line by adding a semicolon at the end of line 240, and RUNning the program again.

FLASHING THE BACKGROUND TO GET ATTENTION

One way to really draw attention to an important message is to make the background flash off and on. You can see how effective this is just by looking at the cursor. No matter how full the screen is, your eye is immediately drawn to the cursor by its flashing.

You can make complete messages stand out on the screen simply by changing the value in one of the background color locations in the VIC-II chip. To see this effect at work, add the following lines to the sample program from the last section:

```
322 REM FLASH BACKGROUND
323 POKE 53284,14
324 FOR I=1 TO 500 : NEXT
325 POKE 53284,7
326 FOR I=1 TO 500 : NEXT
327 GOTO 323
```

When you RUN the program, it displays the messages as before, but the background of the "yellow test message" appears to be flashing off and on. The key is lines 313-316. They change the value in background color 3 from 7 (yellow) to 14 (blue) and back. When the background is blue, it matches the rest of the screen, and disappears. When the color is changed back to yellow, the background flashes on. Even the most determined test tube washer couldn't miss that, especially if you accompanied it with some of the sound effects you'll learn about in Chapter 7. For the experimenter adjusting equipment, you could change the color from red, to yellow, to green, as the computer's measurements showed him getting closer to the right settings.

All our examples have used the built-in character set, but you can use custom characters, too. However, the limitation of 64 possible characters still applies, so you may run short if your program also copies some of the built-in characters for messages.

Multicolor Mode

Multicolor mode is designed for those applications that need even more color than an extended color display. In high-resolution or extended color mode there are eight dots on each line of a character, but each dot is limited to being either the character color or the background color. Multicolor mode trades some of those dots for more colors. In a multicolor character, there are only four dots per line, but each dot can be one of four colors, instead of just two.

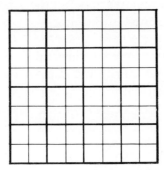

Since a multicolor character is the same size as a high-resolution character, each dot is twice as wide. To get the extra colors of multicolor mode, you must "paint with a broader brush." There are still eight rows in the character, so the height of the dot remains the same.

CHARACTER MEMORY DEFINITIONS OF MULTICOLOR CHARACTERS

The dot patterns of multicolor characters are stored in character memory in the same order as a high-resolution character, but each row (byte) of the pattern looks like this:

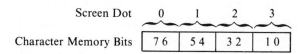

Each dot of a multicolor character is represented by two bits in character memory, rather than one. There are four possible combinations of those two bits (00, 01, 10, and 11), giving four possible colors. The colors selected by those combinations are as follows:

Bit Pair	Color Selected
00	Background color 0
01	Background color 1
10	Background color 2
11	Character color

The pairs of bits select the color of the double-sized dot in the same way that bits 6 and 7 select the background color in extended color mode. Notice, however, that background color 3 is no longer available. Instead, when both bits are on, the dot is displayed in the color stored in the color memory location for that character.

ENABLING MULTICOLOR MODE

Like extended color mode, multicolor mode is enabled by a bit in a location in the VIC-II chip. The controlling bit is bit 4 of location 53270, so the statement

```
100 POKE 53270,PEEK(53270) OR 16
```

will enable multicolor mode, and

```
100 POKE 53270,PEEK(53270) AND 239
```

will return to standard color mode.

MAKING A CHARACTER MULTICOLORED

Enabling multicolor mode does not automatically make the entire screen multicolored. Multicolor mode can be turned on or off for each character.

Whether a character is standard color mode or multicolor mode is controlled by bit 3 in color memory. If that bit is 0, the character is high-resolution. If it has a value of 1, the character is in multicolor mode. This makes it possible to mix multicolor characters with standard or with standard color custom characters. Because that bit has been taken from color memory, only three bits are left for the color code. On a multicolor display, only the first eight colors (black, white, red, cyan, purple, green, blue, and yellow) can be used as character colors.

USING CUSTOM CHARACTER DESIGN TOOLS

Multicolor characters are actually a variation of custom characters, so you'll find the tools for working with them similar. The programs and techniques presented earlier in this chapter, and those you may have developed yourself, will be helpful in multicolor design. However, slight adjustments will be necessary to some of them. For example, to ensure that characters in the test pattern area are in multicolor mode, change the Setup program so it looks like this:

```
100 REM RESERVE MEMORY
110 POKE 52,128 : POKE 56,128 : CLR
120 REM POINT VIC-II AT NEW SCREEN
130 POKE 56576,(PEEK(56576) AND 252) OR 1
140 POKE 53272,32
150 REM POINT BASIC AT NEW SCREEN
160 POKE 648,136
170 PRINT"█▓▒ABCDEFGHIJKLMNOPQRSTUVWXYZ[£]↑←!";
180 PRINT CHR$(34);CHR$(34);CHR$(20);
190 PRINT "#$%&'()*+,-.";
200 PRINT "/0123456789:;<=>?"
210 REM COPY CHARACTER MEMORY ROM TO RAM
220 POKE 56334,PEEK(56334) AND 254
230 POKE 1,PEEK(1) AND 251
240 FOR I=0 TO 2047:POKE 32768+I,PEEK(53248+I) : NEXT
250 POKE 1,PEEK(1) OR 4
260 POKE 56334,PEEK(56334) OR 1
270 REM SET MULTICOLOR MODE
280 POKE 53270,PEEK(53270) OR 16
290 REM MAKE "WORK AREA" CHARACTERS MULTICOLOR
300 FOR I=55296 TO 55359 : POKE I,PEEK(I) OR 8 : NEXT
```

Our character design form needs to be changed, also, to have four double-wide dots per line.

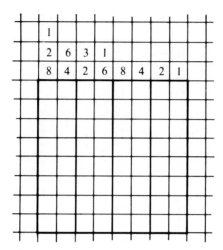

The calculation of the POKE values is not affected by multicolor mode. The columns should be added up just as they are for custom characters. The change in the grouping of the dots is only there to make it easier to visualize the character as it would appear on the screen.

You will probably find it helpful when designing multicolor characters to design the character using two worksheets. Do the first in colored pen or pencil, then translate the colors to their bit values and do the arithmetic on the second. Figure 6-5 displays our old friend, the stick man, in color.

EXPERIMENTING WITH MULTICOLOR CHARACTERS

Before starting to design your own multicolor characters, you will find it helpful to develop a feel for the effects of color. You should start by playing with characters on the screen in multicolor mode.

Load and run the Setup program listed above. As you can see, some of the characters, especially those made up of horizontal and vertical bars (E, F, H, and so on), remain more or less recognizable. The rest are just jumbles of color. As a rule, high-resolution characters must be modified if they are to be used in multicolor mode. By changing the definition of the dots in character memory, multicolor mode tends to turn high-resolution character patterns into gibberish. There are exceptions.Some of the graphic characters, especially the "blocky" ones, will simply change colors in multicolor mode.

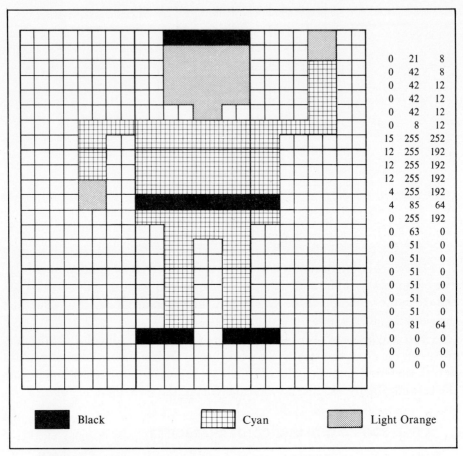

0	21	8
0	42	8
0	42	12
0	42	12
0	42	12
0	8	12
15	255	252
12	255	192
12	255	192
12	255	192
4	255	192
4	85	64
0	255	192
0	63	0
0	51	0
0	51	0
0	51	0
0	51	0
0	51	0
0	81	64
0	0	0
0	0	0
0	0	0

Black   Cyan   Light Orange

FIGURE 6-5. Stick man in color

You can simplify your experimentation by typing the following immediate mode command:

```
POKE 648,9
```

Location 646 contains the value that BASIC puts in color memory for each character it displays on the screen. By changing this value you can put characters into the work area, and BASIC will leave them in multicolor mode. This makes any messages displayed by BASIC multicolor too, but you should have little difficulty recognizing them.

MIXING MULTICOLOR CHARACTERS WITH OTHER MODES

Because multicolor mode is turned on or off for each character on the screen, you can put multicolor characters, custom characters, and normal text on the same screen. For example, try putting the three generations of stick man characters together on a single display.

Multicolor characters give you a great deal of versatility for designing players and playfields, but this is not the end of the multicolor story. As we will see, bit-mapped displays, and even sprites, can be made multicolored.

Multicolored Bit-Mapped Displays

In the section on multicolored character displays, we saw that the formats of screen, character, and color memory were not changed by multicolor mode. Only the way the VIC-II "interpreted" the contents of those memory locations changed.

The same rule applies to multicolored bit map displays: the locations and uses of screen memory and the "bit map" in the "character memory" area are unchanged. The big difference is that the bits in the bit map are used in pairs in multicolor mode.

PUTTING THE DISPLAY IN MULTICOLOR BIT-MAPPED MODE

Setting both the multicolor and bit-map mode bits in the VIC-II chip will give you a multicolored, bit-mapped display. Since these bits are in two separate locations, two POKEs are required.

```
100 POKE 53265,PEEK(53265) OR 32
110 POKE 53270,PEEK(53270) OR 16
```

After executing these two statements, the display will be in multicolor bit-mapped mode. Now let's take a look at what can be done with it.

PROGRAMMING MULTICOLOR BIT-MAPPED DISPLAYS

In our look at bit-mapped displays, we designed a subroutine that would set a bit on the screen based on its "X-Y position": how many dots it was from the top and left edges of the screen. That approach slows down the programs that use it, because it takes time to do the GOSUB and RETURN, but it makes the main program a lot simpler to write and to read.

Using a subroutine for multicolor bit-mapped displays makes sense, too. The calculations are just as complex as for high-resolution bit-mapping and would clutter up the main program. Even though there is a small price to be paid in speed, the benefits in simpler programming are worth it.

Our multicolor subroutine will be very similar to the high-resolution one. It also uses the variables X and Y to point to the dot on the screen. This time, though, the value of X must be between 0 and 159 because the multi-colored screen is only 160 dots wide. We also need a new variable, "DC," to hold the dot color that will be set. Like the "BC" variable that we used for the background color in extended color mode, DC will be a value from 0 to 3, identifying the source of the color code, not the color code itself.

The bit masks for multicolor mode have different values, because we are changing 2 bits at a time. The masks to set a dot to the background color (make both bits 0) are

Dot	0	1	2	3
Bit Pair	7 6	5 4	3 2	1 0
Mask	63	207	243	252

Remember that we are numbering the dots from left to right across the screen, while the bits are numbered from right to left. Since the bits are being set to zero, these masks are used with the AND operator:

```
100 REM SET DOTS TO BACKGROUND COLOR
110 POKE 27450,PEEK(27450) AND 63  : REM DOT 0
120 POKE 27451,PEEK(27451) AND 207 : REM DOT 1
130 POKE 27452,PEEK(27452) AND 243 : REM DOT 2
140 POKE 27453,PEEK(27453) AND 252 : REM DOT 3
```

To set the dots we need 16 different masks (four possible colors for each of the four dots controlled by a byte). These masks are

Dot	0	1	2	3
Background	0	0	0	0
Screen bits 4-7	64	16	4	1
Screen bits 0-3	128	32	8	2
Color memory	192	48	12	3

The following masks are used to set bits to 1, so they work with OR.

```
100 REM SET DOTS TO OTHER COLORS
105 REM DOT 0 FROM SCRREEN MEMORY BITS 4-7
110 POKE 27450,PEEK(27450) AND 63 OR 64
115 REM DOT 1 FROM SCREEN MEMORY BITS 0-3
120 POKE 27451,PEEK(27451) AND 207 OR 32
125 REM DOT 2 FROM COLOR MEMORY
130 POKE 27452,PEEK(27452) AND 243 OR 12
```

THE DOT-SETTING SUBROUTINE

The listing below actually includes two subroutines. The first one, lines 15000-15030, sets the values in the bit-map area. This subroutine is almost identical to the one we used for the high-resolution bit-map. The differences are in calculating the location in the bit-map area (there are four dots per byte instead of eight), and the masking of bits (changing two bits at a time, instead of one).

The second subroutine, lines 16000-16080, sets up the masks. It must be called with a GOSUB 16000 near the beginning of your program. As we have suggested before, this subroutine was put near the end of the program to make the main body easier to read. Line 16040 is a formula that calculates the values of the OR masks. We could have READ them in from DATA statements, but the formula saves memory space and typing.

```
15000 REM MULTICOLOR BIT SETTING SUBROUTINE
15010 PL = BM+(40*(Y AND 248))+(Y AND 7)+2*(X AND 252)
15020 POKE PL,PEEK(PL) AND M0%(X AND 3) OR CM%(X AND 3,DC)
15030 RETURN
16000 REM MULTICOLOR BIT MASK BUILDER
16010 DIM CM%(3,3)
16020 FOR I=0 TO 3
16030 FOR J=0 TO 3
16040 CM%(I,J) = 2↑(2*(3-I))*J
16050 NEXT J
16060 M0%(I) = 255 AND NOT CM%(I,3)
16070 NEXT I
16080 RETURN
```

As an example of how this subroutine works, here's the "triangle program" from the section on bit-mapped displays, modified for a multicolor display:

```
100 REM BIT MAPPED DISPLAY DEMONSTRATION PROGRAM
110 REM PROTECT BIT MAP MEMORY
120 POKE 52,64 : POKE 56,64 : CLR
```

```
130 REM POINT VIC-II AT NEW SCREEN AND BIT MAP MEMORY
140 POKE 56576,(PEEK(56576) AND 252) OR 2
150 POKE 53272,8
160 REM SET VIC-II TO MULTICOLOR BIT-MAPPED MODE
170 POKE 53265,PEEK(53265) OR 32
180 POKE 53270,PEEK(53270) OR 16
190 REM SET POINTER TO BIT MAP AREA
200 BM=24576 : SB=16384
210 REM CLEAR "BIT-MAP" AREA
220 FOR I=BM TO BM+7999 : POKE I,0 : NEXT I
230 REM FILL "SCREEN" MEMORY WITH COLOR CODES
240 FOR I=SB TO SB+999 : POKE I,230 : NEXT I
250 REM BUILD MASK ARRAY
260 GOSUB 16000
270 DC = 1
280 REM DRAW BOTTOM OF TRIANGLE
290 Y=63
300 FOR X=0 TO 63
310 GOSUB 15000
320 NEXT
330 REM DRAW LEFT SIDE OF TRIANGLE
340 FOR X=0 TO 30
350 Y = 63-X*2
360 GOSUB 15000
370 NEXT
380 REM DRAW RIGHT SIDE OF TRIANGLE
390 FOR X=31 TO 62
400 Y = 63-(62-X)*2
410 GOSUB 15000
420 NEXT
430 REM WAIT FOR A KEY TO BE PRESSED
440 GET A$ : IF A$="" THEN 440
450 REM ALL DONE. RESTORE SYSTEM TO NORMAL
460 REM GIVE BIT MAP MEMORY BACK TO BASIC
470 POKE 52,128 : POKE 56,128 : CLR
480 REM POINT VIC-II AT ORIGINAL SCREEN AND CHARACTER
    MEMORY
490 POKE 56576,(PEEK(56576) AND 252) OR 3
500 REM RETURN TO CHARACTER MODE
510 POKE 53265,PEEK(53265) AND 223
520 POKE 53270,PEEK(53270) AND 239
530 POKE 53272,21
540 END
15000 REM MULTICOLOR BIT SETTING SUBROUTINE
15010 PL = BM+(40*(Y AND 248))+(Y AND 7)+2*(X AND 252)
15020 POKE PL,PEEK(PL) AND M0%(X AND 3) OR CM%(X AND 3,
      DC)
15030 RETURN
16000 REM MULTICOLOR BIT MASK BUILDER
16010 DIM CM%(3,3)
```

```
16020 FOR I=0 TO 3
16030 FOR J=0 TO 3
16040 CM%(I,J) = 2↑(2*(3-I))*J
16050 NEXT J
16060 M0%(I) = 255 AND NOT CM%(I,3)
16070 NEXT I
16080 RETURN
```

Compare this program to the high-resolution version. The only change we made to the main body of the program was to assign a value to "DC," the dot color variable! This is a good example of the value of designing and using standard subroutines. Of course, not all programs can be so easily converted from high-resolution to multicolor graphics. We cheated a bit by choosing an example that didn't use all 320 dots of the high-resolution display. Still, the use of standardized subroutines can make new programs easier to write, and existing programs easier to read, maintain, and adapt.

Multicolor Sprites

Multicolor sprites are very similar to multicolor characters, just as standard sprites resemble custom characters. Like multicolor characters and bit maps, the definitions of multicolor sprites are made up of pairs of bits, each calling for one of four colors. The difference between the other multicolor modes and multicolor sprites is where the color codes come from.

Bit Pair	Color Displayed
00	Transparent
01	Location 53285 (in VIC-II Chip)
10	Sprite's color location in VIC-II Chip
11	Location 53286 (in VIC-II Chip)

Locations 53285 and 53286 are used only to hold color codes for multicolor sprites. Like the other color locations, they have only four bits, and must be "masked" when your program PEEKs them.

MAKING A SPRITE MULTICOLOR

Location 53276 identifies which sprites are multicolored. Like most sprite controlling locations, each sprite has a control bit in this byte. When a sprite's bit is a 1, it is displayed in multicolor mode.

Because the sprite's bit in location 53276 determines whether it is multicolor, all four bits of its color location are available, so all 16 color codes can be stored there.

EXPANDED SPRITES

Now that you've spent many hours designing and building your sprite, it's time to learn how to blow it up.

In the case of sprites, "blow up" refers to its photographic, not explosive, meaning (you can, of course, use the animation techniques we described earlier to simulate an explosion).

If you need a larger than normal sprite, you could combine sprites just as you would custom characters. However, there is an easier method. The VIC-II can double the height, width, or both of a sprite with a simple POKE.

Sprite expansion is controlled by locations 53277 and 53271. As with other locations, each sprite is controlled by a bit in these locations. When a sprite's bit in location 53277 is a 1, its width is doubled. Setting its bit in location 53271 to 1 doubles its height.

Doubling the height or width of a sprite is not exactly the same as putting two sprites side by side. Each bit in the sprite definition represents two dots when the sprite is expanded, so there is some loss of resolution. However, expanded sprites are easier to program than multiple combined sprites.

Multicolor sprites can also be expanded. Each bit pair controls an area four dots wide when the width is expanded, or two dots high when the height is doubled.

ADVANCED VIC-II CHIP TOPICS

In this section we will cover some aspects of the VIC-II chip that you will find helpful as you develop more sophisticated programs. If you find some of the information too difficult, just skip over it for now. As you become more familiar with the C-64, this section will become easier to understand.

The VIC-II Chip's Window into Memory

The VIC-II chip and the rest of the computer "see" memory quite differently. The 6502 microprocessor in the C-64 computer can access 65,536 bytes of memory. The VIC-II chip, on the other hand, can access only 16,384 bytes. There is another difference between the two. Most of the computer is based on "normal" bytes of eight bits, but the VIC-II chip uses 12 for screen memory: eight for the character and four for the color. This was done to make the VIC-II chip faster, allowing it to get all the information it needs about a screen character at one time.

To enable the two different chips to communicate through the same memory, the C-64 was designed so the VIC-II chip had a "window" through which it could access only a part of computer memory. This window allows the VIC-II chip to read one of four different "segments" of the C-64's memory, each 16,384 bytes long. The section of memory that the VIC-II uses is selected by two output pins of CIA chip #2. The settings of those pins are controlled by bits 0 and 1 of location 56576. The section of memory selected by the values of these bits are:

Bit Pair	Locations Used
11	0-16383
10	16384-32767
01	32768-49151
00	49152-65535

The other pins associated with location 56576 are used for different purposes, so the values of the other bits must be preserved. To select a section of memory, use one of the statements from the following list:

```
95 REM SELECT 0-16383
100 POKE 56576,PEEK(56576) AND 252 OR 3
105 REM SELECT 16384-32767
110 POKE 56576,PEEK(56576) AND 252 OR 2
115 REM SELECT 32768-49151
120 POKE 56576,PEEK(56576) AND 252 OR 1
125 REM SELECT 49152-65535
130 POKE 56576,PEEK(56576) AND 252
```

THE CHARACTER ROM

If the character ROM chip is at memory location 53248, and the VIC-II can only access 16K of memory at once, how can the VIC-II read the character tables when it is using, for example, locations 0-16383? Through a trick of electronic engineering, Commodore designed the C-64 so that the VIC-II sees the character ROM at locations 4096-8191 and 36864-40959. In fact, the VIC-II doesn't see the character ROM at location 53248! Instead, it sees an area of RAM that is normally invisible to the rest of the computer.

In the two areas where the VIC-II sees the character ROM, it cannot access the RAM. That RAM is available only to the 6502 chip.

When selecting the area of memory you use for storing the screen, the bit map, custom character tables, or sprites, you must keep the fact in mind that the character ROM is only available in certain sections.

WRITING TO THE ROMS

The character table is not the only ROM in the C-64: the built-in software (BASIC and input/output routines for the cassette, screen, etc.) is also stored in ROM chips. These chips occupy locations 40960-49151 and 57344-65535. Plug-in software cartridges, when they are used, occupy locations 32768-40959. The 6502 chip can't read the RAM at these locations, but the VIC-II can.

With certain restrictions, you can use these areas for graphics purposes. When the 6502 reads these locations, it sees the ROM chips, but a write goes to the RAM. As long as you don't need to read back the value stored there, you can use the "hidden" RAM for screens, sprites, or bit maps. A good example would be a bit-mapped background that is set up at the beginning of the program and never changes while the program is running. The bit map could be stored in locations 57344-65343, and the screen and sprites in locations 49152-53247.

To use this technique, you would have to change the bit-setting subroutine used in our examples, because it relies on being able to PEEK the value already in the bit map. Your program would need to calculate the values of all the bits in particular location, then POKE them all at once.

CHANGING THE LOCATION OF SCREEN AND CHARACTER MEMORY

Screen and character memory can be placed anywhere in the VIC-II chip's window. The starting locations are kept in the chip and may be changed with POKE. They are combined into a single location, 53272. Each half of this byte contains a number from 0 to 15, which is the offset in Kbytes (1K = 1024) into the window. The formula to calculate the value to POKE is

$$(\text{character memory location} \ / \ 1024) + $$
$$16 * (\text{screen memory location} \ / \ 1024)$$

Although the character memory location is expressed in units of 1024 bytes, the last bit is ignored. Character memory must begin at offset 0, 2048, 4096, 6144, 8192, 10240, 12288, or 14336 into the window. When you PEEK location 53272, bit 0 will take on unpredictable values. If your program needs to examine the contents of this location, it should mask off the bit by ANDing the value with 254 first.

COLOR MEMORY

The color memory chip has two sets of electronic connections: one that allows the VIC-II chip to read it as the top part of its 12-bit byte, and one that allows the rest of the computer to access it as the lower part of an 8-bit byte. The connections for location numbers also differ. While the rest of the computer perceives color memory only at locations 55296 through 56319, to the VIC-II chip it appears to be everywhere in its window. Byte 0 in the color memory chip, which your program sees as location 55296, is read by the VIC-II chip at locations 0, 1024, 2048, 3072, 4096, and so on up to location 15360 in its window. Byte 1 appears at locations 1, 1025, 2049, etc. Thus, no matter where you move screen memory, the same color memory chip is used.

PRESERVING YOUR MEMORY

In our examples we have shown the POKE statements that keep BASIC from using the memory set aside for custom characters, bit maps, sprites, and so forth. If you write programs that use different areas in memory for custom characters, you will need to understand the rules behind the statements.

Locations 55 and 56 form a pointer to the end of BASIC memory. This is a 16-bit number that is the location of the byte after the last one available for BASIC's use. Locations 51 and 52 are a similar pointer for BASIC's string storage area.

Locations 51 and 55 will normally contain zero after a CLR or a RUN command, and need not be changed. To calculate the POKE value for locations 52 and 56, divide the starting location for your character memory area by 256.

It is essential that the POKEs to limit BASIC's memory be done before any variables are defined in your program, and that they be followed by a CLR. Otherwise, BASIC may not recognize the limits you have attempted to set.

Other software packages may also steal memory from BASIC. It is probable that most of these other packages, from Commodore as well as other manufacturers, will use the 4K of memory from 49152 through 53247, but there will almost certainly be some that do not. If you intend to use custom characters with one of these programs, check its documentation for possible conflicts. In some cases, it may be necessary simply to experiment.

Some programs do not honor the BASIC memory limits. These programs use the value in location 644, which is not checked by BASIC, to determine the last byte of memory in the C-64. This location can be POKEd with the same value used for locations 52 and 56, but some caution is required, because you cannot predict how future cartridges will use this location. If a program that steals memory works without a particular cartridge, but fails when that cartridge is installed, this may be the cause of the problem. If a POKE to location 644 is required, it must be done at the same time as the POKEs to locations 52 and 56, before the CLR.

Saving and Loading Graphics Data

Using DATA statements to store your custom character sets, sprites, and bit maps results in several disadvantages. DATA statements use valuable program space, and BASIC takes a long time to READ and POKE the information into memory. If you are using a Datassette to store your program, it can take two minutes or more to LOAD and run a program that uses a bit-mapped display or custom character set.

A much faster technique is available. Your program can use the same SAVE and LOAD subroutines that are used by BASIC's SAVE and LOAD commands.

Earlier in this chapter, we showed you an example of a program that built the custom character set, then used a LOAD command to bring the main program into memory. This method solves the problem of program space, but not time. It also introduces new problems. You must split your program into 2 parts, and "forget" the variables in the loader program with a CLR before issuing the LOAD.

BASIC programs cannot use the built-in LOAD and SAVE subroutines directly, but machine language programs can. To speed up and shrink those programs that use custom characters and bit-mapped backgrounds, we have written two machine language programs that can be called from BASIC programs to save and retrieve large blocks of data on disk or cassette.

To use these programs, you would build your custom character set, sprites, or bit map, and use the SAVE program to store them on disk. The program that used the data would include the LOAD program as a subroutine.

THE "SAVE" PROGRAM

Before starting to work on your custom character set or display, you should type in and SAVE the SAVE program on tape or disk.

```
100 REM SAVER PROGRAM
110 PS=49152
120 DATA 160,  16,177,253,170,200,177,253
130 DATA 160,   0, 32,186,255,169, 16,166
140 DATA 253,164,254, 32,189,255,160, 18
150 DATA 177,253,133,251,200,177,253,133
160 DATA 252,160, 20,177,253,170,200,177
170 DATA 253,168,169,251, 32,216,255,176
180 DATA   2,169,  0,133,251, 96
190 FOR I=PS TO PS+53 : READ X : POKE I,X : NEXT
200 DCB=50000 : DA=20000 : SIZE=256 : DV=8
210 FI$="LOAD/SAVE TEST   "
220 REM STORE FILE NAME
230 FOR I=1 TO 16 : POKE DCB+I-1,ASC(MID$(FI$,I,1)) :
    NEXT
240 POKE DCB+16,DV  : REM LOAD DEVICE
250 POKE DCB+17,1   : REM IDLE FILE NUMBER
260 POKE DCB+18,DA-256*INT(DA/256) : REM LOW ADDRESS
270 POKE DCB+19,DA/256 : REM HIGH ADDRESS
280 DE=DA+SIZE-1 : REM LAST LOCATION TO SAVE
290 POKE DCB+20,DE-256*INT(DE/256) : REM LOW ADDRESS
300 POKE DCB+21,DE/256 : REM HIGH ADDRESS
310 REM SET UP THE POINTER
320 POKE 253,DCB-256*INT(DCB/256)
330 POKE 254,DCB/256
340 REM TRY THE SAVE
350 SYS PS
360 IF PEEK(251) <>0 THEN 390
370 PRINT "IT WORKED!"
380 END
390 PRINT"ERROR:";PEEK(251)
400 END
```

The SAVE program must be customized before you can use it. There are five variables whose values will depend on the data you are saving. The first four are assigned in line 200:

DCB   is the location of a 22-byte area where values are stored for the machine language subroutine. The example program uses locations 50000-50021. There is no need to change this value, unless you are using this area of memory for other purposes.

DA   is the location of the first byte of data to be saved. This value will probably not match the one you need.

SIZE   is the number of bytes to be saved.

DV   is the device number of the disk or tape drive on which the data will be written. If the data is to be saved to tape, use a value of 1. If you are using a disk drive, use the same number you use with BASIC LOAD and SAVE commands.

The last variable to be changed is FI$. This variable is assigned on line 210 and is the name of the file that will be created by the save. In order to keep the machine language program simple and short, there is a restriction on the file name: it must be exactly 16 characters long. If the name you want to use is shorter, you must add spaces to fill it out to 16 characters. If the name is longer, any characters beyond the 16th are ignored (if you don't want to count characters, just add some extra spaces to make sure that the name is long enough).

The machine language subroutine is stored in locations 49152 through 49205. If you are storing graphics data there, you must move the subroutine. The subroutine is designed so it can be moved anywhere, but the area where it is stored must be protected from BASIC. If you do need to move the program, change the value of the variable PS in line 110 to the memory location where the program is to start.

When the data you want saved is ready, LOAD the SAVE program. Insert the tape or diskette on which the data is to be saved, and RUN the program.

If the built-in SAVE routine indicates an error, the machine language subroutine will store the error code in location 251. Chapter 8 describes these codes (they are the same as those returned in the ST variable). There is one condition that the SAVE program doesn't catch: if you try to replace an existing file on the disk drive, the program will display a message saying that the save worked, but the red light on the disk drive will flash. The original file must be erased, and the program RUN again (see Chapter 8 for a description of how to erase files).

THE "LOAD" PROGRAM

The BASIC portion of the LOAD program is very similar to the SAVE program.

```
100 REM LOADER DEMO PROGRAM
110 PS=49152
120 DATA 160, 16,177,253,170,200,177,253
130 DATA 160,  0, 32,186,255,169, 16,166
```

```
140 DATA 253,164,254, 32,189,255,160, 18
150 DATA 177,253,170,200,177,253,168,169
160 DATA   0, 32,213,255,144,   7,133,251
170 DATA 169,   0,133,252, 96,134,253,133
180 DATA 252, 96
190 FOR I=PS TO PS+49 : READ X : POKE I,X : NEXT
200 DCB=50000 : DA=20000 : DV=8
210 FI$="LOAD/SAVE TEST   "
220 REM STORE FILE NAME
230 FOR I=1 TO 16 : POKE DCB+I-1,ASC(MID$(FI$,I,1)) :
    NEXT
240 POKE DCB+16,DV : REM LOAD DEVICE
250 POKE DCB+17,8 : REM IDLE FILE NUMBER
260 POKE DCB+18,DA-256*INT(DA/256) : REM LOW BYTE
270 POKE DCB+19,DA/256 : REM HIGH BYTE
280 REM SET UP THE POINTER
290 POKE 253,DCB-256*INT(DCB/256)
300 POKE 254,DCB/256
310 REM TRY THE LOAD
320 SYS PS
330 IF PEEK(252) = 0 THEN 360
340 PRINT "IT WORKED!"
350 END
360 PRINT"ERROR:";PEEK(251)
370 END
```

However, it is used differently. The LOAD program is intended to be used as a part of the program that uses the data that is loaded. It can be used as a subroutine, by replacing the END statements with RETURNs, and calling it with a GOSUB.

Like the SAVE program, the LOAD program must be adapted to your use. The DA, DCB, PS, and FI$ variables must be set according to the directions given above. The SIZE variable is not used, because the size is stored with the data when it is saved. Since the LOAD program will be combined with your own, you must make sure that the DATA statements that contain the machine language are properly placed. Remember that the first READ statement gets its information from the first DATA statement. If your program contains READs that are executed before the LOAD program's, their DATA statements must precede the ones containing the machine language subroutine.

If you are using more than one graphics feature in the same program, such as a combination of sprites and custom characters, you will find it convenient to assign the values of DA and FI$ in the main program and call the LOAD subroutine to bring in each block of data. If you call the subroutine more than once, you should skip over the READ statement after the first time, by using a GOSUB to line 200, instead of 100.

THE MACHINE LANGUAGE SUBROUTINES

Listings of the machine language subroutines used by the LOAD and SAVE programs are provided in Figures 6-6 and 6-7. If you are not a machine language programmer, or do not wish to change them, you needn't bother with them. You can use the programs without having to understand the machine code.

```
                        SORCIM 650x Assembler ver  3.2   05/20/83 13:10  Page  1
absolute saver subroutine for C-64 BASIC                    A:C64SAVE .ASM

                        ; This subroutine is designed to allow the BASIC programmer
                        ; to save screen images, sprite defintiions, etc to disk or
                        ;  tape.
                        ;
                        ; When called, it expects a pointer at location $FD to a
                        ; structure of the following form:
                        ;
                        ;  Offset      Contents
                        ;   0    Filename: 16 characters, blank filled.
                        ;        16    Device address
                        ;        17    Logical file number (must not be in use)
                        ;        18    Starting address (in lo-hi format)
                        ;        20    Ending address (in lo-hi format)
                        ;
                        ; On return, location $FB contains the return code from SAVE
                        ;
        = FFD8          SAVE       equ     $FFD8
        = FFBA          SETLFS     equ     $FFBA
        = FFBD          SETNAM     equ     $FFBD
        = OOFD          DCB equ    $FD      ; pointer to ctl block
        = OOFB          START      equ     $FB      ; start of save pointer and
                                                    return code

                        ; set up device address

0000    A010            ldy     #16
0002    B1FD            lda     (dcb),y ; device address
0004    AA              tax             ; stash in x
0005    C8              iny
0006    B1FD            lda     (dcb),y ; logical file number
0008    A000            ldy     #0      ; secondary address of 0 (ignore header)
000A    20BAFF          jsr     setlfs

                        ; set up file name

000D    A910            lda     #16      ; set name length
000F    A6FD            ldx     dcb      ; set name
0011    A4FE            ldy     dcb+1    ;     location
0013    20BDFF          jsr     SETNAM
```

FIGURE 6-6. SAVE subroutine

```
                      ; put starting address into START
0016   A012           ldy     #18      ; point to low byte
0018   B1FD           lda     (dcb),y
001A   85FB           sta     start    ; store it
001C   C8             iny              ; point to high byte
001D   B1FD           lda     (dcb),y
001F   85FC           sta     start+1  ; store it

                      ; set up ending memory address

0021   A014           ldy     #20      ; point to low byte
0023   B1FD           lda     (dcb),y
0025   AA             tax              ; store it in x
0026   C8             iny              ; point to high byte
0027   B1FD           lda     (dcb),y

0029   A8             tay              ; store it in y

002A   A9FD           lda     #dcb     ; point to starting location
002C   20D8FF         jsr     SAVE
```

```
                      SORCIM 650x Assembler ver  3.2   05/20/83 13:10  Page 2
absolute saver subroutine for C-64 BASIC                    A:C64SAVE .ASM

                      ; see if there's an error

002F   B002 ^0033     bcs     error    ; yes
0031   A900           lda     #0       ; no, set code to 0

                      ; done SAVEing. save error code for caller

0033   85FB           error:   sta     start
0035   60             rts              ; and go back

0036           end
```

```
no ERRORs,    6 Labels, 9D7Bh bytes not used. Program LWA = 0036h.
```

FIGURE 6-6. SAVE subroutine (continued)

```
                      SORCIM 650x Assembler ver  3.2   05/20/83 13:10  Page  1
absolute loader subroutine for C-64 BASIC                    A:C64LOAD .ASM

              ; This subroutine is designed to allow the BASIC programmer
              ; to load screen images, sprite defintiions, etc from disk
              ; or tape.
              ;
              ; When called, it expects a pointer at location $FD to a
              ; structure of the following form:
              ;
              ;   Offset       Contents
              ;   0    Filename: 16 characters, blank filled.
              ;        16   Device address
```

FIGURE 6-7. LOAD subroutine

```
                         ;    17    Logical file number (must not be in use)
                         ;    18    Starting address (in lo-hi format)
                         ;
                         ; On return, location $FB contains either the last byte
                         ; loaded, or the return code from LOAD
                         ;
        = FFD5    LOAD        equ     $FFD5
        = FFBA    SETLFS      equ     $FFBA
        = FFBD    SETNAM      equ     $FFBD
        = 00FD    DCB equ     $FD         ; pointer to ctl block
        = 00FB    ENDLD       equ     $FB     ; return code/ending address

                         ; set up device address

0000  A010       ldy         #16
0002  B1FD       lda         (dcb),y ; device address
0004  AA         tax                 ; stash in x
0005  C8         iny
0006  B1FD       lda         (dcb),y ; logical file number
0008  A000       ldy         #0      ; secondary address of 0 (ignore header)
000A  20BAFF     jsr         setlfs

                         ; set up file name

000D  A910       lda         #16     ; set name length
000F  A6FD       ldx         dcb     ; set name
0011  A4FE       ldy         dcb+1   ;      location
0013  20BDFF     jsr         SETNAM

                         ; set up memory address

0016  A012       ldy         #18     ; point to low byte
0018  B1FD       lda         (dcb),y
001A  AA         tax                 ; store it in x
001B  C8         iny                 ; point to high byte
001C  B1FD       lda         (dcb),y
001E  A8         tay                 ; store it in y
001F  A900       lda         #0      ; indicate LOAD
0021  20D5FF     jsr         LOAD

                         ; see if all went well

0024  9007 ^002D  bcc        ok      ; yes

                         ; error LOADing. save error code for caller

0026  85FB       sta         endld
0028  A900       lda         #0      ; set high byte to 0
002A  85FC       sta         endld+1 ;    to show it's an error code.
002C  60         rts                 ; and go back
                         SORCIM 650x Assembler ver  3.2   05/20/83 13:10  Page 2
absolute loader subroutine for C-64 BASIC               A:C64LOAD .ASM

                         ; all is ok, so give back memory address

002D  86FB       ok: stx     endld   ; low byte
002F  84FC       sty         endld+1 ; high byte
0031  60         rts                 ; back to caller

0032             end

no ERRORs,    6 Labels, 9D7Bh bytes not used. Program LWA = 0032h.
```

FIGURE 6-7. LOAD subroutine (continued)

TV Set Limitations

Televisions are designed for moving images of people, places, and things, not for computer displays. Although the C-64 supplies the same electronic signals as your local TV station, the *contents* of the screen are different, and this can cause problems when you are designing displays.

Your TV picture is not nearly as sharp as it appears. Your favorite star may look great from across the room, but from inches away, he or she is just a mass of dots. You've probably seen this same effect, looking at a newspaper photograph through a magnifying glass. Your eyes (and imagination) unconciously fill in and smooth out the picture. Another factor is that the TV picture changes 30 times per second; before you've had a chance to notice the flaws in the picture, they're gone.

When using your TV with the computer, you will almost certainly be much closer than normal "watching" distance. This will emphasize the picture's lack of solidity. Computer displays usually don't change as fast as the 8 o'clock movie, so there's more time to notice how ragged the edges are.

However, there's another factor that is much more important; television picture dots don't usually stand alone. It's very rare for a television picture to contain a line only one dot wide. A dot on the screen is almost always part of a larger object. You'll also notice that there aren't many abrupt contrasts of color. The TV set cannot handle this well.

Computer displays are very different. It's quite common to draw very narrow lines, with pure, contrasting colors side by side. Unfortunately, the TV set cannot handle this well.

The electronics needed to be able to precisely display two dots of any color side by side without distortion is very complex and expensive. Color terminals that can do this typically cost $8000 to $10,000 or more. On the other hand, equipment to do an adequate job for ordinary television watching can be built for a small fraction of that cost. In designing your displays, you must keep in mind the things that TV sets can't do well.

AVOIDING THE TV SET'S WEAKNESSES

There are two things you can do to ensure that your computer displays are pleasing: choose your colors carefully, and avoid vertical lines that are only one dot wide.

Color choices are necessary because the way the TV signal is encoded makes it harder to switch between some colors than between others.

When the square is solid, the switch is easiest. An X means the colors can be used side by side, but the picture won't be quite as sharp. If a square is empty, the colors don't go together well: you may see a fringe around an object as the TV set attempts to change colors.

Remember that the electron beam in the TV is sweeping from left to right. If you use "difficult" colors, the fringe will appear to the right of the color change. This also means that you don't have to worry about dots that are on different rows, because the TV starts out fresh at the beginning of each row.

VERTICAL LINE WIDTHS

The problem of narrow vertical lines is really a symptom of color changes. If the colors are incompatible, it is possible that it will take more than one dot to make the change. For example, it takes almost three dots to change from dark blue to dark red. A single red dot on a blue background is almost invisible, and it doesn't look red at all.

As a rule of thumb, when the chart above shows that it is easy to switch from color A to color B *and* from color B to color A, it may be possible to draw lines one dot wide in those colors. Unfortunately, this is not a hard-and-fast rule. TV sets vary greatly, and what works on one may not work on another. Even changing the settings of the TV controls can affect the appearance of the display. Unless you can be certain that your program will always run on the same type of equipment, you should avoid using isolated dots, and lines only one dot wide.

Sound **7**

This chapter will show you how to produce sound with the C-64. You will learn how to create convincing sound effects to enhance your programs.

You will also learn how to control the sound registers, mix tones, and use sound-shaping techniques to produce variations such as tremolo and vibrato.

In addition to showing you how to produce sounds, this chapter also covers saving and playing back your sounds from either the disk drive or the Datassette.

THE SOUND REGISTERS

The SID Chip

Like the video display, the sounds that the C-64 makes are created by a special integrated circuit. This chip is called the "Sound Interface Device," or "SID." The SID contains three separate sound generators, or "voices," that are blended together to form the sound you hear through your TV speaker.

The SID has twenty-five memory locations, called sound registers, that control sound output. These locations control the volume, the tone, and the type of sounds produced. Table 7-1 shows the memory location and function of each of the sound registers.

TABLE 7-1. Sound Register Memory Locations

Memory Location	Sound Register Description
	54272 - 54278 **VOICE #1**
54272	Lower half of tone frequency value
54273	Upper half of tone frequency value
54274	Lower half of pulse-width value
54275	Upper half of pulse-width value
54276	Waveform control register
54277	Attack and Decay control register
54278	Sustain and Release control register
	54279 - 54285 **VOICE #2**
54279	Lower half of tone frequency value
54280	Upper half of tone frequency value
54281	Lower half of pulse-width value
54282	Upper half of pulse-width value
54283	Waveform control register
54284	Attack and Decay control register
54285	Sustain and Release control register
	54286 - 54292 **VOICE #3**
54286	Lower half of tone frequency value
54287	Upper half of tone frequency value
54288	Lower half of pulse-width value
54289	Upper half of pulse-width value
54290	Waveform control register
54291	Attack and Decay control register
54292	Sustain and Release control register
	54293 - 54296 **SOUND FILTERING FUNCTIONS**
54293	Lower half of cutoff filter value
54294	Upper half of cutoff filter value
54295	Resonance and sound filtering values
54296	Mode and volume controls

Memory location 54296 controls the volume of the sounds produced by the C-64. Sixteen different volume levels can be selected. These range from 0 (off) to 15 (loudest). To control the volume, enter any value between 1 and 15. By itself, however, the volume control register produces no sound. You must also set the voice control registers.

Voice Control Registers

Looking at Table 7-1, you'll notice that each of the 3 "voices" has a set of 7 memory locations associated with it. These locations control the type of sound produced by that voice. All 3 sets of voice control registers work the same way, so even though most of our examples use voice #1, you can use the same values POKEing notes into voices 2 and 3.

SETTING UP THE VOICE CONTROL REGISTERS

When the C-64 is turned on, the voice control registers will take on random values. If the registers are not POKEd with the right values, the SID will make unpredictable sounds or no sound at all. To set up the SID chip properly, enter these POKE statements:

```
POKE 54274,0
POKE 54275,8
POKE 54276,65
POKE 54277,0
POKE 54278,240
```

As you read this chapter, you will learn the uses of the various registers and how to determine your own POKE values. The first two we'll examine control the frequency of the sound.

POKEING A TONE

Table 7-2 shows the frequencies the SID can produce, the approximate musical notes achieved, and the values you must POKE into the tone registers to generate the frequencies.

The lowest audible note the SID can produce is a low C (approximately 16 Hz, or 16 cycles per second). Enter the values for this note into the low tone registers

```
POKE 54272,12:POKE 54273,1
```

and turn on the maximum volume.

```
POKE 54296, 15
```

To turn off the sound, you can use any of the following methods:

- POKE 0 into the tone registers
- POKE 0 into the volume register
- Simultaneously press RUN/STOP and RESTORE.

The first method puts a nonexistent tone value into the tone registers.

The second method turns the volume register to the minimum position, which is off.

The third method resets the system and therefore resets all system variables, such as the tone registers, screen and border colors, and so on. It is better to use one of the first two methods, since the third method may do more than you had in mind.

TABLE 7-2. POKE Values, Frequencies and Musical Equivalents

Upper Tone POKE Value	Lower Tone POKE Value	Frequency Produced	Musical Note
OCTAVE ONE			
1	12	16 Hz	C
1	28	17 Hz	C#
1	45	18 Hz	D
1	62	19 Hz	D#
1	81	21 Hz	E
1	101	22 Hz	F
1	123	23 Hz	F#
1	145	24 Hz	G
1	169	25 Hz	G#
1	195	27 Hz	A
1	221	29 Hz	A#
1	250	31 Hz	B
OCTAVE TWO			
2	24	32 Hz	C
2	56	34 Hz	C#
2	90	37 Hz	D
2	125	39 Hz	D#
2	163	41 Hz	E
2	203	44 Hz	F
2	246	46 Hz	F#
3	35	49 Hz	G
3	83	52 Hz	G#

TABLE 7-2. POKE Values, Frequencies, and Musical Equivalents (continued)

Upper Tone POKE Value	Lower Tone POKE Value	Frequency Produced	Musicap Note
3	134	55 Hz	A
3	187	58 Hz	A#
3	244	62 Hz	B
OCTAVE THREE			
4	48	65 Hz	C
4	112	69 Hz	C#
4	180	73 Hz	D
4	251	76 Hz	D#
5	71	82 Hz	E
5	151	87 Hz	F
5	237	92 Hz	F#
6	71	98 Hz	G
6	167	104 Hz	G#
7	12	110 Hz	A
7	119	117 Hz	A#
7	233	123 Hz	B
OCTAVE FOUR			
8	97	131 Hz	C
8	225	139 Hz	C#
9	104	147 Hz	D
9	247	156 Hz	D#
10	143	165 Hz	E
11	47	175 Hz	F
11	218	185 Hz	F#
12	142	196 Hz	G
13	77	208 Hz	G#
14	24	220 Hz	A
14	238	233 Hz	A#
15	210	247 Hz	B
OCTAVE FIVE			
16	195	262 Hz	C
17	194	277 Hz	C#
18	208	294 Hz	D
19	238	311 Hz	D#
21	30	330 Hz	E
22	95	349 Hz	F
23	180	370 Hz	F#
25	29	392 Hz	G
26	155	415 Hz	G#
28	48	440 Hz	A

TABLE 7-2. POKE Values, Frequencies, and Musical Equivalents (continued)

Upper Tone POKE Value	Lower Tone POKE Value	Frequency Produced	Musicap Note
29	221	466 Hz	A#
31	164	494 Hz	B
OCTAVE SIX			
33	134	523 Hz	C
35	132	554 Hz	C#
37	161	587 Hz	D
39	221	622 Hz	D#
42	60	659 Hz	E
44	191	698 Hz	F
47	104	740 Hz	F#
50	58	784 Hz	G
53	55	831 Hz	G#
56	97	880 Hz	A
59	187	932 Hz	A#
63	72	988 Hz	B
OCTAVE SEVEN			
67	12	1046 Hz	C
71	8	1109 Hz	C#
75	66	1175 Hz	D
79	187	1244 Hz	D#
84	121	1319 Hz	E
89	127	1397 Hz	F
94	209	1480 Hz	F#
100	117	1568 Hz	G
106	110	1661 Hz	G#
112	194	1760 Hz	A
119	118	1865 Hz	A#
126	145	1976 Hz	B
OCTAVE EIGHT			
134	24	2093 Hz	C
142	17	2217 Hz	C#
150	132	2349 Hz	D
159	119	2489 Hz	D#
168	242	2637 Hz	E
178	254	2794 Hz	F
189	163	2960 Hz	F#
200	234	3136 Hz	G
212	220	3322 Hz	G#
225	132	3520 Hz	A
238	237	3729 Hz	A#
253	34	3951 Hz	B

THE COMPONENTS OF SOUND

Pure Tones

With the control register values we have been using, the SID produces continuous frequencies ranging from about 1 Hz to 3995.669 Hz. A cycle, in tonal frequencies, refers to a sound that starts at its minimum volume, rises to its maximum volume, and falls again to its minimum volume.

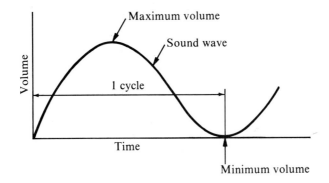

The actual tone of a sound is a direct function of its frequency (how quickly it rises and falls). If you double the frequency, you will have a tone exactly one octave higher than before. Try this program.

```
10 REM: CLEAR SOUND REGISTERS
20 FOR R=54272 TO 54296: POKE R,0: NEXT
30 REM SET UP REGISTER #1
40 POKE 54274, 0: POKE 54275, 8
50 POKE 54278, 240: POKE 54296, 15: T=1
60 POKE 54277, 0: POKE 54276, 65
70 REM: READ FUNCTION KEYS
90 GET A$: IF A$="" THEN 120
100 IF A$=CHR$(133) THEN 160
110 IF A$=CHR$(134) THEN 170
120 IF A$=CHR$(135) THEN 180
130 IF A$=CHR$(136) THEN 200
140 GOTO 90
150 REM: POKE TONES INTO SOUND REG. #1
160 POKE 54272,48:POKE 54273, 4:GOTO 90
170 POKE 54272,97:POKE 54273, 8:GOTO 90
180 POKE 54272,195:POKE 54273,16:GOTO 90
190 REM: TOGGLE VOLUME CONTROL
200 IF T=1 THEN POKE 54296,0:T=-1:GOTO 90
210 POKE 54296, 15: T=1: GOTO 90
```

Line 20 POKEs zero into all the tone registers which clears them. This prevents them from generating random sounds before we enter the sound we want into them. You may have noticed that every time we want to POKE a tone value into a sound register, we must use two values. This is because the C-64 has a range of 65,535 different tones but a single memory location can only hold 256 different numbers (255 if you delete 0 which produces no sound). So to produce the full range of 65,535 different sounds, the C-64 uses two memory locations for each tone value. The numbers in those two locations combine to make a number that is between 0 and 65,535.

The number produced by these two memory locations is represented as a 16-bit binary number, but you don't have to understand binary numbers to use the sound registers; just use Table 7-2 to find the note you want and POKE the indicated values into the sound registers.

Lines 40—60 set up the sound register for continuous tones just as we did earlier.

Lines 90—130 read the function keys and branch to the routines that play the note "C" in one of three different octaves (in lines 160—180).

If you press F7 then you will branch to line 200 which turns the sound ON or OFF. The program then branches back to line 90 and waits for you to press another key.

SWEEPING THE SCALES

You can change the value in a tone register while it is on. This will switch immediately from one note to another. This is especially useful for sliding from one note to the next. Try the following example.

```
10 FOR R=54272 TO 54296: POKE R,0: NEXT
20 POKE 54272, 0: POKE 54273, 0
30 POKE 54274, 0: POKE 54275, 8
40 POKE 54278, 240: POKE 54296, 15
50 POKE 54277, 0: POKE 54276, 65
60 FOR F=0 TO 65535 STEP 256
70 H=INT(F/256): L=INT(F-(256*H))
80 POKE 54272, L: POKE 54273, H
90 NEXT
100 FOR R=54272 TO 54296:POKE R,0: NEXT
```

This program sweeps the entire range of tones in the C-64 in increments of 256. You can make the steps smaller or larger by changing the STEP number in line 50.

Line 60 contains the routine for converting decimal numbers between 65535 and 0 into the correct POKE values for the tone registers. You can use this routine to create any tone you want.

MULTIPLE TONES

By sounding two or more tones at once, you can add depth to many of your sound effects. Adding these lines to the sample program will play two tones at once.

```
25 POKE 54281, 0: POKE 54282, 8
35 POKE 54285, 240
45 POKE 54284, 0: POKE 54283, 65
75 POKE 54279, L: POKE 54280, H
```

You can also harmonize. Type **NEW** and enter the following program:

```
10 REM --- CLEAR SOUND REGISTERS ---
20 FOR R=54272 TO 54296: POKE R,0: NEXT
30.REM --- SET - UP TONE REGISTERS ---
40 POKE 54274, 0: POKE 54275, 8
50 POKE 54281, 0: POKE 54282, 8
60 POKE 54288, 0: POKE 54289, 8
70 POKE 54278, 240: POKE 54296, 15
80 POKE 54285, 240 :POKE 54292, 240
90 POKE 54276, 65: POKE 54283, 65: POKE 54290, 65
100 REM --- TURN ON TONES ---
110 POKE 54273, 16: POKE 54272, 195
120 FOR G=0 TO 500: NEXT
130 POKE 54280, 21: POKE 54279, 30
140 FOR G=0 TO 500: NEXT
150 POKE 54287, 25: POKE 54286, 29
160 FOR G=0 TO 500: NEXT
170 FOR G=0 TO 1500: NEXT
180 REM --- TURN OFF TONE REGISTERS ---
190 FOR R=54272 TO 54296: POKE R,0: NEXT
```

With careful planning, you can make listeners think they are hearing more than three sound registers. Try adding these lines.

```
162 POKE 54273, 33: POKE 54272, 134
165 FOR G=0 TO 500 : NEXT
```

PULSED TONES

Another method of modifying the sound registers involves quickly turning them on and off. This method, called pulsing, can create the effect of a buzzer.

To get a better idea of how pulsing works, look at Figure 7-1 in relation to the following program:

```
10 FOR R=54272 TO 54296: POKE R,0:NEXT
20 POKE 54274, 0: POKE 54275, 8
30 POKE 54278, 240: POKE 54296, 15
40 POKE 54277, 0: POKE 54276, 65
50 FOR T=0 TO 15 STEP .3
60 POKE 54272, 0: POKE 54273, 0
70 FOR F=0 TO 400: NEXT
80 POKE 54272, 67: POKE 54273, 12
90 NEXT
100 POKE 54296, 0
```

Lines 10 through 50 set up the sound registers, but there is no sound output until the tone register is turned on. Line 60 starts the loop that determines the number of pulses produced (we've chosen 50). Line 70 starts the sound at 0 (off), as shown in Figure 7-1. Line 80 is the delay loop that determines the off-time for the pulse. Line 90 turns the sound on. Line 100

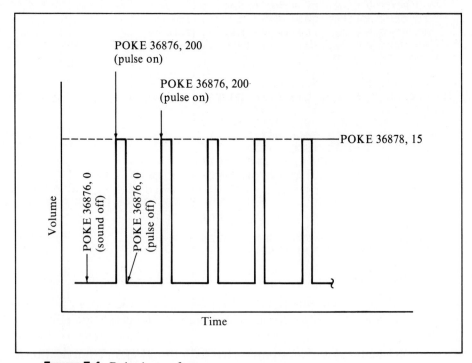

FIGURE 7-1. Pulsed waveforms

completes the loop, sending the program back to line 60. In line 70, the sound is immediately turned off again. After repeating 50 times, the loop ends at line 110 by turning the sound register off.

By increasing the length of the delays between pulses, you can tailor this program to create the sound of a bouncing ping-pong ball. Change line 80 as follows:

```
70 FOR F=0 TO 400: NEXT
```

Volume Adjustments

Up to this point we've been using the volume control as an on/off switch. However, it can also be used to change the nature of the sounds being produced. You can produce a number of effects simply by varying the volume of a tone.

FADING TONES

By slowly reducing the volume of the sound, we can make it sound like the ball is bouncing away. First, change line 50 to read as follows:

```
50 FOR T=0 TO 15 STEP.3
```

This still produces 50 steps through the loop, but in this application, T must never exceed 15 (the highest allowable number in the volume register).

Next, POKE the loop value into the volume register by adding the following line:

```
55 POKE 54296, 15-T
```

This causes the volume to decrease with each pass through the loop.

You can also use the loop variable to decrease the length of the delays between pulses as the volume decreases. This produces a sound resembling a dropping ball. Try changing line 70 to

```
70 FOR F=0 TO 400-T*26: NEXT
```

The number 26 was chosen because 400 divided by 15 is approximately 26. This divides the steps of the delay into 50 even increments. Subtracting the loop value from 400 reduces the delay in the increments each time through the loop.

Try changing the tones used in the first ping-pong program to produce the sound of a clock ticking. This can be accomplished by using two different tone values on alternate loops.

ATTACK/SUSTAIN/DECAY

When you play a note on a piano, the sound begins loudly and slowly fades until it finally fades away completely. The start of the sound is called the *attack*. The portion of the sound in which the volume is maintained is called *sustain,* and the last part of the sound, in which it fades, is called *decay*.

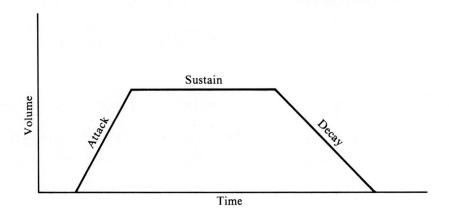

All of the sounds we've produced so far have had a very fast attack and a very fast decay. When these parameters are changed, the sounds become quite different. Here is the original bouncing ball program again.

```
10 FOR R=54272 TO 54296: POKE R,0:NEXT
20 POKE 54274, 0: POKE 54275, 8
30 POKE 54278, 240: POKE 54296, 15
40 POKE 54277, 0: POKE 54276, 65
50 FOR T=0 TO 15 STEP .3
60 POKE 54272, 0: POKE 54273, 0
70 FOR F=0 TO 400: NEXT
80 POKE 54272, 67: POKE 54273, 12
90 NEXT
100 POKE 54296, 0
```

One way to produce a decay in the sound being produced is by adding a loop that causes the volume to sweep down each time the tone is produced.

```
85 FOR V=0 TO 15: POKE 54296,15-V:NEXT
```

If we also add some lines to provide attack, the program looks like this.

```
5 INPUT "ATTACK"; A
7 INPUT "DECAY"; D
10 FOR R=54272 TO 54296: POKE R,0:NEXT
20 POKE 54274, 0: POKE 54275, 8
30 POKE 54278, 240: POKE 54296, 15
40 POKE 54277, 0: POKE 54276, 65
50 FOR T=0 TO 15 STEP .3
60 POKE 54272, 0: POKE 54273, 0
70 FOR F=0 TO 400: NEXT
80 POKE 54272, 67: POKE 54273, 12
85 FOR V=0 TO 15 STEP A: POKE 54296, V:NEXT
87 FOR V=0 TO 15 STEP D: POKE 54296, 15-V:NEXT
90 NEXT
100 POKE 54296, 0
```

Listen to the differences introduced by different attack/decay ratios. You can enter any positive number, including fractions, in the input statement. If you enter 0 for either the attack or decay, however, the note will never end.

Sustain can be added by including a delay between the attack and the decay as follows:

```
9 INPUT "SUSTAIN"; S
86 FOR SS=1 TO S: NEXT
```

DECAYS USING THE BUILT-IN FUNCTIONS

The only real disadvantage of producing attacks and decays this way is that any of the effects that you produce will affect all of the tone registers. Depending on the sounds you want to produce, this may cause problems.

The C-64 has another way to change the attack, decay and sustain of a tone. The key to these features is in the sound registers we looked at in Table 7-1.

Figure 7-2 shows the attack and decay control registers for sound register #1. They are located in memory location 54277.

By POKEing values between 0 and 15 into the lower four bits of this memory location (the decay register), we can create decays of different lengths.

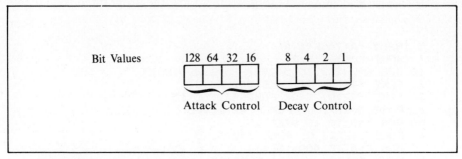

FIGURE 7-2. Memory location 54277: attack/decay control

```
 5 INPUT "DECAY"; D
10 FOR R=54272 TO 54296: POKE R,0:NEXT
20 POKE 54274, 0: POKE 54275, 8
30 POKE 54278, 0: POKE 54296, 15
40 POKE 54277, D
50 FOR T=1 TO 1
60 POKE 54272, 67: POKE 54273, 12: POKE 54276, 65
70 FOR F=0TO 1000 :NEXT:POKE54273,0: POKE54272,0:
   POKE 54276, 64
80 NEXT
90 POKE 54296, 0
```

Notice what happens as you use different decay values. The smaller values (shorter decays) drop to a very low sound level much sooner than the length of the note (which is determined by the loop in line 85). On the other hand, the longer delays drop so slowly that they are still fairly loud when the note stops. You'll need to be aware of the amount of decay you are introducing whenever you use this function and make the note last as long as your decay requires.

ATTACKS USING THE BUILT-IN FUNCTIONS

Producing attacks using the built-in attack function is nearly identical to producing decays. The only real difference is that we need to place the attack values into the upper portion of memory location 54277. The simplest way to do this is to multiply the attack value by 16 and POKE that value into memory location 54277. Try changing lines 5 and 40 as follows:

```
 5 INPUT "ATTACK"; A
40 POKE 54277, A*16
```

SUSTAIN

When you run this program you will find another interesting feature of the built-in sound functions. The shorter attack functions cause the sound volume to rise abruptly and then fall just as abruptly, maintaining a very low volume level until the end of the note. This is because the sound register turns the volume down at the end of the attack function. To make it continue after the attack, you will need to include a sustain value as well. This will keep the tone at its peak value until the sound times out. This can be accomplished by POKEing a large value into the upper half of the Sustain/Release register (memory location 54278 if you are using sound register #1) in line 30.

```
30 POKE 54278, 240: POKE 54296, 15
```

Another thing to look at is the longer attack functions. If the time-out value in your delay loop is too short, the sound may turn off before it reaches maximum volume. To compensate for this, you may need to increase the length of the time-out delay if you are using very long attack values.

Sustain can also be accomplished by using standard delay loops. Here is a routine that produces attacks, decays and sustains using only delay loops.

```
10 INPUT "ATTACK"; A
20 INPUT "DECAY"; D
30 INPUT "SUSTAIN"; S
40 FOR R=54272 TO 54296: POKE R,0:NEXT
50 POKE 54274, 0: POKE 54275, 8
60 POKE 54278, 240: POKE 54296, 15
70 POKE 54277, 0: POKE 54276, 65
80 POKE 54272, 0: POKE 54273, 0
100 POKE 54272, 67: POKE 54273, 12
110 FOR V=0 TO 15 STEP A: POKE 54296, V:NEXT
120 FOR L=0 TO S
125 NEXT
130 FOR V=0 TO 15 STEP D: POKE 54296, 15-V:NEXT
140 POKE 54296, 0
```

VIBRATO/TREMOLO

Vibrato and tremolo take place during the sustain portion of the tone. *Vibrato* is a passage in which the volume is raised and lowered quickly to produce a wavering effect. Enter the following lines to produce vibrato:

```
121 FOR V=0 TO S
122 FOR W=0 TO 7:POKE 54296, 15-W: NEXT
123 FOR W=8 TO 15:POKE 54296, W: NEXT
125 NEXT
```

Tremolo is a fast vibrato. If you change lines 122 and 123 to

```
122 FOR W=15 TO 8 STEP -J: POKE 54296, W: NEXT
123 FOR W=8 TO 15 STEP J: POKE 54296, W: NEXT
```

and add an input line to enter the vibrato rate

```
1 INPUT "VIB. RATE"; J
```

you will be able to vary these parameters at the start of each tone. Entering larger numbers will increase the speed of the vibrato, and smaller numbers will slow it down. Do not enter numbers larger than 15; they will have no effect. Entering a 0 will result in an endless loop.

Mixing Tones

Earlier in this chapter we put three harmonizing tones together to create a chord. It is also possible to combine tones to create entirely new sounds. Let's take a look at some of these.

BEAT FREQUENCY

A *beat frequency* is a sound that is produced when two tones that are very close together are played at the same time. Try the following simple experiment:

```
10 FOR R=54272 TO 54296: POKE R,0: NEXT
20 POKE 54275, 8: POKE 54296, 15
25 POKE 54282, 8
30 POKE 54278, 240: POKE 54276, 65
35 POKE 54285, 240: POKE 54283, 65
40 INPUT " STARTING FREQUENCY."; F
50 FF=F/.06097
60 H=INT(FF/256):L=INT((FF/256-H)*256)
70 POKE 54272, L: POKE 54273, H
80 FOR G=F-100 TO F+100
85 FO=G/.06097
87 HO=INT(FO/256):LO=INT((FO/256-HO)*256)
88 POKE 54279, LO: POKE 54280, HO: NEXT
90 FOR R=54272 TO 54296: POKE R,0: NEXT
```

This will allow you to hear the effects of different notes (frequencies) on each other. Listen for the "beat" that occurs at certain frequencies. This is caused by the interaction of the two tones.

Selecting Waveforms

Up to this point, we've been making sounds using only one waveform—square waves. In addition to these, the C-64 can produce three other kinds of sounds. These sounds are produced by the different kinds of waveforms produced. They are: triangle, sawtooth and white noise.

Looking at the shapes of the waveforms, it is easy to see how they affect the sound. For example, the square waves we have been using up to this point rise sharply, stay at that high level for exactly half of their period and then fall sharply, staying low for the other half.

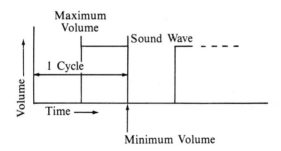

These kinds of square waves are called symmetrical square waves because they are at their high level for exactly as long as they are at their low level. We can modify this symmetry by changing the pulse-width registers. For sound register #1, these are memory locations 54274 and 54275. Here is a routine that sounds a single tone while sweeping the pulse width from one end of its range to the other in increments of 16.

```
10 FOR R=54272 TO 54296: POKE R,0: NEXT
20 POKE 54272, 15: POKE 54273, 10
30 POKE 54296, 15: POKE 54278, 240
40 POKE 54276, 65
50 FOR R=0 TO 4095 STEP 16
60 H=INT(R/256):L=R-256*H
70 POKE 54274, L: POKE 54275, H: NEXT
80 FOR G=F-100 TO F+100
90 FOR R=54272 TO 54296: POKE R,0: NEXT
```

When you run this program, the sound begins as a buzzy, tinny sound. As the pulse width becomes more symmetrical, the sound becomes fuller. Finally, at the upper end of the pulse-width sweep, the sound becomes buzzy again.

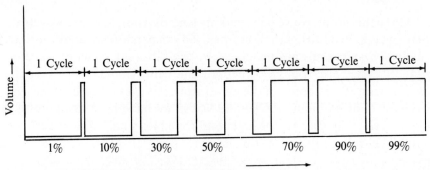

Pulse width ratio (per 100%) sweep up

The triangle, sawtooth and noise registers are not affected by the pulse width. To turn on the triangle waveform, change line 40 to POKE the waveform control register (54276) with 17 instead of 65.

```
40 POKE 54276, 17
```

For a sawtooth, POKE 54276 with 33 instead of 17.

```
40 POKE 54276, 33
```

To turn on the noise register, use 129 instead of 33.

```
40 POKE 54276, 129
```

USING THE NOISE REGISTER

The noise register operates exactly like the tone registers. Here's a bouncing ball program, this time using the noise register.

```
10 FOR R=54272 TO 54296: POKE R,0:NEXT
20 POKE 54274, 0: POKE 54275, 8
30 POKE 54278, 240: POKE 54277, 0
40 POKE 54296, 15
50 POKE 54272, 67: POKE 54273, 12
60 FOR T=0 TO 15
70 POKE 54276, 128
80 FOR F=0 TO 400: NEXT
```

```
90 POKE 54276, 129
100 NEXT
110 FOR R=54272 TO 54296: POKE R,0:NEXT
```

Now let's add some decay to the sound.

```
30 POKE 54278, 0: POKE 54277, 9
95 FOR N=0TO500: NEXT
```

By also modifying the repeat rate, we can create a sound similar to a train as follows:

```
80 FOR F=0 TO 400-26*T: NEXT
```

By mixing sound we can also add a train whistle. Add the following lines to your program:

```
11 POKE 54285, 0: POKE 54284, 13
12 POKE 54280, 16: POKE 54279, 195
110 FOR T=0 TO 150
120 POKE 54276, 128
125 IF T=30 OR T=35 OR T=70 OR T=75 THEN 180
130 POKE 54276, 129
140 POKE 54296, 15-T/10
150 FOR N=0TO500-T*3: NEXT
160 NEXT
170 GOTO 200
180 POKE 54283, 32: POKE 54283, 33
190 GOTO 130
200 FOR R=54272 TO 54296: POKE R,0:NEXT
```

PROGRAMMING MUSIC ON THE C-64

By POKEing values and delays into the sound registers we can write song programs.

```
5 REM ----- SET UP REGISTERS -----
10 FOR R=54272 TO 54296: POKE R,0:NEXT
20 POKE 54278, 240: POKE 54277, 0
30 POKE 54296, 15
35 REM ----- START PLAYING MUSIC -----
40 POKE 54272, 134: POKE 54273, 33
50 POKE 54276, 17
60 FOR R=0 TO 200: NEXT
70 POKE 54276, 16
80 FOR R=0 TO 100: NEXT
90 POKE 54276, 17
```

```
100 FOR R=0 TO 200: NEXT
110 POKE 54276, 16
120 FOR R=0 TO 100: NEXT
130 POKE 54272, 161: POKE 54273, 37
140 POKE 54276, 17
150 FOR R=0 TO 200: NEXT
160 POKE 54276, 16
170 FOR R=0 TO 100: NEXT
180 POKE 54272, 60: POKE 54273, 42
190 POKE 54276, 17
200 FOR R=0 TO 200: NEXT
210 POKE 54276, 16
220 FOR R=0 TO 100: NEXT
230 POKE 54272, 134: POKE 54273, 33
240 POKE 54276, 17
250 FOR R=0 TO 200: NEXT
260 POKE 54276, 16
270 FOR R=0 TO 100: NEXT
280 POKE 54272, 60: POKE 54273, 42
290 POKE 54276, 17
300 FOR R=0 TO 200: NEXT
310 POKE 54276, 16
320 FOR R=0 TO 100: NEXT
330 POKE 54272, 161: POKE 54273, 37
340 POKE 54276, 17
350 FOR R=0 TO 600: NEXT
360 POKE 54276, 16
370 FOR R=0 TO 100: NEXT
380 POKE 54272, 134: POKE 54273, 33
390 POKE 54276, 17
400 FOR R=0 TO 200: NEXT
410 POKE 54276, 16
420 FOR R=0 TO 100: NEXT
430 POKE 54276, 17
440 FOR R=0 TO 200: NEXT
450 POKE 54276, 16
460 FOR R=0 TO 100: NEXT
470 POKE 54272, 161: POKE 54273, 37
480 POKE 54276, 17
490 FOR R=0 TO 200: NEXT
500 POKE 54276, 16
510 FOR R=0 TO 100: NEXT
520 POKE 54272, 60: POKE 54273, 42
530 POKE 54276, 17
540 FOR R=0 TO 200: NEXT
550 POKE 54276, 16
560 FOR R=0 TO 100: NEXT
570 POKE 54272, 134: POKE 54273, 33
580 POKE 54276, 17
590 FOR R=0 TO 600: NEXT
600 POKE 54276, 16
```

```
610 FOR R=0 TO 100: NEXT
620 POKE 54272, 164: POKE 54273, 31
630 POKE 54276, 17
640 FOR R=0 TO 600: NEXT
650 POKE 54276, 16
660 FOR R=0 TO 100: NEXT
670 POKE 54272, 134: POKE 54273, 33
680 POKE 54276, 17
690 FOR R=0 TO 200: NEXT
700 POKE 54276, 16
710 FOR R=0 TO 100: NEXT
720 POKE 54276, 17
730 FOR R=0 TO 200: NEXT
740 POKE 54276, 16
750 FOR R=0 TO 100: NEXT
760 POKE 54272, 161: POKE 54273, 37
770 POKE 54276, 17
780 FOR R=0 TO 200: NEXT
790 POKE 54276, 16
800 FOR R=0 TO 100: NEXT
810 POKE 54272, 60: POKE 54273, 42
820 POKE 54276, 17
830 FOR R=0 TO 200: NEXT
840 POKE 54276, 16
850 FOR R=0 TO 100: NEXT
860 POKE 54272, 191: POKE 54273, 44
870 POKE 54276, 17
880 FOR R=0 TO 200: NEXT
890 POKE 54276, 16
900 FOR R=0 TO 100: NEXT
910 POKE 54272, 60: POKE 54273, 42
920 POKE 54276, 17
930 FOR R=0 TO 200: NEXT
940 POKE 54276, 16
950 FOR R=0 TO 100: NEXT
960 POKE 54272, 161: POKE 54273, 37
970 POKE 54276, 17
980 FOR R=0 TO 200: NEXT
990 POKE 54276, 16
1000 FOR R=0 TO 100: NEXT
1010 POKE 54272, 134: POKE 54273, 33
1020 POKE 54276, 17
1030 FOR R=0 TO 200: NEXT
1040 POKE 54276, 16
1050 FOR R=0 TO 100: NEXT
1060 POKE 54272, 164: POKE 54273, 31
1070 POKE 54276, 17
1080 FOR R=0 TO 200: NEXT
1090 POKE 54276, 16
1100 FOR R=0 TO 100: NEXT
1120 POKE 54272, 29: POKE 54273, 25
```

```
1130 POKE 54276, 17
1140 FOR R=0 TO 200: NEXT
1150 POKE 54276, 16
1160 FOR R=0 TO 100: NEXT
1170 POKE 54272, 48: POKE 54273, 28
1180 POKE 54276, 17
1190 FOR R=0 TO 200: NEXT
1200 POKE 54276, 16
1210 FOR R=0 TO 100: NEXT
1220 POKE 54272,.164: POKE 54273, 31
1230 POKE 54276, 17
1240 FOR R=0 TO 200: NEXT
1250 POKE 54276, 16
1260 FOR R=0 TO 100: NEXT
1270 POKE 54272, 134: POKE 54273, 33
1280 POKE 54276, 17
1290 FOR R=0 TO 600: NEXT
1300 POKE 54276, 16
1310 FOR R=0 TO 100: NEXT
1320 POKE 54276, 17
1330 FOR R=0 TO 600: NEXT
1340 POKE 54276, 16
1350 FOR R=54272 TO 54296: POKE R,0:NEXT
```

This isn't a very long song, but the program is quite long. If you attempted to put all of the notes of a song into a program this way, you would probably run out of memory.

Another way to enter music into a song program is by using DATA statements. A program of this type requires three short sections: a routine that reads the notes, one that plays them, and one that contains the notes as data. Try this version of the song.

```
10 FOR R=54272 TO 54296: POKE R,0: NEXT
20 POKE 54278, 240: POKE 54296, 15
30 DATA 134,33,200,134,33,200,161,37,200,60,42,200,134,33,
   200,60,42,200,161,37
40 DATA 600,134,33,200,134,33,200,161,37,200,60,42,200,
   134,33,600,164,31,600
50 DATA 134,33,200,134,33,200,161,37,200,60,42,200,191,44,
   200,60,42,200,161,37
60 DATA 200,134,33,200,164,31,200,29,25,200,48,28,200,
   164,31,200,134,33,600,134
70 DATA 33,600,999,999,999
80 READ A,B,C
90 IF A=999 THEN 160
100 POKE 54272, A: POKE 54273, B
110 POKE 54276, 17
120 FOR R=0 TO C: NEXT
130 POKE 54276, 16
```

```
140 FOR R=0 T0100: NEXT
150 GOTO 80
160 FOR R=54272 TO 54296: POKE R,0: NEXT
```

By changing the values in the DATA statement, you can play almost any song you like. Enter 999 to signal the end of the song, as shown above.

Programming Rhythm

Programming rhythm on the C-64 is much like programming the train sound we made earlier. Let's start with a simple drum sound.

```
10 FOR R=54272 TO 54296: POKE R,0: NEXT
20 POKE 54277, 6: POKE 54296, 15
30 POKE 54272, 15: POKE 54273, 2
40 DATA 375,150,165,999
50 READ A
60 IF A=999 THEN 100
70 POKE 54276, 129
80 FOR R= 0 TO A: NEXT
90 POKE 54276, 128: GOTO 50
100 RESTORE: GOTO 50
```

By using another tone in the same register we can add a bass drum:

```
10 FOR R=54272 TO 54296: POKE R,0: NEXT
20 POKE 54277, 6: POKE 54296, 15
30 POKE 54272, 15: POKE 54273, 2
40 DATA 33,375,129,150,129,165,999,999
50 READ A,B
60 IF A=999 THEN 100
70 POKE 54276, A
80 FOR R=0 TO B: NEXT
90 POKE 54276, 0: GOTO 50
100 RESTORE: GOTO 50
```

Changing the loop variable will vary the speed of the rhythm.

```
80 FOR R=0 TO B/2: NEXT
```

By adding some additional READ and DATA statements to the rhythm program we can include a melody. Here's the complete listing.

```
10 FOR R=54272 TO 54296: POKR R, 0: NEXT R
20 POKE 54277, 40: POKE 54296, 15
30 POKE 54272, 15: POKE 54273, 3
35 POKE 54285, 240: POKE 54283, 17
40 DATA 16,185,17,375,   18,208,129,150,   18,208,129,
   150,    19,238,17,375
```

```
50 DATA 19,238,129,150,    19,238,129,150,    18,208,17,
   375,      18,208,129,150
60 DATA 18,208,129,150,    16,195,17,375,    16,195,129,
   150,      16,195,129,150
70 DATA 16,195,17,375,    18,208,129,150,    18,208,129,
   150,      19,238,17,375
80 DATA 25,29,129,150,    25,29,129,150,    18,208,17,
   375,      19,238,129,150
90 DATA 19,238,129,150,    16,195,17,375,    16,195,129,
   150,      16,195,129,150
100 DATA 999,999,999,999
160 READ H,L,R,N
170 IF H=999 THEN 230
180 POKE 54279,L: POKE 54280, H
190 POKE 54276, R
200 FOR M=0 TO N: NEXT
210 POKE 54276, 0
220 GOTO 160
230 RESTORE: GOTO 160
```

The most important thing to keep in mind when working with this kind of program is that doing more things within your loops (such as adding more READ statements) adds time to the loop. Test statements, such as the one on line 170, also take some time. Be sure to account for every line. If you are unsure of your timing, run the program and listen for timing problems. By adding to or subtracting from the timing loops, you can usually compensate for timing errors.

The C-64 Electronic Organ

Here's a program that "GETs" notes from the keyboard and plays them. We've used the note values from Table 7-2 and POKEd them into the upper and lower tone registers of sound register #1.

```
10 FOR R=54272 TO 54296: POKE R,0: NEXT
20 POKE 54278, 240
30 GET A$: IF A$="" THEN 30
40 IF A$="Q" THEN U=8:L=97
50 IF A$="2" THEN U=8:L=225
60 IF A$="W" THEN U=9:L=104
70 IF A$="3" THEN U=9:L=247
80 IF A$="E" THEN U=10:L=143
90 IF A$="R" THEN U=11:L=47
100 IF A$="5" THEN U=11:L=218
110 IF A$="T" THEN U=12:L=142
120 IF A$="6" THEN U=13:L=77
```

```
130 IF A$="Y" THEN U=14:L=24
140 IF A$="7" THEN U=14:L=238
150 IF A$="U" THEN U=15:L=210
160 IF A$="I" THEN U=16:L=195
170 POKE 54272,L:POKE 54273,U
180 POKE 54296,15: POKE 54276, 17
190 FOR G=0 TO 500: NEXT
200 POKE 54296,0: POKE 54276, 16
210 GOTO 30
```

This program was written for only one octave. By increasing the number of keys read, you can add more octaves. To make the keys play longer, you can increase the length of the delay loop at line 190 making the fractional STEP smaller.

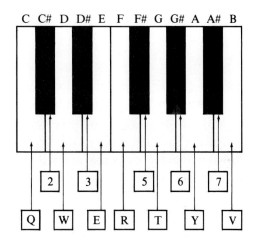

Saving Music

An alternative to writing DATA statements by hand is to use the electronic organ to store your musical values. Let's look at how these can be saved.

CREATING MUSIC ARRAYS

Adding the following lines to your program will allow you to store the notes you play into an array. For the purposes of this program, we'll use an array with 100 notes in it. You can create arrays with more notes in them if you like, but remember, each note is two bytes, and you won't be able to dimension an array that is larger than your available memory space.

```
5 DIM U(100), L(100)
31 IF A$=" {F3} " THEN U(X)=U: L(X)=L: X=X+1: GOTO 30
32 IF A$<>" {F1} " THEN 40
33 FOR Z=0 TO X
34 POKE 54272, L(Z): POKE 54273, U(Z)
35 POKE 54296, 15: POKE 54276, 17
36 FOR G=0 TO 500: NEXT
38 POKE 54296,0: POKE 54276, 16: NEXT
39 GOTO 30
```

Each time you press one of the keys on the keyboard, it will be played. Pressing F1 will play back all of the notes stored in memory. To add a note to the song, press F3 after pressing the note you want.

STORING MUSIC ON THE DATASSETTE OR DISK

When you turn the C-64 off, any music you have stored into an array will be lost. If you want to save your songs and play them back later, you will need to store them on either the disk drive or the Datassette.

Adding the following lines to your program will allow you to store the music data in your array into a data file on either the Datassette or disk drive:

```
45 IF A$=" {F5} "THEN 300
300 INPUT "FILE NAME"; F$
310 INPUT "STORE ON {REVERSE ON}D {REVERSE OFF}ISK OR
    {REVERSE ON} C {REVERSE OFF}ASSETTE";S$
320 IF S$="D" THEN 350
330 IF S$="C" THEN 360
340 PRINT"{CURSOR UP}";:GOTO 310
350 OPEN1,8,4,F$+",W": GOTO 370
360 OPEN1,1,1,F$
370 FOR Z=0 TO X
380 PRINT#1, U(Z): PRINT#1,L(Z): NEXT
390 CLOSE 1: GOTO 30
1000 OPEN15,8,15:INPUT#15,A,B$,C,D: PRINTB$:CLOSE15: END
```

Now, when you press the F5 function key, the program will ask you for a file name and whether you want to save the song on disk or Datassette. It will then store the contents of the song array in the file you've specified.

**READING MUSIC FROM THE
DATASSETTE OR DISK**

To read a song from a music file, you will need to read the information back into an array that can be read by your electronic organ program. The following routine accomplishes this.

```
55 IF A$=" {F7} "THEN 400
400 INPUT "FILE NAME"; F$
410 INPUT "LOAD FROM {REVERSE ON} D {REVERSE OFF} ISK OR
    {REVERSE ON} C{REVERSE OFF} ASSETTE"; S$
420 IF S$="D" THEN 450
430 IF S$="C" THEN 460
440 PRINT" {CURSOR UP}";:GOTO 410
450 OPEN1,8,4,F$+",R": GOTO 470
460 OPEN1,1,0,F$ : J=0
470 INPUT#1, U(J): INPUT#1,L(J):BB=ST:J=J+1
480 IF BB=0 THEN 470
490 X=J:CLOSE 1: GOTO 30
1000 OPEN15,8,15:INPUT#15,A,B$,C,D: PRINTB$:CLOSE15: END
```

Once you have added these lines to the program, you can use the F7 function key to load songs that you have stored. When you press the F7 function key, the program will ask you for a file name, and whether you want to load from disk or Datassette. It will then load the song array from the file you've specified.

COMBINING SOUND WITH
ANIMATION

Most video games use sound very effectively. The sounds can be used to create a mood or to give the player more information about the action that is taking place on the screen.

Timing

When playing a video game, the player is more dependent on the timing of the sound than on the visual portion of the game. Try this bouncing ball program with no sound.

```
5 PRINT"{CLEAR HOME}"
10 A$="                                        "
20 FOR R=0 TO 2: PRINT A$;: NEXT
30 FOR T=1104 TO 1143
40 FOR Y=0 TO 10: NEXT
50 POKE T-1,32: POKE T,81: NEXT
60 FOR T=1143 TO 1104 STEP -1
70 FOR Y=0 TO 10: NEXT
80 POKE T+1,32: POKE T, 81: NEXT
90 GOTO 30
```

Now we will add sound with the following lines:

```
15 FOR I=54272 TO 54296: POKE I,0: NEXT
16 POKE 54272, 12: POKE 54273,36
17 POKE 54296, 15: POKE 54278, 240
55 POKE 54276, 17: POKE 54276, 0
85 POKE 54276, 17: POKE 54276, 0
```

The addition of sound helps create the effect of a bouncing ball.

To synchronize the sound with a visual event on the screen, you will have to be aware of the position of the objects on the screen. In the example above, the timing was straightforward because the sound was created at the end of each loop. To make simple sounds synchronize with movements, the sounds should generally take place when one object collides with another. The following program determines object movement and sound based on the numeric position on the screen:

```
10 FOR I=54272 TO 54296: POKE I,0: NEXT
20 POKE 54272, 12: POKE 54273,36
25 POKE 54279, 12: POKE 54280,100
30 POKE 54296, 15: POKE 54278, 240
35 POKE 54285, 240
40 A$="                                        "
50 PRINT"{CLEAR HOME}";:FOR R=0 TO 5: PRINTA$;: NEXT
60 B1=1104: B2=1144: R1=1: R2=.7
70 POKE B1,81: POKE B1-1,32: POKE B1+1,32
80 POKE B2,81: POKE B2-1,32: POKE B2+1,32
90 B1=B1+R1: B2=B2+R2
100 IF B1=1104 OR B1=1143 THEN R1=R1*-1:POKE 54276,17:
    POKE 54276,0
110 IF B2<1144.5 OR B2>1182.5 THEN R2=R2*-1:POKE 54283,
    17: POKE 54283,0
120 GOTO 70
```

Because different tone values are used, it is immediately apparent which object has just hit the wall.

CHAPTER 8
Peripheral Devices

The C-64 can be connected to many peripheral devices, including the 1525 Printer, the VIC Datassette, and the 1541 Disk Drive. These devices expand the capabilities of the C-64 by giving it the ability to produce permanent copies of its output on either paper or magnetic media such as cassette tape or floppy diskettes. Storing information on magnetic media can also increase the amount of memory space available.

With the addition of a modem, the C-64 can communicate by telephone with any other computer that has a similar device. The modem also allows access to computer networks, which provide services such as stock market updates, computer shopping, and electronic mail.

Storing Data

The most common media for storing data on microcomputers are floppy diskettes and magnetic tape. Diskettes have the advantage of being *random-access* devices. That is, they can directly store or retrieve data at any location on their surface. Tapes store data sequentially (one file after another) and must be manually rewound to access data that have already been passed. What they lack in speed and flexibility, however, tape systems make up in cost. They are much less expensive than disk systems.

FILES

Computer data are stored in *files*. This allows you to locate information you have placed in a certain category. To look up a word beginning with "C" in the dictionary, you would turn to the section with the heading "C." Similarly, to find information on a cassette or diskette, you would instruct the computer to locate a section (file) with a heading (file name) you assigned.

C-64 data files can have names that are much longer than the single-letter headings in the dictionary: file names can be up to 16 characters long. The length of the files is limited only by the space available on the diskette or cassette tape. The number of file names on a 1541 diskette is limited to 144.

There are two kinds of files: program files and data files.

Program Files

Whenever you have a program in the computer memory that you wish to save in order to use it again, you may SAVE it on tape or diskette. To read it back into the computer, you LOAD it into memory. You should give each program a unique name so the computer can differentiate one from the other. When you are using the Datassette to store programs, you don't have to use file names, since the computer can simply be instructed to LOAD the first program it encounters. This is not true of the disk drive. You *must* tell the computer which file you want when you load or save on a disk.

To use a program file, you load and run it, just as if you had entered the program by hand. The advantage is that you do not need to enter the program by hand. In general, the size of a program you store on disk or tape will be limited to the amount of memory available in your computer. This is because a program is normally saved in its entirety. You cannot easily save part of a program and then save the rest of the program later.

One way to handle programs that will not fit into your computer's available memory space is to break them into shorter programs and simply load each section of the program separately and run it. In this fashion, you can execute programs that are much larger than the memory space in your C-64.

If you decide to do this, make sure that the first program section that you load is longer than any of the sections it calls. This is necessary because the program variables will be stored at the end of your program's first section; if a longer routine is loaded into memory, either your variables or part of the new program segment will be lost.

To load the next program segment from within a program, just end your first segment with

LOAD "second program name",8

This will load and run the next segment.

Data Files

Data files do not contain programs, so they cannot be loaded and run. They contain data that must be loaded into memory by a program or entered by you in immediate mode.

RECORDS AND FIELDS

The information in a data file can be broken up into *records* and *fields*. This is determined by the program reading the data from the file. To better understand this concept, consider a data file that contains a passenger's flight information for a trip from New York to San Francisco and back.

XYZ AIRLINES June 7, 1982

John Doe
1234 Home Place
Small Town, New Jersey

FLIGHT #303

LEAVES JFK Int'l   1:45 PM   EST
ARRIVE SFO Int'l   4:28 PM   PST

XYZ AIRLINES June 9, 1982

John Doe
1234 Home Place
Small Town, New Jersey

FLIGHT #215

LEAVES SFO Int'l   9:15 AM   PST
ARRIVE JFK Int'l   4:45 PM   EST

The file contains information for the departure and arrival of the flights John Doe is taking to and from San Francisco. For simplicity, we will say it is a single file that contains two records: the trip to San Francisco and the trip back to New York.

Each record contains several fields. The fields are the groups of characters that form either complete words or numbers. For instance, the word "JUNE" contains four characters (or bytes) that are stored on the tape or diskette as the individual characters J, U, N, and E. Logically, however, the characters should be taken as the whole word: JUNE. Similarly, the numbers 2, 1, and 5 should be taken as the number 215. To distinguish the data within a record, it is important that the fields be separated.

Data Transfer

The first time you access a tape or diskette file, you may be misled into thinking that the system is not operating correctly. It would seem logical that the disk drive or Datassette would operate each time the program reads or writes from it. This will occasionally be the case, but not always. This is because the C-64 has a small section of memory allocated as a data buffer. Each time information is read from the disk or Datassette, the buffer is filled. Until those data are exhausted, the drive or Datassette will not be accessed again. Similarly, when you write to the disk or Datassette, data are first stored in a buffer. When the buffer is full, all the data it contains will be stored at once.

Logical Files and Physical Units

Input/output programming describes any programming that controls the transfer of data between the computer and a peripheral device such as the Datassette, disk drive, or printer. These are all external physical units. In order to transfer data to or from one of these physical units, it is necessary to indicate which one you are accessing. This is because each unit has a specific kind of interface and a particular way in which it must receive its input (the computer's output). In addition, if more than one device is connected to the computer, you will need to indicate which device you are "talking to."

The computer can also receive data from the Datassette and disk drive, and the data it receives must be put somewhere. Look at the problem in programming terms. If you want to input data from the keyboard, you would use a BASIC statement such as

```
10 INPUT A
```

This line stops program execution and waits for you to enter some data from the keyboard and press RETURN. The data are assigned to the variable A. Unless the C-64 is told otherwise, all input statements such as the one above look for data coming from the keyboard.

If you want to output some data to the video screen, you might use the following statement:

```
20 PRINT A
```

The value of variable A will appear on the screen.

The INPUT statement tells the computer it is to receive some data, and the PRINT statement instructs the computer to output some data. Although data are usually sent from the keyboard and received by the video screen, these are not the only devices available.

To "talk" or "listen" to another device, you will first need to open a *logical channel* to that device. This is accomplished using the OPEN statement. With this statement, you designate what channel you are using and what device number you are addressing. Every physical unit (peripheral device) has a unique device number. The channel you open is called the file and the number you assign to it is its file number. The format for an OPEN statement is as follows:

10 OPEN *fn, dn, sa, filename*

where:

fn	The file number is the number you use to access the file. You may choose any number between 0 and 255
dn	The device number is the number of the peripheral device you are addressing
sa	The secondary address sets up certain parameters for the device being used
filename	The file name is used to specify the file during a read operation. If you specify a file name when you write the file and when you read it on the Datassette, all files will be skipped until the one you specified is found.

Table 8-1 shows the device numbers and secondary addresses that correspond to the C-64's logical devices.

TABLE 8-1. Device Numbers and Secondary Addresses

Device	Device Number	Secondary Address	Operation Performed
Keyboard	0	None	
Cassette Drive #	1	0 1	Open for read Open for write
	2	2	Open for write, but add End-of-Table mark (EOT) on close
Video Display	3	None	
Line Printer Models 1515 or 1525	4 or 5	7	Alternate character set
Disk Drives (all models)	8*	0 1 2-14 15	Load a program file to the computer Save a program file from the computer Unassigned Open command/status channel
Other devices connected to IEEE 488 Bus	5,6,7 and 9 through 31		Device numbers and secondary addresses are selected and assigned by the manufacturer of the device connecting to the IEEE 488 Bus.
	12 to 255 unavailable at this time		

*Normally 8, but may be set to 9, 10, or 11 (see the section on multiple disk systems).

Datassette Files

Now that you have had a chance to look at files in a general way, you can apply them to reading from and writing to the Datassette. The VIC Datassette is the default external storage device. That means that if you don't specify which device you are writing to, the information will go to the Datassette.

For example, to save a program called FILENAME on the Datassette, you would type

```
SAVE "FILENAME"
```

and press RETURN. If you have pressed the PLAY and RECORD keys on the Datassette, the Datassette will start operating. After your program has been saved, the Datassette will stop, the cursor will start flashing again, and the computer will display READY on the screen.

To load the program from the Datassette, type

```
LOAD "FILENAME"
```

If the PLAY button has been depressed, the Datassette will operate and the computer will display

```
SEARCHING FOR FILENAME
```

As it passes the various programs that precede the one being looked for, it will display their names.

```
FOUND OTHERFILE
FOUND WRONGFILE
FOUND NEXTFILE
```

When the program requested is found, it will display

```
FOUND FILENAME
LOADING
```

WRITING DATA FILES

Writing program files into a Datassette file is a simple task. Putting data into a Datassette file is almost as easy, but it does require a basic understanding of how the information is put onto tape.

The most common method of storing data is by simply printing the data one item at a time to the Datassette. This can be done by entering the following statements.

First, you will need to open a file.

```
10 OPEN 1,1,2,"DATA FILE"
```

This will open a Datassette file with the number 1 and the name DATA FILE. When the file is closed, it will write an *end-of-file* marker onto the tape, which indicates to the C-64 that no more records exist in the file.

Now you can enter the data from the keyboard.

```
20 INPUT A$
```

If you were entering numeric data, you could use a numeric variable such as A.

At some point you will want to end the data entry. Let's say that if you enter **XXX** the computer will branch out of the routine.

```
30 IF A$ = "XXX" THEN 60
```

If the input was not XXX, you'll want to save it on tape

```
40 PRINT#1, A$
```

and go back for more input.

```
50 GOTO 20
```

If you are done entering data, close the file.

```
60 CLOSE 1
```

To run this program, you should first wind a fresh tape all the way forward and rewind it again until you can see where the nonmagnetic leader and the actual magnetic tape meet. Make sure that this is in the center of the cassette opening (see Figure 8-1).

Here's the complete program.

```
10 OPEN 1,1,2,  "DATA FILE"
20 INPUT A$
30 IF A$ = "XXX" THEN 60
40 PRINT#1, A$
50 GOTO 20
60 CLOSE 1
```

Now close the lid and run the program. The program will pause (and the cursor will disappear) for a few moments while the file is opened and the name of the file is written onto the tape. The cursor will return and a question mark will appear. Enter some characters and press RETURN.

After entering a few items, enter **XXX**. The cursor should disappear again; this time the file is being closed and the data and end-of-file marker are being written onto the tape.

PHOTO BY HARVEY SCHWARTZ

Leader

Magnetic surface

FIGURE 8-1. Tape position

READING DATA FILES

To read the data back from the tape you will need to open a Datassette file for reading. Add the following lines to the end of your Write Data program:

```
70 PRINT "REWIND TAPE"
80 PRINT "WHEN THE TAPE IS"
90 PRINT "REWOUND, PRESS STOP"
100 PRINT "ON THE DATASSETTE"
110 PRINT "THEN HIT <RETURN>"
120 INPUT C
130 OPEN 1,1,0, "DATA FILE"
```

Lines 70 through 110 tell the operator to rewind the tape and to signal the C-64 when the rewinding is completed by pressing RETURN. Line 120 makes the computer wait until the tape has been rewound, and line 130 opens the data file for reading.

Now you can begin reading data from the Datassette.

```
140 INPUT#1, A$
```

This inputs the first record you entered and assigns it to the string variable A$. The statement

```
150 PRINT A$
```

takes the data that you just put into A$ and displays them on the screen.

Status Register

There is a special variable name (similar to TI and TI$) that indicates the status of the external devices connected to the C-64. This is the variable ST. Table 8-2 interprets the values of ST.

To determine whether you have reached the end of a file, you can check the value of ST from inside your program. If the value of ST is 64 you have run out of data. Add the following line:

```
160 IF ST <> 64 THEN 150
```

Your program will branch back to read another record from the file.

If ST equals 64, all the data have been read and displayed. Close the file.

```
170 CLOSE 1
```

Then follow the instructions on the screen. The computer will display all of the items you entered in the previous section.

Using GET# to Read Files

It is also possible to use the GET command, just as you would from the keyboard. The GET# instruction reads one byte at a time from the Datassette. Change line 140 to

```
140 GET#1, A$
```

and, in immediate mode, type

```
GOTO 70
```

This time all the data are printed in a vertical column. Why?

Look at line 140. The GET# function inputs only one character at a time. That character is then assigned to variable A$ and printed. The

TABLE 8-2. Status Byte Returned by External Devices via Variable ST

Device Operation	00000001 Read as 1	00000010 Read as 2	00000100 Read as 4	00001000 Read as 8	00010000 Read as 16	00100000 Read as 32	01000000 Read as 64	10000000 Read as 128
Status								
Read from cassette drive	Operation OK	Operation OK	Short Block. Data block read had fewer bytes than expected	Long Block. Data block read had more bytes than expected	Unrecoverable read error	Checksum error. One or more data bits read incorrectly	End of file encountered	End of tape encountered
Verify cassette drive					Any verify mismatch		None	
Disk drives (all models)	Receiving device not available	Transmitting device not available	None	None	None	None	End of file	Disk drive not present

computer then does a carriage return, and the next character is input with the next GET#.

At the end of each string, the computer automatically adds a carriage return, which acts as a delimiter separating one string from the next. This is usually desirable, since it causes the computer to separate the variables. In some applications, however, you may want to eliminate the trailing carriage returns. For example, you may want to conserve space in a tightly-packed file in which all the variables or strings are of the same length. In such a case, you could leave out the carriage returns and separate the variables yourself.

Remember, however, if you create a file that has no delimiters (carriage returns) you must separate the data yourself in your program. To suppress the carriage returns you could change line 40 to read

```
40 PRINT#1, A$;
```

Note: Generally the best programs are the ones that are the simplest. Therefore, before you use this method be sure that you need to. Also be aware that a file with no delimiters cannot be read by an INPUT# statement unless it contains less than 80 characters because the INPUT buffer holds only 80 characters.

Disk Files

The disk drive can store data and programs just as the Datassette does. The major differences between the disk drive and the Datassette are speed and accessibility.

The disk drive can access data much faster than the Datassette, and can access them randomly. That is, the drive can access any location on the disk's surface to read or write data, while the Datassette must read and write all data sequentially.

HOW DATA ARE STORED ON DISKETTE

The data are stored on the diskette in concentric rings called *tracks*. The 1541 Disk Drive has a total of 35 tracks. Each track may be addressed directly and therefore may be quickly accessed. In general, the disk drive will not record data onto an entire track. This would make the files needlessly long. To avoid this, each track is divided up into *sectors*, each of which contains 256 bytes.

Look at Figure 8-2. You will see that the tracks on the diskette are not all the same length. The ones nearest the outer edge of the diskette are longer than the ones near the center. To make the most of the space available on the diskette, the 1541 Disk Drive puts more sectors into each of the outer tracks. The number of sectors per track varies from 17 on the inner tracks to 21 in the outer tracks. This means that one 1541 diskette can hold 176,640 bytes.

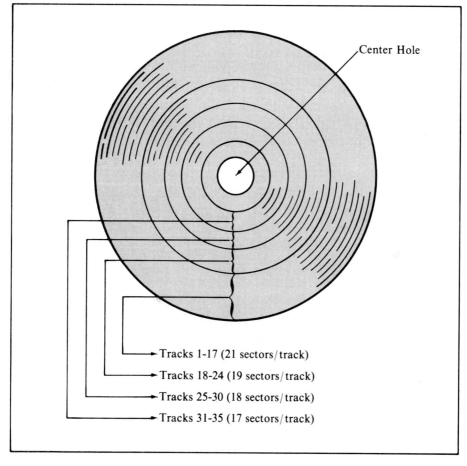

FIGURE 8-2. 1541 Diskette sectoring pattern (by tracks)

DISKETTE SECTORING

If you manually rotate the diskette inside its jacket, you will find one or more small holes in the diskette which come into alignment with the small hole in the jacket. If there is only one hole, the diskette is *soft-sectored.* If there are several holes, the diskette is *hard-sectored.* The holes in the hard-sectored diskette are used on some disk systems to position the sectors on the diskette. Since the 1541 Disk Drive provides its own special sectoring, you should only use soft-sectored diskettes.

DISKETTE DIRECTORY

Track 18 on the 1541 diskettes is used for the directory. The directory contains the names, starting sector addresses, and file types of all the files on the diskette.

To list a diskette's directory, load it into memory by entering

```
LOAD "$",8
```

The name of the directory file is $ (dollar sign), and we are loading it from device number 8 (the disk drive). To list the diskette directory, simply type

```
LIST
```

and the directory will be displayed on the screen.

THE BLOCK AVAILABILITY MAP (BAM)

The BAM resides on track 18 of the diskette. It contains information pertaining to memory space allocation on the diskette.

INITIALIZATION

Each time the disk drive is accessed, it compares the identifier number on the diskette with the ID number stored in disk memory. If the ID numbers match, the disk drive proceeds with the instruction it was given. If there is a mismatch, the disk drive automatically *initializes* the diskette.

When the diskette is initialized, the contents of the BAM are copied into disk memory. This tells the disk drive which sectors are available to be written to. If the ID numbers of two diskettes are the same, the disk drive will not initialize automatically. It will not update the BAM with the allocation information and may write over sections of other programs or data. To avoid this, format your diskettes with different ID numbers whenever possible.

To manually initialize a diskette, use the following statements:

```
OPEN 1,8,15
PRINT#1, "INITIALIZE"
```

A shorter version of this command is

```
OPEN 1,8,15, "I"
```

FORMATTING A DISKETTE

Before you can use a new diskette, you must format it. Formatting writes a disk name, an ID number, and all of the track and sector information onto the diskette so that data may be written onto it by the C-64.

To format a diskette that has never been used before, use the following commands:

```
OPEN 1,8,15
PRINT#1,"NEW:DISKNAME,ID"
```

The disk name can be any 16-character string you choose. The ID can be any number you choose. The Disk Operating System (DOS) uses the ID number to determine which diskette is in your drive. Remember to use a different number for each of your diskettes; that way the disk drive will always be able to determine whether it should initialize or not. If the IDs of your diskettes are all different, the initialization will be automatic; otherwise, you will need to do it manually each time you change diskettes.

A good way to ensure that all of your diskettes have different IDs is to format an entire box of diskettes at once, numbering them sequentially. When you need to use them, you can perform a short version of the FORMAT instruction which erases all data on the diskette and renames it, leaving the ID number the same. That way, no two diskettes in the box will have the same ID number. To do this, use the following FORMAT instruction.

Note: This will not work on new (previously unformatted) diskettes.

```
OPEN 1,8,15
PRINT#1, "N:DISKNAME"
```

Notice that in the above examples the letter "N" is used instead of the word NEW. N is an acceptable abbreviation for the NEW (disk) command.

Renaming Files

If you have a file with a name that you feel is inappropriate, you may change its name using the RENAME instruction. To rename a file, use the following format:

```
OPEN 1,8,15
PRINT#1, "RENAME: NEW FILENAME = OLD FILENAME"
```

You may use the abbreviation R in place of the word RENAME. Thus, if you wanted to change a file named DOG.1 to CAT.1, you would enter

```
OPEN 1,8,15
PRINT#1, "R: CAT.1 = DOG.1"
```

Erasing Files

To erase a file from your diskette, use the SCRATCH command. Its format is shown here.

```
OPEN 1,8,15
PRINT#1, "SCRATCH: FILENAME"
```

The abbreviation S may be used in place of the instruction SCRATCH. Therefore, you can also use

```
PRINT#1, "S: FILENAME"
```

to erase programs or data.

The VALIDATE Command

The VALIDATE command may be used to "clean up" a diskette. After a time there may be some files on your diskette that were not properly closed, or various files that were used as temporary storage and are not even part of another file. To perform this housekeeping, use the VALIDATE command. It deletes any unclosed files and frees any blocks that were previously allocated but not associated with any specific file.

Copying Files

You can make a copy of any file on your diskettes by using the COPY command. The same command with slightly different syntax will concatenate diskette files as well.

To make a copy of a program on the same diskette, use the following command sequence:

```
OPEN 15,8,15
PRINT#15, "COPY: NEW FILENAME = OLD FILENAME"
```

You may use the abbreviation C in place of the word COPY, as in the following example:

```
OPEN 15,8,15
PRINT#15, "C.DOG.2 = DOG.1"
```

Disk File Concatenation

Two or more files may be joined together, or concatenated, to form a single file. To create a new file named NEWFILE, for instance, out of the data files OLDFILE.0, OLDFILE.1, and OLDFILE.2 on diskette, use the following command:

```
PRINT#1, "C: NEW FILE = OLD FILE 1, OLD FILE 2"
```

Note: The maximum length of a disk command string is 40 characters, so keep your file names short.

Multiple-Disk Systems

If you have a system with more than one disk drive, you may copy files from one diskette to another. Before you do, however, you will first need to differentiate between disk drives.

When the 1541 Disk Drives are first powered up, they all have a device number of 8. If you connect more than one disk drive to your system, each drive will need a different device number. The device number may be either 8, 9, 10, or 11. To change the device number of a disk drive, follow these instructions.

1. Turn off all drives except the one you are changing.

2. Open a command file, such as

```
OPEN 15,8,15
```

3. Enter the following command sequence. **Note:** Don't worry if you don't understand this sequence; this kind of instruction is covered in more detail in the section on advanced disk commands.

```
PRINT#15,"M-W"CHR$(119)CHR$(0)CHR$(2)CHR$(9+32)CHR$(9+64)
```

This instruction will change the disk to device number 9. To change the disk drive to another device number, add that number, instead of 9, to 32 and 64 at the end of the command.

4. Turn on the next drive and repeat the command sequence above, using a different device number for each drive added.

Note: Do not turn off any drive that has been changed. This will erase the new device number.

Disk Data Files

Just as there is a difference in the way that data files and program files are handled by the Datassette, there is a difference in the way that data files and program files are handled by the disk drive.

There are three different kinds of information that can be stored on the disk drive. The first, program files, has already been covered. The second type is sequential data files, and the third, random access files.

SEQUENTIAL FILES

Like sequential data files on the Datassette, sequential data files on the 1541 Disk Drive must be opened before they can be accessed. To open a sequential data file to the disk, use the following format:

OPEN *lfn, dn, sa, "drn:file name,*SEQ,W"

where:

lfn   is the logical file number

dn   is the device number for the disk drive

    sa   is the secondary address. You can use any number between 2 and 14. Both 0 and 1 are reserved by the C-64 for LOAD and SAVE operations and 15 is used to open the command channel

    drn   is the drive number. This may be omitted if you have a one-drive system

file name   is the name of the file you are accessing

    SEQ   indicates that this will be a sequential data file

    W   indicates the write mode. You may also read. The READ command may be abbreviated as R.

Here's an example of writing to a file named AIRLINE.

```
OPEN 2,8,4,"0:AIRLINE,SEQ,W"
```

Whenever you open a file on the disk drive, the red activity light on the front of the drive will light until the file is closed. If you try to open in write mode a sequential file that already exists, the red activity light will flash, indicating an error condition.

If you want to write over a file that already exists, you can modify the above OPEN command as follows:

```
OPEN 1,8,10,"@0:AIRLINE,SEQ,W"
```

The @ tells the disk drive that you want to overwrite the data in the specified file.

If the file does not exist, the normal OPEN procedure will be carried out by the disk drive.

USING STRING VARIABLES AS FILE NAMES

You can use a string in place of a file name if you want to generate file names from within a program.

Here's an example of a program that asks you for the name of the file before it is opened. This allows you to use the same program to open different files. You might do this in a word processing program that has different names for each text file.

```
10 INPUT "FILE NAME"; FN$
20 OPEN 2,8,4, "0:"+FN$+ ",W"
```

Line 10 requests a file name. In line 20, the file name is concatenated to the OPEN file string. This is important, because the OPEN command must be a single string. Using the Plus (+) operator accomplishes this.

CLOSING DISK FILES

As a program writes data to a disk file, the data are first written to a buffer. When the buffer is full, the data are written onto the diskette. If you are done writing data to the diskette and the buffer is not yet filled, the data will not be written onto the diskette unless you close the file. Closing a file writes the data in the buffer onto the diskette whether or not the buffer is full. It is therefore very important that you close all files when you are done writing data to them.

Note: You may keep only ten files open with the C-64, and only five of them to the disk drive. Therefore, it is advisable to close channels after reading them as well as after writing to them, even though leaving a channel that you have read will not cause the same kind of catastrophic failures as failing to close a file that has been written to.

The PRINT# Command

The PRINT# command is used to transfer data to the disk drive or any other peripheral device. The C-64 automatically sends a carriage return at the end of each file record to terminate it properly. In some cases, such as printing to the 1525 printer, you may want to send a carriage return and a line feed to terminate the records in a file.

Use logical file numbers 1 through 127 to send a carriage return only, and logical file numbers 128 through 255 to send a carriage return-line feed after each record.

Reading a Data File

The INPUT# and GET# statements work in basically the same way on disk files as they do on Datassette files. The INPUT# statement can read strings no longer than 80 characters. To read longer strings, it will be necessary to use GET# and read the strings one byte at a time.

Random Access Files

You can create random access files by directly addressing diskette data blocks and memory buffers. Each data block occupies a single sector of the diskette. There are eight buffers available on the C-64, but four of them are used for the Block Availability Map, variable space, command channel I/O, and the disk controller. This leaves you with only four buffers for random access files. Be sure not to open more than four buffers at a time. Opening more than four will result in a system error.

Information is written to diskette random access files using the PRINT# command. The files are specified through parameters in the OPEN statement. The format for opening a random access file is as follows:

> OPEN *lfn, dn, sa,* "*# buf*"

where:

> *lfn*   is the logical file number. For performing data transfers, use logical file numbers between 2 and 14. To perform any utility command, use logical file 15. In general, it is a good idea to open the command channel (15) and a data channel for each operation
>
> *dn*   is the device number
>
> *sa*   is the secondary address (it must have a value between 2 and 14)
>
> *buf*   is the buffer number allocated to the specified secondary address. You do not need to use this specification. If you leave it out, DOS will automatically select a buffer.

DISK UTILITY INSTRUCTIONS

The C-64's disk utility instructions are described in this section. Table 8-3 provides a summary of these commands.

BLOCK-READ

The BLOCK-READ command reads any sector (block) into one of the memory buffers. To read a block, you would first need to open the command channel (15) as follows:

```
10 OPEN 15,8,15
```

Now a direct access channel must be opened.

```
20 OPEN 2,8,4,"#"
```

You can select which block you want to read (by track and sector).

```
30 INPUT "TRACK"; A
40 INPUT "SECTOR"; B
```

TABLE 8-3. Disk Utility Instruction Set

Command	Abbreviation	Format
BLOCK-READ	B-R	PRINT#15, "B-R:"ch;dr;t;s·
BLOCK-ALLOCATE	B-A	PRINT#15, "B-A:"dr;t;s
BLOCK-WRITE	B-W	PRINT#15, "B-W:"ch;dr;t;s
BLOCK-EXECUTE	B-E	PRINT#15, "B-E:"ch;dr;t;s
BUFFER-POINTER	B-P	PRINT#15, "B-P:"ch;byte
BLOCK-FREE	B-F	PRINT#15, "B-F:"dr;t;s
MEMORY-WRITE*	M-W	PRINT#15, "M-W:"CHR$(adr1)CHR$ (adrh) CHR$(#bytes)CHR$(data)CHR$ (data)...
MEMORY-READ*	M-R	PRINT#15, "M-R"CHR$(adr1)CHR$ (adrh)
MEMORY-EXECUTE*	M-E	PRINT#15, "M-E"CHR$(adrl)CHR$ (adrh)
U1	UA	Replacement for BLOCK-READ
U2	UB	Replacement for BLOCK-WRITE
U3	UC	Disk Processor JMP $0500
U4	UD	Disk Processor JMP $0503
U5	UE	Disk Processor JMP $0506
U6	UF	Disk Processor JMP $0509
U7	UG	Disk Processor JMP $050C
U8	UH	Disk Processor JMP $050F
U9	UI	Disk Processor JMP $FFFA
U:	UJ	Disk Processor JMP power-up vector

*You *must* use the abbreviation for these instructions.

The following statement reads a block of data into the buffer:

```
50 PRINT#15, "B-R:"4;0;A;B
```

Let's look at the components of this instruction.

PRINT#15 to perform any of the commands in this section, you must use the command channel (15)

"B-R:"   is the abbreviation for "BLOCK-READ:". The colon within the quotation marks positions the data that follow the instruction

4   is the secondary address from line 20 above

0   is the drive number. This is mandatory when you are using the direct access instructions

A   is the track number that was input in line 30. Although you may use variables to designate track and sector in these instructions, a constant can be used as well

B   is the sector number.

All of the data—secondary address, drive number, track number, and sector number—in this instruction must be separated by semicolons, as shown in the example.

Now that the data in your selected block has been transferred to the buffer, you will need to use a GET# or an INPUT# statement to extract it from the buffer.

The INPUT# statement retrieves all bytes up to and including the first carriage return it finds. Since you may not know the exact data in a sector before you read it, you may overrun the length of the INPUT#, which can hold only 80 bytes.

Because of this limitation of the INPUT# statement, it is preferable to use the GET# statement when you are unsure of the data you will read. It will read the data one byte at a time.

```
60 GET#2, A$
```

There are 256 bytes of data in each block, but not every block is full. To read all the data in a block and stop at the end of the file, test the status variable (ST) to see if it is zero.

```
70 IF ST=0 THEN PRINT A$; :GOTO 60
```

Note: Although there is a trailing semicolon in the PRINT statement, the display will jump to the next line whenever it reaches a carriage return in the data, separating the data just as they were entered.

If ST = 0, there are still more data, and you can go back and get another byte. Otherwise, close all channels when you are done with them.

```
80 CLOSE2: CLOSE15
```

Here is the whole BLOCK-READ program.

```
10 OPEN 15,8,15
20 OPEN 2,8,4, "#"
30 INPUT "TRACK"; A
40 INPUT "SECTOR"; B
50 PRINT#15, "B-R:"4;0;A;B
60 GET#2, A$
70 IF ST=0 THEN PRINT A$;: GOTO 60
80 CLOSE 2: CLOSE 15
```

BLOCK-ALLOCATE

The BAM keeps a record of all blocks that have been allocated (contain data). In the higher-level instructions (SAVE and so forth) the DOS (Disk Operating System) uses this information to determine where data can be written on the diskette.

When you are using the direct-access functions, however, the DOS does not use the BAM and you can write anything into any block on the diskette, whether or not it already contains data. You can write data anywhere, even over the directory and BAM, but you should avoid this. You can lose normal access to everything on your diskette if you write to it indiscriminately. It is therefore advisable to perform a BLOCK-ALLOCATE instruction before attempting to write a block.

The BLOCK-ALLOCATE instruction checks a sector to determine if it already contains data. If it is available (as indicated in the BAM), it marks the sector as allocated. If it is already allocated, it leaves the BAM unchanged and indicates the next available sector in the error channel.

Here is a routine to perform a BLOCK-ALLOCATE.

```
10 OPEN 15,8,15
20 INPUT "TRACK"; A
30 INPUT "SECTOR"; B
40 PRINT#15, "B-A:"0;A;B
```

The components of the BLOCK-ALLOCATE instruction are as follows:

PRINT#15,	activates the command channel
"B-A:"	is the BLOCK-ALLOCATE instruction
0	is the drive number
A	is the track number
B	is the sector number.

```
60 INPUT#15,E,EM$,T,S
70 PRINT E,EM$
80 PRINT T,S
90 CLOSE 15
99 END
```

After every disk operation the disk status can be read through the error channel. This is accessed by reading the values of four variables available to the command channel (15). In the case of a BLOCK-ALLOCATE instruction, the error channel will tell you if the track and sector you chose are available. If they are not available, it will give you the number of the next available track and sector.

Line 60 checks the error channel, putting the information contained in it into variables E (error code), EM$ (error message), T (track), and S (sector). Lines 70 and 80 print the data and lines 90 and 99 close the channel and end the program.

If you were using this as a subroutine within a program, you could use the data obtained from the error channel to allocate another block if the one you wanted was already occupied, since the next available track and sector will have been placed into the error channel. If the sector is free, the message "OK" will be displayed.

BLOCK-WRITE

Whenever you use BLOCK-WRITE, you should perform a BLOCK-ALLOCATE first to determine if the sector you want to write to is available. If it isn't, you will know the next available sector.

The following BLOCK-WRITE program uses BLOCK-ALLOCATE to check the selected sector:

```
10 OPEN 15,8,15
20 INPUT "TRACK"; A
30 INPUT "SECTOR"; B
40 PRINT#15, "B-A:"0;A;B
50 INPUT#15,E,EM$,T,S
```

Now you must look at EM$ to determine whether the sector you selected is available.

```
60 IF EM$ = "OK" THEN 100
```

If it isn't, then use the values obtained through the error channel as your new track and sector.

```
70 A=T
80 B=S
```

Note: If there are no more available sectors on the diskette, the error channel will return track 0 and sector 0. These do not designate a real sector and will cause an error if you try to write to that location. To make sure you don't have this problem, recheck the error channel. If there are zeros in variables T and S, then you need to check for sectors with lower numbers.

```
90 IF A=0 AND B=0 THEN PRINT "DISK FULL":GOTO 160
```

If you don't get this error, continue with your BLOCK-WRITE.

```
100 PRINT "TRACK";A;"";"SECTOR";B
105 OPEN 2,8,4,"#"
110 INPUT A$
```

If you input an X, the program will terminate data input.

```
120 IF A$="X" THEN 150
```

If not, then put the data into your file

```
130 PRINT#2, A$
```

and go back for more.

```
140 GOTO 110
```

Use the following statement to put the data into your selected sector:

```
150 PRINT#15, "B-W:"4;0;A;B
```

Note: The format of the BLOCK-WRITE instruction is the same as that of the BLOCK-READ instruction.

Once more, you must close your files and end the program.

```
160 CLOSE 2: CLOSE 15
```

BUFFER-POINTER

As you have seen, the data buffer stores information that is read in from the diskette. The *buffer pointer* keeps track of which byte is being read and advances by one each time a byte is read.

Suppose you wanted to read the data in a specific 240-byte file as separate records. The first record resides in bytes 1 through 120 and the other is stored in bytes 121 through 240. Reading the files in order would be easy because the BUFFER-POINTER would already be at the point where the second file starts after reading the first file. But what if you only wanted to read the second file?

One way to read the second file would be to perform 120 GET# instructions, using a short loop, until you got to byte 121.

This can be accomplished more easily, however. The BUFFER-POINTER instruction will allow you to point at any byte in the buffer. Its format is

PRINT#15, "B-P:" *sa;byte*

where:

PRINT#15,   activates the command channel

"B-P:"   is the BUFFER-POINTER command

sa;   is the secondary address

byte   is the byte you want to access.

For example, if you wanted to GET the 120th byte of a block, you would use

```
PRINT#15, "B-P:"4;15
```

BLOCK-FREE

The BLOCK-FREE instruction will deallocate any block on the diskette. This instruction tells the BAM to mark the block specified as available, thus allowing data to be written to the block.

To perform a BLOCK-FREE, use the following format:

OPEN 15,8,15

PRINT#15, "B-F:" *dr;trk;sec*

where:

PRINT#15,   activates the command channel

"B-F:"   is the BLOCK-FREE command

dr   is the drive number

trk   is the track number

sec   is the sector number.

Here is a routine you can use to free any block on the diskette.

```
10 OPEN 15,8,15
20 INPUT "TRACK"; A
30 INPUT "SECTOR"; B
40 PRINT#15, "B-F:"0;A;B
50 CLOSE 15
99 END
```

DISKETTE MEMORY MANIPULATION

The 1541 *controller* interprets external commands and causes the disk drive mechanism to carry them out. The controller contains a 6502 micro-processor, similar to the one inside the C-64. It has 2K of RAM and the Disk Operating System (DOS), which is contained on two ROM chips.

Some of this memory is used for the buffers discussed in the last few sections; some is used for housekeeping purposes such as maintaining the BAM data and special file information; and some is available for you to use for special applications.

The RAM that is available for you to write routines on is the same RAM that is used by DOS for the buffers. If you decide to write a special machine language program into those areas you will have to keep track of which areas you are using and which areas you will reserve for buffers. There are five *pages* of memory, each of which contains 256 bytes.

Buffer	Memory Location (Hexadecimal)
#1	300—3FF
#2	400—4FF
#3	500—5FF
#4	600—6FF
#5	700—7FF

It is not advisable to use buffer #5, because this buffer is often used by DOS for various housekeeping activities. Although it is not always in use, data placed there may alter DOS procedures or may be written over by DOS.

The memory space in buffers 1 through 4 is used only by the buffers. If you haven't requested a buffer, and you know that one has not been opened by the system, you may use that memory freely. One method is to specify which buffers you want when you open a disk channel and write your routines in one or two of the buffers that are not in use.

The information that follows is not intended for beginning programmers. The use of the MEMORY-READ, MEMORY-WRITE, and MEMORY-EXECUTE commands requires a thorough understanding of machine language programming and the Disk Operating System.

MEMORY-WRITE

To store data into the disk drive memory, you will need to use the MEMORY-WRITE command. Like POKE in BASIC, this instruction puts whatever data you specify into any memory location you want. Take the example of a POKE statement.

```
POKE 768, 255
```

There is only one byte transferred with each POKE statement. The MEMORY-WRITE command allows you to transfer up to 34 bytes with a single statement. To perform the same operation using MEMORY-WRITE you would need to convert the decimal memory location into a hexadecimal number; 300 is the hexadecimal equivalent of decimal 768. Since you can transfer only one byte at a time with a POKE command, BASIC always knows how many bytes to expect. With the MEMORY-WRITE command, you will need to indicate how many bytes are going to be transferred. In this case, only one byte is going to be transferred, so the command will be quite short.

There are some special constraints that must be used with these instructions since they are actually just extensions of machine code.

1. The memory address must be entered as two bytes, low byte first, then high byte.

2. All of the data must be transferred as character strings (CHR$).

3. The 6502 understands only binary data. The instruction allows you to enter numbers in hexadecimal; but BASIC doesn't use that notation. For instance,

    65536 decimal = FFFF hexadecimal

    This is two hexadecimal bytes (FF and FF). To represent them in this mode, take the two bytes and convert each to its decimal equivalent, 255. The number 65536 would then be stored into the 1541's memory as CHR$(255)CHR$(255). Any number that can be expressed in only one byte (0 to 255) must be entered that way.

4. You must indicate how many bytes are being transferred. This should also be expressed as hexadecimal numbers converted to decimal notation, as above.

5. The MEMORY-WRITE instruction must be abbreviated "M-W". No colon or other punctuation is allowed.

The code, then, to store 255 into memory location 768 ($0300) is as follows:

```
OPEN 15,8,15
PRINT#15,"M-W"CHR$(00)CHR$(03)CHR$(1)CHR$(255)
CLOSE 15
```

MEMORY-READ

It is possible to read any memory location in the 1541 using the MEMORY-READ instruction. This instruction allows you to read one byte at a time from the disk drive memory, similar to the way PEEK allows you to read one byte at a time from the C-64's memory.

The BASIC instruction to read memory location 768 would be

```
PRINT PEEK(768)
```

The same instruction using the MEMORY-READ instruction would look like this.

```
40 OPEN 15,8,15
50 PRINT#15,"M-R"CHR$(00)CHR$(03)
60 GET#15, A$
70 PRINT A$
80 CLOSE 15
```

This is what happened: first, we opened the command (error) channel and then requested the MEMORY-READ instruction. On the same line (with no additional punctuation) the byte to be read was specified (low byte first, then high byte). This is memory location 300—the same as 768 decimal.

Note: The instruction "M-R" is the *only* valid way to invoke this instruction. Spelling out the instruction will cause an error.

After the data in that location are read, they can be transferred to the computer through the error channel (#15). To read them from the error channel we used the instruction GET# 15, A$. The values were then available as variable A$, which we printed to the screen. Finally, we closed the command (error) channel.

Since the data read from the 1541 memory are transmitted through the error channel, you should not try to read an error condition from the error channel again until you have closed it and reopened it. If you do not do this, you will get the data which were transmitted instead of the error message.

MEMORY-EXECUTE

The MEMORY-EXECUTE instruction is used to run a machine language program that has been entered into the 1541's memory. The program *must* end with an RTS instruction so that the processor will return control to the C-64; otherwise the 1541's internal memory will probably go into an endless loop—if not worse.

The format of the MEMORY-EXECUTE (M-E) instruction is essentially the same as that of the MEMORY-READ instruction.

```
40 OPEN 15,8,15
50 PRINT#15,"M-E"CHR$(00)CHR$(03)
60 CLOSE 15
```

This sequence will send the DOS into a routine that begins at the 1541's memory location 300 (768 decimal).

USER COMMANDS

The 1541 makes use of a number of commands called user commands (do not mistake these for USR routines, which are a part of BASIC). These commands perform a number of convenient functions that are similar to the other commands in this section.

U1

The U1 command is similar to BLOCK-READ. In fact, its format is identical. Look at the BLOCK-READ command. B-R is simply replaced with U1. The B-R command reads only the data in a particular block (sector). The U1 command reads all the information in the block, including the two bytes that precede the 254 data bytes. These bytes contain the link to the next block. The link is the track and sector to go to next.

U2

The U2 command is similar to BLOCK-WRITE. The format of the U2 command is identical to that of B-W. The difference between these two commands is that invoking B-W terminates the file. That is, the track and sector link (the two bytes that precede the 254 bytes of data in the block) are set to indicate that this block is the end of a file. The next track and sector are not pointed to.

Obviously, this can cause some problems. If, for instance, you wanted to write some data into the middle of some existing data, using the B-W instruction would end the file in the middle. U2, however, would not. It allows you to write in the next track and sector or to leave it the same.

U3-U9

The next few user commands are similar to the MEMORY-EXECUTE command. They jump to a specific location in memory and begin executing at that location. The locations they jump to are listed in Table 8-3.

The syntax for the U3 command, for example, is

```
OPEN 15,8,15
PRINT#15, "U3:"
CLOSE 15
```

The command U: (or UJ) will jump the DOS to its power-up routine. The locations that the user commands jump to are only three bytes long. This is because they are intended to contain a JMP machine code instruction to go to a program that you define.

THE MODEM

The modem allows your C-64 computer to communicate with other computers over telephone lines. This will allow your C-64 to talk to other C-64's directly and to access the various computer networks. These allow you to use your C-64 as a terminal to a large mainframe computer some-where in the network. The networks give you access to informtion such as stock market reports, articles from a variety of publications, airline sche-dules, and messages from other computer users.

Installing the Modem

To install the modem, perform the following steps:

1. Turn *off* the power to your C-64.

2. Plug the modem into the C-64's user port (see Figure 1-2).

3. Turn the C-64 back *on.*

4. Load a program to operate the modem.

5. Dial the appropriate phone number to reach either the network you wish to access or the other computer you are calling.

    If you are accessing one of the networks, you will need to code in, on the C-64, your ID and access code numbers.

    If you are accessing another computer, you will need to set your modem to "O" (originate), and the computer you are calling must be set to "A" (answer).

6. When you hear a high-pitched tone, unplug the telephone receiver and plug the cord into the modem.

    Note: If you have a Trimline telephone, you will need a special adapter for the modem; it will not work with this kind of telephone because the telephone electronics are in the handset, which you unplug when you disconnect the cable.

7. Put the handset aside. Do not hang it up; this will disconnect the modem.

Terminology

The following is a list of common terms used in telecommunications:

Modem The peripheral device used to convert the signals output by your computer into information that can be transmitted over the telephone lines. ("Modem" stands for "modulate/demodulate.")

Handshaking The process of sending data and waiting for an acknowledgement from the receiving computer.

Full/half duplex These are two modes of handshaking. In full duplex mode, a computer sends some data and the receiving computer repeats the data back to the originating computer. If the data returned are the same as those sent, the originating computer sends the next byte. If they are incorrect, the data are sent again. In half duplex mode, the originating computer sends data and the receiving computer simply acknowledges that the data have been received.

Baud rate This indicates the maximum speed at which data are transmitted and received. The VIC Modem sends and receives data at 300 baud. Another way of describing baud rate is in BPS, or bits per second. A system running at 300 baud will send/receive 300 bits of data per second.

Answer/originate When you connect to one of the networks, you will be calling the system. Since you are originating the call, your modem should be set to "originate." This sets up the "introductory" protocol in the electronics. If you are communicating directly with another computer, one computer must be in originate mode and the other in answer mode. Once communications have been established, it makes no difference which is which.

Parity In order to verify that the data transmitted are correct, some computers will send an extra bit called the *parity bit* along with the data. If the total of all the "ON" (or 1) bits, including the parity bit, is an even number, the transmission is odd parity. If the parity bit is missing, the transmission has no parity. To communicate properly, both computers must be set to the same parity.

Word length This is the number of bits in each byte. Most computers use a word length of seven or eight bits.

Start/stop bits Some computers require that a certain number of null bits be transmitted after each byte. These null bits are called stop bits. If the system uses these, the most common number is one stop bit and one start bit. If this is the case, the total number of bits per byte increases to ten. This will slow the effective transmission rate slightly, but will not impair the operation of the C-64 or the modem.

Line feed At the end of a line of data, the computer will typically send a carriage return. Some systems also require a line feed after each line or data file.

ASCII This is the standard coding used to communicate the numbers 1 through 9 and upper- and lower-case letters. There are also a number of standard symbols and special characters used in the ASCII (American Standard Code for Information Interchange) system. The C-64 uses an extension of the ASCII character set for its extended character set, but should use this extended set only when communicating with other Commodore computers.

THE 1525 PRINTER

The 1525 Printer has a built-in character set that closely resembles the character set of the C-64. It includes upper- and lower-case letters, numbers, and graphic symbols. You can use the 1525 printer to print fully programmable custom graphics of almost any size.

OPEN Statement

In order to access the 1525 printer you must open a file to it. The OPEN statement for the printer has the following format:

OPEN *fn, dn, sa*

where:

fn	The file number is the number you choose to access the file. You may choose any number between 0 and 255
dn	The device number for the printer may be either 4 or 5. This number may be selected using a switch at the rear of the printer
sa	In most cases, you will not use a secondary address when you access the printer. The one exception to this is covered in the section on the 1515 printer's character sets.

Once you have opened a file to the printer, all you need to do to print to the printer is put your data in a PRINT# statement, such as

PRINT#1, "YOUR DATA GOES HERE"

The printer will print

YOUR DATA GOES HERE

CLOSE Statement

After you have finished accessing a file, whether it is to the printer or any other device, you should always close the file. To close a file you would use the following format:

CLOSE *file number*

If you opened a file with a file number of 1, such as

OPEN 1,4

then you would close with

CLOSE 1

CMD Statement

Everything the C-64 outputs will normally be sent to the video display. The video display is known as the *primary output device*. It is possible, however, to change this to some other device, such as the printer, so you can print listings instead of merely looking at them on the screen.

This is done with the CMD instruction. The format of a CMD instruction is

CMD *device number*

Let's instruct the C-64 to use the printer as the primary output device. First we'll need to OPEN a file to the printer.

OPEN 1,4

Then we can use the CMD instruction as follows:

CMD 1

Now everything that the C-64 would normally display on the screen will be printed on the printer, including the READY message, the display, and error messages. Your entries will still be displayed on the screen. To see this, try performing some PRINT statements.

EXITING THE CMD MODE

There are three ways to exit the CMD mode.

1. Press RUN/STOP and RESTORE at the same time. This will reset the entire system and restore the computer to its default condition.

2. Redirect the CMD instruction to another device, such as the video screen, device #3.

    ```
    CMD 3
    ```

3. Enter a PRINT# instruction to the primary device. For example, if you had made the primary device #1 with CMD 1, you would exit this mode with

    ```
    PRINT#1
    ```

Of the three methods, the last—using a PRINT# instruction—is preferred because it will exit the CMD mode and also empty the printer buffer. Characters may have been left there from an incomplete PRINT statement (one that was terminated with a semicolon).

THE 1525 Printer's Character Sets

Type your name at the C-64's keyboard. Press RETURN and type some hearts (SHIFTS) on the next line. Now press the Commodore symbol key and SHIFT at the same time. The letters of your name will become lower-case letters and the hearts will become upper-case S's.

Both the C-64 and the 1525 have two separate character sets available, and you can select either set at any time. There are two ways to select the different character sets.

1. Specify a secondary address of 7 when you OPEN the printer file.

    ```
    OPEN 1,4,7
    ```

    This will select the alternate character set.

To access the default character set (the one that is displayed when you first turn the C-64 on), OPEN your printer file with

```
OPEN 1,4
```

leaving out the secondary address.

2. Print the command CHR$(14) for the alternate character set or CHR$(142) for the standard character set, as in the following example:

```
10 OPEN 1,4
20 PRINT#1,CHR$(17);"LOWER CASE"
30 PRINT#1,CHR$(145);"UPPER CASE"
40 CLOSE 1
```

Print Formatting

The formatting instructions TAB and SPC and the comma and semicolon help you to position data on the video screen. Although the printer also uses these instructions, it does not treat them exactly as the video display does.

THE COMMA

The comma starts data in two specific locations on the video screen: column 0 and column 11. Try this example.

```
10 FOR T=0 TO 30
20 PRINT T,
30 NEXT
```

Notice that two even columns are displayed, even though the numbers in them are of different lengths. On the printer, a comma will put 11 spaces between your entries, but they will not necessarily wind up in even columns. Try the same program on the printer.

```
5 OPEN 1,4
10 FOR T=0 TO 30
20 PRINT#1, T,
30 NEXT
40 CLOSE 1
```

THE SEMICOLON

The semicolon operates in the same way on the printer as it does on the video display. It is used to separate variables without putting spaces between them. Remember, however, that numeric variables will still be preceded by a space even with the semicolon. To see this, try the following program:

```
10 OPEN 1,4
20 A=21 : B=300 : AB=57
30 PRINT#1,A;B;AB
```

TAB and SPC

The TAB and SPC instructions are so similar that they are often confused. The TAB function designates an absolute position, and the SPC function indicates a relative position. The following TAB statement will print an asterisk in column 10 of the screen:

```
PRINT TAB(10);"*"
```

Now try the following statement. It will print one asterisk in column 10 and another in column 11.

```
PRINT TAB(10);"*";TAB(10);"*"
```

The SPC instruction begins at the current cursor position and counts the indicated number of spaces over from that point. Try the following SPC statement:

```
PRINT SPC(10);"*";SPC(10);"*"
```

Although this line looks almost identical to the TAB statement above, it prints one asterisk in column 10 and another in column 21. This happens because the SPC function starts counting at the space immediately after the first asterisk (column 11) and puts the next asterisk ten spaces away.

Using POS to Tab the Printer

When used in PRINT# statements, TAB and SPC both act like SPC. Note, however, that TAB and SPC cannot appear directly after PRINT# (for example, PRINT#1, TAB(20)).

To take a look at these two functions, first open the printer file with

```
OPEN 1,4
```

Now type in the following line:

```
PRINT#1,""SPC(10);"*";SPC(10);"*"
```

This will print one asterisk in column 10 and another in column 21 on the printer.

If you replace the SPC instruction with TAB, you will get exactly the same results. Try the following example:

```
PRINT#1,"";TAB(10);"*";TAB(10);"*"
```

To produce the TAB function on the printer, you will need to use the POS instruction. POS is sent to the printer as CHR$(16). Try the following example:

```
PRINT#1,CHR$(16);"10*";CHR$(16);"10*"
```

CHR$(16) is the POS instruction. When the printer encounters this command, it uses the two characters immediately following the command to determine where on the line to begin printing.

You can also use the character codes of the numbers to indicate the position.

```
PRINT#1, CHR$(16); CHR$(49); CHR$(48); "*"
```

Note: CHR$(49) is 1 and CHR$(48) is 0.

Printer Graphics

The printer has several different modes, which are described in Table 8-4. The characters it receives will be treated differently in each mode.

By using the various modes, you can print anything from standard text to full dot graphics.

DOUBLE/SINGLE-WIDTH CHARACTERS

To print double-width characters on the 1525 printer, use the command CHR$(14) before the string you want printed.

```
PRINT#1,CHR$(14);"THIS SHOULD PRINT WIDE"
```

To return to normal width, use the command CHR$(15).

```
PRINT#1,CHR$(14);"WIDE";CHR$(15);"NARROW"
```

REVERSE CHARACTERS

Reverse field characters can be printed using the command CHR$(18). Try it with this example.

```
PRINT#1,CHR$(18);"REVERSE CHARACTERS"
```

TABLE 8-4. Printer Modes

Mode	Printer Command
PRINT DOUBLE-WIDTH CHARACTERS	CHR$(14)
PRINT SINGLE-WIDTH CHARACTERS	CHR$(15)
PRINT REVERSE CHARACTERS	CHR$(18)
PRINT NON-REVERSE CHARACTERS	CHR$(146)
GRAPHICS MODE	CHR$(8)
ALTERNATE CHARACTER SET	CHR$(17)
STANDARD CHARACTER SET	CHR$(145)
REPEAT GRAPHICS MODE	CHR$(26)

Notice that the command CHR$(18) is the same as the CHR$ function, which prints reverse characters on the video screen. On the screen, typing CTRL RVS ON switches to reverse characters. This also works on the printer if you put the instruction in a PRINT# statement like the following:

```
PRINT#1,"<CTRL><RVS ON>";"REVERSE CHARACTERS"
```

You can use either CHR$(146) or CTRL RVS OFF to leave reverse mode.

GRAPHICS

The command CHR$(8) causes the printer to enter the graphics mode. Graphics are created by printing patterns of dots. For instance, a smiling face could be made up of dots in the following pattern:

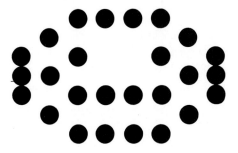

This pattern is converted into a set of numbers to be sent to the printer. This is done as follows: the rows (horizontal dots) are each given a numeric value. The top row is 1, the next row down is 2, and so forth, with each successive row being double the value of the one above it. The value of the seventh row is 64. Add up the numbers in the places that you want to print dots. To this number you then add 128, and that is the number that you put into the printer.

Let's examine the smiling face and determine what the value of each row should be to print it on the printer.

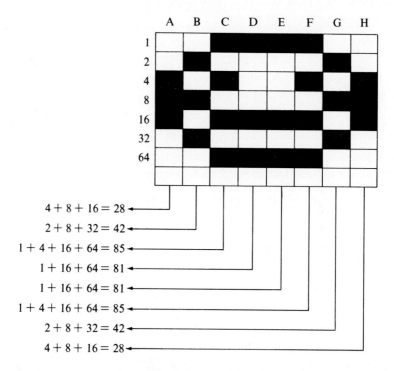

$$4 + 8 + 16 = 28$$
$$2 + 8 + 32 = 42$$
$$1 + 4 + 16 + 64 = 85$$
$$1 + 16 + 64 = 81$$
$$1 + 16 + 64 = 81$$
$$1 + 4 + 16 + 64 = 85$$
$$2 + 8 + 32 = 42$$
$$4 + 8 + 16 = 28$$

Look at column A. The dark squares represent locations in which the printer should print dots. Adding up the values of the locations in column A we get: $4 + 8 + 16 = 28$. Column B is $2 + 8 + 32 = 42$.

If you continue through all eight columns you will get the values 28, 42, 85, 81, 81, 85, 42, and 28.

To print these as a graphic shape, put the values into CHR$ statements, such as the following:

```
10 DATA 28,42,85,81,81,85,42,28
20 OPEN 1,4
30 PRINT#1, CHR$(8);
40 FOR R=1 TO 8
50 READ A
60 PRINT#1,CHR$(A+128);
70 NEXT
80 PRINT#1
90 PRINT#1
```

This will print a smiling face on the printer. You can print more smiling faces by repeating this pattern.

You can also use the function keys to produce the special characters. Here's a short program that prints whatever text you enter into it, plus a smiling face.

The smiling face will be printed (on the printer only—an asterisk will be printed on the screen) each time you hit the F1 key.

```
10 OPEN 1,4
20 GET A$: IF A$="" THEN 20
30 IF A$ = "<F1>" THEN 70
40 PRINT#1, A$
50 PRINT A$;
60 GOTO 20
70 DATA 28,42,85,81,81,85,42,28
80 PRINT#1,CHR$(8);
90 FOR R=1 TO 8
100 READ A
110 PRINT#1, CHR$(A+128);
120 NEXT:PRINT "*";
130 PRINT#1, CHR$(15)
140 RESTORE: GOTO 20
```

GRAPHICS REPEAT FUNCTION

The graphics repeat function allows you to print any pattern of seven vertical dots as many times as you like (up to 255 times per command).

Here's an example of a repeat function.

```
OPEN 1,4
PRINT#1, CHR$(26)CHR$(10)CHR$(255)
```

This will print a solid horizontal bar seven dots high by ten dots long.

CHR$(26) is the repeat function, CHR$(10) is the number of times to repeat, and CHR$(255) produces the dot pattern containing seven vertical dots.

This function can easily be incorporated into the smiling face routine above and used to expand the face.

```
10 DATA 28,42,85,81,81,85,42,28
20 OPEN 1,4
30 INPUT "WIDTH";W
40 PRINT#1,CHR$(8);
50 FOR R=1 TO 8
60 READ A
70 PRINT#1,CHR$(26) CHR$(W) CHR$(A+128);
80 NEXT
90 PRINT#1
```

Put different values into the width variable when the program requests it and notice how the picture changes. Of course, this becomes impractical at some point, since it can become so wide that it is no longer recognizable.

System Architecture

Figure A-1 is a block diagram of the C-64's design architecture. It illustrates the relationships between several of the system elements described in Chapter 1. The arrows show the flow of data between these elements.

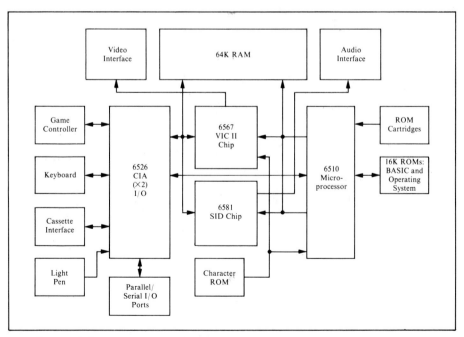

FIGURE A-1. System block diagram

Memory Usage

The main function of any memory map is to help you utilize the many built-in functions of your computer. The following memory guide does not catalog every memory location in the C-64 map. Instead, it indicates those locations that are the most useable and includes a detailed explanation of what each location does and how it works.

INTERPRETING POINTERS

Many of the memory locations included in this guide are paired. Instead of performing the indicated function, these locations point to the location of the function listed. This allows you to move certain functions around in memory. For example, location 648 (which contains a 1-byte address) points to the beginning of the screen memory. By changing this number, you can use different parts of memory for the screen. By doing this you can set up different screens and switch between them by changing the number in this location.

In addition, some of these locations keep track of functions within the computer such as location 144, which monitors the status of the current I/O device logged onto the system. By reading the value in this location, you can determine an OK condition or, if necessary, an error condition.

Those locations that are organized as address pairs contain two numbers which represent a single hexadecimal number. To convert these two numbers into a decimal value (for PEEKing or POKEing) use the following formula:

value = lower memory location + (upper memory location × 256)

Here is a short BASIC routine that will perfom this function for you.

```
10 INPUT "VALUE IN LOWER MEMORY LOCATION"; L
20 INPUT "VALUE IN HIGHER MEMORY LOCATION"; H
30 PRINT "DECIMAL VALUE ="; L+256*H
```

Memory Location	Function
43 & 44	These locations contain the address of the first byte of your BASIC program.
45 & 46	These locations contain the address of the first byte of the variables in your BASIC program.
47 & 48	These locations contain the address of the beginning of the BASIC arrays.
49 & 50	The number stored in these locations is one byte higher than the end of BASIC arrays.
51 & 52	The number in these locations point indicate the lowest memory location used for storing the strings in your BASIC program.
55 & 56	These two locations indicate the highest memory location used by BASIC.
144	The I/O status byte. This location stores a number which indicates the condition I/O device in operation. A zero in this location indicates a OK condition. Table 8-2 (in Chapter eight) gives the error codes for any other number in this location.
160 — 162	The jiffy clock. The number in these three locations is a straight binary number. To interpret its value, use the following routine:

```
10 A=PEEK(160)
20 B=PEEK(161)
```

```
30 C=PEEK(162)
40 D=C+((256)*B)+(65536*A)
50 PRINT D
```

192	This is the cassette motor interlock. Ordinarily it is used to turn the Datassette on and off during read and write operations. It can also be used as an I/O line to control other low current devices. See Figure C-6 for the location of the CASSETTE MOTOR line of the cassette port.
197	The value of the current key being pressed can be read in this location.
198	This location can be read to determine how many characters are currently in the keyboard buffer (there are a maximum of ten). Any keystrokes after the tenth entry will be lost.
631 − 641	The keyboard buffer.
641 − 642	These locations point to the lowest memory location of the operating system.
643 − 644	These locations point to the highest memory location of the operating system.
648	This location controls the location of screen memory. The actual location of the screen can be found by multiplying the number stored here by 256.
649	This location controls the size of the keyboard buffer. By changing this value (which is initialized to ten whenever the system is reset) you can control the number of keystrokes that will be stored while the computer is operating.
650	Repeat key ON/OFF. ON = 128, OFF = 0
651	Repeat rate. This location controls the speed of the repeat function.

652	Repeat delay. This location determines how long a key must be depressed before it will begin repeating.
567	Enable/Disable SHIFT function. This location controls the keyboard access to the alternate character set obtained through (COMMODORE/SHIFT).
770 − 771	Warm start vector. A SYS to this location has the same effect as hitting RUN/STOP-RESTORE.
788 − 789	Hardware IRQ (Interrupt Request) vector.
1024 − 2023	Location of Screen Memory at power up.
2040 − 2047	These locations control the locations of the sprites in memory.
2048 − 40959	Free RAM space.
32768 − 40959	These memory locations can be used by an external cartridge. If they are used, the RAM will be overlaid.
40960 − 49151	BASIC interpreter.
49152 − 53247	4K Buffer RAM. This RAM is available for your use. If you place data in this area it will not affect the normal BASIC RAM down at 2048 − 40959.
53248 − 54271	**VIC II Chip Control Registers**
53248	Sprite #0: X position
53249	Sprite #0: Y position
53250	Sprite #1: X position
53251	Sprite #1: Y position
53252	Sprite #2: X position
53253	Sprite #2: Y position
53254	Sprite #3: X position
53255	Sprite #3: Y position
53256	Sprite #4: X position

53257	Sprite #4: X position
53258	Sprite #5: X position
53259	Sprite #5: Y position
53260	Sprite #6: X position
53261	Sprite #6: X position
53262	Sprite #7: X position
53263	Sprite #7: Y position
53264	Sprites 0—7 MSB of X position

53265   VIC II Chip Control Register
                                Bits 0-2: Smooth Scroll (Y direction)
                                Bit 3: 24/25 Row Select (24=0)
                                Bit 4: Screen Blanking (Blank=0)
                                Bit 5: Enable Bit Map Mode (1=ON)
                                Bit 6: Extended Color Text (1=ON)
                                Bit 7: Raster Value Register (MSB)

53266   Raster Value Register (Bits 0-7)

53267   Light Pen (X Value)

53268   Light Pen (Y Value)

53269   Sprite Display Control Register
                                Bit 0: Sprite #0 (1=ON)
                                Bit 1: Sprite #1 (1=ON)
                                Bit 2: Sprite #2 (1=ON)
                                Bit 3: Sprite #3 (1=ON)
                                Bit 4: Sprite #4 (1=ON)
                                Bit 5: Sprite #5 (1=ON)
                                Bit 6: Sprite #6 (1=ON)
                                Bit 7: Sprite #7 (1=ON)

53270   VIC II Control Register #2
                                Bits 0-2: Smooth Scroll (X direction)
                                Bit 3: 38/40 Column Select (1=40)
                                Bit 4: Multicolor Mode (1=ON)
                                Bits 5-7: Not Used

53271   Sprite Expansion Register (Y direction)
                                Bit 0: Sprite #0 (1=2X)

Bit 1: Sprite #1 (1=2X)
Bit 2: Sprite #2 (1=2X)
Bit 3: Sprite #3 (1=2X)
Bit 4: Sprite #4 (1=2X)
Bit 5: Sprite #5 (1=2X)
Bit 6: Sprite #6 (1=2X)
Bit 7: Sprite #7 (1=2X)

53272   VIC II Address Control Register
Bit 0: Not Used
Bits 1-3: Character Set Location
Bits 4-7: Screen Location

53273   VIC II Interrupt Control Register
Bit 0: Raster Compare
Bit 1: Sprite-Background Collision
Bit 2: Sprite-Sprite Collision
Bit 3: Light Pen Interrupt
Bits 4-6: Not Used

53274   VIC II Interrupt Enable Register
Bit 0: Raster Compare (1=ON)
Bit 1: Sprite-Background Collision (1=ON)
Bit 2: Sprite-Sprite Collision (1=ON)
Bit 3: Light Pen Interrupt (1=ON)
Bits 4-6: Not Used (1=ON)

53275   Sprite-Background Priority Register
Bit 0: Sprite #0 (1=SPRITE)
Bit 1: Sprite #1 (1=SPRITE)
Bit 2: Sprite #2 (1=SPRITE)
Bit 3: Sprite #3 (1=SPRITE)
Bit 4: Sprite #4 (1=SPRITE)
Bit 5: Sprite #5 (1=SPRITE)
Bit 6: Sprite #6 (1=SPRITE)
Bit 7: Sprite #7 (1=SPRITE)

53276   Sprite Multicolor Control Register
Bit 0: Sprite #0 (1=Multicolor)
Bit 1: Sprite #1 (1=Multicolor)
Bit 2: Sprite #2 (1=Multicolor)

	Bit 3: Sprite #3 (1=Multicolor)
	Bit 4: Sprite #4 (1=Multicolor)
	Bit 5: Sprite #5 (1=Multicolor)
	Bit 6: Sprite #6 (1=Multicolor)
	Bit 7: Sprite #7 (1=Multicolor)
53277	Sprite Expansion Register (X direction)
	Bit 0: Sprite #0 (1=2X)
	Bit 1: Sprite #1 (1=2X)
	Bit 2: Sprite #2 (1=2X)
	Bit 3: Sprite #3 (1=2X)
	Bit 4: Sprite #4 (1=2X)
	Bit 5: Sprite #5 (1=2X)
	Bit 6: Sprite #6 (1=2X)
	Bit 7: Sprite #7 (1=2X)
53278	Sprite-Sprite Collision Register
	Bit 0: Sprite #0 (1=Collision Detect)
	Bit 1: Sprite #1 (1=Collision Detect)
	Bit 2: Sprite #2 (1=Collision Detect)
	Bit 3: Sprite #3 (1=Collision Detect)
	Bit 4: Sprite #4 (1=Collision Detect)
	Bit 5: Sprite #5 (1=Collision Detect)
	Bit 6: Sprite #6 (1=Collision Detect)
	Bit 7: Sprite #7 (1=Collision Detect)
53279	Sprite-Background Collision Register
	Bit 0: Sprite #0 (1=Collision Detect)
	Bit 1: Sprite #1 (1=Collision Detect)
	Bit 2: Sprite #2 (1=Collision Detect)
	Bit 3: Sprite #3 (1=Collision Detect)
	Bit 4: Sprite #4 (1=Collision Detect)
	Bit 5: Sprite #5 (1=Collision Detect)
	Bit 6: Sprite #6 (1=Collision Detect)
	Bit 7: Sprite #7 (1=Collision Detect)
53280	Screen Border Color
	0 = BLACK
	1 = WHITE
	2 = RED

```
                          3 = CYAN
                          4 = PURPLE
                          5 = GREEN
                          6 = BLUE
                          7 = YELLOW
                          8 = 0RANGE
                          9 = BROWN
                         10 = LIGHT RED
                         11 = DARK GREY
                         12 = MEDIUM GREY
                         13 = LIGHT GREEN
                         14 = LIGHT BLUE
                         15 = LIGHT GREY

53281              Background Color #1
                          0 = BLACK
                          1 = WHITE
                          2 = RED
                          3 = CYAN
                          4 = PURPLE
                          5 = GREEN
                          6 = BLUE
                          7 = YELLOW
                          8 = 0RANGE
                          9 = BROWN
                         10 = LIGHT RED
                         11 = DARK GREY
                         12 = MEDIUM GREY
                         13 = LIGHT GREEN
                         14 = LIGHT BLUE
                         15 = LIGHT GREY

53282              Background Color #2
                          0 = BLACK
                          1 = WHITE
                          2 = RED
                          3 = CYAN
                          4 = PURPLE
                          5 = GREEN
```

```
                        6 = BLUE
                        7 = YELLOW
                        8 = 0RANGE
                        9 = BROWN
                       10 = LIGHT RED
                       11 = DARK GREY
                       12 = MEDIUM GREY
                       13 = LIGHT GREEN
                       14 = LIGHT BLUE
                       15 = LIGHT GREY
```

53283   Background Color #2

```
                        0 = BLACK
                        1 = WHITE
                        2 = RED
                        3 = CYAN
                        4 = PURPLE
                        5 = GREEN
                        6 = BLUE
                        7 = YELLOW
                        8 = 0RANGE
                        9 = BROWN
                       10 = LIGHT RED
                       11 = DARK GREY
                       12 = MEDIUM GREY
                       13 = LIGHT GREEN
                       14 = LIGHT BLUE
                       15 = LIGHT GREY
```

53284   Background Color #3

```
                        0 = BLACK
                        1 = WHITE
                        2 = RED
                        3 = CYAN
                        4 = PURPLE
                        5 = GREEN
                        6 = BLUE
                        7 = YELLOW
                        8 = 0RANGE
```

	9 = BROWN
	10 = LIGHT RED
	11 = DARK GREY
	12 = MEDIUM GREY
	13 = LIGHT GREEN
	14 = LIGHT BLUE
	15 = LIGHT GREY
53285	Sprite Multicolor Register #0
53286	Sprite Multicolor Register #1
53287—53294	Sprite Color Registers 0-7

    0 = BLACK
    1 = WHITE
    2 = RED
    3 = CYAN
    4 = PURPLE
    5 = GREEN
    6 = BLUE
    7 = YELLOW
    8 = ORANGE
    9 = BROWN
    10 = LIGHT RED
    11 = DARK GREY
    12 = MEDIUM GREY
    13 = LIGHT GREEN
    14 = LIGHT BLUE
    15 = LIGHT GREY

54272 — 55295	**SID Chip Control Registers**
54272 — 54278	Sound Register #1
54272	Frequency Control (Low Byte)
54273	Frequency Control (High Byte)
54274	Pulse Width Value (Low Byte)
54275	Pulse Width Value (High Byte)
54276	Sound Control Register Bit 0: Sound ON/OFF (1=ON)

	Bit 1: Sync Bit (1=ON)
	Bit 2: Ring Modulation (1=ON)
	Bit 3: Test Bit (Normally not used)
	Bit 4: Triangle Wave (1=ON)
	Bit 5: Sawtooth Waveform (1=ON)
	Bit 6: Square Wave (1=ON)
	Bit 7: White Noise (1=ON)
54277	Attack/Decay Control Register
	Bits 0-3: Decay Value
	Bits 4-7: Attack Value
54278	Sustain/Release Control Register
	Bits 0-3: Release Value
54279 — 54285	Sound Register #2
54279	Frequency Control (Low Byte)
54280	Frequency Control (High Byte)
54281	Pulse Width Value (Low Byte)
54282	Pulse Width Value (High Byte)
54283	Sound Control Register
	Bit 0: Sound ON/OFF (1=ON)
	Bit 1: Sync Bit (1=ON)
	Bit 2: Ring Modulation (1=ON)
	Bit 3: Test Bit (Normally not used)
	Bit 4: Triangle Wave (1=ON)
	Bit 5: Sawtooth Waveform (1=ON)
	Bit 6: Square Wave (1=ON)
	Bit 7: White Noise (1=ON)
54284	Attack/Decay Control Register
	Bits 0-3: Decay Value
	Bits 4-7: Attack Value
54285	Sustain/Release Control Register
	Bits 0-3: Release Value
	Bits 4-7: Sustain Value
54286 — 54292	Sound Register #3
54286	Frequency Control (Low Byte)

54287	Frequency Control (High Byte)
54288	Pulse Width Value (Low Byte)
54289	Pulse Width Value (High Byte)
54290	Sound Control Register

      Bit 0: Sound ON/OFF (1=ON)
      Bit 1: Sync Bit (1=ON)
      Bit 2: Ring Modulation (1=ON)
      Bit 3: Test Bit (Normally not used)
      Bit 4: Triangle Wave (1=ON)
      Bit 5: Sawtooth Waveform (1=ON)
      Bit 6: Square Wave (1=ON)
      Bit 7: White Noise (1=ON)

54291	Attack/Decay Control Register

      Bits 0-3: Decay Value
      Bits 4-7: Attack Value

54292	Sustain/Release Control Register

      Bits 0-3: Release Value
      Bits 4-7: Sustain Value

54293 − 54296	Sound Filter Functions
54293	Filter Cutoff Value (Low Byte)
54294	Filter Cutoff Value (High Byte)
54295	Filter/Resonance Control Register

      Bit 0: Sound Register #1 Filter (1=ON)
      Bit 1: Sound Register #2 Filter (1=ON)
      Bit 2: Sound Register #3 Filter (1=ON)
      Bit 3: External Filter (1=ON)
      Bits 4-7: Resonance Value
      Bits 4-7: Sustain Value

54296	Mode/Volume Control

      Bits 0-3: Volume Control Register
      Bit 4: Low Pass Filter
      Bit 5: Band Pass Filter
      Bit 6: High Pass Filter
      Bit 7: Sound Register #3 ON/OFF (1=OFF)

54297	Paddle Controller X-value
54298	Paddle Controller Y-value
54299	Oscillator #3 Random Number Generator
54300	Envelope Register
56320 — 56335	**CIA (Complex Interface Adapter) #1**
56320	Port A

      Bits 0-7: Keyboard Column Key Values
      Bits 0-3: (alt) Direction (Joystick A)
      Bits 2&3: (alt) Paddle Fire Buttons
      Bit 4: (alt) Fire Button (Joystick A)
      Bits 6&7: (alt) Port A Paddle Values

56321	Port B

      Bits 0-7: Keyboard Row Key Values
      Bits 0-3: (alt) Direction (Joystick B)
      Bits 2&3: (alt) Paddle Fire Buttons
      Bit 4: (alt) Fire Button (Joystick B)
      Bits 6&7: (alt) Port B Paddle Values

56322	Port A Input/Output Direction Register
56323	Port B Input/Output Direction Register
56324 — 56327	Timers
56324	Timer A (Low Byte)
56325	Timer A (High Byte)
56326	Timer B (Low Byte)
56327	Timer B (High Byte)
56328 — 56331	Real Time Clock
56328	0.1 Seconds
56329	Seconds
56330	Minutes
56331	Bits 0-6: Hours
	Bit 7: AM/PM Indicator
56332	Serial I/O Buffer (Synchronous)

56333	Interrupt Control Register
	Bit 0: Timer A
	Bit 1: Timer B
	Bit 2: Clock Alarm
	Bit 3: Serial Port
	Bit 4: Cassette Read/Serial Bus SRQ Input
	Bit 7: Interrupt Detect Bit
56334	Control Register A
	Bit 0: Start/Stop Timer (1=Start)
	Bit 1: Timer Output (1=ON)
	Bit 2: Timer Mode (1=Toggle 0=Pulse)
	Bit 3: Timer Run Mode (1=One Shot 0=Cont)
	Bit 4: Preset Timer (1=Preset)
	Bit 5: Timer Clock Source (1=Int 0=System)
	Bit 6: Serial Port I/O Mode (1=Output)
	Bit 7: Real Time Clock Freq (0=60Hz)
56335	Control Register B
	Bit 0: Start/Stop Timer (1=Start)
	Bit 1: Timer Output (1=ON)
	Bit 2: Timer Mode (1=Toggle 0=Pulse)
	Bit 3: Timer Run Mode (1=One Shot 0=Cont)
	Bit 4: Preset Timer (1=Preset)
	Bits 5&6: Timer B Mode Select
	0 = Clock Source: System
	1 = Clock On Positive Pulses
	2 = Carry From Timer A
	3 = Carry From Timer A Positive Pulses
	Bit 7: Set Alarm (1=Set)
	2 = Carry From Timer A
	3 = Carry From Timer A Postive Pulses
	Bit 7: Set Alarm (1=Set)
56576 – 56831	**CIA (Complex Interface Adapter) #2**
56576	Data Port A
	Bits 0&1: VIC II Chip Bank Select
	0 = Bank 3 (49152-65535)
	1 = Bank 2 (32768-49151)

	2 = Bank 1 (16384-32767)
	3 = Bank 0 (00000-16383)
	Bit 2: RS-232 User Data Output
	Bit 3: ATN Output Signal
	Bit 4: Serial Bus Output Clock Pulse
	Bit 5: Serial Bus Output
	Bit 6: Serial Bus Input Clock Pulse
	Bit 7: Serial Bus Input
56577	Data Port B (RS-232 User Port)
	Bit 0: Data Received
	Bit 1: Request to Send
	Bit 2: Data Terminal Ready
	Bit 3: Ring Indicator
	Bit 4: Carrier Detect
	Bit 6: Clear to Send
	Bit 7: Data Set Ready
56378	Port A Input/Output Direction Register
56379	Port B Input/Output Direction Register
56380 − 56383	Timers
56380	Timer A (Low Byte)
56381	Timer A (High Byte)
56382	Timer B (Low Byte)
56383	Timer B (High Byte)
56384 − 56387	Real Time Clock
56384	0.1 Seconds
56385	Seconds
56386	Minutes
56387	Bits 0-6: Hours
	Bit 7: AM/PM Indicator
56388	Serial I/O Buffer (Synchronous)
56389	Interrupt Control Register
	Bit 0: Timer A
	Bit 1: Timer B

Bit 2: Clock Alarm
Bit 3: Serial Port
Bit 4: Cassette Read/Serial Bus SRQ Input
Bit 7: Interrupt Detect Bit

56390   Control Register A
Bit 0: Start/Stop Timer (1=Start)
Bit 1: Timer Output (1=ON)
Bit 2: Timer Mode (1=Toggle 0=Pulse)
Bit 3: Timer Run Mode (1=One Shot 0=Cont)
Bit 4: Preset Timer (1=Preset)
Bit 5: Timer Clock Source (1=Int 0=System)
Bit 6: Serial Port I/O Mode (1=Output)
Bit 7: Real Time Clock Freq (0=60Hz)

56391   Control Register A
Bit 0: Start/Stop Timer (1=Start)
Bit 1: Timer Output (1=ON)
Bit 2: Timer Mode (1=Toggle 0=Pulse)
Bit 3: Timer Run Mode (1=One Shot 0=Cont)
Bit 4: Preset Timer (1=Preset)
Bits 5&6: Timer B Mode Select
     0 = Clock Source: System
     1 = Clock On Positive Pulses
     2 = Carry From Timer A
     3 = Carry From Timer A Positive Pulses
Bit 7: Set Alarm (1=Set)

C-64 I/O Pinouts

This section contains the pinouts of all the I/O connectors on the C-64. Using this information you can design your own interfaces for devices that do not hook up directly to the C-64.

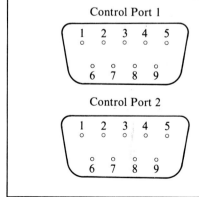

Pin No.	Type
1	JOY0
2	JOY1
3	JOY2
4	JOY3
5	POT Y
6	Fire Button
7	+5 V (50 mA max)
8	GND
9	POT X

FIGURE C-1. Game port pinout

Pin No.	Type
1	GND
2	+5v
3	+5v
4	$\overline{\text{IRQ}}$
5	R/$\overline{\text{W}}$
6	DOT CLOCK
7	I/O 1
8	$\overline{\text{GAME}}$
9	$\overline{\text{EX ROM}}$
10	I/O 2
11	$\overline{\text{ROM L}}$

Pin No.	Type
12	BA
13	$\overline{\text{DMA}}$
14	D7
15	D6
16	D5
17	D4
18	D3
19	D2
20	D1
21	D0
22	GND

Pin No.	Type
A	GND
B	$\overline{\text{ROM H}}$
C	$\overline{\text{RESET}}$
D	$\overline{\text{NMI}}$
E	S 02
F	A 15
H	A 14
J	A 13
K	A 12
L	A 11
M	A 10

Pin No.	Type
N	A9
P	A8
R	A7
S	A6
T	A5
U	A4
V	A3
W	A2
X	A1
Y	A0
Z	GND

Figure C-2. Expansion port pinout

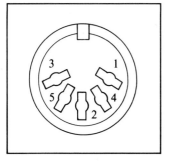

Pin No.	Type
1	LUMINANCE
2	GND
3	AUDIO OUT
4	VIDEO OUT
5	AUDIO IN

FIGURE C-3. Audio/video port pinout

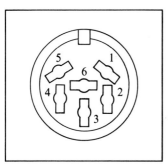

Pin No.	Type
1	SERIAL SRQ IN
2	GND
3	SERIAL ATN IN/OUT
4	SERIAL CLK IN/OUT
5	SERIAL DATA IN/OUT
6	RESET

FIGURE C-4. Serial I/O port pinout

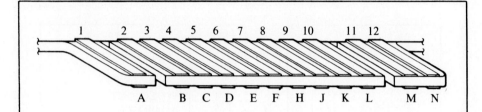

Pin No.	Type
1	GND
2	+5 V
3	$\overline{\text{RESET}}$
4	CONTROL 1
5	SP 1
6	CONTROL 2
7	SP 2
8	$\overline{\text{PC 2}}$
9	SERIAL ATN IN
10	+9 V (100 mA max)
11	+9 V (100 mA max)
12	GND
A	GND
B	$\overline{\text{FLAG 2}}$
C	PB0
D	PB1
E	PB2
F	PB3
H	PB4
J	PB5
K	PB6
L	PB7
M	PA2
N	GND

FIGURE C-5. User port pinout

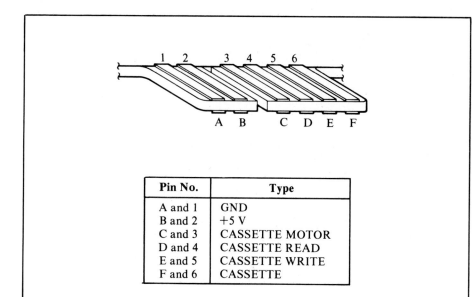

Pin No.	Type
A and 1	GND
B and 2	+5 V
C and 3	CASSETTE MOTOR
D and 4	CASSETTE READ
E and 5	CASSETTE WRITE
F and 6	CASSETTE

FIGURE C-6. Cassette interface pinout

Conversion Tables
Trigonometric Functions

The tables in this section are intended as an aid to mathematical programming.

Hexadecimal-Decimal Integer Conversion

Table D-1 provides for direct conversions between hexadecimal integers in the range 0-FFF and decimal integers in the range 0-4095. For conversion of larger integers, the table values may be added to the figures in Table D-2.

Hexadecimal fractions may be converted to decimal fractions as follows:

1. Express the hexadecimal fraction as an integer times 16^{-n}, where n is the number of significant hexadecimal places to the right of the hexadecimal point.

$$0. \text{CA9BF3}_{16} = \text{CA9 BF3}_{16} \times 16^{-6}$$

2. Find the decimal equivalent of the hexadecimal integer

$$\text{CA9 BF3}_{16} = 13\ 278\ 195_{10}$$

3. Multiply the decimal equivalent by 16^{-n}

$$
\begin{array}{ccc}
13 & 278 & 195 \\
\times\ 596 & 046 & 448 \times 10^{16} \\
\hline
0.791 & 442 & 096_{10}
\end{array}
$$

TABLE D-1. Hexadecimal-Decimal Integer Conversion

	0	1	2	3	4	5	6	7	8	9	A	B	C	D	E	F
00	0000	0001	0002	0003	0004	0005	0006	0007	0008	0009	0010	0011	0012	0013	0014	0015
01	0016	0017	0018	0019	0020	0021	0022	0023	0024	0025	0026	0027	0028	0029	0030	0031
02	0032	0033	0034	0035	0036	0037	0038	0039	0040	0041	0042	0043	0044	0045	0046	0047
03	0048	0049	0050	0051	0052	0053	0054	0055	0056	0057	0058	0059	0060	0061	0062	0063
04	0064	0065	0066	0067	0068	0069	0070	0071	0072	0073	0074	0075	0076	0077	0078	0079
05	0080	0081	0082	0083	0084	0085	0086	0087	0088	0089	0090	0091	0092	0093	0094	0095
06	0096	0097	0098	0099	0100	0101	0102	0103	0104	0105	0106	0107	0108	0109	0110	0111
07	0112	0113	0114	0115	0116	0117	0118	0119	0120	0121	0122	0123	0124	0125	0126	0127
08	0128	0129	0130	0131	0132	0133	0134	0135	0136	0137	0138	0139	0140	0141	0142	0143
09	0144	0145	0146	0147	0148	0149	0150	0151	0152	0153	0154	0155	0156	0157	0158	0159
0A	0160	0161	0162	0163	0164	0165	0166	0167	0168	0169	0170	0171	0172	0173	0174	0175
0B	0176	0177	0178	0179	0180	0181	0182	0183	0184	0185	0186	0187	0188	0189	0190	0191
0C	0192	0193	0194	0195	0196	0197	0198	0199	0200	0201	0202	0203	0204	0205	0206	0207
0D	0208	0209	0210	0211	0212	0213	0214	0215	0216	0217	0218	0219	0220	0221	0222	0223
0E	0224	0225	0226	0227	0228	0229	0230	0231	0232	0233	0234	0235	0236	0237	0238	0239
0F	0240	0241	0242	0243	0244	0245	0246	0247	0248	0249	0250	0251	0252	0253	0254	0255
10	0256	0257	0258	0259	0260	0261	0262	0263	0264	0265	0266	0267	0268	0269	0270	0271
11	0272	0273	0274	0275	0276	0277	0278	0279	0280	0281	0282	0283	0284	0285	0286	0287
12	0288	0289	0290	0291	0292	0293	0294	0295	0296	0297	0298	0299	0300	0301	0302	0303
13	0304	0305	0306	0307	0308	0309	0310	0311	0312	0313	0314	0315	0316	0317	0318	0319
14	0320	0321	0322	0323	0324	0325	0326	0327	0328	0329	0330	0331	0332	0333	0334	0335
15	0336	0337	0338	0339	0340	0341	0342	0343	0344	0345	0346	0347	0348	0349	0350	0351
16	0352	0353	0354	0355	0356	0357	0358	0359	0360	0361	0362	0363	0364	0365	0366	0367
17	0368	0369	0370	0371	0372	0373	0374	0375	0376	0377	0378	0379	0380	0381	0382	0383
18	0384	0385	0386	0387	0388	0389	0390	0391	0392	0393	0394	0395	0396	0397	0398	0399
19	0400	0401	0402	0403	0404	0405	0406	0407	0408	0409	0410	0411	0412	0413	0414	0415
1A	0416	0417	0418	0419	0420	0421	0422	0423	0424	0425	0426	0427	0428	0429	0430	0431
1B	0432	0433	0434	0435	0436	0437	0438	0439	0440	0441	0442	0443	0444	0445	0446	0447
1C	0448	0449	0450	0451	0452	0453	0454	0455	0456	0457	0458	0459	0460	0461	0462	0463
1D	0464	0465	0466	0467	0468	0469	0470	0471	0472	0473	0474	0475	0476	0477	0478	0479
1E	0480	0481	0482	0483	0484	0485	0486	0487	0488	0489	0490	0491	0492	0493	0494	0495
1F	0496	0497	0498	0499	0500	0501	0502	0503	0504	0505	0506	0507	0508	0509	0510	0511
20	0512	0513	0514	0515	0516	0517	0518	0519	0520	0521	0522	0523	0524	0525	0526	0527
21	0528	0529	0530	0531	0532	0533	0534	0535	0536	0537	0538	0539	0540	0541	0542	0543
22	0544	0545	0546	0547	0548	0549	0550	0551	0552	0553	0554	0555	0556	0557	0558	0559
23	0560	0561	0562	0563	0564	0565	0566	0567	0568	0569	0570	0571	0572	0573	0574	0575
24	0576	0577	0578	0579	0580	0581	0582	0583	0584	0585	0586	0587	0588	0589	0590	0591
25	0592	0593	0594	0595	0596	0597	0598	0599	0600	0601	0602	0603	0604	0605	0606	0607
26	0608	0609	0610	0611	0612	0613	0614	0615	0616	0617	0618	0619	0620	0621	0622	0623
27	0624	0625	0626	0627	0628	0629	0630	0631	0632	0633	0634	0635	0636	0637	0638	0639
28	0640	0641	0642	0643	0644	0645	0646	0647	0648	0649	0650	0651	0652	0653	0654	0655
29	0656	0657	0658	0659	0660	0661	0662	0663	0664	0665	0666	0667	0668	0669	0670	0671
2A	0672	0673	0674	0675	0676	0677	0678	0679	0680	0681	0682	0683	0684	0685	0686	0687
2B	0688	0689	0690	0691	0692	0693	0694	0695	0696	0697	0698	0699	0700	0701	0702	0703
2C	0704	0705	0706	0707	0708	0709	0710	0711	0712	0713	0714	0715	0716	0717	0718	0719
2D	0720	0721	0722	0723	0724	0725	0726	0727	0728	0729	0730	0731	0732	0733	0734	0735
2E	0736	0737	0738	0739	0740	0741	0742	0743	0744	0745	0746	0747	0748	0749	0750	0751
2F	0752	0753	0754	0755	0756	0757	0758	0759	0760	0761	0762	0763	0764	0765	0766	0767

TABLE D-1. Hexadecimal-Decimal Integer Conversion (continued)

	0	1	2	3	4	5	6	7	8	9	A	B	C	D	E	F
30	0768	0769	0770	0771	0772	0773	0774	0775	0776	0777	0778	0779	0780	0781	0782	0783
31	0784	0785	0786	0787	0788	0789	0790	0791	0792	0793	0794	0795	0796	0797	0798	0799
32	0800	0801	0802	0803	0804	0805	0806	0807	0808	0809	0810	0811	0812	0813	0814	0815
33	0816	0817	0818	0819	0820	0821	0822	0823	0824	0825	0826	0827	0828	0829	0830	0831
34	0832	0833	0834	0835	0836	0837	0838	0839	0840	0841	0842	0843	0844	0845	0846	0847
35	0848	0849	0850	0851	0852	0853	0854	0855	0856	0857	0858	0859	0860	0861	0862	0863
36	0864	0865	0866	0867	0868	0869	0870	0871	0872	0873	0874	0875	0876	0877	0878	0879
37	0880	0881	0882	0883	0884	0885	0886	0887	0888	0889	0890	0891	0892	0893	0894	0895
38	0896	0897	0898	0899	0900	0901	0902	0903	0904	0905	0906	0907	0908	0909	0910	0911
39	0912	0913	0914	0915	0916	0917	0918	0919	0920	0921	0922	0923	0924	0925	0926	0927
3A	0928	0929	0930	0931	0932	0933	0934	0935	0936	0937	0938	0939	0940	0941	0942	0943
3B	0944	0945	0946	0947	0948	0949	0950	0951	0952	0953	0954	0955	0956	0957	0958	0959
3C	0960	0961	0962	0963	0964	0965	0966	0967	0968	0969	0970	0971	0972	0973	0974	0975
3D	0976	0977	0978	0979	0980	0981	0982	0983	0984	0985	0986	0987	0988	0989	0990	0991
3E	0992	0993	0994	0995	0996	0997	0998	0999	1000	1001	1002	1003	1004	1005	1006	1007
3F	1008	1009	1010	1011	1012	1013	1014	1015	1016	1017	1018	1019	1020	1021	1022	1023
40	1024	1025	1026	1027	1028	1029	1030	1031	1032	1033	1034	1035	1036	1037	1038	1039
41	1040	1041	1042	1043	1044	1045	1046	1047	1048	1049	1050	1051	1052	1053	1054	1055
42	1056	1057	1058	1059	1060	1061	1062	1063	1064	1065	1066	1067	1068	1069	1070	1071
43	1072	1073	1074	1075	1076	1077	1078	1079	1080	1081	1082	1083	1084	1085	1086	1087
44	1088	1089	1090	1091	1092	1093	1094	1095	1096	1097	1098	1099	1100	1101	1102	1103
45	1104	1105	1106	1107	1108	1109	1110	1111	1112	1113	1114	1115	1116	1117	1118	1119
46	1120	1121	1122	1123	1124	1125	1126	1127	1128	1129	1130	1131	1132	1133	1134	1135
47	1136	1137	1138	1139	1140	1141	1142	1143	1144	1145	1146	1147	1148	1149	1150	1151
48	1152	1153	1154	1155	1156	1157	1158	1159	1160	1161	1162	1163	1164	1165	1166	1167
49	1168	1169	1170	1171	1172	1173	1174	1175	1176	1177	1178	1179	1180	1181	1182	1183
4A	1184	1185	1186	1187	1188	1189	1190	1191	1192	1193	1194	1195	1196	1197	1198	1199
4B	1200	1201	1202	1203	1204	1205	1206	1207	1208	1209	1210	1211	1212	1213	1214	1215
4C	1216	1217	1218	1219	1220	1221	1222	1223	1224	1225	1226	1227	1228	1229	1230	1231
4D	1232	1233	1234	1235	1236	1237	1238	1239	1240	1241	1242	1243	1244	1245	1246	1247
4E	1248	1249	1250	1251	1252	1253	1254	1255	1256	1257	1258	1259	1260	1261	1262	1263
4F	1264	1265	1266	1267	1268	1269	1270	1271	1272	1273	1274	1275	1276	1277	1278	1279
50	1280	1281	1282	1283	1284	1285	1286	1287	1288	1289	1290	1291	1292	1293	1294	1295
51	1296	1297	1298	1299	1300	1301	1302	1303	1304	1305	1306	1307	1308	1309	1310	1311
52	1312	1313	1314	1315	1316	1317	1318	1319	1320	1321	1322	1323	1324	1325	1326	1327
53	1328	1329	1330	1331	1332	1333	1334	1335	1336	1337	1338	1339	1340	1341	1342	1343
54	1344	1345	1346	1347	1348	1349	1350	1351	1352	1353	1354	1355	1356	1357	1358	1359
55	1360	1361	1362	1363	1364	1365	1366	1367	1368	1369	1370	1371	1372	1373	1374	1375
56	1376	1377	1378	1379	1380	1381	1382	1383	1384	1385	1386	1387	1388	1389	1390	1391
57	1392	1393	1394	1395	1396	1397	1398	1399	1400	1401	1402	1403	1404	1405	1406	1407
58	1408	1409	1410	1411	1412	1413	1414	1415	1416	1417	1418	1419	1420	1421	1422	1423
59	1424	1425	1426	1427	1428	1429	1430	1431	1432	1433	1434	1435	1436	1437	1438	1439
5A	1440	1441	1442	1443	1444	1445	1446	1447	1448	1449	1450	1451	1452	1453	1454	1455
5B	1456	1457	1458	1459	1460	1461	1462	1463	1464	1465	1466	1467	1468	1469	1470	1471
5C	1472	1473	1474	1475	1476	1477	1478	1479	1480	1481	1482	1483	1484	1485	1486	1487
5D	1488	1489	1490	1491	1492	1493	1494	1495	1496	1497	1498	1499	1500	1501	1502	1503
5E	1504	1505	1506	1507	1508	1509	1510	1511	1512	1513	1514	1515	1516	1517	1518	1519
5F	1520	1521	1522	1523	1524	1525	1526	1527	1528	1529	1530	1531	1532	1533	1534	1535

TABLE D-1. Hexadecimal-Decimal Integer Conversion (continued)

	0	1	2	3	4	5	6	7	8	9	A	B	C	D	E	F
60	1536	1537	1538	1539	1540	1541	1542	1543	1544	1545	1546	1547	1548	1549	1550	1551
61	1552	1553	1554	1555	1556	1557	1558	1559	1560	1561	1562	1563	1564	1565	1566	1567
62	1568	1569	1570	1571	1572	1573	1574	1575	1576	1577	1578	1579	1580	1581	1582	1583
63	1584	1585	1586	1587	1588	1589	1590	1591	1592	1593	1594	1595	1596	1597	1598	1599
64	1600	1601	1602	1603	1604	1605	1606	1607	1608	1609	1610	1611	1612	1613	1614	1615
65	1616	1617	1618	1619	1620	1621	1622	1623	1624	1625	1626	1627	1628	1629	1630	1631
66	1632	1633	1634	1635	1636	1637	1638	1639	1640	1641	1642	1643	1644	1645	1646	1647
67	1648	1649	1650	1651	1652	1653	1654	1655	1656	1657	1658	1659	1660	1661	1562	1663
68	1664	1665	1666	1667	1668	1669	1670	1671	1672	1673	1674	1675	1676	1677	1678	1679
69	1680	1681	1682	1683	1684	1685	1686	1687	1688	1689	1690	1691	1692	1693	1694	1695
6A	1696	1697	1698	1699	1700	1701	1702	1703	1704	1705	1706	1707	1708	1709	1710	1711
6B	1712	1713	1714	1715	1716	1717	1718	1719	1720	1721	1722	1723	1724	1725	1726	1727
6C	1728	1729	1730	1731	1732	1733	1734	1735	1736	1737	1738	1739	1740	1741	1742	1743
6D	1744	1745	1746	1747	1748	1749	1750	1751	1752	1753	1754	1755	1756	1757	1758	1759
6E	1760	1761	1762	1763	1764	1765	1766	1767	1768	1769	1770	1771	1772	1773	1774	1775
6F	1776	1777	1778	1779	1780	1781	1782	1783	1784	1785	1786	1787	1788	1789	1790	1791
70	1792	1793	1794	1795	1796	1797	1798	1799	1800	1801	1802	1803	1804	1805	1806	1807
71	1808	1809	1810	1811	1812	1813	1814	1815	1816	1817	1818	1819	1820	1821	1822	1823
72	1824	1825	1826	1827	1828	1829	1830	1831	1832	1833	1834	1835	1836	1837	1838	1839
73	1840	1841	1842	1843	1844	1845	1846	1847	1848	1849	1850	1851	1852	1853	1854	1855
74	1856	1857	1858	1859	1860	1861	1862	1863	1864	1865	1866	1867	1868	1869	1870	1871
75	1872	1873	1874	1875	1876	1877	1878	1879	1880	1881	1882	1883	1884	1885	1886	1887
76	1888	1889	1890	1891	1892	1893	1894	1895	1896	1897	1898	1899	1900	1901	1902	1903
77	1904	1905	1906	1907	1908	1909	1910	1911	1912	1913	1914	1915	1916	1917	1918	1919
78	1920	1921	1922	1923	1924	1925	1926	1927	1928	1929	1930	1931	1932	1933	1934	1935
79	1936	1937	1938	1939	1940	1941	1942	1943	1944	1945	1946	1947	1948	1949	1950	1951
7A	1952	1953	1954	1955	1956	1957	1958	1959	1960	1961	1962	1963	1964	1965	1966	1967
7B	1968	1969	1970	1971	1972	1973	1974	1975	1976	1977	1978	1979	1980	1981	1982	1983
7C	1984	1985	1986	1987	1988	1989	1990	1991	1992	1993	1994	1995	1996	1997	1998	1999
7D	2000	2001	2002	2003	2004	2005	2006	2007	2008	2009	2010	2011	2012	2013	2014	2015
7E	2016	2017	2018	2019	2020	2021	2022	2023	2024	2025	2026	2027	2028	2029	2030	2031
7F	2032	2033	2034	2035	2036	2037	2038	2039	2040	2041	2042	2043	2044	2045	2046	2047
80	2048	2049	2050	2051	2052	2053	2054	2055	2056	2057	2058	2059	2060	2061	2062	2063
81	2064	2065	2066	2067	2068	2069	2070	2071	2072	2073	2074	2075	2076	2077	2078	2079
82	2080	2081	2082	2083	2084	2085	2086	2087	2088	2089	2090	2091	2092	2093	2094	2095
83	2096	2097	2098	2099	2100	2101	2102	2103	2104	2105	2106	2107	2108	2109	2110	2111
84	2112	2113	2114	2115	2116	2117	2118	2119	2120	2121	2122	2123	2124	2125	2126	2127
85	2128	2129	2130	2131	2132	2133	2134	2135	2136	2137	2138	2139	2140	2141	2142	2143
86	2144	2145	2146	2147	2148	2149	2150	2151	2152	2153	2154	2155	2156	2157	2158	2159
87	2160	2161	2162	2163	2164	2165	2166	2167	2168	2169	2170	2171	2172	2173	2174	2175
88	2176	2177	2178	2179	2180	2181	2182	2183	2184	2185	2186	2187	2188	2189	2190	2191
89	2192	2193	2194	2195	2196	2197	2198	2199	2200	2201	2202	2203	2204	2205	2206	2207
8A	2208	2209	2210	2211	2212	2213	2214	2215	2216	2217	2218	2219	2220	2221	2222	2223
8B	2224	2225	2226	2227	2228	2229	2230	2231	2232	2233	2234	2235	2236	2237	2238	2239
8C	2240	2241	2242	2243	2244	2245	2246	2247	2248	2249	2250	2251	2252	2253	2254	2255
8D	2256	2257	2258	2259	2260	2261	2262	2263	2264	2265	2266	2267	2268	2269	2270	2271
8E	2272	2273	2274	2275	2276	2277	2278	2279	2280	2281	2282	2283	2284	2285	2286	2287
8F	2288	2289	2290	2291	2292	2293	2294	2295	2296	2297	2298	2299	2300	2301	2302	2303

TABLE D-1. Hexadecimal-Decimal Integer Conversion (continued)

	0	1	2	3	4	5	6	7	8	9	A	B	C	D	E	F
90	2304	2305	2306	2307	2308	2309	2310	2311	2312	2313	2314	2315	2316	2317	2318	2319
91	2320	2321	2322	2323	2324	2325	2326	2327	2328	2329	2330	2331	2332	2333	2334	2335
92	2336	2337	2338	2339	2340	2341	2342	2343	2344	2345	2346	2347	2348	2349	2350	2351
93	2352	2353	2354	2355	2356	2357	2358	2359	2360	2361	2362	2363	2364	2365	2366	2367
94	2368	2369	2370	2371	2372	2373	2374	2375	2376	2377	2378	2379	2380	2381	2382	2383
95	2384	2385	2386	2387	2388	2389	2390	2391	2392	2393	2394	2395	2396	2397	2398	2399
96	2400	2401	2402	2403	2404	2405	2406	2407	2408	2409	2410	2411	2412	2413	2414	2415
97	2416	2417	2418	2419	2420	2421	2422	2423	2424	2425	2426	2427	2428	2429	2430	2431
98	2432	2433	2434	2435	2436	2437	2438	2439	2440	2441	2442	2443	2444	2445	2446	2447
99	2448	2449	2450	2451	2452	2453	2454	2455	2456	2457	2458	2459	2460	2461	2462	2463
9A	2464	2465	2466	2467	2468	2469	2470	2471	2472	2473	2474	2475	2476	2477	2478	2479
9B	2480	2481	2482	2483	2484	2485	2486	2487	2488	2489	2490	2491	2492	2493	2494	2495
9C	2496	2497	2498	2499	2500	2501	2502	2503	2504	2505	2506	2507	2508	2509	2510	2511
9D	2512	2513	2514	2515	2516	2517	2518	2519	2520	2521	2522	2523	2524	2525	2526	2527
9E	2528	2529	2530	2531	2532	2533	2534	2535	2536	2537	2538	2539	2540	2541	2542	2543
9F	2544	2545	2546	2547	2548	2549	2550	2551	2552	2553	2554	2555	2556	2557	2558	2559
A0	2560	2561	2562	2563	2564	2565	2566	2567	2568	2569	2570	2571	2572	2573	2574	2575
A1	2576	2577	2578	2579	2580	2581	2582	2583	2584	2585	2586	2587	2588	2589	2590	2591
A2	2592	2593	2594	2595	2596	2597	2598	2599	2600	2601	2602	2603	2604	2605	2606	2607
A3	2608	2609	2610	2611	2612	2613	2614	2615	2616	2617	2618	2619	2620	2621	2622	2623
A4	2624	2625	2626	2627	2628	2629	2630	2631	2632	2633	2634	2635	2636	2637	2638	2639
A5	2640	2641	2642	2643	2644	2645	2646	2647	2648	2649	2650	2651	2652	2653	2654	2655
A6	2656	2657	2658	2659	2660	2661	2662	2663	2664	2665	2666	2667	2668	2669	2670	2671
A7	2672	2673	2674	2675	2676	2677	2678	2679	2680	2681	2682	2683	2684	2685	2686	2687
A8	2688	2689	2690	2691	2692	2693	2694	2695	2696	2697	2698	2699	2700	2701	2702	2703
A9	2704	2705	2706	2707	2708	2709	2710	2711	2712	2713	2714	2715	2716	2717	2718	2719
AA	2720	2721	2722	2723	2724	2725	2726	2727	2728	2729	2730	2731	2732	2733	2734	2735
AB	2736	2737	2738	2739	2740	2741	2742	2743	2744	2745	2746	2747	2748	2749	2750	2751
AC	2752	2753	2754	2755	2756	2757	2758	2759	2760	2761	2762	2763	2764	2765	2766	2767
AD	2768	2769	2770	2771	2772	2773	2774	2775	2776	2777	2778	2779	2780	2781	2782	2783
AE	2784	2785	2786	2787	2788	2789	2790	2791	2792	2793	2794	2795	2796	2797	2798	2799
AF	2800	2801	2802	2803	2804	2805	2806	2807	2808	2809	2810	2811	2812	2813	2814	2815
B0	2816	2817	2818	2819	2820	2821	2822	2823	2824	2825	2826	2827	2828	2829	2830	2831
B1	2832	2833	2834	2835	2836	2837	2838	2839	2840	2841	2842	2843	2844	2845	2846	2847
B2	2848	2849	2850	2851	2852	2853	2854	2855	2856	2857	2858	2859	2860	2861	2862	2863
B3	2864	2865	2866	2867	2868	2869	2870	2871	2872	2873	2874	2875	2876	2877	2878	2879
B4	2880	2881	2882	2883	2884	2885	2886	2887	2888	2889	2890	2891	2892	2893	2894	2895
B5	2896	2897	2898	2899	2900	2901	2902	2903	2904	2905	2906	2907	2908	2909	2910	2911
B6	2912	2913	2914	2915	2916	2917	2918	2919	2920	2921	2922	2923	2924	2925	2926	2927
B7	2928	2929	2930	2931	2932	2933	2934	2935	2936	2937	2938	2939	2940	2941	2942	2943
B8	2944	2945	2946	2947	2948	2949	2950	2951	2952	2953	2954	2955	2956	2957	2958	2959
B9	2960	2961	2962	2963	2964	2965	2966	2967	2968	2969	2970	2971	2972	2973	2974	2975
BA	2976	2977	2978	2979	2980	2981	2982	2983	2984	2985	2986	2987	2988	2989	2990	2991
BB	2992	2993	2994	2995	2996	2997	2998	2999	3000	3001	3002	3003	3004	3005	3006	3007
BC	3008	3009	3010	3011	3012	3013	3014	3015	3016	3017	3018	3019	3020	3021	3022	3023
BD	3024	3025	3026	3027	3028	3029	3030	3031	3032	3033	3034	3035	3036	3037	3038	3039
BE	3040	3041	3042	3043	3044	3045	3046	3047	3048	3049	3050	3051	3052	3053	3054	3055
BF	3056	3057	3058	3059	3060	3061	3062	3063	3064	3065	3066	3067	3068	3069	3070	3071

TABLE D-1. Hexadecimal-Decimal Integer Conversion (continued)

	0	1	2	3	4	5	6	7	8	9	A	B	C	D	E	F
C0	3072	3073	3074	3075	3076	3077	3078	3079	3080	3081	3082	3083	3084	3085	3086	3087
C1	3088	3089	3090	3091	3092	3093	3094	3095	3096	3097	3098	3099	3100	3101	3102	3103
C2	3104	3105	3106	3107	3108	3109	3110	3111	3112	3113	3114	3115	3116	3117	3118	3119
C3	3120	3121	3122	3123	3124	3125	3126	3127	3128	3129	3130	3131	3132	3133	3134	3135
C4	3136	3137	3138	3139	3140	3141	3142	3143	3144	3145	3146	3147	3148	3149	3150	3151
C5	3152	3153	3154	3155	3156	3157	3158	3159	3160	3161	3162	3163	3164	3165	3166	3167
C6	3168	3169	3170	3171	3172	3173	3174	3175	3176	3177	3178	3179	3180	3181	3182	3183
C7	3184	3185	3186	3187	3188	3189	3190	3191	3192	3193	3194	3195	3196	3197	3198	3199
C8	3200	3201	3202	3203	3204	3205	3206	3207	3208	3209	3210	3211	3212	3213	3214	3215
C9	3216	3217	3218	3219	3220	3221	3222	3223	3224	3225	3226	3227	3228	3229	3230	2231
CA	3232	3233	3234	3235	3236	3237	3238	3239	3240	3241	3242	3243	3244	3245	3246	3247
CB	3248	3249	3250	3251	3252	3253	3254	3255	3256	3257	3258	3259	3260	3261	3262	3263
CC	3264	3265	3266	3267	3268	3269	3270	3271	3272	3273	3274	3275	3276	3277	3278	3279
CD	3280	3281	3282	3283	3284	3285	3286	3287	3288	3289	3290	3291	3292	3293	3294	3295
CE	3296	3297	3298	3299	3300	3301	3302	3303	3304	3305	3306	3307	3308	3309	3310	3311
CF	3312	3313	3314	3315	3316	3317	3318	3319	3320	3321	3322	3323	3324	3325	3326	3327
D0	3328	3329	3330	3331	3332	3333	3334	3335	3336	3337	3338	3339	3340	3341	3342	3343
D1	3344	3345	3346	3347	3348	3349	3350	3351	3352	3353	3354	3355	3356	3357	3358	3359
D2	3360	3361	3362	3363	3364	3365	3366	3367	3368	3369	3370	3371	3372	3373	3374	3375
D3	3376	3377	3378	3379	3380	3381	3382	3383	3384	3385	3386	3387	3388	3389	3390	3391
D4	3392	3393	3394	3395	3396	3397	3398	3399	3400	3401	3402	3403	3404	3405	3406	3407
D5	3408	3409	3410	3411	3412	3413	3414	3415	3416	3417	3418	3419	3420	3421	3422	3423
D6	3424	3425	3426	3427	3428	3429	3430	3431	3432	3433	3434	3435	3436	3437	3438	3439
D7	3440	3441	3442	3443	3444	3445	3446	3447	3448	3449	3450	3451	3452	3453	3454	3455
D8	3456	3457	3458	3459	3460	3461	3462	3463	3464	3465	3466	3467	3468	3469	3470	3471
D9	3472	3473	3474	3475	3476	3477	3478	3479	3480	3481	3482	3483	3484	3485	3486	3487
DA	3488	3489	3490	3491	3492	3493	3494	3495	3496	3497	3498	3499	3500	3501	3502	3503
DB	3504	3505	3506	3507	3508	3509	3510	3511	3512	3513	3514	3515	3516	3517	3518	3519
DC	3520	3521	3522	3523	3524	3525	3526	3527	3528	3529	3530	3531	3532	3533	3534	3535
DD	3536	3537	3538	3539	3540	3541	3542	3543	3544	3545	3546	3547	3548	3549	3550	3551
DE	3552	3553	3554	3555	3556	3557	3558	3559	3560	3561	3562	3563	3564	3565	3566	3567
DF	3568	3569	3570	3571	3572	3573	3574	3575	3576	3577	3578	3579	3580	3581	3582	3583
E0	3584	3585	3586	3587	3588	3589	3590	3591	3592	3593	3594	3595	3596	3597	3598	3599
E1	3600	3601	3602	3603	3604	3605	3606	3607	3608	3609	3610	3611	3612	3613	3614	3615
E2	3616	3617	3618	3619	3620	3621	3622	3623	3624	3625	3626	3627	3628	3629	3630	3631
E3	3632	3633	3634	3635	3636	3637	3638	3639	3640	3641	3642	3643	3644	3645	3646	3647
E4	3648	3649	3650	3651	3652	3653	3654	3655	3656	3657	3658	3659	3660	3661	3662	3663
E5	3664	3665	3666	3667	3668	3669	3670	3671	3672	3673	3674	3675	3676	3677	3678	3679
E6	3680	3681	3682	3683	3684	3685	3686	3687	3688	3689	3690	3691	3692	3693	3694	3695
E7	3696	3697	3698	3699	3700	3701	3702	3703	3704	3705	3706	3707	3708	3709	3710	3711
E8	3712	3713	3714	3715	3716	3717	3718	3719	3720	3721	3722	3723	3724	3725	3726	3727
E9	3728	3729	3730	3731	3732	3733	3734	3735	3736	3737	3738	3739	3740	3741	3742	3743
EA	3744	3745	3746	3747	3748	3749	3750	3751	3752	3753	3754	3755	3756	3757	3758	3759
EB	3760	3761	3762	3763	3764	3765	3766	3767	3768	3769	3770	3771	3772	3773	3774	3775
EC	3776	3777	3778	3779	3780	3781	3782	3783	3784	3785	3786	3787	3788	3789	3790	3791
ED	3792	3793	3794	3795	3796	3797	3798	3799	3800	3801	3802	3803	3804	3805	3806	3807
EE	3808	3809	3810	3811	3812	3813	3814	3815	3816	3817	3818	3819	3820	3821	3822	3823
EF	3824	3825	3826	3827	3828	3829	3830	3831	3832	3833	3834	3835	3836	3837	3838	3839

TABLE D-1. Hexadecimal-Decimal Integer Conversion (continued)

	0	1	2	3	4	5	6	7	8	9	A	B	C	D	E	F
F0	3840	3841	3842	3843	3844	3845	3846	3847	3848	3849	3850	3851	3852	3853	3854	3855
F1	3856	3857	3858	3859	3860	3861	3862	3863	3864	3865	3866	3867	3868	3869	3870	3871
F2	3872	3873	3874	3875	3876	3877	3878	3879	3880	3881	3882	3883	3884	3885	3886	3887
F3	3888	3889	3890	3891	3892	3893	3894	3895	3896	3897	389C	3899	3900	3901	3902	3903
F4	3904	3905	3906	3907	3908	3909	3910	3911	3912	3913	3914	3915	3916	3917	3918	3919
F5	3920	3921	3922	3923	3924	3925	3926	3927	3928	3929	3930	3931	3932	3933	3934	3935
F6	3936	3937	3938	3939	3940	3941	3942	3943	3944	3945	3946	3947	3948	3949	3950	3951
F7	3952	3953	3954	3955	3956	3957	3958	3959	3960	3961	3962	3963	3964	3965	3966	3967
F8	3968	3969	3970	3971	3972	3973	3974	3975	3976	3977	3978	3979	3980	3981	3982	3983
F9	3984	3985	3986	3987	3988	3989	3990	3991	3992	3993	3994	3995	3996	3997	3998	3999
FA	4000	4001	4002	4003	4004	4005	4006	4007	4008	4009	4010	4011	4012	4013	4014	4015
FB	4016	4017	4018	4019	4020	4021	4022	4023	4024	4025	4026	4027	4028	4029	4030	4031
FC	4032	4033	4034	4035	4036	4037	4038	4039	4040	4041	4042	4043	4044	4045	4046	4047
FD	4048	4049	4050	4051	4052	4053	4054	4055	4056	4057	4058	4059	4060	4061	4062	4063
FE	4064	4065	4066	4067	4068	4069	4070	4071	4072	4073	4074	4075	4076	4077	4078	4079
FF	4080	4081	4082	4083	4084	4085	4086	4087	4088	4089	4090	4091	4092	4093	4094	4095

TABLE D-2. Conversion Values

Hexadecimal	Decimal	Hexadecimal	Decimal	Hexadecimal	Decimal	Hexadecimal	Decimal
01 000	4 096	11 000	69 632	30 000	196 608	400 000	4 194 304
02 000	8 192	12 000	73 728	40 000	262 144	500 000	5 242 880
03 000	12 288	13 000	77 824	50 000	327 680	600 000	6 291 456
04 000	16 384	14 000	81 920	60 000	393 216	700 000	7 340 032
05 000	20 480	15 000	86 016	70 000	458 752	800 000	8 388 608
06 000	24 576	16 000	90 112	80 000	524 288	900 000	9 437 184
07 000	28 672	17 000	94 208	90 000	589 824	A00 000	10 485 760
08 000	32 768	18 000	98 304	A0 000	655 360	B00 000	11 534 336
09 000	36 864	19 000	102 400	B0 000	720 896	C00 000	12 582 912
0A 000	40 960	1A 000	106 496	C0 000	786 432	D00 000	13 631 488
0B 000	45 056	1B 000	110 592	D0 000	851 968	E00 000	14 680 064
0C 000	49 152	1C 000	114 688	E0 000	917 504	F00 000	15 728 640
0D 000	53 248	1D 000	118 784	F0 000	983 040	1 000 000	16 777 216
0E 000	57 344	1E 000	122 880	100 000	1 048 576	2 000 000	33 554 432
0F 000	61 440	1F 000	126 976	200 000	2 097 152		
10 000	65 536	20 000	131 072	300 000	3 145 728		

Decimal fractions may be converted to hexadecimal fractions by successively multiplying the decimal fraction by 16_{10}. After each multiplication, the integer portion is removed to form a hexadecimal fraction by building to the right of the hexadecimal point. However, since decimal arithmetic is used in this conversion, the integer portion of each product must be converted to hexadecimal numbers.

Example:

Convert 0.895_{10} to its hexadecimal equivalent

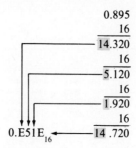

Functions that are not intrinsic to C-64 BASIC may be calculated as in Table D-3.

TABLE D-3. Deriving Mathematical Functions

Function	VIC BASIC Equivalent
Secant	SEC(X) = 1/COS(X)
Cosecant	CSC(X) = 1/SIN(X)
Cotangent	COT(X) = 1/TAN(X)
Inverse sine	ARCSIN(X) = ATN(X/SQR(− X*X + 1))
Inverse cosine	ARCCOS(X) = −ATN(X/SQR (−X*X + 1)) + π/2
Inverse secant	ARCSEC(X) = ATN(X/SQR(X*X − 1))
Inverse cosecant	ARCCSC(X) = ATN(X/SQR(X*X − 1)) + (SGN(X) − 1)* π/2
Inverse cotangent	ARCOT(X) = ATN(X) + π/2
Hyperbolic sine	SINE(X) = (EXP(X) − EXP(− X))/2
Hyperbolic cosine	COSH(X) = (EXP(X) + EXP(− X))/2
Hyperbolic tangent	TANH(X) = EXP(− X)/EXP(X) + EXP (−X))*2 + 1
Hyperbolic secant	SECH(X) = 2/(EXP(X) + EXP(− X)
Hyperbolic cosecant	CSCH(X) = 2/(EXP(X) − EXP(− X))
Hyperbolic cotangent	COTH(X) = EXP(− X)/(EXP(X) − EXP(− X)*2 + 1
Inverse hyperbolic sine	ARCSINH(X) = LOG(X + SQR(X*X + 1)
Inverse hyperbolic cosine	ARCCOSH(X) = LOG(X + SQR(X*X − 1)
Inverse hyperbolic tangent	ARCTANH(X) = LOG((1 + X)/(1 − X))/2
Inverse hyperbolic secant	ARCSECH(X) = LOG((SQR (− X*X + 1) + 1/X)
Inverse hyperbolic cosecant	ARCCSCH(X) = LOG((SGN(X)*SQR (X*X + 1)/X
Inverse hyperbolic cotangent	ARCCOTH(X) = LOG((X + 1)/(X − 1))/2

Sound and Display
Characters and Codes

Two of the more powerful functions of the C-64 are its display and sound generation capabilities. The tables in this appendix cover all of the C-64 character codes, screen POKE values, sound register equivalents, and color values.

Table E-1 covers all of the characters and functions that are displayed using the CHR$ instruction. In many instances, the use of the CHR$ function is optional; however, some functions, such as RETURN and RUN/STOP, are not programmable with the PRINT function. To program using these functions you will need to use the CHR$ function and the codes in this table.

The codes used in the CHR$ instruction are not the same as those used in the POKE-to-screen commands. The codes shown in Table E-2 are listed in the same order as the characters in memory. Notice that all of the control characters are omitted from this list. This is because there is no display code for them; control codes use the codes of standard reverse characters (for example, reverse-heart for CLR/HOME).

The C-64 can use certain keyword abbreviations. These can save time when entering lines of code. In most cases, they consist of the first letter of the command and the shifted second letter of the command. In some cases you need to enter the first two letters of the command and the shifted third letter. See Table E-3 for each command and note that the display does not contain the second (or third) character, but a graphic character instead.

TABLE E-1. C-64 Character Codes

Prints	CHR$	Prints	CHR$	Prints	CHR$	Prints	CHR$
	0	CLR HOME	19	&	38	:	58
	1	INST DEL	20	'	39	;	59
	2			(	40	<	60
	3		21	)	41	=	61
	4		22	*	42	>	62
WHT	5		23	+	43	?	63
	6		24	,	44	@	64
	7		25	−	45	A	65
	8		26	.	46	B	66
	9		27	/	47	C	67
	10	RED	28	0	48	D	68
	11	CRSR →	29	1	49	E	69
	12	GRN	30	2	50	F	70
RETURN	13	BLU	31	3	51	G	71
SWITCH TO LOWER-CASE	14		32	4	52	H	72
	15	!	33	5	53	I	73
	16	"	34	6	54	J	74
CRSR ↓	17	#	35	7	55	K	75
RVS ON	18	$	36	8	56	L	76
		%	37	9	57	M	77

TABLE E-1. C-64 Character Codes (continued)

Prints	CHR$	Prints	CHR$	Prints	CHR$	Prints	CHR$
N	78	(graphic)	98	(graphic)	118	f4	138
O	79	(graphic)	99	(graphic)	119	f6	139
P	80	(graphic)	100	(graphic)	120	f8	140
Q	81	(graphic)	101	(graphic)	121	SHIFT RETURN	141
R	82	(graphic)	102	(graphic)	122	SWITCH TO UPPER-CASE	142
S	83	(graphic)	103	(graphic)	123		143
T	84	(graphic)	104	(graphic)	124	BLK	144
U	85	(graphic)	105	(graphic)	125	↑ CRSR	145
V	86	(graphic)	106	(graphic)	126	RVS OFF	146
W	87	(graphic)	107	(graphic)	127	CLR HOME	147
X	88	(graphic)	108	(graphic)	128	INST DEL	148
Y	89	(graphic)	109	ORANGE	129	BROWN	149
Z	90	(graphic)	110		130	LT RED	150
[	91	(graphic)	111		131	DK GREY	151
£	92	(graphic)	112		132	MED GREY	152
]	93	(graphic)	113	f1	133	LT GREEN	153
↑	94	(graphic)	114	f3	134	LT BLUE	154
←	95	(graphic)	115	f5	135		
(graphic)	96	(graphic)	116	f7	136		
(graphic)	97	(graphic)	117	f2	137		

TABLE E-1. C-64 Character Codes (continued)

Prints	CHR$	Prints	CHR$	Prints	CHR$	Prints	CHR$
LT GREY	155		175		195		215
PUR	156		176		196		216
CRSR ←	157		177		197		217
YES	158		178		198		218
CYN SPACE	159		179		199		219
	160		180		200		220
	161		181		201		221
	162		182		202		222
	163		183		203		223
	164		184		204		224
	165		185		205		225
	166		186		206		226
	167		187		207		227
	168		188		208		228
	169		189		209		229
	170		190		210		230
	171		191		211		231
	172		192		212		232
	173		193		213		233
	174		194		214		234

TABLE E-1. C-64 Character Codes (continued)

Prints	CHR$	Prints	CHR$	Prints	CHR$	Prints	CHR$
	235		241		246		251
	236		242		247		252
	237		243		248		253
	238		244		249		254
	239		245		250		255
	240						

TABLE E-2. Screen Codes

Set 1	Set 2	POKE	Set 1	Set 2	POKE	Set 1	Set 2	POKE
@		0	J	j	10	T	t	20
A	a	1	K	k	11	U	u	21
B	b	2	L	l	12	V	v	22
C	c	3	M	m	13	W	w	23
D	d	4	N	n	14	X	x	24
E	e	5	O	o	15	Y	y	25
F	f	6	P	p	16	Z	z	26
G	g	7	Q	q	17	[		27
H	h	8	R	r	18	£		28
I	i	9	S	s	19	]		29

TABLE E-2. Screen Codes (continued)

Set 1	Set 2	POKE	Set 1	Set 2	POKE	Set 1	Set 2	POKE
↑		30	2		50		F	70
←		31	3		51		G	71
		32	4		52		H	72
!		33	5		53		I	73
"		34	6		54		J	74
#		35	7		55		K	75
$		36	8		56		L	76
%		37	9		57		M	77
&		38	:		58		N	78
'		39	;		59		O	79
(		40	<		60		P	80
)		41	=		61		Q	81
*		42	>		62		R	82
+		43	?		63		S	83
,		44			64		T	84
-		45		A	65		U	85
.		46		B	66		V	86
/		47		C	67		W	87
0		48		D	68		X	88
1		49		E	69		Y	89

TABLE E-2. Screen Codes (continued)

Set 1	Set 2	POKE	Set 1	Set 2	POKE	Set 1	Set 2	POKE
		90			103			116
		91			104			117
		92			105			118
		93			106			119
		94			107			120
		95			108			121
		96			109			122
		97			110			123
		98			111			124
		99			112			125
		100			113			126
		101			114			127
		102			115			

TABLE E-3. Keyword Abbreviations

Command	Abbreviation		Characters That Appear On Screen	Command	Abbreviation		Characters That Appear On Screen
AND	A	SHIFT N	A⁄	PRINT#	P	SHIFT R	P＿
NOT	N	SHIFT O	N⌐	READ	R	SHIFT E	R⁻
CLOSE	CL.	SHIFT O	CL⌐	RESTORE	RE	SHIFT S	RE♣
CLR	C	SHIFT L	CL	RETURN	RE	SHIFT T	REI
CMD	C	SHIFT M	C⟍	RUN	R	SHIFT U	R⁄
CONT	C	SHIFT O	C⌐	SAVE	S	SHIFT A	S♠
DATA	D	SHIFT A	D♠	STEP	ST	SHIFT E	ST⁻
DEF	D	SHIFT E	D⁻	STOP	S	SHIFT T	SI
DIM	D	SHIFT I	D⟍	SYS	S	SHIFT Y	S I
END	E	SHIFT N	E⁄	THEN	T	SHIFT H	T I
FOR	F	SHIFT O	F⌐	VERIFY	V	SHIFT E	V⁻
GET	G	SHIFT E	G⁻	WAIT	W	SHIFT A	W♠
GOSUB	GO	SHIFT S	GO♣	ABS	A	SHIFT B	AI
GOTO	G	SHIFT O	G⌐	ASC	A	SHIFT S	A♣
INPUT#	I	SHIFT N	I⁄	ATN	A	SHIFT T	AI
LET	L	SHIFT E	L⁻	CHR$	C	SHIFT H	C I
LIST	L	SHIFT I	L⟍	EXP	E	SHIFT X	E♠
LOAD	L.	SHIFT O	L⌐	FRE	F	SHIFT R	F＿
NEXT	N	SHIFT E	N⁻	LEFT$	LE	SHIFT F	LE＿
OPEN	O	SHIFT P	O⌐	MID$	M	SHIFT I	M⟍
POKE	P	SHIFT O	P⌐	PEEK	P	SHIFT E	P⁻
PRINT	?		?	RIGHT$	R	SHIFT I	R⟍
RND	R	SHIFT N	R⁄	STR$	ST	SHIFT R	ST＿
SGN	S	SHIFT G	SI	TAB(	T	SHIFT A	T♠
SIN	S	SHIFT I	S⟍	USR	U	SHIFT S	U♣
SPC(	S	SHIFT P	S⌐	VAL	V	SHIFT A	V♠
SQR	S	SHIFT Q	S♣				

Error Messages

F

C-64 error messages may be displayed in response to almost anything you key in at the keyboard. They may also appear when your program is running. This Appendix lists and explains error messages issued by the C-64 BASIC interpreter and by the operating system.

Whenever the C-64 BASIC interpreter detects an error, it displays a diagnostic message, headed by a question mark, in the general form

    ?message ERROR IN LINE *number*

where *message* is the type of error (listed alphabetically below) and *number* is the line number in the program where the error occurred (not present in immediate mode). Following any error message, C-64 BASIC returns to immediate mode and displays the READY prompt.

Here is an alphabetical list of error messages accompanied by a two-part description that explains the cause of the error and possible ways of correcting it.

BAD SUBSCRIPT

An attempt was made to reference an array element that is outside the dimensions of the array. This can result from specifying the wrong number of dimensions (different from the DIM statement), using a subscript larger than specified in the DIM statement, or using a subscript larger than 10 for a nondimensioned array.

Correct the array element number to remain within the original dimensions or change the array size to allow more elements.

CAN'T CONTINUE

A CONT command was issued, but program execution cannot be resumed because the program has been altered, added to, or cleared in immediate mode, or because execution was stopped by an error. Program execution cannot be continued past an error message.

Correct the error. The most prudent course is to type **RUN** and start over. However, you can attempt to reenter the program at the point of interruption by a directed GOTO.

DEVICE NOT PRESENT

No device on the bus was present to handshake an attention sequence. The status variable (ST) will have a value of 2, indicating a timeout. This message may occur for any I/O command.

If the device identification is in error, correct the OPEN (or other) statement. If the statement is correct, especially if it has worked before, check the addressed device for malfunction, misconnection, or power off.

DIVISION BY ZERO

An attempt was made to perform a division operation with a divisor of zero. Dividing by zero is not allowed.

Check the values of variables (or constants) in the indicated line number. Change the program so that the divisor can never be evaluated to zero, or add a check for zero before performing the division.

FILE ALREADY EXISTS

The name of the source file being copied with the COPY statement already exists on the destination diskette.

FILE NOT FOUND

The filename given in the LOAD or OPEN statement was not found on the specified device.

Check that you have the correct tape or diskette in the device. Check the filenames on the tape or diskette for a possible spelling error in the program statement.

FILE NOT OPEN

An attempt was made to access a file that was not opened via the OPEN statement.

Open the file.

FILE OPEN

An attempt was made to open a file that had already been opened via a previous OPEN statement.

Check the logical file number (first parameter in the OPEN statement) to be sure that a different number is used for each file. Insert a CLOSE statement if you want to reopen the same file for a different I/O operation.

FORMULA TOO COMPLEX

This is not a program error but indicates that a string expression in the program is too intricate for C-64 BASIC to handle.

Break the indicated expression into two or more parts and rerun the program. (This will also tend to improve program readability.)

ILLEGAL DIRECT

A command was given in immediate mode that is valid only in program mode. The following are invalid in immediate mode: DATA, DEF FN, GET, GET#, INPUT, and INPUT#.

Enter the desired operation as a (short) program and run it.

ILLEGAL QUANTITY

A function has passed one or more parameters that are out of range. This often occurs in POKE statements that use input variables greater than 255 or less than 0.

This message also occurs if the USR function is referenced before storing the subroutine address at memory locations 1 and 2.

LOAD

An unacceptable number of tape errors (more than 31) were accumulated on a tape load. They were not cleared on reading the redundant block. This message is issued in connection with the LOAD command.

NEXT WITHOUT FOR

A NEXT statement is encountered that is not tied to a preceding FOR statement. Either there is no FOR statement or the variable in the NEXT statement is not in a corresponding FOR statement.

The FOR part of a FOR-NEXT loop must be inserted or the offending NEXT statement deleted. Be sure that the index variables are the same at both ends of the loop.

NOT INPUT FILE

An attempt was made to read from a tape file that has been opened for output only.

Check the READ# and OPEN statement parameters for correctness. Reading requires a zero as the third parameter of the OPEN statement. (This is the default option.)

NOT OUTPUT FILE

An attempt was made to write to a tape file that has been opened for input only.

Check the PRINT# and OPEN statement parameters for correctness. Writing to a file requires a 1 (or a 2 if you want an EOT at the end of the file) as the third parameter in the OPEN statement.

OUT OF DATA

A READ statement is executed but all of the DATA statements in the program have already been read. For each variable in a READ statement, there must be a corresponding DATA element.

Add more DATA elements or restrict the number of READs to the current number of DATA elements. Insert a RESTORE statement to reread the existing data. Or add a flag at the end of the last DATA statement (any value not used as a DATA element may be used for the flag value) and stop READing when the flag has been read.

OUT OF MEMORY

The user program area of memory has been filled and a request is given to add a line to the program. This message may also be caused by multiple FOR-NEXT or GOSUB nestings that fill up the stack; this is the case if ?FRE(0) shows a considerable program area storage left.

Simplify the program. Pay particular attention to reducing array sizes. It may be necessary to restructure the program into overlays.

OVERFLOW

A calculation has resulted in a number outside the allowable range, meaning that the number is too big. The largest number allowed is 1.70141183E+38.

Check your calculations. It may be possible to eliminate this error just by changing the order in which the calculations are programmed.

REDIM'D ARRAY

An array name appears in more than one DIM statement. This error also occurs if an array name is used (given a default size of 11) and later appears in a DIM statement.

Place DIM statements near the beginning of the program. Check to see that each DIM statement is executed only once. DIM must not appear inside a FOR-NEXT loop or in a subroutine where either may be executed more than once.

REDO FROM START

This is a diagnostic message during an INPUT statement operation and is not a fatal error. It indicates that the wrong type of data (string for numeric or vice versa) was entered in response to an INPUT request.

Reenter the correct type of data. INPUT will continue prompting until an acceptable response is entered.

RETURN WITHOUT GOSUB

A RETURN statement was encountered without a previous matching GOSUB statement being executed.

Insert a GOSUB statement or delete the RETURN statement. The error may be caused by dropping into the subroutine code inadvertently. In this case, correct the program flow. An END or STOP statement placed just ahead of the subroutine serves as a debugging aid.

STRING TOO LONG

An attempt was made by use of the concatenation operator (+) to create a string longer than 255 characters.

Break the string into two or more shorter strings as part of the program operation. Use the LEN function to check string lengths before concatenating them.

SYNTAX

There is a syntax error in the line just entered (immediate mode) or scanned for execution (program mode). This is the most common error message. It is caused by such things as misspellings, incorrect punctuation, unmatched parentheses, and extraneous characters.

Examine the line carefully and make corrections. Note that syntax errors in a program are diagnosed at run time, not at the time the lines are entered from the keyboard. You can eliminate many syntax error messages by carefully scrutinizing newly entered program lines before running the program.

TYPE MISMATCH

An attempt was made to enter a string into a numeric variable or vice versa, or an incorrect type was given as a function parameter.

Change the offending item to the correct type.

UNDEF'D FUNCTION

Reference was made to a user-defined function that has not previously been defined by appearing in a DEF FN statement. The definition must precede the function reference.

Define the function. Place DEF FN statements near the beginning of the program.

UNDEF'D STATEMENT

An attempt was made to branch to a nonexistent line number.

Insert a statement with the necessary line number or branch to another line number.

VERIFY ERROR

The program in memory and the specified file do not compare. This message is issued in connection with the VERIFY command.

BASIC Statements

This appendix explains the syntax of all the C-64 BASIC statements. They are presented in alphabetical order and include both internal functions and I/O commands.

CLOSE

The CLOSE statement closes a logical file.

Format:

CLOSE *lf*

The CLOSE statement closes logical file *lf*. Every file should be closed after all file accesses have been completed. An open logical file may be closed only once. The particular operations performed in response to a CLOSE statement depend on the open file's physical device and the type of access that occurred.

Example:

CLOSE 1	*Close logical file 1*
CLOSE 14	*Close logical file 14*

CLR

The CLR statement sets all numeric variables to zero and assigns null values to all string variables. All array space in memory is released. This is equivalent to turning the computer off, then turning it back on and reloading the program into memory. CLR closes all logical files that are currently open within the executing program.

Format:

CLR

A program will continue to run following execution of a CLR statement if the statement's execution does not adversely affect program logic.

Example:

100 CLR

CMD

The CMD statement sends all output that would have gone to the display to another specified unit. Output goes to that unit, instead of the display, until a PRINT# statement specifying the same logical file number that was opened is executed. At least one PRINT# statement must follow a CMD statement.

Format:

CMD *lf*

The CMD statement assigns a line printer output channel to logical file *lf*. After execution of a CMD statement, PRINT and LIST both print data instead of displaying it.

Example:

The following sequence uses CMD to print program listings:

OPEN 5,4	*Open logical file 5 selecting the printer*
CMD 5	*Direct subsequent output to the printer*
LIST	*Print the program listing*
PRINT#5	*Print a carriage return and deselect the printer*
CLOSE 5	*Close logical file 5*

CONT

The CONT statement, typed at the keyboard in immediate mode, resumes program execution after a BREAK.

Format:

CONT

A break is caused by execution of a STOP statement or an END statement that has additional statements following it. Depressing the STOP key while a program is running also causes a break. Program execution continues at the exact point where the break occurred.

Pressing the RETURN key in response to an INPUT statement will also cause a break. Typing **CONT** after this break reexecutes the INPUT statement.

Example:

CONT

DATA

The DATA statement declares constants that are assigned to variables by READ statements.

Format:

DATA *constant[,constant,constant,...,constant]*

DATA statements may be placed anywhere in a program. The DATA statement specifies either numeric or string constants. String constants are usually enclosed in double quotation marks; the quotes are not necessary unless the string contains graphic characters, blanks (spaces), commas, or colons. Blanks, commas, colons, and graphic characters are ignored unless the string is enclosed in quotes. A double quotation mark cannot be represented in a DATA string; it must be specified using a CHR$(34) function. The DATA statement is valid in program mode only.

Example:

10 DATA NAME,"C.D."   *Defines two string variables*

50 DATA 1E6,-10,XYZ   *Defines two numeric variables and one string variable*

Refer to the READ statement for a description of how DATA statement constants are used within a program.

DEF FN

The DEF function (DEF FN) allows special purpose functions to be defined and used within BASIC programs.

Format:

DEF FN*nvar(arg)=expression*

Floating point variable *nvar* identifies the function, which is subsequently referenced using the name FN*nvar(data)*. (If *nvar* has more than five letters, a syntax error is reported. A syntax error is also reported if *nvar* is a string or integer variable.)

The function is specified by *expression*, which can be any arithmetic expression containing any combination of numeric constants, variables, or operators. The dummy variable name *arg* can (and usually does) appear in *expression*.

arg is the only variable in *expression* that can be specified when FN*nvar(data)* is referenced. Any other variables in expression must be defined before FN*nvar(data)* is referenced for the first time. FN*nvar(data)* evaluates *expression* using *data* as the value for *arg*.

The entire DEF FN statement must appear on a single 80-character line; however, a previously defined function can be included in *expression*, so user-defined functions of any complexity can be developed.

The function name *var* can be reused and therefore redefined by another DEF FN statement appearing later in the same program.

The DEF FN definition statement is illegal in immediate mode. However, a user-defined function that has been defined by a DEF FN statement in the current stored program can be referenced in an immediate mode statement.

Example:

```
10 DEF FNC(R)=π*R↑2
```
Defines a function that calculates the circumference of a circle. It takes a single argument R, the radius of the circle, and returns a single numeric value, the circumference of the circle

```
?FNC(1)
```
Prints 3.141159265 (the value of π)

```
55 IF FNC(X)>60 GOTO 150
```
Uses the value calculated by the user-defined function FNC as a branch condition. The current contents of variable X are used when calculating the user-defined function

DIM

The Dimension statement DIM allocates space in memory for array variables.

Format:

DIM *var(sub)*[,*var(sub)*,...,*var(sub)*]

The DIM statement identifies arrays with one or more dimensions as follows:

var(sub$_i$)	Single-dimensional array
var(sub$_i$,sub$_j$)	Two-dimensional array
var(sub$_i$,sub$_j$,sub$_k$)	Multiple-dimensional array

Arrays with more than 11 elements must be dimensioned in a DIM statement. Arrays with 11 elements or less (subscripts 0 through 10 for a one-dimensional array) may be used without being dimensioned by a DIM statement; for such arrays, 11 array spaces are automatically allocated in memory when the first array element is encountered in the program. An array with more than 11 elements must occur in a DIM statement before any other statement references an element of the array.

If an array is dimensioned more than once, or if an array having more than 11 elements is not dimensioned, an error occurs and the program is aborted. A CLR statement allows a DIM statement to be reexecuted.

Example:

`10 DIM A(3)`	*Dimension a single-dimensional array of 3 elements*
`45 DIM X$(44,2)`	*Dimension a two-dimensional array of 88 elements*
`1000 DIM MU(X,3*B),N(12)`	*Dimension a two-dimensional array of X times 3*B elements and a single-dimensional array of 12 elements. X and B must have been assigned values before the DIM statement is executed*

END

The END statement terminates program execution and returns the computer to immediate mode.

Format:

END

The END statement can provide a program with one or more termination points at locations other than the physical end of the program. END statements can be used to terminate individual programs when more than one program is in memory at the same time. An END statement at the physical end of the program is optional. The END statement is used in program mode only.

Example:

```
20001 END
```

FOR-NEXT STEP

All statements between the FOR statement and the NEXT statement are reexecuted the same number of times.

Format:

FOR *nvar* = *start* TO *end* STEP *increment*
[*statements in loop*]
NEXT[*nvar*]

where

nvar	is the index of the loop. It holds the current loop count. *nvar* is often used by the statements within the loop.
start	is a numeric constant, variable, or expression that specifies the beginning value of the index.
end	is a numeric constant, variable, or expression that specifies the ending value of the index. The loop is completed when the index value is equal to the end value, or when the index value is incremented or decremented past the end value.
increment	if present, is a numeric constant, variable, or expression that specifies the amount by which the index variable is to be incremented with each pass. The step may be incremental (positive) or decremental (negative). If STEP is omitted, the increment defaults to 1.

nvar may optionally be included in the NEXT statement. A single NEXT statement is permissible for nested loops that end at the same point. The NEXT statement then takes the form

NEXT $nvar_1, nvar_2, \ldots$

The FOR-NEXT loop will always be executed at least once, even if the beginning *nvar* value is beyond the end *nvar* value. If the NEXT statement is omitted and no subsequent NEXT statements are found, the loop is executed once.

The *start, end,* and *increment* values are read only once, on the first execution of the FOR statement. You cannot change these values inside the loop. You can change the value of *nvar* within the loop. This may be used to terminate a FOR-NEXT loop before the *end* value is reached: Set *nvar* to the *end* value and on the next pass the loop will terminate itself. Do not jump out of the FOR-NEXT loop with a GOTO. Do not start the loop outside a subroutine and terminate it inside the subroutine.

FOR-NEXT loops may be nested. Each nested loop must have a different *nvar* variable name. Each nested loop must be wholly contained within the next outer loop; at most, the loops can end at the same point.

GET

The GET statement receives single characters as input from the keyboard.

Format:

GET *var*

The GET statement can be executed in program mode only. When a GET statement is executed, *var* is assigned a 0 value if numeric, or a null value if a string. Any previous value of the variable is lost. Then GET fetches the next character from the keyboard buffer and assigns it to *var*. If the keyboard buffer is empty, *var* retains its 0 or null value.

GET is used to handle one-character responses from the keyboard. GET accepts the RETURN key as input and passes the value (CHR$(13)) to *var*.

If *var* is a numeric variable and no key has been pressed, 0 is returned. However, a 0 is also returned when 0 is entered at the keyboard.

If *var* is a numeric variable and the character returned is not a digit (0-9), a ?SYNTAX ERROR message is generated and the program aborts.

The GET statement may have more than one variable in its parameter list, but it is hard to use if it has multiple parameters.

GET *var,var,...,var*

Example:

```
10 GET C$
10 GET D
10 GET A,B,C
```

GET#

The GET External statement (GET#) receives single characters as input from an external storage device identified via a logical file number.

Format:

GET#*lf,var*

The GET# statement can only be used in program mode. GET# fetches a single character from an external device and assigns this character to variable *var*. The external device is identified by logical file number *lf*. This logical file must have been previously opened by an OPEN statement.

GET# and GET statements handle variables and data input identically. For details see the GET statement description.

Example:

```
10 GET#4,C$:IF C$="" GOTO 10
```
Get a keyboard character. Reexecute if no character is present

GOSUB

The GOSUB statement branches program execution to a specified line and allows a return to the statement following GOSUB. The specified line is a subroutine entry point.

Format:

GOSUB *ln*

The GOSUB statement calls a subroutine. The subroutine's entry point must occur on line *ln*. A subroutine's entry point is the beginning of the subroutine in a programming sense; that is to say, it is the line containing the statement (or statements) that are executed first. The entry point need not necessarily be the subroutine line with the smallest line number.

Upon completing execution the subroutine branches back to the line following the GOSUB statement. The subroutine uses a RETURN statement in order to branch back in this fashion.

A GOSUB statement may occur anywhere in a program; in consequence a subroutine may be called from anywhere in the program.

Example:

```
100 GOSUB 2000
110 A=B*C
```
Branch to subroutine at line 2000

```
    .                   Subroutine branches back here
    .

2000                    Subroutine entry point

    .
    .

2090 RETURN             Branch back to line 110
```

GOTO

The GOTO statement branches unconditionally to a specified line.

Format:

GOTO *ln*

Example:

```
10 GOTO 100
```

Executed in immediate mode, GOTO branches to the specified line in the stored program without clearing the current variable values. GOTO cannot reference immediate mode statements, since they do not have line numbers.

IF-THEN

The IF-THEN statement provides conditional execution of statements based on a relational expression.

Format:

IF *condition* THEN *statement*[:*statement*...] *Conditionally execute statement(s)*

IF *condition* $\begin{Bmatrix} \text{THEN} \\ \text{GOTO} \end{Bmatrix}$ *line*   *Conditionally branch*

If the specified condition is true, then the statement or statements following the THEN are executed. If the specified condition is false, control passes to the statement(s) on the next line and the statement or statements following the THEN are not executed. For a conditional branch, the branch line number is placed after the word THEN or after the word GOTO. The compound form THEN GOTO is also acceptable.

IF A = 1 THEN 50
IF A = 1 GOTO 50   } *Equivalent*
IF A = 1 THEN GOTO 50

If an unconditional branch is one of many statements following THEN, the branch must be the last statement on the line, and it must have "GOTO line" format. If the unconditional branch is not the last statement on the line, then statements following the unconditional branch can never be executed.

The following statements cannot appear in an immediate mode IF-THEN statement: DATA, GET, GET#, INPUT, INPUT#, REM, RETURN, END, STOP, WAIT.

If a line number is specified, or any statement containing a line number, there must be a corresponding statement with that line number in the current stored program.

The CONT and DATA statements cannot appear in a program mode IF-THEN statement. If a FOR-NEXT loop follows the THEN, the loop must be completely contained on the IF-THEN line. Additional IF-THEN statements may appear following the THEN as long as they are completely contained on the original IF-THEN line. However, Boolean connectors are preferred to nested IF-THEN statements. For example, the two statements below are equivalent, but the second is preferred.

```
10 IF A$="X" THEN IF B=2 THEN IF C>D THEN 50
10 IF A$="X" AND B=2 AND C>D THEN 50
```

Example:

```
400 IF X>Y THEN A=1
500 IF M+1 THEN AG=4.5 GOSUB 1000
```

INITIALIZE

You can use PRINT# to initialize a diskette before performing any operation on it.

Format:

PRINT#*file*,"[INITIALIZE][*dr*]"

The diskette in drive *dr* is initialized. If the *dr* parameter is not present, the diskette in drive 0 will be initialized. You do not need to initialize a diskette after preparing it; the preparation process also initializes the diskette.

Example:

```
OPEN 1,8,15        Open the diskette command channel
```

```
PRINT#1,"I"          Initialize diskettes in drive 0
```

INPUT

The INPUT statement receives data input from the keyboard.

Format:

INPUT $\begin{Bmatrix} (blank) \\ \text{"}message\text{"}; \end{Bmatrix}$ *var[,var,...,var]*

INPUT can be used in program mode only. When the INPUT statement is executed, C-64 BASIC displays a question mark on the screen requesting data input. The user must enter data items that agree exactly in number and type with the variables in the INPUT statement parameter list. If the INPUT statement has more than one variable in its parameter list, then keyboard entries must be separated by commas. The last entry must be terminated with a carriage return.

```
?1234 <CR>              Single data item response
?1234,567.89,NOW<CR>    Multiple data item response
```

If "*message*" is present, it is displayed before the question mark. "*message*" can have as many as 80 characters.

If more than one but less than the required number of data items are input, C-64 BASIC requests additional input with double question marks (??) until the required number of data items have been input. If too many data items are input, the message ?EXTRA IGNORED is displayed. The extra input is ignored, but the program continues execution.

Example:

Statement	Operator Response	Result
10 INPUT A,B,C$	? 123,456,NOW	A=123,B=456,C$="NOW"
10 INPUT A,B,C$	? 123 ?? 456 ?? NOW	A=123 B=456 C$="NOW"
10 INPUT A,B,C$	? NOW ?REDO FROM START ? 123 ?? 456 ?? 789	 A=123 B=456 C="789"
10 INPUT "A= ";A	A= ? 123	A=123

Note that you must input numeric data for a numeric variable, but you can input numeric or string data for a string variable.

INPUT#

The INPUT External statement (INPUT#) inputs one or more data items from an external device identified via a logical file number.

Format:

INPUT#*lf var*[,*var*,...,*var*]

The INPUT# statement inputs data from the selected external device and assigns data items to variable(s) *var*. Data items must agree in number and kind with the INPUT# statement parameter list.

If an end-of-record is detected before all variables in the INPUT# statement parameter list have received data, then an OUT OF DATA error status is generated, but the program continues to execute.

INPUT# and INPUT statements execute identically, except that INPUT# receives its input from a logical file. Also, INPUT# does not display error messages; instead, it reports error statuses that the program must interrogate and respond to.

Input data strings may not be longer than 80 characters (79 characters plus a carriage return) because the input buffer has a maximum capacity of 80 characters. Commas and carriage returns are treated as item separators by the computer when processing the INPUT# statement; they are recognized, but are not passed on to the program as data. INPUT# is valid in program mode only.

Example:

`1000 INPUT#10,A`	*Input the next data item from logical file 10. A numeric data item is expected; it is assigned to variable A*
`946 INPUT#12,A$`	*Input the next data item from logical file 12. A string data item is expected; it is assigned to variable A$*
`900 INPUT#5,B,C$`	*Input the next two data items from logical file 5. The first data item is numeric; it is assigned to numeric variable B. The second data item is a string; it is assigned to string variable C$*

LET=

The Assignment statement LET=, or simply =, assigns a value to a specified variable.

Format:

$$\begin{Bmatrix} (blank) \\ \text{LET} \end{Bmatrix} var = data$$

Variable *var* is assigned the value computed by resolving *data*. The word LET is optional; it is usually omitted.

Example:

```
10 A=2
450 C$="."

300 M(1,3)=SGN(X)
310 XX$(I,J,K,L)="STRINGALONG"
```

LIST

LIST displays one or more lines of a program. Program lines displayed by the LIST statement may be edited.

Format:

$$\text{LIST} \begin{cases} (blank) \\ line \\ line_1 - line_2 \\ -line \\ line- \end{cases}$$

The entire program is displayed in response to LIST. Use line-limiting parameters for long programs to display a section of the program that is short enough to fit on the screen.

Example:

LIST	*List entire program*
LIST 50	*List line 50*
LIST 60-100	*List all lines in the program from lines 60 to 100, inclusive*
LIST -140	*List all lines in the program from the beginning of the program through line 140*
LIST 20000-	*List all lines in the program from line 20000 to the end of the program*

Listed lines are reformatted as follows:

1. ?'s entered as a shorthand for PRINT are expanded to the word PRINT. Example:

   ?A *becomes* PRINT A

2. Blanks preceding the line number are eliminated. Example:

   50 A=1   *becomes*   50 A=1
   100 A=A+1   100 A=A+1

3. A space is inserted between the line number and the rest of the statement if none was entered. Example:

   55A=B−2 *becomes* 55 A=B−2

LIST is always used in immediate mode. A LIST statement in a program will list the program but then exit to immediate mode. Attempting to continue program execution via CONT simply repeats the LIST indefinitely.

Printing a Program Listing

To print a program listing instead of displaying it, OPEN a printer logical file and execute a CMD statement before executing the LIST statement. Here is the necessary immediate mode sequence:

```
OPEN 4,4      Open the printer specifying logical file 4
CMD 4         Deflect display output to the printer
LIST          Print the program listing
PRINT#4       Deflect output back to the display
CLOSE 4
```

LOAD

The LOAD statement loads a program from an external device into memory.

Cassette Program Format

LOAD [*"file name"*][*,dev*]

The LOAD statement loads into memory the program file specified by *file name* from the cassette unit selected by device number *dev*. If no device is specified, device 1 is assumed by default; cassette unit 1 is then selected. If no file name is given, the next file detected on the selected cassette unit is loaded into memory.

Example:

LOAD	*Load into memory the next program found on cassette unit #1. If you start a LOAD when the cassette is in the middle of a program, the cassette will read past the remainder of the current program, then load the next program*
LOAD "",2	*Load into memory the next program found on cassette unit #2*
LOAD "EGOR"	*Search for the program named EGOR on tape cassette #1 and load it into memory*
N$="WHEE!LS" LOAD N$	*Search for the program named WHEE!LS on cassette unit #1 and load it into memory*
LOAD "X"	*Search for a program named X on cassette unit #1 and load it into memory*

Diskette Drive Program Format

LOAD "*dr:file name*",*dev*

The LOAD statement loads into computer memory the program file with the *file name* on the diskette in drive *dev.* The device number for the diskette drive unit is 8 in the C-64. If *dev* is not present, the default value is 1, which selects the primary tape cassette unit.

A single asterisk can be included instead of the file name, in which case the first program found on the selected diskette drive is loaded into memory.

Example:

LOAD"0:*",8	*Load the first program found on disk drive 0*
LOAD"0:FIREBALL",8	*Search for the program named FIREBALL on disk drive 0 and load it into memory*
T$="0:METEOR" LOAD T$,8	*Search for the program named METEOR on disk drive 0 and load it into memory*

When a LOAD is executed in immediate mode, C-64 BASIC automatically executes CLR before the program is loaded. Once a program has been loaded into memory, it can be listed, updated, or executed.

The LOAD statement can also be used in program mode to build program overlays. A LOAD statement executed from within a program causes that program's execution to stop and another program to be loaded. In this case the C-64 computer does not perform a CLR; therefore, the old program can pass on all of its variable values to the new program.

When a LOAD statement accessing a cassette unit is executed in program mode, LOAD message displays are suppressed unless the tape PLAY key is up (off). If the PLAY key is off, the PRESS PLAY ON TAPE #1 message is displayed so that the load can proceed. All LOAD messages are suppressed when loading programs from a diskette in program mode.

NEW

The NEW statement clears the current program from memory.

Format:

    NEW

When a NEW statement is executed, all variables are initialized to zero or null values and array variable space in memory is released. The pointers that keep track of program statements are reinitialized, which has the effect of deleting any program in memory; in fact the program is not physically deleted. NEW operations are automatically performed when a LOAD statement is executed.

If there is a program in memory, you should execute a NEW statement in immediate mode before entering a new program at the keyboard. Otherwise, the new program will overlay the old one, replacing lines if their numbers are duplicated, but leaving other lines. The result is a scrambled mixture of two unrelated programs.

Example:

    NEW

NEW is always executed in immediate mode. If a NEW statement is executed from within a program, the program will "self-destruct," or clear itself out.

NEW (DOS Command)

Use PRINT# to prepare and format a new diskette or to erase and reformat an old diskette.

Format:

    PRINT#*lf*,"N[EW]*dr:disk name,vv*"

The diskette in drive *dr* is prepared. When a diskette is prepared, sectors are laid out on the diskette surface. The diskette directory and Block

Availability Map (BAM) are initialized. The diskette is assigned the name *disk name* and the number *vv*.

The diskette name and number are displayed in the reverse field at the top of a directory display.

Example:

```
OPEN 1,8,15                    Open the diskette command channel
.
PRINT#1,"N0:NEWDATA,02"        A diskette has been prepared for use in
                               drive 0. The diskette is given the
                               name NEWDATA and the number 02
```

ON-GOSUB

The ON-GOSUB statement provides conditional subroutine calls to one of several subroutines in a program, depending on the current value of a variable.

Format:

ON *byte* GOSUB *line*$_1$[,*line*$_2$,...,*line*$_n$]

ON-GOSUB has the same format as ON-GOTO. Refer to the ON-GOTO statement description for branching rules. *byte* is evaluated and truncated to an integer number, if necessary.

For *byte*=1, the subroutine beginning at *line*$_1$ is called. That subroutine completes execution with a RETURN statement that causes program execution to continue at the statement immediately following ON-GOSUB. If *byte*=2, the subroutine beginning with *line*$_2$ is called, and so on.

ON-GOSUB is normally executed in program mode. It may be executed in immediate mode as long as there are corresponding line numbers to branch to in the current stored program.

Example:

```
10 ON A GOSUB 100,200,300
```

ON-GOTO

The ON-GOTO statement causes a conditional branch to one of several points in a program, depending on the current value of a variable.

Format:

ON *byte* GOTO *line*$_1$[,*line*$_2$,...,*line*$_n$]

byte is evaluated and truncated to an integer number, if necessary.

If *byte* = 1, a branch to line number *line*₁ occurs. If *byte* = 2, a branch to line number *line*₂ occurs, and so on.

If *byte* = 0, no branch is taken. If *byte* is in the allowed range but there is no corresponding line number in the program, then no branch is taken. If a branch is not taken, program control proceeds to the statement following the ON-GOTO; this statement may be on the same line as the ON-GOTO (separated by a colon) or on the next line.

If index has a nonzero value outside of the allowed range, the program aborts with an error message. As many line numbers may be specified as will fit on the 80-character line.

ON-GOTO is normally executed in program mode. It may be executed in immediate mode as long as there are corresponding line numbers in the current stored program that may be branched to.

Example:

```
40 A=B<10
50 ON A+2 GOTO 100,200
```
Branch to statement 100 if A is true (−1) or branch to statement 200 if A is false (0)

```
50 X=X+1
60 ON X GOTO 500,600,700
```
Branch to statement 500 if X=1, statement 600 if X=2, or to statement 700 if X=3. No branch is taken if X>3

OPEN

The OPEN statement opens a logical file and readies the assigned physical device.

Cassette Data File Format

OPEN *lf* [,*dev*][,*sa*][,*"file name"*]

The file named *file name* on the tape cassette unit identified by *dev* is opened for the type of access specified by the secondary address *sa;* the access is assigned the logical file number *lf.*

If no file name is specified, the next file encountered on the selected tape cassette is opened. If no device is specified, device number 1 is selected by default; this device number selects cassette unit 1. If no secondary address is specified, a default value of 0 is assumed and the file is opened for a read access only. A secondary address of 1 opens the file for a write access, while a secondary address of 2 opens the file for a write access with an end-of-tape mark written when the file is subsequently closed.

Example:

OPEN 1	*Open logical file 1 at cassette drive #1 (default) for a read access (default) from the first file encountered on the tape (no file name specified)*
OPEN 1,1	*Same as above*
OPEN 1,1,0	*Same as above*
OPEN 1,1,0,"DAT"	*Same as above but access the file named DAT*
OPEN 3,1,2	*Open logical file 3 for cassette #1 for a write with EOT (End Of Tape) access. The new file is unnamed and will be written at the current physical tape location*
OPEN 3,1,2,"PENTAGRAM"	*Same as above but access the file named PENTAGRAM*

Disk Data File Format

OPEN *lf,dev,sa,* "*dr:file name,type*[*,access*]"

The file named *file name* on the diskette in drive *dr* is opened and assigned logical file number *lf. type* identifies the file as sequential (SEQ), program (PRG), or random (USR). If the file is sequential, access must be WRITE to specify a write access or READ to specify a read access. Access is not present for a program or random access file.

An existing sequential file can be opened for a write access if *dr* is preceded by an @ sign. The existing sequential file contents are replaced entirely by new written data.

The device number *dev* must be present; it is 8 for all standard disk units. If *dev* is absent, a default value of 1 is assumed and the primary tape cassette unit is selected.

For a data file the secondary address *sa* can have any value between 2 and 14, but every open data file should have its own unique secondary address. A secondary address of 15 selects the disk unit command channel. Secondary addresses of 0 and 1 are used to access program files. Secondary address 0 is used to load a program file; secondary address 1 is used to save a program file.

Example:

```
OPEN 1,8,2,"0:DAT,SEQ,READ"          Open logical file 1 on a diskette in drive
                                     0. Read from sequential file DAT
OPEN 5,8,3,"1:NEWFILE,SEQ,WRITE"     Open logical file 5 on a diskette in drive
                                     1. Write to sequential file NEWFILE
OPEN 4,8,4,"@1:NEWFILE,SEQ,WRITE"    Open logical file 4 on diskette drive 1.
                                     Write to sequential file NEWFILE
                                     replacing prior contents
```

POKE

The POKE statement stores a byte of data in a specified memory location.

Format:

POKE *memadr,byte*

A value between 0 and 255, provided by *byte,* is loaded into the memory location with the address *memadr.*

Example:

```
10 POKE 1,A                 POKE value of variable A into memory
                            at address 1
POKE 32768,ASC("A")-64      POKE 1 (the value of ASC ("A")−64)
                            into memory at address 32768
```

PRINT

The PRINT statement displays data; it is also used to print to the line printer.

Format:

$$\left\{ {PRINT \atop ?} \right\} \ data \ \left\{ {, \atop ;} \right\} \ data... \left\{ {, \atop ;} \right\} \ data$$

PRINT Field Formats

Numeric fields are displayed using standard numeric representation for numbers greater than 0.01 and less than or equal to 999999999. Scientific notation is used for numbers outside of this range. Numbers are preceded by a sign character and are followed by a blank character.

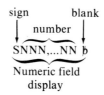

The sign is blank for a positive number and a minus sign (−) for a negative number.

Strings are displayed without additions or modifications.

PRINT Formats

First data item. The first data item is displayed at the current cursor position. The PRINT format character (comma or semicolon) following the first data item specifies the location of the second data item's display. The location of each subsequent data item's display is determined by the punctuation following the preceding data item. Data items may be in the same PRINT statement or in a separate PRINT statement.

New line. When no comma or semicolon follows the last data item in a PRINT statement, a carriage return occurs after the last data item is displayed.

Tabbing. A comma following a data item causes the next data item to be displayed at the next default tab column. Default tabs are at columns 1, 11, and 21. If a comma precedes the first data item, a tab will precede the first item display.

Continuous. A semicolon following a data item causes the next display to begin immediately in the next available column position. Numeric data always has one trailing blank character. For string data, items are displayed continuously with no forced intervening spaces.

Example:

```
40 PRINT A
40 PRINT A,B,C
40 PRINT A;B;C
40 PRINT, A;B;C
40 PRINT "NUMBERS",A;B;C
40 PRINT "NUM";"BER";
41 PRINT "S",A;B;C
```

PRINT#

The PRINT External statement (PRINT#) outputs one or more data items from the computer to an external device (cassette tape unit, disk unit, or printer) identified by a logical file number.

Format:

PRINT#*lf*,*data*;*CHR$(13)*;*data*;*CHR$(13)*,...;*CHR$ (13)*;*data*

Data items listed in the PRINT# statement parameter list are written to the external device identified by logical unit number *lf.*

Very specific punctuation rules must be observed when writing data to external devices. A brief summary of punctuation rules is given below.

PRINT# Output to Cassette Files

Every numeric or string variable written to a cassette file must be followed by a carriage return character. This carriage return character is automatically output by a PRINT# statement that has a single data item in its parameter list. But a PRINT# statement with more than one data item in its parameter list must include characters that force carriage returns. For example, use CHR$(13) to force a carriage return, or a string variable that has been equated to CHR$(13) such as *c$*=CHR$(13).

PRINT# Output to Diskette Files

The cassette output rules described above apply also to diskette files with one exception: Groups of string variables can be separated by comma characters (CHR$(44)). The comma character separators, like the carriage return separators, must be inserted using CHR$. String variables written to diskette files with comma character separators must subsequently be read back by a single INPUT# statement. The INPUT# statement reads all text from one carriage return character to the next.

PRINT# Output to the Line Printer

When the PRINT# statement outputs data to a line printer CHR$ must equal CHR$(29). No punctuation characters should separate CHR$ from data items, as illustrated in the PRINT# format definition.

Caution: The form ?# cannot be used as an abbreviation for PRINT#.

READ

The READ statement assigns values from a DATA statement to variables named in the READ parameter list.

Format:

> READ *var*[,*var*,...,*var*]

READ is used to assign values to variables. READ can take the place of multiple assignment statements (see LET=).

READ statements with variable lists require corresponding DATA statements with lists of constant values. The data constants and corresponding variables have to agree in type. A string variable can accept any type of constant; a numeric variable can accept only numeric constants.

The number of READ and DATA statements can differ, but there must be an available DATA constant for every READ statement variable. There can be more data items than READ statement variables, but if there are too few data items the program aborts with an ?OUT OF DATA error message.

READ is generally executed in program mode. It can be executed in immediate mode as long as there are corresponding DATA constants in the current stored program to read from.

Example:

```
10 DATA 1,2,3        On completion, A=1, B=2, C=3
20 READ A,B,C

150 READ C$,D,F$     On completion, C$="STR", D=14.5, F$="TM"
160 DATA STR
170 DATA 14.5,"TM"
```

REM

The Remark statement (REM) allows comments to be placed in the program for program documentation purposes.

Format:

> REM *comment*

where

> *comment*   is any sequence of characters that will fit on the
>   current 80-column line.

REM statements are reproduced in program listings, but they are otherwise ignored. A REM statement may be placed on a line of its own, or it may be placed as the last statement on a multiple-statement line.

A REM statement cannot be placed ahead of any other statements on a multiple-statement line, since all text following the REM is treated as a comment. REM statements may be placed in the path of program execution, and they may be branched to.

Example:

```
10 REM *** * * * * ***
20 REM ***PROGRAM EXCALIBUR***
30 GOTO 55 REM BRANCH IF OUT OF DATA
```

RESTORE

The RESTORE statement resets the DATA statement pointer to the beginning of data.

Format:

RESTORE

RESTORE may be given in immediate or program mode.

Example:

```
10 DATA 1,2,N44
20 READ A,B,B$        A=1, B=2, B$="N44"
30 RESTORE
40 READ X,Y,Z$        X=1, Y=2, Z$="N44"
```

RETURN

The RETURN statement branches program control to the statement in the program following the most recent GOSUB call. Each subroutine must terminate with a RETURN statement.

Format:

RETURN

Example:

```
100 RETURN
```

Note that the RETURN statement returns program control from a subroutine, whereas the RETURN key moves the cursor to the beginning of the next display line. The two are not related in any way.

RUN

RUN begins execution of the program currently stored in memory. RUN closes any open files and initializes all variables to 0 or null values.

Format:

RUN[*line*]

When RUN is executed in immediate mode, the computer performs a CLR of all program variables and resets the data pointer in memory to the beginning of data (see RESTORE) before executing the program.

If RUN specifies a line number, the computer still performs the CLR and RESTOREs the data, but execution begins at the specified line number. RUN specifying a line number should not be used following a program break — use CONT or GOTO for that purpose.

RUN may also be used in program mode. It restarts program execution from the beginning of the program with all variables cleared and data pointers reinitialized.

Example:

RUN   *Initialize and begin execution of the current program*

RUN 1000   *Initialize and begin execution of the program starting at line 1000*

SAVE

The SAVE statement writes a copy of the current program from memory to an external device.

Cassette Unit Format

SAVE ["*file name*"][,*dev*][,*sa*]

The SAVE statement writes the program that is currently in memory to the tape cassette drive specified by *dev*. If the *dev* parameter is not present, the assumed value is 1 and the primary cassette drive is selected. The *file name,* if specified, is written at the beginning of the program. If a nonzero secondary address (*sa*) is specified, an end-of-file mark is written on the cassette after the saved program.

Although no SAVE statement parameters are required when writing to a cassette drive, it is a good idea to name all programs. A named program can be read off cassette tape either by its name or by its location on the cassette tape. A program with no name can be read off cassette tape by its location only.

The SAVE statement is most frequently used in immediate mode, although it can be executed from within a program.

Example:

SAVE	*Write the current program onto the cassette in drive 1, leaving it unnamed*
SAVE "RED"	*Write the current program onto the cassette in drive 1, assigning the file name of RED*
A$="RED" SAVE A$	*Same as above*
SAVE "BLACKJACK",2,1	*Write the current program onto the cassette in drive 2, naming the program BLACKJACK. Write an end-of-file mark after the program*

Diskette Drive Format

SAVE *"dr;file name",dev*

The SAVE statement writes a copy of the current program from memory to the diskette in the drive specified by *dr*. The program is given the name *file name. dev* must be present; normally, it has the value 8. If *dev* is absent, a default value of 1 is assumed and the cassette is selected.

The file name assigned to the program must be new. If a file with the same name already exists on the diskette, a syntax error is reported. However, a program file can be replaced; if an @ sign precedes *dr* in the SAVE statement text string, the program replaces the contents of a current file named *file name.*

The diskette SAVE statement is also used primarily in immediate mode although it can be executed out of a program.

STOP

The STOP statement causes the program to stop execution and return control to C-64 BASIC. A break message is displayed on the screen.

Format:

STOP

Example:

655 STOP   *Will cause the message BREAK IN 655*
                  to be displayed

VALIDATE

Format:

PRINT#*lf*,"V[ALIDATE][*dr*]"

The diskette in drive *dr* is validated. If the *dr* parameter is absent, the diskette in the most recently selected drive is validated.

When a diskette is validated, a new Block Availability Map is created for all valid data files on the diskette. Any files that were improperly closed or were not closed become invalid files; they are deleted from the diskette and their diskette space is released.

Do not validate a diskette that contains random access files; validation will erase the random access file. If a read error occurs during validation, the validation operation is aborted and the diskette is left in its initial state. A diskette must be initialized after it is validated.

Example:

OPEN 1,8,15   *Open the diskette command channel*

PRINT#1,"I0"   *Initialize the diskette in drive 0*

PRINT#1,"V0"   *Validate the diskette in drive 0*

VERIFY

The VERIFY statement compares the current program in memory with the contents of a program file.

Cassette Unit Format

VERIFY ["*file name*"][*,dev*]

The program currently in memory is compared with the program named *file name* on the cassette in the unit specified by *dev*. If *dev* is not present, a default of 1 is assumed and cassette unit 1 is selected. If *file name* is not present, the next file on the cassette in the selected unit is verified.

You should always verify a program immediately after saving it. The VERIFY statement is almost always executed in immediate mode.

Example:

VERIFY	*Verify the next program found on the tape*
VERIFY "CLIP"	*Search for the program named CLIP on cassette unit #1 and verify it*
A$="CLIP" VERIFY A$	*Same as above*

Diskette Drive Format

VERIFY *"dr;file name",dev*

The program currently stored in memory is compared with the program file named *file name* on the diskette in drive *dr*. The *dev* parameter must be present and unless otherwise specified it must have the value 8. If the *dev* parameter is absent, a default value of 1 is assumed and the primary cassette drive is selected.

In order to verify the program most recently saved, use the following version of the VERIFY statement:

VERIFY "*",8

You should always verify programs as soon as you have saved them. The VERIFY statement is nearly always executed in immediate mode.

Example:

VERIFY "*",8	*Verify the program just saved*
VERIFY"0:SHELL",8	*Search for the program named SHELL on disk drive 0 and verify it*
C$="0:SHELL" VERIFY C$	*Same as above*

WAIT

The WAIT statement halts program execution until a specified memory location acquires a specified value.

Format:

WAIT *memadr, mask[,xor]*

where

mask	is a one-byte mask value
xor	is a one-byte mask value

The WAIT statement executes as follows:

1. The contents of the addressed memory location are fetched.

2. The value obtained in step 1 is Exclusive-ORed with *xor,* if present. If *xor* is not specified, it defaults to 0. When *xor* is 0, this step has no effect.

3. The value obtained in step 2 is ANDed with the specified mask value.

4. If the result is 0, WAIT returns to step 1, remaining in a loop that halts program execution at the WAIT.

5. If the result is not 0, program execution continues with the statement following the WAIT statement.

The STOP key will not interrupt WAIT statement execution.

APPENDIX **H**

BASIC Functions

The C-64 can define a great number of functional operations directly from BASIC. These functions include mathematical derivations, screen formatting instructions, and string manipulators. They are listed in alphabetical order.

ABS

ABS returns the absolute value of a number.

Format:

ABS(*data n*)

Example:

`A=ABS(10)`	Results in A=10
`A=ABS(-10)`	Results in A=10
`PRINT ABS(X),ABS(Y),ABS(Z)`	

ASC

ASC returns the ASCII code number for a specified character.

Format:

ASC(*data$*)

If the string is longer than one character, ASC returns the ASCII code for the first character in the string. The returned argument is a number and may be used in arithmetic operations. ASCII codes are listed in Appendix A.

Example:

```
?ASC("A")        Prints 65
X=ASC("S")
?X               Prints the ASCII value of "S," which is 83
```

ATN

ATN returns the arctangent of the argument.

Format:

ATN(*data n*)

ATN returns the value in radians in the range ±17.

Example:

```
A=ATN(AG)
?180π*ATN(A)
```

CHR$

CHR$ returns the string representation of the specified ASCII code.

Format:

CHR$(*byte*)

CHR$ can be used to specify characters that cannot be represented in strings. These include a carriage return and the double quotation mark.

Example:

```
IF C$=CHR$(13) GOTO 10        Branch if C$ is a carriage return (CHR$(13))
```

```
?CHR$(34):"HOHOHO":CHR$(34)   Print the eight characters "HOHOHO" (where
                              CHR$(34) represents a double quotation mark)
```

COS

COS returns the cosine of the argument.

Format:

COS(*data n*)

EXP

EXP returns the value e^{arg}. The value of e used is 2.71828183.

Format:

EXP(*arg n*)

arg n must have a value in the range ±88.029691. A number larger than +88.029691 will result in an overflow error message. A number smaller than −88.029691 will yield a zero result.

Example:

?EXP(0)	Prints 1
?EXP(1)	Prints 2.71828183
EV=EXP(2)	Results in EV=7.3890561
EB=EXP(50.24)	Results in EB=6.59105247E+21
?EXP(88.0296919)	Largest allowable number, yields 1.70141183E+38
?EXP(-88.0296919)	Smallest allowable number, yields 5.87747176E−39
?EXP(88.029692)	Out of range, overflow error message
?EXP(-88.029692)	Out of range, returns 0

FRE

FRE is a system function that collects all unused bytes of memory into one block (called "garbage collection") and returns the number of free bytes.

Format:

FRE(*arg*)

arg is a dummy argument. It may be string or numeric.

FRE can be used anywhere a function may appear, but it is normally used in an immediate mode PRINT statement.

Example:

```
?FRE(1)
```
Institute garbage collection and print the
number of free bytes

INT

INT returns the integer portion of a number, rounding to the next lower signed number.

Format:

INT(*arg n*)

For positive numbers, INT is equivalent to dropping the fractional portion of the number without rounding. For negative numbers, INT is equivalent to dropping the fractional portion of the number and adding 1. Note that INT does *not* convert a floating point number (5 bytes) to integer type (2 bytes).

Example:

```
A=INT(1.5)      Results in A=1
A=INT(-1.5)     Results in A=-2
X=INT(-0.1)     Results in X=-1
```

A caution here: since floating point numbers are only close approximations of real numbers, an argument may not yield the exact INT function value you might expect. For instance, consider the number 3.89999999. The function INT(3.89999999) would yield a 3 answer, not 4 as would be expected.

```
?INT(3.89999999)
3
```

LEFT$

LEFT$ returns the leftmost characters of a string.

Format:

LEFT$(*arg$,byte*)

byte specifies the number of leftmost characters to be extracted from the *arg$* character string.

Example:

```
?LEFT$("ARG",2)       Prints AR
```

```
A$=LEFT$(B$,10)       Prints leftmost ten characters of the string B$
```

LEN

LEN returns the length of the string argument.

Format:

LEN(*arg$*)

LEN returns a number that is the count of characters in the specified string.

Example:

```
?LEN("ABCDEF")        Displays 6
```

```
N=LEN(C$+D$)          Displays the sum of characters in strings C$ and D$
```

LOG

LOG returns the natural logarithm, or log, to the base e. The value of e used is 2.71828183.

Format:

LOG(*arg n*)

An ILLEGAL QUANTITY ERROR message is returned if the argument is zero or negative.

Example:

```
?LOG(1)               Prints 0
```

```
A=LOG(10)             Results in A=2.30258509
```

```
A=LOG(1E6)            Results in A=13.8155106
```

```
A=LOG(X)/LOG(10)      Calculates log to the base 10
```

MID$

MID$ returns any specified portion of a string.

Format:

MID$(*data$,byte*₁[,*byte*₂])

Some number of characters from the middle of the string identified by *data$* are returned. The two numeric parameters *byte*₁ and *byte*₂ determine the portion of the string which is returned. String characters are numbered from the left, with the leftmost character having position 1. The value of *byte*₁ determines the first character to be extracted from the string. Beginning with this character, *byte*₂ determines the number of characters to be extracted. If *byte*₂ is absent then all characters up to the end of the string are extracted.

An ILLEGAL QUANTITY ERROR message is printed if a parameter is out of range.

Example:

`?MID$("ABCDE",2,1)`	Prints B
`?MID$("ABCDE",3,2)`	Prints CD
`?MID$("ABCDE",3)`	Prints CDE

PEEK

PEEK returns the contents of the specified memory location. PEEK is the counterpart of the POKE statement.

Format:

PEEK(*mem adr*)

Example:

`?PEEK(1)`	Prints contents of memory location 1
`A=PEEK(20000)`	

POS

POS returns the column position of the cursor.

Format:

POS(*data*)

data is a dummy function; it is not used and therefore can have any value.

POS returns the current cursor position. If no cursor is displayed, the current character position within a program line or string variable is returned. Character positions begin at 0 for the leftmost character.

Recall that program logic processes 80-character lines even though the C-64 computer has a 40-character display. If program logic in such a computer is processing a character in the second half of the line, the POS function will return a value between the beginning and end of the line (in other words, 41 to 80).

By concatenation, string variables with up to 255 characters may be generated. If program logic is processing a long string, then the POS function will return the character position currently being processed. Under these circumstances the POS function will return a value ranging between 0 and 255.

Example:

```
?POS(1)
```
At the beginning of a line, returns 0

```
?"ABCABC";POS(1)
```
With a previous POS value of 0, displays a POS value of 6

RIGHT$

RIGHT$ returns the rightmost characters in a string.

Format:

RIGHT$(*arg$,byte*)

byte identifies the number of rightmost characters that are extracted from the string specified by *arg$*.

Example:

```
RIGHT$(ARG,2)
```
Displays RG

```
MM$=RIGHT$(X$+"#",5)
```
MM$ is assigned the last four characters of X$, plus the character #

RND

RND generates random number sequences ranging between 0 and 1.

Format:

RND(*arg n*)   Return random number
RND(−*arg n*)   Store new seed number

Example:

```
A=RND(-1)
```
Store a new seed based on the value −1

```
A=RND(1)
```
Fetch the next random number in sequence

An argument of zero is treated as a special case; it does not store a new seed, nor does it return a random number. RND(0) uses the current system time value TI to introduce an additional random element into play.

A pseudo-random seed is stored by the following function:

```
RND(-TI)
```
Store pseudo-random seed

RND(0) can be used to store a new seed that is more truly random by using the following function:

```
RND(-RND(0))
```
Store random seed

For a complete discussion of the RND function see Chapter 5.

SGN

SGN determines whether a number is positive, negative, or zero.

Format:

SGN(*arg n*)

The SGN function returns +1 if the number is positive or nonzero, 0 if the number is zero, or −1 if the number is negative.

Example:

```
?SGN(-6)
```
Displays −1

```
?SGN(0)
```
Displays 0

```
?SGN(44)
```
Displays 1

```
IF A>C THEN SA=SGN(X)

IF SGN(M)>=0 THEN PRINT "POSITIVE NUMBER"
```

SIN

SIN returns the sine of the argument.

Format:

SIN(*arg n*)

Example:

```
A=SIN(AG)
?SIN(45*π/180)      Displays the sine of 45 degrees
```

SPC

SPC moves the cursor right a specified number of positions.

Format:

SPC(*byte*)

The SPC function is used in PRINT statements to move the cursor some number of character positions to the right. Text which the cursor passes over is not modified.

The SPC function moves the cursor right from whatever column the cursor happens to be in when the SPC function is encountered. This is in contrast to a TAB function, which moves the cursor to some fixed column measured from the leftmost column of the display. (See TAB for examples.)

SQR

SQR returns the square root of a positive number. A negative number returns an error message.

Format:

SQR(*arg n*)

Example:

```
A=SQR(4)          Results in A=2
A=SQR(4.84)       Results in A=2.2
?SQR(144E30)      Displays 1.2E+16
```

ST

ST returns the current value of the I/O status. This status is set to certain values depending on the results of the last input/output operation.

Format:

ST

ST values are shown in Table H-1.

Status should be checked after execution of any statement that accesses an external device.

Example:

```
10 IF ST<>0 GOTO 500          Branch on any error

50 IF ST=4 THEN ?"SHORT BLOCK"
```

STR$

STR$ returns the string equivalent of a numeric argument.

Format:

STR$(*arg n*)

STR$ returns the character string equivalent of the number generated by resolving *arg n*.

TABLE H-1. ST Values for I/O Devices

ST Bit Position	ST Numeric Value	Cassette Tape Read	Cassette Tape Verify and Load
0	1		
1	2		
2	4	Short block	Short block
3	8	Long block	Long block
4	16	Unrecoverable read error	Any mismatch
5	32	Checksum error	Checksum error
6	64	End of file	
7	128	End of tape	End of tape

Example:

`A$=STR$(14.6)`	Displays 14.6
`?A$`	
`?STR$(1E2)`	Displays 100
`?STR$(1E10)`	Displays 1E+10

SYS

SYS is a system function that transfers program control to an independent subsystem.

Format:

SYS(*mem adr*)

mem adr is the starting address at which execution of the subsystem is to begin. The value must be in the range 0 <address <65535.

TAB

TAB moves the cursor right to the specified column position.

Format:

TAB(*arg n*)

TAB moves the cursor to the n+1 position, where n is the number obtained by resolving *arg n*.

Example:

`?"QUARK";SPC(10);"W"` `QUARK        W`	These two examples show the difference between SPC and TAB. SPC skips ten positions from the last cursor location, whereas TAB skips to the 10+1th position on the row
`?"QUARK";TAB(10);"W"` `QUARK     W`	

TAN

TAN returns the tangent of the argument.

Format:

TAN(*arg n*)

Example:

> ?TAN(3.2)   Displays 0.0584738547
>
> XY(1)=TAN(180*π/180)

TI, TI$

TI and TI$ represent two system time variables.

Format:

> TI   Number of jiffies since current startup
> TI$ Time of day string

Example:

> ?TI
>
> TI$="081000"

USR

USR is a system function that passes a parameter to a user-written assembly language subroutine whose address is contained in memory locations 1 and 2. USR also fetches a return parameter from the subroutine.

Format:

> USR(*arg*)

VAL

VAL returns the numeric equivalent of the string argument.

Format:

> VAL(*data*$)

The number returned by VAL may be used in arithmetic computations.

VAL converts the string argument by first discarding any leading blanks. If the first nonblank character is not a numeric digit (0-9), the argument is returned as a value of 0. If the first nonblank is a digit, VAL begins converting the string into real number format. If it subsequently encounters a nondigit character, it stops processing so that the argument returned is the numerical equivalent of the string up to the first nondigit character.

Example:

```
A=VAL("123")
NN=VAL(B$)
```

Index

439

Other Osborne/McGraw-Hill Publications